About this Series: General Editor, Abdullahi A. An-Na'im

The present book is the outcome of two related research projects led by Professor Abdullahi A. An-Na'im at the School of Law, Emory University, and funded by the Ford Foundation. Both projects deploy the notion of cultural transformation to promote human rights in African and Islamic societies. The first explores this notion in theoretical terms and then focuses on issues of women and land in Africa from customary, religious and statutory rights perspectives, with a view to linking research to advocacy, for securing the rights of women to own or control land as a vital economic resource. The second project is a global study of Islamic family law, including some country studies and thematic studies, from a human rights perspective. Four volumes are being published at this stage of these on-going projects:

VOLUME I *Cultural Transformation and Human Rights in Africa*, edited by Abdullahi A. An-Na'im

VOLUME II *Islamic Family Law in a Changing World: A Global Resource Book*, edited by Abdullahi A. An-Na'im

VOLUME III *Women and Land in Africa: Culture, Religion and Realizing Women's Rights*, edited by L. Muthoni Wanyeki

VOLUME IV *Islamic Family Law in Comparative Perspective*, edited by Lynn Welchman

D1167290

Women and Land in Africa: Culture, Religion and Realizing Women's Rights

**edited by
L. Muthoni Wanyeki**

Zed Books Ltd
LONDON • NEW YORK

David Philip Publishers
CAPE TOWN

Women and Land in Africa: Culture, Religion and Realizing Women's Rights was first published in South Africa by David Philip Publishers (Pty Ltd), 99 Garfield Road, Claremont 7700, and in the rest of the world by Zed Books Ltd, 7 Cynthia Street, London N1 9JF, UK and Room 400, 175 Fifth Avenue, New York, NY 10010, USA in 2003.

www.zedbooks.demon.co.uk

Cover designed by Andrew Corbett
Set in Monotype Baskerville and Univers Black by Ewan Smith, London
Printed and bound in Malaysia

Distributed in the USA exclusively by Palgrave, a division of St Martin's Press, LLC, 175 Fifth Avenue, New York, NY 10010, USA

A catalogue record for this book is available from the British Library
Library of Congress Cataloging-in-Publication Data: available

ISBN 1 84277 096 9 cased
ISBN 1 84277 097 7 limp

in South Africa
ISBN 0 86486 625 9 limp

Contents

Tables

Abbreviations

ACAFEJ	Association of Cameroonian Women Lawyers
ACFODE	Action for Development
CEDAW	Convention on the Elimination of All Forms of Discrimination Against Women
CFA	Communauté financiaire africaine franc
ECWA	Evangelical Churches of West Africa
EWLA	Ethiopian Women Lawyers' Association
FAO	Food and Agriculture Organisation
FEMNET	African Women's Development and Communications Network
FGM	female genital mutilation
FIDA	Federation of Women Lawyers
FRELIMO	Front for the Liberation of Mozambique
GAD	gender and development
GDP	gross domestic product
GNP	gross national product
GOR	Government of Rwanda
ICJ	International Court of Justice
IDR	Institute of Development Research
IFI	international financial institution
IGO	intergovernmental organisation
IMF	International Monetary Fund
LRD	Land Reform Decree
NAC	National African Company
NEPU	Northern Elements Progressive Union
NGO	non-governmental organisation
NPC	Northern People's Congress
NPN	National Party of Nigeria
NRM	National Resistance Movement
OMM	Mozambican Women's Organisation
PA	Peasant Association
PIV	Perimètre irrigué villageois
PRA	participatory rural appraisal

PRP	People's Redemption Party
REWA	Revolutionary Ethiopian Women's Association
RIG	Rural Interest Group
RISD	Rwanda Initiative for Sustainable Development
RNC	Royal Niger Company
RPF	Rwandan Patriotic Front
SAED	Société d'aménagement et d'exploitation des terres du delta du fleuve Sénégal
SAP	Structural Adjustment Programme
SNNPR	Southern Nations, Nationalities and Peoples Region
TPLF	Tigray People's Liberation Front
UNHCR	United Nations High Commission for Refugees
UWONET	Ugandan Women's Network
WID	women in development

Contributors

Hussaina J. Abdullah, a sociologist, is an independent scholar. She has published extensively on the effects of economic and political reforms on Nigerian women.

Winifred Bikaako holds an MA in public administration and management and a BA in social sciences from Makerere University, Kampala. She is a research fellow at the Centre for Basic Research in Kampala, Uganda, and coordinator of the HIV/AIDS project. Her research focus is mainly on livelihoods, gender and HIV/AIDS.

Elise-Henriette Bikie is the coordinator of Global Forest Watch (GFW)-Cameroon, founded in 1999. She implements GFW activities in Cameroon, developing partnerships with and providing backstopping to local NGOs and research institutions. She maintains close contacts with the key stakeholders involved in forestry in Cameroon within the administration, civil society and the private sector. She has co-authored two reports on Cameroon's logging sector, 'An Overview of Logging in Cameroon' and '1999–2000 Allocation of Logging Permits in Cameroon: Fine-tuning Central Africa's First Auction System'. Prior to joining GFW-Cameroon, she conducted several village surveys, first with a local NGO, INADES-Formation, and then with CIFOR. The results of this work were published in 'L'impact de la crise économique sur les systèmes agricoles et le changement du couvert forestier dans la zone forestière humide du Cameroun'. She holds a masters in social anthropology.

Liazzat Bonate is pursuing a PhD in African history at Northwestern University. She has an MA in Islamic societies and cultures from the School of Oriental and African Studies (SOAS) at the University of London. She taught history at the Eduardo Mondlane University from 1993–97 and was a research assistant at the Law Department of the Centre for Middle Eastern and Islamic Law at SOAS at the University of London from 1998–99.

Ibrahim Hamza holds BA and MA degrees in African history from Usmanu Dan Fodiyo University in Sokoto, Nigeria. He currently works as a research assistant on a UNESCO/York University Nigerian Hinterland Project and is studying for a PhD in African history at York University. His areas of interest are African social and political history and the African diaspora.

Rachel Kagoiya is an intern with the African Women's Development and Communication Network (FEMNET) in Nairobi.

Patrice Bigombe Logo is a political scientist, lecturer and researcher at the Group for Administrative, Political and Social Science Research (GRAPS) in the Department of Political Science of the Faculty of Judicial and Political Science at the University of Yaoundé II, Cameroon's Chapter of the African Association of Political Science (AAPS). He has worked with the FAO in Cameroon in the Forests, Trees and People Programme (FTPP). He is now an associate researcher with the WRI-CIFOR research programme on environmental decentralisation in Africa and the Director of the Centre for Research and Action for Sustainable Development in Central Africa (CERAD-Afrique Centrale). He has edited and written on the Pygmies of south-eastern Cameroon, political identities in Cameroon and forest management in Cameroon.

Rwanda Initiative for Sustainable Development (RISD) is a local NGO established in 1994 by Rwandan professionals from different academic backgrounds. RISD envisages a country where all citizens are in charge of their own destiny and exercise social accountability regardless of difference and the atrocities that have characterised Rwanda and its people. RISD seeks to promote and foster social and economic transformation in Rwanda by Rwandans and works towards poverty eradication. It aims to enhance community participation in improving their living conditions and contributing to national policy debates and promotes gender equality, Participatory Rural Approaches (PRA) and self-reliance. RISD is managed by a director, Annie Kairaba, who holds an MA in development studies and a programme coordinator, John Muyenzi, who holds an MSc in agriculture.

John Ssenkumba is a graduate in political science from Makerere University. He is a research fellow at Centre for Basic Research, where he has, over the years, focused on peace, democracy and human rights. In addition to his current research on poverty, he is very active in mainstream Ugandan politics.

Mohamadou Sy is the director of the Department of Economic Planning and Organisations Management of the National School of Applied Economics (ENEA), Senegal. He works in research and training, particularly in support of civil society activities.

Zenabaworke Tadesse studied international relations and sociology. Her areas of specialisation include gender, poverty and governance. She has written a book on *Women in Ethiopia* and co-authored a book on *Children in Zambia*. Her recent publications are on the democratisation process in Africa and the struggles for gender justice. She is a founding member and first executive secretary of the

Association of African Women for Research and Development (AAWORD) as well as the first deputy executive secretary in charge of publications of the Council for the Development of Social Sciences in Africa (CODESRIA). She serves on numerous international, regional and local boards of advisers. She has served as visiting scholar at the African Studies Department of Emory University and the Carter Center as well as the African Gender Institute in the University of Cape Town. Presently, she serves as a member of the Management Committee and editor of the Forum for Social Studies, Addis Ababa.

Ngoné Diop Tine is an economist and a gender expert. She has done extensive work on mainstreaming gender into poverty eradication programmes, including engendering budgets and sectoral policies. She also undertakes training in gender analysis and gender mainstreaming. Her areas of interest include women's economic empowerment, engendering structural adjustment programmes and the impact of macroeconomic policies on women. She has worked with the Council for the Development of Social Science Research in Africa (CODESRIA) and has undertaken extensive work for the United Nations system, including FAO and UNDP. She is a member of the Executive Board of Akina Mama wa Afrika, an international NGO promoting African women's leadership. She is currently the gender analyst and adviser to the government of Rwanda with Department for International Development (DfID) support.

Introduction

L. Muthoni Wanyeki

§ THIS book is the result of collaboration in action-oriented research among African researchers on the continent, under the Law and Religion Programme of the Faculty of Law at Emory University and the African Women's Development and Communication Network (FEMNET). Its primary objective is to examine women's land rights and evolutionary prospects with respect to the customary, religious and statutory regulation of land in Africa. Secondary objectives are to propose activities and regulatory reforms to improve women's land rights (with regard both to access and control) and to share the results of communications and advocacy activities undertaken on the basis of the research.

The book includes original research on the relationship between culture, religion and human rights as these impact on women's enjoyment of land rights in seven African countries: Cameroon, Ethiopia, Mozambique, Nigeria, Rwanda, Senegal and Uganda. The aim was not only to assess the ways in which culture and religion impede human rights, but also to assess how they might reinforce human rights.

The first section of the book covers the empirical and primary research was carried out in all the countries except Cameroon, by African researchers from the country concerned, using Participatory Rural Appraisal (PRA) techniques: questionnaires, interviews and focus group discussions. Secondary research was also carried out, using archival, ethnographic, historical, legal, religious and other research sources.

The second section of the book includes outputs of communications and advocacy work conducted around the research in five of the selected countries (excluding Mozambique and Rwanda, where the research was completed much later). The communications work aimed to summarise the research findings and key recommendations and to present them in relation to international human rights and women's legal standards for all five countries. The advocacy packages were prepared for circulation to gender and development practitioners, as well as to the broad range of stakeholders (environmentalists, human rights practitioners, legal reformers and policy-makers) pushing for land reform in the countries researched.

Also included in this section are two reports from a pilot advocacy process conducted in Ethiopia on the basis of the research and the advocacy packages. Two advocacy and training workshops were held in Ethiopia. The first was targeted solely at stakeholders and aimed simply to present the research findings and recommendations, as well as the advocacy packages, for feedback and initial strategising. The second was targeted both at stakeholders and relevant policy-makers and included training on gender and development, on women's human rights and on advocacy with respect to land. A national advocacy plan was developed and entrusted to a local women's human rights and legal organisation for follow-up action.

The second section thus tries to present the challenges of the processes of disseminating the research and of transforming it into implementable and practical policy advocacy options. It is included to enable lessons to be derived from the process now under way.

Women's identities, social status and land rights are presented throughout the book from the intersection of ethnic, gender and religious perspectives. Women's marital status is used as a determining variable, as marriage is a primary means through which women (and men) access land. However, women's land rights are dependent on their relations with men (not vice versa), and divorced and widowed women are particularly vulnerable to dispossession.

Land rights are usually conceived of as the rights to use (usus), enjoy (fructus), and exploit (abusus) land. Here, taking gender analysis into account, land rights are conceptualised not only as the rights to access and control land as a productive resource, but also as information about, decision-making around (for example, to mortgage, lease, sell or bequeath land) and benefits from land.

The research revealed key contradictions. Almost without exception, the practice of customary regulation of land, including inheritance, has been accommodated by religious (Islamic) regulation of land to women's detriment. Similarly, and without exception, customary law is accommodated by statutory law, also to women's detriment. Within statutory law itself, there are unresolved tensions with implications for women's land rights. Implicit in all statutory land regulation and reform efforts examined is the attempt to balance the civil rights of the landed (through which land is viewed as private property) with the economic and social rights of the landless (through which land is viewed as a communal source of livelihood). The lack of resolution on this issue – the private versus the public – is especially critical now in the context of population expansion, land scarcity, liberalisation and privatisation. For even the nominal land rights customarily or religiously enjoyed by women are diminishing within this context.

Cameroon

The chapter on Cameroon was written by Patrice Bigombe Logo and Elise-Henriette Bikie.

Land is a critical issue in Cameroon, which has a population growth of 2 per cent a year and which has seen a reduction in per capita income of 25 per cent as a result of structural adjustment, liberalisation and privatisation. Although 40 per cent of the population is now employed in the agricultural and informal sectors, there has been a decrease in income from both food and export crops.

A key tension around land relates to the different perceptions of it held by communities on the one hand and the state on the other. The former view land as a spiritual heritage and community resource that is managed by particular lineages and communities under customary law. The latter views land as a practical economic resource that should be managed by the state under statutory law. This tension dates back to changes in land tenure introduced under colonialism.

Under the German Imperial Crown, the British governor and then the French, colonial policies authorised the appropriation of land deemed as being 'without a master' for the colonial state. The objectives of the appropriation were to extend individual land ownership and to consolidate the colonial state's monopoly over land. Thus European-style individual property rights (in which land was seen as private property) were introduced and set against African collective use and management rights (in which land was seen as a common resource). The transformation from customary land tenure to individual land tenure was achieved through a process of registration of land ownership.

The post-colonial state essentially maintained the dualism of land tenure brought about under colonialism. In 1974, land was deemed to be either exploited and/or occupied (in which case either individual or customary rights could apply), or empty/virgin (in which case it became public land under the state).

Decree Number 76-164 of 24 April 1976 set out the methods through which land could be acquired: by protecting customary rights accrued through exploitation/occupation, or by donation, inheritance, purchase or receipt of a state grant for development. Ownership was to be registered with an administrative judge, and this process was the sole justiciable form of ownership. But due to ignorance of the law, the complexity and costs of the process, registration was not widely carried out in rural areas. Further, under Article 1, Ordinance Number 74-1 of 6 July 1977, the state was declared the ultimate owner of all land.

In practice, however, customary land tenure persists, especially regarding user rights to forests. As far as communities were concerned, the land they occupied and/or used was not 'free' or 'undeveloped'. The failure to consult with communities in formulating post-colonial land law and policy has led to misunderstandings about the evidence of development required to register land and the state's expressed intention of monopolising land for development purposes.

The research in Cameroon focused on women of varied marital status in semi-urban and rural areas. Two research sites were selected: the northwest and the south. The northwest is characterised by centralised, hierarchical and syncretic communities. It is 80 per cent agricultural and densely populated, resulting in competition for land between indigenous people and foreigners on the one hand, and indigenous people and agro-industries and manufacturers on the other. Home to the Christian Habes/Kirdis, the Muslim Peulh and others, traditionally, land is managed by the *fons* (chiefs), their chieftains/nobles (who are responsible for taxing land) and their *fawties*.

The south is characterised by communal/'segmental' communities and has a low population density. Home to animist 'Pygmies' and others, traditionally land was managed communally. Today, however, it is managed by 'chiefs' who are nominated by the administration on the basis of customary criteria in consultation with 'boards' (councils of elders). The 'chiefs' are either elders or individuals with exceptional moral and/or political qualities.

Women in Cameroon constitute 52 per cent of the population, 38 per cent of which is urbanised. Women are dominant in agriculture, although 71 per cent live below the poverty line. Traditionally, women play inferior roles to men publicly (except in the south, where older women can participate in public decision-making). However, they have important roles privately, in that they and children are the means by which men acquire influence and power. As in many African (and other) countries, women's reproductive roles include taking care of their husbands and families. Their community roles include the organisation of marriages, and their productive roles include farming, fishing, hunting and small trading.

With respect to statutory law, the 1974 land reforms appear on the surface to affirm women's land rights and not to discriminate against women. In practice, however, barriers exist to the equal application and impact of the reforms on women. Women's lower literacy and higher poverty levels compound the difficulties relating to the registration of land, adding to the complexity and length of time required. Cultural barriers exist as well. Customarily, men manage land (with some individual exceptions). Men are responsible for the growing of export crops (cocoa, coffee, cotton), which are used as evidence of 'development' of land. Women are responsible for the cultivation of food crops. In addition, the possibility of counterclaims from relatives regarding women's succession and fear of retaliation prevent women from making claims to land ownership under the 1974 reforms.

Under customary law and practice, women do not receive donations of land. Women do have user rights to land, acquired from their fathers or husbands. However, these rights are precarious in the event of divorce/widowhood. Inheritance for women is restricted because succession is patrilineal, from fathers to sons. However, wives can inherit land from their husbands if they have male children (in which case they do not own the land, but hold it in trust for their sons), or if they have no land of their own to grow food to sustain their family (in which case their user rights may be left intact). Women tend not to take loans of land or to purchase land, as they have to pay in money or kind for such transactions.

There is an evident need for information and knowledge among women, and among those responsible for land registration, about the impact of statutory law on women's access to and control over land. In addition, exceptional customary practices or innovations that support women's land rights need to be identified and promoted at the community level to improve the enjoyment of women's land rights. Finally, land law reform that takes this into account is also necessary.

In advocating such change, new opportunities for women should be considered. The economic crisis has forced women to seek to diversify household incomes. They are therefore increasingly involved in the production and marketing of export crops. As land is also rapidly being commodified, new opportunities exist for women to buy land, particularly through their mobilisation and organisation into *tontines* (mutual self-help groups) to work large farms.

This has both facilitated the beginning of role reversals within households and created a local basis for women's mobilisation and organisation nationally. There is therefore more political space, both rural and urban, in which women can question male power and advance women's power. This political space is critical for land reform efforts in favour of women's land rights.

Ethiopia

The chapter on Ethiopia was written by Zenabaworke Tadesse.

Five-sixths of Ethiopia's population is rural, with agriculture accounting for 81 per cent of employment, 51 per cent of Ethiopia's gross national product (GNP) and 85 per cent of its export earnings. The majority of the population gains its livelihood from sedentary agriculture, with mixed farming being the norm. Pre-1974, all land was under the imperial government, with a well-established system of landlord–tenant relations. Land was acquired through inheritance or communal use. Women (of means) could purchase land. But women also acquired land as gifts and could inherit it.

From 1975–91, 'land to the tiller' reforms were carried out under the Derg military regime, resulting in an increase in smallholdings, any benefits of which were undermined by civil war, drought and famine. The Derg's Land Reform Proclamation made no differentiation between men and women. However, land was distributed according to family size to male heads of households, without distinction between residential and agricultural land. The predisposition of the administration responsible for land distribution was towards customary inheritance, meaning that in many cases female heads of households were given smaller sizes. The residential requirements meant that married women (who tended to move to the homes of their husbands rather than vice versa) lost shares of land that they were entitled to in their natal homes. In addition, men in polygamous marriages tended to register only one wife, making other wives vulnerable in the event of separation, divorce or widowhood. Divorce rates were high because of early marriage.

Finally, women's right to control land (decision-making around land and benefits derived from land) remained unaddressed. The cultural taboo against women ploughing or sowing was not challenged, so that the gender division of labour in agriculture was reinforced.

Despite these failings with respect to gender, the land reforms of 1975 nevertheless loosened some taboos and allowed some space for the creation of new female identities.

From 1991 to the present, following the fall of the Derg, new statutory law regarding land has come into being. The Land Law of 1987 was to facilitate redistribution of land to both men and women, with allocations being made to individuals within households. The Constitution of 1994 entrenched equality rights regarding access to land as well as the use, administration, transfer and inheritance of land. And the Federal Rural Land Administration Proclamation requires the creation and implementation of a land administration law from each regional council, without differentiation on the basis of gender.

So far, however, it has not been implemented except in Amhara Regional State.[1] Article 9 of the Rural Land Redistribution Proclamation of Amhara Regional State of 1997 provides for the redistribution of land to both men and women. But redistribution is limited to single women and excludes any beneficiaries of the past two regimes, thus including women both as individual beneficiaries and as wives of beneficiaries.

A pressing challenge is the need to close the gap between regulatory goals and implementation. The near absence of civil society advocacy on this issue compounds the problem.

The research was conducted in 30 households in each of two *weredas* (the smallest administrative unit) in three regions. Wello in Amhara Regional State is home to the Muslim Haiq, with Islamic succession law being followed. It produces largely cereals on smallholdings, with 54 per cent of landholdings being less than one hectare. North Shoa in Oromia Regional State produces cereals and root crops, with 53 per cent of landholdings being less than one hectare. And Wollaitta in Southern Regional State has 82 per cent of landholdings under one hectare. As in North Shoa, women inherit only if there are no male siblings. They can exercise control over land if they are not married, have no sons and do not live with adult males (that is, if they do not live in male-headed households).

The research found that women's labour is generally more demanding than that of men as they are responsible for the reproductive work of fuel and water collection as well as housework, which consumes both energy and time. In addition, they engage in the productive work of weeding and harvesting. As custom prevents them ploughing or sowing, some women engage in sharecropping, which limits their food security and earnings. Control over cereals is held by men.

Women are also involved in animal husbandry. However, men are responsible for herding and control the produce of hides and skins. Women are responsible for the small animals and control the produce of milk and milk products. Although this brings them additional income, the work is considered reproductive and they therefore have no access to agricultural and veterinary extension services.

Marital status emerged as a determining variable for the enjoyment of women's land rights. The type of marriage was also important, as polygamy in all three research sites constrains women's land rights. Women's land rights varied across the sites. In Wello, women have nominal rights to land due to the influence of Islam. In North Shoa, they have no rights to land, and in Wollaitta there are restrictions on women's land rights originating from Christianity (that practised by the Orthodox Ethiopian Church). Female heads of household with adolescent/grown male children were less disadvantaged with respect to land than those with small children/daughters.

There is a clear need to focus on addressing the barriers to girls' education. But there must also be a move away from interventions based solely on practical needs. Agricultural information, knowledge, capital and markets must be found for women, accompanied by a change in state perceptions of agricultural production and its planning. This could be supported by the development of more autonomous women's organisations.

Opportunities exist to support these changes. The stigma formerly faced by unmarried women has diminished. The increased sale of cereals (as local brew) and milk products, the introduction and sale of new food crops such as vegetables, and drought response interventions such as the 'food for work' programmes have increased women's incomes. Although women do not necessarily control such income, whatever funds they generate are rarely valued by men. Nevertheless, both of these changes are positive signals for women's autonomy.

Mozambique

The chapter on Mozambique was written by Liazzat Bonate.

Statutory law on land was introduced under Portuguese colonialism. The Portuguese designated land either as non-indigenous, regulated under Article 7 of Decreto Lei Number 23 of 1993, or as indigenous, regulated according to indigenous customs and traditions (which were, however, not codified) by local chiefs, who were included in the administrative system.

Article 4 of the post-colonial Constitution of 1975 banned dualism. However, Law 12/1978 re-established dualism by setting up Judicial Courts and Popular Courts, with judges for the latter being elected locally and required to consult with local communities about their decisions. Land was nationalised without redistribution to peasants. Private farms became state cooperatives and rural families were allowed landholdings of half a hectare of wetland and one hectare of dryland.

Articles 200 and 203 of the Constitution of 1990 re-endorsed dualism. In 1992, Community Courts replaced the Popular Courts, without mechanisms for legal or national coordination. Under Article 3 of the Land Law of 1997, land became the property of the state. Article 5 required testimonial proof for the individual registration of land. But Articles 7 and 9 allowed for community use/benefit under customary norms and practices. In addition, Article 24 facilitated community participation in land administration. However, the land reforms had some problems. The definition of 'local community' was ambiguous and without legal precedent, and Article 27 facilitated a later definition of terms and mechanisms.

However, due to the civil war, most of the rural population exists and functions outside state control. Although the population is predominantly Muslim, customary law plays a larger role than religious law. Customary law has not been codified, so that norms cannot be identified nor rights established.

Nampula province of northern Mozambique, where the research was carried out, is 75 per cent rural. The two main ethnic groups are the Koti and the Makua. Both are Bantu, with their languages being variants of Kiswahili. The Koti are originally from the Angoche/Koti islands and claim Shirazi descent from Kilwa/Zanzibar, while the Makua trace their ancestors to the Zambezi.

Both have different *n'loko* (clans) under the authority of the *mwene n'loko* (paramount chief) and different *nihimo* (kinship groups) under the authority of the *humu/mwene nihimo* (chief). Some *n'loko/nihimo* are dominant, as they were the firstcomers to the area. Both are matrilineal, with inheritance being through the maternal line to the niece/nephew or other family member on the maternal side.

Traditionally, women's authority and leadership was recognised through the *apyamwene* (female paramount chiefs). The *apyamwene* accompanies each *mwene*, with an older *apyamwene* selecting a niece from her maternal side to succeed her. The *apyamwene* play a spiritual role regarding the ancestors, fertility and land. Although the post-colonial political party FRELIMO banned traditional structures and created the Mozambican Women's Organisation as a forum for women's political participation, the institution of the *apyamwene* persists.

N'loko and *nihimo* land is owned collectively by kinship groups and cannot be alienated. Only usufruct rights are granted, without gender discrimination. Everyone has access to land, as user rights are allocated by the *mwene* in consultation with the *humu/mwene nihimo*. Virgin lands can, however, be acquired by clearing and cultivating. Land so acquired can be alienated (bequested/inherited by direct descendants). Trees are owned individually and can also be alienated. However, this has become a means of accessing land, thus bypassing customary and statutory prohibitions on the sale of land without prior community consultation (Article 9 of the Land Law of 1997).

The research was conducted in four research sites. The first was Inguri zone of Angoche city, home to the Muslim Koti (who constitute 38 per cent of the population). They acquired land in exchange for access to Indian Ocean trade. The area is of high population density and there is conflict over land and water. Livelihoods include agriculture (of both food and cash crops) and fishing. The second was Anchilo administrative post of Nampula city, home to the Catholic Makua (who make up 27 per cent of the population). The third was Corrane administrative post in Meconta district, home to the Makua who follow indigenous religion (and constitute 1.6 per cent of the population). Livelihoods include agriculture (both food and cash crops) and animal husbandry. The fourth and final was Muecate administrative post in Muecate district.

A total of 150 households was surveyed. Women respondents ranged from 18–97 years of age, with generally low literacy levels. Seventy per cent were married, 16 per cent divorced and 14 per cent widowed. Landholdings varied from 0.25–30 hectares, with an average size of 1.7 hectares.

Women's access to and control over land varied in the four research sites. Customarily, because of matrilineal inheritance, kinship land was the domain of wives. For married women, this is fine. But for divorced/widowed women, this was satisfactory only when the couple lived on the wife's kinship land (under uxorilocal marriages). Such marriages accounted for 34 per cent of the total, but were especially prevalent in Corrane and Muecate. The matrilineal inheritance was also unsatisfactory for local women whose mothers were not in uxorilocal marriages.

Customarily, user rights are not transferable to spouses or children. This is illegal under Article 13 of the Land Law of 1997, which provides for succession. In theory, women can customarily inherit land from the maternal side. But in practice, this was observed only in Muecate. In both Anchilo and Corrane, inheritance went to men.

Apart from inheritance, land can be acquired through registration and titling (as per Article 10 of the 1997 Land Law). In practice, the process of registration and titling is slow and the number of women who had acquired land in this way was fewer than that of men.

Land can also be bought. This is increasingly being done to secure children's futures, to increase the land for food crop production and to grow cash crops. Land can also be acquired through the state (possible but rare) or culturally (through certifying its availability with the *mwene*, then clearing and working it). However, these methods of acquisition are difficult for women as they have limited labour and money to spare. Nevertheless, bartering for land by women is common, especially among Koti women in Inguri and divorced/widowed women in Corrane.

In Inguri, such self-acquired land is increasingly becoming individually owned. There, land is also self-acquired through establishing marriage/kinship relations with local people or by renting land on a yearly basis (94 per cent of land in Inguri has been so acquired, and 81 per cent of such owners are women). However, there is a problem with renting. Sometimes, the tenants are allowed to clear land and use it for one year. But the following year it is rented to somebody else at a higher rent.

In Anchilo and Corrane, land is increasingly being self-acquired through the buying of trees, although this is both culturally unacceptable (newcomers not allowed to plant trees, especially cash crops) and illegal (under Article 13 of the Land Law of 1997). Self-acquired land tends to revert upon divorce/widowhood to husbands and their matrilineal families. But disposal can be by those in whose name the land was acquired, male or female, including *mahari* (dowry). Trees are generally seen as women's property.

Land can also be rented. However, this is difficult for women, who are culturally responsible for food production and therefore have little spare time. This is not the case in Inguri, where the majority of those who rented were women, as women are responsible for agriculture overall and men for other income-generating activities (in Inguri, women could also rent out land, although the presence and witness of a male relative on the maternal side was required). This was also not the case in Anchilo, where women – especially Maconde women – have some money from waged labour. One successful woman cotton producer was observed in Corrane. Also in Corrane, one divorced and two widowed women rent 'land' (technically trees) to grow cash crops. Land tends to be rented jointly, although money is men's responsibility.

Among the Koti, control over land (decision-making about land) was in the hands of women, but they tended to consult with their husbands. In Anchilo, consultation is required with the women's families or the *mwene*, except about trees. In Corrane, however, men control decision-making, with women being consulted only if they are divorced/widowed and without means.

In general, women exercised autonomy over the benefits accrued from their own activities. Control over food crop production was in the hands of women, except in Inguri (among the Koti, according to Islam, men provide and women are obedient, therefore men exercise control to fulfil their religious obligation to provide). Women controlled their own land. However, with respect to benefits from land, husbands and wives tended to consult. Although men are expected to control money, in practice women do, except for large purchases when consultation occurs. Control is especially an issue for divorced/widowed women in virilocal marriages, where women lose their family belongings, shares of the harvest and land.

Conflicts around land occurred between families, between individuals and the community, or between the community and private enterprises. Such cases concern lending or renting agreements, occupancy through trees (especially among the Koti of Inguri), land limits and the occupation of private or vacant land during the civil war. The majority of cases were settled by the community (the *mwene/apyamwene*) or the shaykhs (religious leaders) in Inguri and were unregistered. But the Community Courts were revealed to be more important in dispute settlement than the Judicial Courts.

No cases involving women were found or observed. Women's perceptions were that women's groups were not helpful, that religious leaders were not interested in women, especially divorced/widowed women (particularly the Muslim leaders, who consider that women are not meant to bring the private into the public under Islam, but also the Catholic leaders) and that the police and the courts were corrupt. In Anchilo and Corrane, women who had tried to defend their land rights had been accused of adultery, murder (if widowed) and witchcraft.

Nigeria

The chapter on Nigeria was written by Hussaina J. Abdullah and Ibrahim Hamza.

The research was conducted in northern Nigeria, home to the federal capital of Abuja, containing 19 of Nigeria's 36 states and home to 55 per cent of Nigeria's population, over half of whom are women. The majority of people are Hausa, who converted to Islam under the Sokoto Caliphate after the 1804 jihad. However, there are also Christians and followers of indigenous religions, termed Maguzawa, meaning non-Muslims under a Muslim state. Agriculture is the predominant economic activity.

When the Royal Niger Company (RNC) sold the land it had acquired from agreements with the local population to the British colonial government in 1903, Islam and Islamic courts already existed. In 1804, Shehu Uthman Dan Fodio, a Fulani scholar, had established the Sokoto Caliphate based on the Maliki doctrine of Sharia, with its own courts and judges. Sources of Islamic law included the Qur'an, Hadith (sayings of the Prophet) and ijma (consensus of the ulama). However, in civil matters, particularly with respect to marriage and inheritance, Islam did not replace custom. Under British colonialism, some non-Muslims converted to Christianity, with the numbers of Christians rising post-1945 after the inclusion of education and health care in missionary work.

Under the Caliphate, land was regulated according to Islam, which applied to both Muslims and non-Muslims in this respect. The state had control of all mineral lands, and the inheritance or sale of land was forbidden. Individuals were granted user rights to exploit land for population settlement, to increase the land under agriculture, to develop agricultural production and to raise revenue for the state through the taxation of non-Muslims and the imposition of royalties on mining. Muslims living on *waqf* (conquered) land were exempt from paying tax, but paid *zakkat* (a tenth of all produce), and the emirates under the Caliphate paid an annual land tax to the Caliphate. Non-Muslims also paid tax to the Caliphate for protection.

There were six categories of land under the Caliphate. *Waqf* (conquered) land could not be inherited or sold as it was for all Muslims. *Suhr* (non-Muslim) land required recognition of the state in order to be protected, and it could be alienated. *Ushr* was abandoned state land. Usufruct rights were gained through building and/or cultivating *waqf* land, and ownership rights were gained by the same means for *suhr* and *ushr* land. Additional categories of land were *al-hima* (protected) land, under the control of the imam for charitable or communal grazing purposes, *iqta* (virgin) land which could be gained by Muslims from non-Muslims without immovable property and *mawat* (dead) land, which was left fallow or vacant or used for pasture.

After the defeat of the Caliphate, land under British colonialism was regulated by statutory law. The Land Proclamation Act of 1902 established two categories of land. Crown land was that purchased from the RNC. Public land was gained from the Caliphate and non-Muslims for the exercise of usufruct rights according to customary law, and could only be alienated with the consent of the colonial governor. The Land and Native Rights Proclamation of 1910 placed customary lands under the government.

The Land Tenure Law of 1962 was followed by the Land Use Act of 1978, which is the prevailing statute today. Under the 1978 Act, land falls into two categories. Urban or statutory land covers urban and government land, for which renewable leaseholds of 99 years can be acquired through registration. However, the registration process is both costly and time-consuming. All statutory titles are vested in the state governors and rights are dependent on payment for the certificate of registration. Other land covers customary land, to be used according to customary land rights, which are defensible in the Sharia Court. Other land falls under the jurisdiction of customary leadership and local government authorities.

A problem is posed by the fact that the 1978 Land Use Act does not define what is urban and what is other land. In addition, northern Nigeria experiences land scarcity as a result of urbanisation, the demand for land by the government for irrigation and the extension of World Bank rural development programmes and projects. This has led to the gradual disappearance of grazing lands and to environmental degradation. The 1978 Act thus limits to half a hectare the amount of undeveloped land that any one person can hold.

The research was carried out in three sites. The first site included the Muslims of Kano and Sokoto states. Dawakin Tofa is a local government area in Kano state where the *tijanniya* (populist radical) Islamic brotherhood dominates (it supports women's equality under the Qur'an) and where agriculture and pottery-making are key economic activities. The Yabo local government area in Sokoto state is dominated by the *quadriyya* (conservative) Islamic brotherhood.

The second site included the Mugazawa of Kano state. The Tudun Wada local government area is marginalised and retains no independent political authority, having been under the Muslim authority of the Caliphate. There is some Christian and Islamic conversion. Women are not secluded nor treated as legal and social minors. They participate in economic and social life, engage in agricultural work (they are responsible for food production most of the year, with men taking over during the rainy season), can own and dispose of money earned from agriculture and are relatively prosperous, if overworked.

The third and final site included the Christians of the southern Zaria emirate. The Kamurun Ikulu and Zango Kataf local government areas were the first

Christian converts under British colonialism. The churches play social as well as religious roles. However, women do not customarily inherit.

Among the Muslims of Kano and Sokoto states, land is regulated according to Islam. Land is viewed as a gift from God and belongs to the whole community. Usufruct rights are granted for three categories. Occupied land is acquired by grants from the emir, by clearing, cultivating and fencing, or by inheritance. Unoccupied land within the town is under the emir and cannot be alienated without his approval. However, unoccupied land outside the town can be acquired by clearing, cultivating or fencing. *Waqf* (common) land is that acquired beforehand by war and/or treaty and is now under the emir, and in consultation with the elders it can be used for grazing, marketing or prayers.

Under Islam, women can hold property received as a gift or through purchase, and can inherit property as a wife, mother, daughter and relative, sibling or slave. Daughters receive half of the male share and wives one-quarter of property if there are no children, but one-eighth if there are. Wives can also give away up to one-third of their property without their husbands' consent. If divorced, women are entitled to their personal property, including their dowry and gifts received during the marriage.

Despite these religious provisions for women's land rights, in practice Hausa women do not inherit land, except as trustees for their sons. Hausa men believe women's inheritance of land is unnecessary, as they are catered for by their husbands or male guardians and do not farm.

The perception is that women do not own or have access to or control over land due to *kalle* (seclusion). Although women's right to inherit was established by the jihad, it was not uniformly enforced. It was enforced in Sokoto state, but not in Kano and southern Zaria. Women's land was not intended to be sold. But as land became expensive, women's inheritance was threatened, except for the fruit of trees on their land. Some judges refused to recognise women's inheritance rights, until the British colonial government insisted that both English and Islamic law allowed inheritance.

In Muslim areas, inheritance is based on Sharia. However, in Kano state, Hausa custom invalidated Islamic rights. In general, all customary practices in a conquered society that are not contradictory to Sharia are accepted. However, the principle of *ahafu dharayn* (choosing a lesser evil) was applied with respect to women's inheritance, in order to maintain societal equilibrium. It was believed that women's inheritance would lead to economic destruction, as there would be too many heirs and male power would be reduced. In 1954, this was changed by Sarki Sanusi. His decree was not backed by the principle of *radd al-Mazahlim* (redressing of injustices) to restore individual/group rights violated by previous regimes. However, following his decree, the courts were inundated with women's land claims, some dating back to the 1800s.

In non-Muslim areas, inheritance is patrilineal, with male children inheriting their father's property. Wives and daughters are excluded, although females can be considered for inheritance if there are no male children. Women can also purchase and develop land.

Among the Mugazawa of Kano state, land is regulated according to customary law. Land is viewed as inalienable, as it belongs to the whole community. These rights are acquired by grants from the head of the family and/or community. Usufruct rights are restricted for non-members of the community. As the Mugazawa are patrilineal, males inherit land through male descent.

Women gain access to land through their families and/or marriage. They have usufruct rights and cannot alienate the land that they use. They can inherit land from their parents, but not equally, although this is not customary. They cannot alienate inherited land, which reverts back to their families upon marriage, re-marriage or death. If they are divorced, they are expected to return the bride-price and they lose their user rights to their husbands' lands. Their children lose their inheritance rights. However, they can retain acquired property, and some-times their own families will take them back. If they are widowed, they are inherited by a male relative of their husbands, unless they are old and choose to stay on their husbands' lands with their children. If they are without children, they can choose to return to their families. Outside of marriage, they lose all land rights, although there are exceptions if the husbands' families are responsible (due to the influence of Christianity).

Among the Christians of southern Zaria, land is regulated by customary law. Christianity has had no impact on women's land rights, as Christian marriages are not deemed to be synonymous with civil marriages under the Marriage Act of 1914, which facilitates women's inheritance. Widowed women from civil marriages are entitled to one-quarter of their husbands' properties if they have children and to one-half without.

In summary, women can acquire land in northern Nigeria as: an allocation of abandoned or uncleared land from the village head; a purchase (*saye*); a gift (*kayuta*); an inheritance (*gado*); an acceptance of pledge (*jingine*); a loan (*aro*); a lease (*aro*); or through sharecropping (*kashi/nomamuraba*). However, women's access to land is determined by their relationships with men. It is assumed that women will be married, although marriage is fluid – two-thirds of the respondents had been married more than once – especially among the Hausa and Maguzawa, because the Christianity practised in southern Zaria does not allow divorce. And women's land rights are dependent on marriage.

Eighty-eight per cent of the female respondents had access to land, mostly through their husbands. Only 12.5 per cent had purchased land and enjoyed individual land rights. Acquiring land through clearing is no longer an option, as there is no longer any vacant land. Acquiring land through registration did not take place, due to the costs and time involved in registration. Acquiring land through group formation was limited, as many women's groups were not perceived as being the result of their own initiative but the result of cultural and religious (seclusion) constraints.

Although women largely enjoy access to land, they do not enjoy control over land because of social constraints. The defence of women's land rights has happened historically among the Hausa, but is now undertaken only by the Maguzawa, through their rejection of Christian marriages that forbid divorce, as well as legally. Women said they did not defend their land rights because they either did not have land rights, or their land rights were not socially recognised, or they did not want to create trouble.

Customary law determines women's access to and control over land. Christianity is conservative in northern Nigeria, enforcing subservient monogamy and disallowing divorce. It does not promote or protect women's land rights. Islam contains positive provisions to enhance women's land rights, but the seclusion of women militates against them making use of such provisions.

With respect to women, statutory law provides little relief. The Land Use Act of 1978 grants women equal access to land in a context of inequality and therefore reinforces that inequality. It stereotypes men as earners and women as dependants, and does not recognise the de facto ownership that is the situation of many women. In addition, the provision for the registration of customary land rights threatens women who customarily have only secondary rights. Civil marriage provides some protection for women's land rights, as the Matrimonial Clauses Act of 1970 and the Administration of Estate Law allow women to inherit, whether testate or intestate.

What is needed is gender-responsive law and policy reform to ensure that women's land rights are protected through occupancy (with and without title deeds), and reform of customary law to ensure gender equality in inheritance as well as uniform inheritance. In addition, education in environmental rights, human and legal rights and women's rights needs to be provided for traditional, religious and government leaders.

Rwanda

The research in Rwanda was conducted by the Rwanda Initiative for Sustainable Development (RISD).

Rwanda experiences land scarcity, with a population density of 300 people/ km^2, 91 per cent of whom are involved in agriculture. Women's land rights are now critical, given the increase in (girl) child/female-headed households as a result of the genocide and war of 1994, the 1996–99 insurgency in the northwest and HIV/AIDS. Thirty-four per cent of households are now female-headed and women have taken on new roles as a result of men being killed or imprisoned. In response to these changes, the Rwandan government passed a new rural settlement policy in 1994 and a new inheritance law in 1999.

In the pre-colonial period, two customary land tenure systems were found in Rwanda: *ubukonde* in the north and northwest; and *igikingi* in the centre, east and south. Both depended on collective ownership of land by different patrilineages (*imiryango*). Under the *ubukonde* system, land was acquired by the first person to clear it. Ownership was collective under the lineage chief (*umukonde*), who granted user rights through *ubugererwa* (payments of a portion of the harvest or labour). There were three categories of land based on agricultural, grazing or hunting usage. Under the *igikingi* system, all land was under the *mwami* (chief), who distributed large grazing lands to war heroes or other respected individuals in exchange for regular gifts. Such lands could be alienated for cultivation in return for gifts. Rights to hunting lands were also granted by the *mwami*.

During the colonial period, laws applying to foreigners were introduced, by which title deeds to land were granted to the colonisers and (at least in theory) to 'civilised' Africans. Through such laws, the majority of landowners became religious groups and Indian traders. With the backing of first the German and then the Belgian colonisers, the central *mwami* consolidated and asserted his control in the northwest. The *ubukonde* system was transformed. Gifts of cattle and produce were given in exchange for land and virgin land was brought under the *mwami*. In the 1930s, the *ubukonde* system was replaced by the *igikingi* system. New landowners from the centre moved into the northwest and conflict was frequent until independence, when the central landowners were finally evicted.

In the 1950s, the *ubukonde* system was abolished. The outcome was the loss of common lands and a move from collective lineage to nuclear family ownership. A head tax was imposed on male heads of households, ensuring adherence to labour requirements and investment in cash crops. For women, these changes meant that control and responsibility was vested in adult men, whose labour went to their rulers and to the state.

However, in the 1960s, following independence, the *igikingi* system was also suspended and suppressed. Control over land was granted first to the *sous-chefferies* and then to community authorities. They were to protect user rights to land and facilitate its partition into individual plots that could be registered.

During the First and Second Republics, the *paysannat* system was adopted. Land was distributed to nuclear families (young men) with certificates and communal fields were to be used for cash crops. This was implemented where the population density was low (in the former hunting grounds); inhabitants were required to grow specific hectares of coffee and not to partition the land (although this was not respected). Unmarried daughters and widows were also allowed to inherit land.

Following the genocide and war of 1994, the return of refugees heightened land scarcity. These refugees were first settled on land abandoned in 1994 and then in the villages administered by the United Nations High Commissioner for Refugees (UNHCR). Those who had been absent for more than ten years were not allowed to reclaim land.

A villagisation policy was introduced to group the population for the purposes of modern agriculture, providing services and reducing land conflicts. But the redistribution of land required a new land policy (currently being drafted). The result of the villagisation policy was the provision of housing to female heads of households without discrimination. However, problems were experienced by the disabled, the elderly and widows. In addition, obtaining construction materials and supplies has been difficult. And while the politically connected were not as affected in terms of land seized for the redistribution, they tended to get bigger shares of what was distributed.

Citizens continue to perceive customary land as being their own, although the state is clear that all land is available for use. Under statutory law, women remain vulnerable in property disputes. It is assumed that women are under men's protection and that there are limits on property for women. Women could not previously do community work, engage in paid labour or enter into contracts without their husbands' consent. The relevant statutes were slightly modified in 1998 to allow women to open and hold bank accounts in their own names, and a new inheritance law was passed in 1998.

The research was carried out in four sites covering both of the two customary land tenure systems, *ubukonde* and *igikingi*, as well as the new villagisation policy. Kinigi commune in Ruhengeri prefecture in the northwest was traditionally under the *ubukonde* land tenure system. Polygamy is common and the insurgency affected implementation of the villagisation policy. Mugina commune in Gitarama prefecture in the centre was traditionally under the *igikingi* land tenure system. It has experienced two different post-colonial land policies, the *paysannat* policy of the First Republic and the villagisation policy of the post-genocide government. Kahi commune in Umutara prefecture is semi-arid, with pastoralism and some agriculture being the predominant economic activities. It is now home to old-caseload refugee settlements from Uganda. Finally, Kigarama commune of Kibungi prefecture is undergoing the villagisation policy and is home to both old- and new-caseload refugees.

Women can now access land by joining agricultural cooperatives or women's groups, which are allocated land by the state, or else pay rent for land from the income received from their produce. However, men are not generally supportive of such access. Women are often exploited by men in mixed agricultural co-operatives and marketing of produce continues to be a problem, causing women to sell their produce to middlemen for low prices. In addition, land scarcity and the fees required to register allocated land impose further constraints.

Customarily, women's land rights are held only temporarily. If they have never been married or are divorced, women access land through their fathers. For divorced women, such access is dependent on good conduct, as they are expected to abstain from sexual relationships or to remarry. Males inherit patrilineally. Levirate marriage (wife inheritance) is practised, although land can be held by widows in trust for their sons. But if there are no children, the widows can return to their own families and their lands revert to their husbands' families. As their rights are only usufruct in all instances, they cannot alienate their lands. An exception was found in the northwest, where women could acquire land as gifts before, at, or during marriage. However, this practice is under attack and now only occurs when there is land available that is not needed.

As inheritance is now by the head of the family rather than of the lineage, some joint decision-making around land takes place within marriages, although women tend to defer to men. This deference is backed by traditional proverbs equating women's identities to those of their husbands, and also by the Bible (Catholicism is the dominant religion). The perception is that women cannot own land because they cannot be war heroes (under the *igikingi* land tenure system). However, as a result of the genocide, women can now inherit family land if all the men of their families or lineages were killed.

Customary land tenure systems provided for the protection of the vulnerable, for example, girls rejected by their husbands (*indushyi*), widows and orphans. This custom persists today through the villagisation policy. However, post-genocide, where the vulnerable are the majority, it is difficult to implement. A particularly vulnerable population is that of the Batwa, who were formerly hunter gatherers. However, with the depletion of the forests, they have been forced into agriculture. But they have no land and have been ignored in all policies.

Under the Constitution of 1979, civil marriages alone are legally recognised. However, most marriages are only customary and religious, with the exchange of bridewealth being sufficient for social recognition, due to the costs of civil marriages. These costs are incurred in obtaining identification papers and marriage certificates, to meet the requirement of having a house or a plot before marriage (although this is not enforced) and the cost of parties. Civil marriages are also seen as not being relevant. In the northwest, polygamy is common, although it is illegal. Under the law, therefore, additional wives are not legally recognised and are vulnerable in cases of divorce or widowhood. Their children have some legal recourse, although the legally recognised wife must agree to their paternity. There is also no common law providing legal recognition to cohabitation, which is the situation in which the majority of women find themselves.

Marriage law thus impedes women's land rights. For example, at the time of this research, the Canton Court in Kinigi commune was dealing with 200 cases, 190 of which were about land and 30 per cent of which involved women's land rights. In recognition of this, the new inheritance law of 1999 provided for equal inheritance by girls and boys. There are three property regimes to be followed, the choice of which is supposed to be made during civil marriage ceremonies: common property (under which all property is shared); separation of property (under which all property remains separate); and limited common property (under which what is to be shared is listed).

The problem is that the law applies to civil marriages, although most marriages are not in this category. It also applies only to legitimate children. In practice, the choice of property regime (common) is usually assumed. Land not included as land is the property of the state. In addition, land scarcity makes the division of property difficult.

The law is seen as unfair, in that women are now entitled to two shares, from their fathers and from their husbands. The belief is that women should use their husbands' share, but retain their customary rights if not married, divorced or widowed. The law is also seen as impractical, as women do not exploit land.

Customarily, conflict resolution about land occurs through the family councils (*gacaca*). However, these have no legal basis; their decisions are not binding and implementation is dependent on the goodwill of the parties involved. The local authorities are also involved in conflict resolution. But they are susceptible to influence and tend to use both customary and statutory law as the basis for their decisions, allowing for inconsistency and partiality. The courts are a final recourse. They rely on statutory law, unless the issue in question is not covered.

There is therefore a need for law and policy reform that recognises the rights of illegitimate children and women in informal, including polygamous, marriages. Such reform needs to cover equality rights, the law on marriage, family law, family planning and land policy and law.

Senegal

The research in Senegal was carried out by Ngoné Diop Tine and Mouhamadou Sy.

Seventy-five per cent of Senegal's population lives in the rural areas, with women providing 81 per cent of agricultural labour and accounting for 70 per cent of agricultural production. Customarily, land could be acquired by fire (burning vegetation on virgin land) or by the axe (clearing vegetation on unused land). In both instances, land so acquired was under the *lamane* (landlord) and could be rented out to farmers in return for payment (usually of millet). Among the Wolof, women did not own land as they were assumed to be under men's protection, but they could use land. There was also a traditional conception of public land, with land that was used publicly for ten years reverting to the individual user. If it was family land, this period extended to 40 years. Among the Serer – a matriarchal and matrilineal community – women could inherit their mothers' rice fields (according to the gender division of labour, women grew rice while men grew millet), although this is changing with the shift to patriarchy and patrilineality brought about by modernisation. However, among the Peul land was owned communally, with user rights being granted by the community to both men and women.

Christianity, under which men and women are considered equal, has had little impact on land ownership patterns among the Christian Serer. Islam has had more impact, particularly among the Islamic Wolof as compared to the Islamic Peul. Islam grants women the right to inherit from their fathers (they get one-half of the men's share) as well as from their husbands (a one-eighth portion if they have children and one-quarter if they do not). However, as women are expected to stay at home, the perception is that they cannot work and therefore cannot own land.

Land is regulated by the National Land Law 64-46 of 1964. It brings all unclassified and unregistered land under the control of the state, as land in the national domain. Classified and registered land can be urban, local (under the control of communities through their locally elected authorities), pioneer (intended for agricultural companies) or classified (forests). Law 72-25 of 1972 established rural communities with Rural Councils. The Rural Councils can allocate local land to its inhabitants, or for development for unspecified durations. These allocations can be revoked if the land is not developed, or be reintegrated into state land.

The research in Senegal was carried out in three sites. The first included the Muslim Wolof of Medina Sabakh. The second focused on the Christian Serer of Joal Fadiouth, a traditionally matriarchal and matrilineal community where women could inherit land but do not own it. The third included the Muslim Peul of Medina Ndiathbe, a caste-organised and hierarchical community that tends to follow customary law more than Islamic law.

Among the Wolof, 42.85 per cent of women own land acquired through marriage (when divorced or widowed) or through the Rural Council allocations to women's groups. The community complies with Islamic succession law, although there is some application of customary law (with divorced or widowed women being expected to marry/remarry and thus having their right to land threatened). The commercialisation of land has meant that in theory women can also buy land. However, they tend not to do so, as land is seen as belonging to the community. The shortage of land compounds gender-based constraints to women's acquisition of land, as does the lack of women's leadership (education and training, knowledge of law regarding the Rural Councils) and the lack of female representation on the Rural Councils. Customary law is still used as a reference with respect to inheritance, and there is non-implementation of land law with regard to speculation in land.

Among the Serer, 88.46 per cent of women own land acquired through marriage (when divorced or widowed), through inheritance (especially rice fields) and through the Rural Council. One-quarter of the Rural Council is female and they are literate and follow clear procedures with respect to land allocations. Christianity is not relevant for women's land rights among the Serer. However, constraints to women's land rights include shortage of land, its salinisation/tannification, the cost of demarcation fees and the lack of permanent title deeds. Exploitation permits of only one or two years are given to prevent the sale of land.

Among the Peul, 32 per cent of women own land. Customary law predominates, with Islam being flouted so that order prevails. Land is inalienable and is therefore not inherited. It cannot be owned by individuals, so that women access land either through marriage (when widowed as divorce is not common), through Rural Council allocations with family or community consent (the Rural Council relies on customary law to make its decisions), or through women's groups. Although there is no shortage of land, constraints to women's land rights include the conservatism of the community, the lack of organisation of the Rural Council (which is illiterate, has no land register and provides little or no follow-up to applications) and lack of the fees required to register land.

Factors positively impacting women's land rights in Senegal thus seem to be women's knowledge and organisation, the attention of traditional, religious, administrative or local government leaders, and support for development programmes and projects run by women. Tradition benefits Serer women.

What is needed to enhance women's land rights is therefore the education and literacy of women in decision-making and improved organisation of women. In addition, the implementation of the provisions in the Convention to Eliminate All Forms of Discrimination Against Women (CEDAW) pertaining to the development of customary law and rural women, and the harmonisation of national domain and rural community laws in accordance with CEDAW, should be undertaken. Finally, the implementation of religious and statutory law is critical.

Uganda

The research in Uganda was carried out by Winnie Bikaako and John Ssenkumba.

Ninety per cent of the Ugandan population is involved in agriculture, with women providing up to 80 per cent of agricultural labour and accounting for 90 per cent of food production. Prior to 1900, land was regulated by customary law. While this varied from community to community, in general, land in its natural state was owned communally, or owned individually where this had been approved. Three land tenure systems were identified. The communal land tenure system was found in the centralised and feudal kingdoms of the Ankole, Buganda, Bunyoro, Toro, with the king serving as the overall owner or trustee of land. The clan land tenure system was found among the Bakigga, the nilotic and nilo-hamitic peoples and the Sudanese, with the clan elders serving as the overall owners or trustees. The nomadic or pastoralist land tenure system was found among the Karamoja, with land being owned by the whole community for grazing purposes. However, some pastures and wells were restricted.

Under all three tenure systems, individuals had rights to their own homes, fields and trees for produce and trapping. Community rights were held over virgin land, grazing lands and forests. In general, uncultivated land was not owned. Among the nilotic peoples, such land was used for hunting. Land could thus be acquired through settlement, conquest or seizure. The owners could allocate land and settle land disputes. In Bunyuro, tributes were paid to the king for individual use. Men were thus entitled to privacy within their own homes. They controlled produce and could inherit land. Women did not inherit land. Widows retained user rights to their husbands' lands unless they returned to their own families or remarried outside their husbands' families. Inheritance was thus patrilineal, with some matrilineal exceptions.

Other exceptions also existed among royal women in the kingdoms. For example, in Buganda, royal women could own and inherit land, consistent with their right to become chiefs or family heads. In Toro, royal women could inherit in the absence of male heirs, as uxorilocal marriage was practised. They could also obtain customary land from the king if they proved they could build on it.

From 1890–94, under British colonisation, three new land tenure systems were introduced to complement customary tenure – which continued to exist during the colonial period. The first was the *mailo* land tenure system in Buganda, brought in by the 1890 Uganda Agreement and upheld in the 1980 Buganda Land Law. Under the *mailo* land tenure system, the Lukiiko (Buganda Parliament) had the authority to allocate land on chiefs' recommendations; 4,138 individuals benefited from this provision, each obtaining up to 30 km^2 with a title deed. However, they could not alienate this land without approval from the Lukiiko and the colonial governor. The Land Succession Law and 1927 Busuulu and Envujjo Laws were later passed to regulate relations between *mailos* (landowners) and peasants. The 1967 Constitution gave the national Parliament the power to regulate land and granted the state control of all minerals and water on *mailo* lands.

The second was the leasehold land tenure system, which gave individuals the right to own and occupy or use land for a specific duration (99 years), subject to development conditions such as building or agriculture. The leasehold land tenure system was statutory, introduced by the Crown Lands Ordinance, the 1969 Public Lands Act and the 1975 Land Reform Decree. Individual leases were controlled by urban authorities. Private arrangements could be sought with individuals or organisations and *mailo*/freehold owners. However, arrangements involving more than 500 acres required the approval of the minister, especially if customary land was involved.

The third was the freehold land tenure system, established by the 1962 Public Lands Ordinance. This set up district and federal land boards to control public land and supervise customary land registration. The 1967 Constitution established the Uganda Land Commission to regulate both freeholds and leaseholds on the advice of District Land Committees. They could make grants of these lands, but had to compensate the original owners, and ministerial approval was required for grants of more than 500 acres. Under the Registration of Titles Act, individual lands could be alienated, subject to development conditions and with all mineral and water rights reverting to the state. The Land Transfer Act placed restrictions on land ownership for non-Africans, who required ministerial consent to ownership. Freeholds were not widespread, however, with only the elite and agricultural companies benefiting from them.

Post-independence, from 1975 to the present, some changes to the colonial land tenure systems were made. The 1975 Land Reform Decree abolished the *mailo* land tenure system (although in practice *mailos* continued to pay ground and commodity rent to the state) and transformed freeholds into leaseholds of 99 and 199 years. These changes contradicted the 1967 Constitution, under which Article 126 had entrenched *mailos* and Article 13 had disallowed nationalisation without compensation.

The effect on women of the colonial and post-independence changes was that their land rights were effectively restricted to usufruct. Men obtained more control over land as women's customary land rights were made less secure. The changes also facilitated an increase in nuclear families, by giving individual decision-making priority over community consultation about land. The legal dualism thus adversely affected rights of access to land and security of tenure.

With the Succession (amendment) Decree Number 22 of 1972, women's inheritance rights were slightly improved. The decree provided for the inheritance by women of 15 per cent of their husbands' estates should they die intestate, and it also established the right of dependent women to inherit. However, in practice only 7 per cent of land is owned by women, and a majority of the 16 per cent with no access to land are female heads of households. Further changes in land tenure and in women's land rights are now expected, following reforms under the new Land Law.

The research in Uganda was carried out in two sites. The first site included the Kakanju and Mazinga parishes of Bushenyi district in Ankole, to the west of the country. The population density is 150 people/km^2, and both customary and leasehold land tenure systems exist. The second site included the Lutete and Nakaseta parishes of Mubende district in Buganda in the centre of the country. It has a population density of 89 people/km^2, and both customary and *mailo* land tenure systems.

With regard to access to land, the research findings were as follows. Although women can statutorily inherit, this inheritance occurs through male mediation, and customary law disallowing women's inheritance continues to dominate. For example, the Federation of Women Lawyers (FIDA) in Uganda found that 40 per cent of their cases in 1995 involved women's inheritance. In addition, inheritance by widows of their husbands' land is dependent on length of marriage, number of children and the sex of those children.

Both men and women could customarily be donated land from their families, with women receiving smaller shares. However, in practice women are increasingly being donated land: they are perceived as more loyal and useful to their families than men, and marital instability is more and more taken into account. But married women do not necessarily reside near their families, and men therefore remain the custodians and exercise effective control over women's land. In addition, some families are choosing to sell land to provide for their daughters' education rather than to donate that land to their daughters. Finally, the traditional protection of battered, separated, divorced or widowed women is being eroded, particularly with the practice of polygamy.

Nevertheless, a shift in custom can be observed. Whereas customarily only men were the subject of land transfers, women are now being considered, as families make individual decisions about what is appropriate for them. However, this shift is still minimal in terms of its effect on women's overall access to land. With the population increase and land scarcity, different avenues are being pursued to ensure women's security.

Women can also purchase land, but land accessed in this way is still limited, due to women's lack of money and the perception of their husbands. Secrecy about such purchases is common, leading to reluctance among land sellers and making women buyers vulnerable. In addition, men can claim joint ownership of land purchased by women.

Finally, women can access land by borrowing it, although such arrangements tend to be short term and tenuous. Since most lenders are male, the negotiations can be difficult for women, who are often obliged to give part of their produce to lenders, making borrowing arrangements rather risky.

With respect to control over land, the research findings were that men tend to control benefits from cash crops and livestock. Women earn less money, as they are responsible for food crops. Women have the rights to use land and the resources on land for their families, such as surplus food crops. They can grow cash crops and rear livestock, but the decision to do so is determined by men. Their right to participate in decision-making over produce, the income derived from it and use of that income is not absolute, as such decisions are made in consultation with their husbands. This decision-making affects activities carried out on land, land transactions and incomes. Nevertheless, there is an upward trend towards joint responsibility and control, especially where women contribute to household income and the acquisition of property. It is important to note that wills are generally respected and could therefore serve to enhance women's land rights.

Land rights can be lost when illegal land transactions are performed, or when children (both male and female, but usually male) are ill-mannered and irresponsible. Land rights acquired through marriage can also be lost if women remain childless; when their husbands take another wife; if they are separated or divorced; or when women make mistakes (such as using land as a surety for loans they cannot repay).

To defend land rights, women have used wills, legal aid and the help of chiefs, as well as the Local Councils and the law courts. Women have guaranteed seats on the Local Councils and 16 cases had been brought before these councils in

Bushenyi by widows. Awareness of their rights, having women on the Local Councils, the existence of women's groups and the enactment of land law reform are critical to assure women's land rights. However, the new Land Law, which hinges on the economic privatisation of land, has failed to abolish patriarchal customary law with regard to land.

Concerns about women's land rights therefore persist. Women's land rights are fragile and transient, being dependent upon age and marital status (including type of marriage and the success of that marriage), whether they had children (including the number and sex of those children) and their sexual conduct. The impact of inequality in land rights has aggravated women's poor socio-economic status, increased the number of women engaging in sex work, allowed for sexual harassment and violence against women and contributed towards marital instability, separation and divorce. The lack of appropriate conflict-resolution mechanisms is key. Women's claims to land continue to be insignificant and unprotected, because the customary courts, the Local Council courts and the law courts continue to be corrupt and male-dominated, favouring men, costing money and requiring time.

Common Themes

The research, the communications and advocacy work all point to the need for gender-responsive land reform within the seven countries surveyed. Land reform can be defined as legal and policy-led changes with respect to rights affecting access to and control over land, with the aim of ultimately transforming land ownership patterns. Gender-responsive land reform would therefore ensure equal access to and control over land for both men and women, and be aimed at ensuring equal land ownership patterns between men and women.

Land reform is usually understood as being either conservative, liberal or revolutionary in terms of the rights being promoted and protected, as well as in terms of the process through which these rights are guaranteed. However, such understandings have tended to assume homogeneity among the poor, the rural and women as well as among households and communities. In reality, these categories or groupings are differentiated both in terms of interests and power. As the research shows, an increasing number of households are now female-headed for various reasons, including increased marital instability. Or, in the case of Rwanda, as a result of the genocide and ensuing war and insurgency. Land reform efforts that fail to take this differentiation into account will fail to improve (and indeed may aggravate) gender relations with respect to access to land.

Gender also interplays or intersects with age, caste, class, ethnicity and race. Again, the research points to the need to take this interplay into account. For example, the Batwa women of Rwanda face discrimination not just on the basis of gender, but also on the basis of their ethnic group's traditional hunting and gathering livelihood, which is no longer tenable because of the depletion of forest land.

The research also demonstrates that gender-based divisions of labour with respect to land significantly impact upon women's rights not just to access land, but to exercise control over it. While women's responsibilities for reproductive labour in relation to land are fairly homogeneous, their responsibilities for productive labour are heterogeneous. Control over food crops and poultry or goats (and benefits derived from surpluses of food crops and small farm animals) tended to rest with women in the countries surveyed. However, control over the type of cash crop and livestock (and benefits derived therefrom) tended to rest with men, even where women had made an exceptional and direct contribution to the labour involved. Again, the point made was that gender-based divisions of labour are important to take into account during land reform, so as not inadvertently to increase women's workloads without commensurately increasing the benefits derived by women.

Tadesse draws from research on gender and land reform in South Asia and Latin America to highlight some of the requirements typical to land reform processes that can inadvertently preclude the possibility of women benefiting from such reforms. These requirements can pertain to a history of residence on the land in question, to farming experience, formal education and permanent employment, or to the nomination of a specific household member as the beneficiary. In addition, requirements pertaining to modesty, a good reputation and seclusion can militate against women's increased access to and control over land. In sub-Saharan Africa, requirements of registration and titling can similarly preclude increased access to and control over land for women. Finally, limiting the objectives of land reform processes to settlement or the development of land markets also precludes women from benefiting from land reform processes.

Tadesse also points to the need for such reforms intended to benefit women to distinguish between the legal and social recognition of women's land rights, between recognition and enforcement and between access or ownership and control. The temporal nature of women's land rights must also be clearly stipulated, and a distinction made between lifelong, hereditary and less important women's land rights.

Without exception, the research findings were that in rural areas (as well as in some peri-urban areas), customary law supersedes positive law with respect to women's land rights. The notion of ownership is understood differently by communities and by the law, with customary law perceiving ownership in more custodial or trusteeship terms. Customary law does allow for women's access to land. However, such access is gender-based and dependent upon customary marriage and inheritance norms. Women's access to land was in relation to men; it was not tied to specific landholdings and was not heterogeneous. With the exception of the Serer in Senegal, no substantial difference was found in regard to women's access to land in both matrilineal and patrilineal communities.

However, women's customary land rights are changing, evolving as a result of economic and social change in the communities covered by the research. This change was most notable in Uganda, where individual families are increasingly making individual decisions around granting land to their daughters. The research thus concludes that tradition and modernity are not mutually exclusive. Tradition can be and is dynamic, being influenced by modernity.

Christianity has a minimal influence on women's land rights, with mixed impacts depending on whether the variant of Christianity practised is in favour of women's equality, as in Nigeria and Senegal, or not (as in Rwanda). Islam, however, has a far greater influence on women's land rights. Or rather, a far greater potential influence. For the findings of the research were that, in principle, Islam grants women greater land rights than customary law. However, in practice, these rights are generally not respected.

Abdullah proffers an explanation for this failure of respect, noting that customary law gains precedence in accordance with the principle of *ahafu dharayn* (choosing a lesser evil). Islam allows for syncretism, with all customary practices in a (conquered) community not contradictory to Sharia being accepted. However, although women's rights are protected by Sharia, they were overturned so as to maintain societal equilibrium. Where this gap between theory and practice has eventually been acknowledged, such acknowledgement has not been on the basis of the principle of *radd al-Mazahlim* (redressing of injustices) to restore women's collective land rights. Instead, individual Muslim women have put forward cases that are still being dealt with by the Sharia courts.

Conclusion

Both customary and religious law offer some (albeit limited) opportunities to enhance women's enjoyment of rights in relation to law. The non-codification and orality of customary law is presented as being an obstacle to the possibility of evolution of this type of law and its harmonisation with statutory law. However, the non-codification and orality also provide the possibility for customary law's adaptation by individuals and individual families and for regional variations. Such adaptation occurs particularly in the absence of strong customary conflict-resolution mechanisms, and where a multiplicity of conflict-resolution mechanisms are being referred to.

There is contestation about custom and tradition. Therefore, if moves are taken to codify customary law with respect to women's land rights, the exceptions that exist in practice can also be used to illustrate interpretations of customary law that are more favourable to women's land rights.

Contestation over interpretations of Christianity also exist with regard to women's equality and can be similarly exploited to enhance women's land rights. Islam is clearer in its provision for (albeit nominal) women's land rights. The possibility therefore exists to close the gap between theory and practice and end the flouting of Sharia in favour of tradition.

The lesson is that land reform processes that address not only statutory law (and its supporting policies), but also customary and religious law, are critical to enhancing women's enjoyment of their land rights. Among women, legal literacy and political education and understanding not just of statutory law, but also of customary and religious entitlements, are essential to strengthen their relative bargaining power. Women's ability to act in their own self-interest with respect to land is also dependent on their sense of self-worth, their ability to accrue resources and the value assigned to those resources. This ability can therefore be realised through land reform processes that address both the external (the constraints to the realisation of their self-interest, to their collective organisation) and the internal (their own perception and understanding of their land rights).

Factors that would enhance women's enjoyment of their land rights include legitimising women's claims to these land rights through changing gender stereotypes, roles and the gender-based division of labour. The customary social support mechanisms and support from development actors and the state are critical. Reform in inheritance laws, access to the administration regarding land economics and access to legal mechanisms are also important.

Although both customary and religious law can be used to guarantee limited land rights for women, their independent land rights with respect to both ownership and control are the ultimate goal.

Note

1. At the time this research was done.

Part I

Women's Land Rights in Rural Africa: Law and Practice

ONE

Women and Land in Cameroon: Questioning Women's Land Status and Claims for Change

Patrice Bigombe Logo and Elise-Henriette Bikie

Gender roles and behaviour and culturally ascribed status develop the sub-jective awareness that one is a member of the male or female sex. They create the motivation to conform to culturally determined expectations and deter-mine rights, duties and power relations within the socio-economic system of society. Women's subordination, existing in societies of every degree of complexity, is not something that can be changed by rearranging certain tasks and roles in the social system. The potential for change lies in changing social institutions at the same time as changing cultural assumptions through consciousness-raising and involvement by both men and women. (Berhane-Selassie 1991: 3)

Theoretical Framework and Context

This research seeks to draw an inventory of women's land status in Cameroon and to note possible evolutionary prospects. It also seeks to propose and analyse activities to be undertaken to improve women's land status in Cameroon. It is therefore an action-research project.

Locating the theoretical framework of the research, presenting and analysing its political, economic, socio-anthropological and cultural contexts, is a prerequisite for the above and even more for understanding the fluctuating and unstable environment of the land in general and women's land status in particular.

Determining the theoretical framework will help to understand the meaning and content of the research, the problem area and the methodological considera-tions, as well as the project's limitations.

Conceptualisation and Definition

Any research is based on the assumption that explanation is not dependent on immediate data. It is therefore necessary to define the fundamental concepts of the research and to landmark its spatial field.

Defining the research's core concepts is necessary to launch the research, break with preconceptions, determine what to study and define the nomenclature. As Emile Durkheim has explained, 'la première démarche du sociologue doit ... être de définir les choses dont il traite, afin que l'on sache et qu'il sache bien de quoi il est question' (Durkheim 1981: 34). For this research, what do notions of women and land entail?

At present, two tendencies dominate definitions of women. The naturalist tendency insists on a biological definition. The socio-anthropological tendency favours the role and social status of women as determining their definition.

The biological definition, or definition by sexual difference, valorises the 'real' being of women. In this sexualised sense, women are human beings of the female sex, that is, the sex that gives birth. From this perspective, the operative character-ising and differential element of women lies in their sex, in biological difference.

The socio-anthropological approach definition of women places emphasis on their social role and status, their social existence. Women are known as actors with the same capacities as men. Women are thought of in a multidimensional way, going beyond the classic opposition between the domestic and the political and integrating the feminine dimension in understandings of societies.

However, it is worth acknowledging that neither sex, nor roles and status alone, are sufficient to account for the extent of the differentiation between the sexes and the functions that are specific to women. Roles and status refer back in each socio-cultural milieu to a world of representations that are inherent in conceptions and visions of the world. Games of symbolism, ideology and power that ensure a society's internal equilibrium and reproduction should therefore also be considered. The social status of women and the relationships between them and men cannot be thought of outside the power that determines social dynamics. 'Women' must at once be naturalised and socialised. To be a woman is to be both a biological being and a social actor. The biological and the social are linked. They influence, and sometimes determine each other.

This research privileges the socio-anthropological approach. Women's land status is fundamentally determined by the socio-anthropological nature of women's condition through the regulation of power between women and men in society. The socio-anthropological perspective enables an operational categorisation of women in Cameroon to be sketched out.

The endeavour to define, categorise or draw a typology of Cameroonian women carries both certainties and uncertainties. With certainty, it is known that Cameroonian women are complex and diversified. There is no unique category or type of woman in Cameroon. There are many categories and types, according to their social origins, training, professions, marital status and so on. However, there are uncertainties, because of change and the dynamic character of women's identities in Cameroon. Women's identities are not primordial, intangible and immovable. In so far as women are social creations, their identities are changing, dynamic and moving. In one milieu, a woman can valorise her peasant identity, and in another she can display her professional status, all in relation to her personal expectations of a given situation and the interests at stake in it.

In Cameroon, it is women who most use land and who most need it for different productive activities. This research makes an operational choice that takes into account women's living place and matrimonial status. The category of women considered comprises women who live in rural zones or in partially urban zones, whether single, married, divorced or widowed. Rural women are therefore at the heart of this research. This choice is not only operational. It is also ideological, related to the project's philosophical and professional goals.

In Cameroon, land is both a heritage and a resource. Under civil law, heritage is defined as the sum of goods and obligations of a person. It is an entity whose assets and liabilities cannot be separated.

Here, it is necessarily considered in a wider sense, going beyond the individual to embrace the community. In almost all Cameroonian societies, land is considered as a common heritage, that is, as a cultural and physical collective space inherited from the ancestors. It is a community resource transmitted from generation to generation. In the name of the community, land is managed by the community's legitimate representatives. This management ensures the social reproduction of the group, in terms both of its identity and its survival. As communal heritage, land has a cosmological function. It is a visible link with the invisible. As a communal resource, land is not property. It is not to be commercially appropriated, and in both judicial and farming terms is identified with a lineage or a community, a resource to be used or managed, without a right to be owned.

In this sense, this heritage is peculiar. It is different from heritage under civil law and is dependent on community, rather than being universal. The land is nobody's property, but is common to all. It is shared wealth (Barrière and Barrière 1997: 15–25; Le Roy 1991: 338).

However, land is also conceptualised as property. In present practice, land (farming, forestry, judicial) is a property resource highly solicited by both the state and its population. It is the object of many interests – cultural, economic, political and social.

For the state, it is an economic and political stake. The state poses as the owner of the land. The land is the spatial expression of the state's power and sovereignty and is also a source of financial revenues.

For the population, land is an economic and political stake, but also a cultural and social one. Land is a factor of power and strength. The withholder, owner or user of land has power and controls the dynamics of production and reproduction of social groups. Land is a vital resource. But culturally and symbolically, land is a sacred object that ensures the mediation of men and women to the sacred. It is an element of social status in the sense that it determines the relationships of individuals to the different social networks to which they belong. Economically and socially, land is a means of subsistence, ensuring life, and is indispensable for survival.

Although land is understood both as a heritage and a resource, it is also more and more understood merely as an exploitable resource. Accordingly, land in Cameroon has come to mean predominantly farming and forestry lands. These lands, as exploitable resources, are the centre of growing covetousness, on local, regional and national scales.

This research covers the whole country, but divides it into two main socio-anthropological zones. The first is that of centralised communities in north and west Cameroon; the second is that of segmentary communities in south Cameroon. Preference is given to the rural and almost rural areas, where most of the struggles for access to and control over land take place. The conception of the rural is fairly extensive, taking into account land integrated into urban areas that is controlled and managed by traditional communities, for example, the suburbs of cities such as Bafoussam, Douala, Garoua and Yaounde. In these areas, the perenisation of the rural in an urban environment can be noticed and, at this point, traditional systems of land management prevail over the prescriptions of positive law.

Problematic and Aim

This research on women and land in Cameroon is part of a regional process questioning and analysing cultural transformation in Africa from a human rights perspective. Its task is to show that the protection and promotion of human rights are both a means to and an end of cultural transformation. Law and religion are appropriate institutions to encourage this transformation.

An analysis of women's land status is an example to question the dynamics of integrating human rights into cultural transformation. This research therefore poses the question of whether or not the use of the human rights paradigm is appropriate to evaluate social change in Africa as seen from the relationship between women and land (An-Na'im, Madigan and Minkley 1997: 287–9). It aims to contribute to the analysis of the roles played by customary, religious and judicial norms and practices in the building and promotion of women's economic, social and cultural rights. It also aims to develop attempts to question limitations to women's total enjoyment of these rights. And finally, it seeks to propose concrete reforms that are realistic and achievable in order to change women's land status for the better. These reform proposals are aimed at political and social (customary and religious) policy-makers, so as to ensure effective implementation in the geographical areas from which they have emerged. It is therefore action-research.

As a local process, this research is preoccupied with systematising, questioning and demanding accountability for discriminatory customs and practices affecting women. The reform proposals are therefore to be integrated into the process of valorising and claiming women's human rights in general, and their land rights in particular, as demanded by women's non-governmental organisations (NGOs) and organisations in Cameroon and the government of Cameroon itself. Indeed, the emergence of gender in NGO activities has contributed to a renewal of questioning women's land status. The involvement of NGOs in gender has helped to increase recognition of the pivotal role of women in development and to revive debates on the expansion of women's human rights in Cameroon.

Thus, for two successive years, 1997 and 1998, celebrations of International Women's Day have been devoted to analysing, questioning and denouncing discriminatory judicial norms and customary practices. Women's land status in Cameroon was raised and questions raised as follows:

- What explains the difficulties experienced by women in Cameroon in accessing, acquiring and appropriating land?
- What justifies the fact that women, who constitute 52 per cent of the total population and who work preponderantly in farming, the main productive activity in the rural areas, have difficulties obtaining access to land and are almost totally excluded from land ownership?
- Is it possible to remedy this situation?
- What is to be done?
- How to do it?

The process of action-research suggested and retained for the endeavour identified and denounced discriminatory judicial and customary practices. An appropriate methodological approach was developed and its insufficiencies and limitations noted.

Methodological Considerations

Outlining the methodology of this research and its limitations allows for an objective and scientific assessment of its findings. The theoretical paradigms and the data collection and research techniques are outlined below.

The theoretical paradigms used are those of syncretic and interdisciplinary logic. As this research aims to assess both the present situation and the evolutionary prospectives of women's land status, land cannot be studied by itself, outside its environment and setting. Land is a reflection of social relationships, and the problems raised by its exploitation are political. These political problems are correlated to the structure and functioning dynamics of societies, the interactions between them and their environment and their individual evolution. Pre-eminence is thus given to dialectical and systemic analysis. Women's land status is analysed as an element of social systems and determined by their internal laws, but subject to the influence of external factors that have a dialectical evolutionary effect. This evolution is caused not only by contradictions resulting from the internal functioning of social systems, but also by environmental constraints that impose adaptation, adjustment and cooperation. The research is contextual, systemic and dialectical, as a result of the dynamic between tradition and modernity.

Gender analysis is therefore integrated into this research. In contrast to its predecessor, Women in Development (WID), developed during the 1975–85 Decade for Women and intended to account for women's contribution to development, the Gender and Development (GAD) approach refuses to appraise the women as an entity isolated from the social unit, and takes into account relationships between women and men. It analyses unequal relationships symbolised by gender-based divisions of labour, and poses the problems created by the roles and status of both women and men and the impact of gender relationships.

With GAD, notions of gender-based differences that are fundamentally socially constructed are pointed out. Gender analysis is therefore an activist research approach to the socially structured relations between men and women in all domains of economic, political and social life. It is based on empowerment (the acquisition of power), a concept developed by Latin American feminists. It postulates that women's situations can only be improved, and equality between genders promoted, if the historically and socially valorised power relations between men and women are questioned (Hesseling and Locoh 1997: 3–5; Sow 1995: 1–17; Locoh, Labourie-Racapé and Tichict 1996). Therefore, women's access to and control over land in Cameroon is at the heart of this action-research, because land is a major stake in gender relations.

This study has also considered the heuristic contributions of institutional and comparative analysis. These have permitted clarification and presentation of the extreme hold of traditional and modern institutional dynamics on women's land status. These methods of analysis have also facilitated appraisal of the similarities, differences and contradictions among various customary land systems and the modern land system and their respective approaches to management of women's land status.

Beyond the methodological syncretism, the research was enriched by the contribution of many fields (law, sociology, anthropology, economy, geography, political science, history and, to some extent, agronomy). Until very recently, law was seen as the authorised field for researching land. But legal analysis was based on the study of status and practice, without reference to the social relationships of production, and a strictly legal approach is thus largely outdated. Land questions can no longer be confined to purely judicial analysis or even to economic analysis.

The contributions of the different fields mentioned have become essential. As

Etienne, Le Roy explains, 'land is a social relationship, having the soil or the territory as foundation and stake; whereby economic and judicial variables and the improvement techniques of nature are levelled out by political factors at different local, national and international scales' (Le Roy 1997: 455). An interdisciplinary approach helps to appraise the influence of social organisation on land and the relationships between women and men concerning land, and emphasises the historic building of land status and the power relations that determine such status. It helps to consider land dynamics in the framework of agrarian systems and to appraise land tenure in terms of localisation, spatial disposition and the efficency of agrarian systems. Thus, by means of a syncretic, interdisciplinary approach, the normative dispositions and the concrete realities faced by actors within the areas studied may be better reconciled.

The collection of data and information in the field was part of the action-research process, which is orientated towards solving practical problems in local contexts by those who are involved. This approach made it possible to involve all actors with stakes in land (those at the top and those at the bottom). Surveys in the field referred to local and regional administrative, political and traditional authorities, as well as to women's organisations, NGOs and the populations themselves. The field surveys, conducted through field visits, interviews and focus groups, were complemented by bibliographical and documentary material as well as by attendance at national and international seminars. About fifty publications were read, some related to land in general and others specifically to women and land. And four seminars on land women were attended, two at the national level and two at the international level, organised by the government of Cameroon, women's organisations, an environmental organisation and the UN respectively.

Limitations

Despite the above, the research was constrained by methodological insufficiencies and by time. The researchers were compelled to complete their work within six months. To follow up, they have integrated the research into a local environmental organisation, Planet Survey, which has developed a pilot project in the southeast of Cameroon for the promotion of women's land rights. Rather than wait for the government of Cameroon to implement the proposed reforms, it was imperative to undertake local actions for the sensitisation and training of women and traditional leaders at the community level.

With respect to methodological insufficiencies, the researchers faced two difficulties: the unavailability or weakness of reliable statistics and difficulties with quantification. The research therefore does not include statistics regarding women's land rights.

Political and Economic Context

Land in Cameroon is a complex and problematic area, unfolding in a dynamic and fluctuating cultural, economic, political and social environment. It is important to outline these dynamics and to measure their effects on women's land status.

The evolution of the economic and political context in Cameroon is marked by the imposition of neoliberalism. Cameroon's economic life was suffocated for a long time by political monolithism and the state's economic interventionism. Both Cameroon's economics and politics were, however, gradually liberalised at the beginning of the 1990s as a result of the mobilisation of the local populations, international pressure and the government's adaptive measures.

Internationally, the political context is marked by liberalisation and the movement for women's political emancipation. The liberalisation of Cameroon's political system dates from the 1990s. Responding to pressure from the local population and the international community, the ruling political party progressively reduced its authoritarianism. This slow mutation was characterised by a commitment to political liberties, the creation and functioning of opposition parties, the institutionalisation of political competition and the participation of citizens in the management of public affairs.

This process was not linear. It was contradictory and included movements both forward and backward. And the questioning and reduction of authoritarianism were not total. As in most parts of Africa, the emergence of neoliberal change was accompanied by the persistence of authoritarian traditions of governance. Cameroon practises an authoritarian democratisation. This problematic construction of democracy contained at the same time liberal innovations and 'authoritarian repetitions'. The liberalisation was marked by order and disorder, by liberal discussion and authoritarianism (Mbembe 1997; Sindjoun 1994; Bigombe Logo and Menthong 1996).

The liberalisation was expressed in the recognition of socio-cultural pluralism and the recomposition and construction of a state of law. The commitment to pluralism in the legitimate socio-political space is considerably advanced. Pluralism shapes the socio-political at various levels. It is manifested through a proliferation of associations for human rights, political associations and groupings, unions and so on. The organisational or structural emancipation of society has contributed to the slowing down of the totalitarianism of the state and to the failure of the Jacobean enterprise.

Pluralism is also evident in the media. Media pluralism has contributed to the development of the public sphere and the destruction of the founding myths of the post-colonial state. Newspapers such as *Le Messager*, *La Nouvelle Expression*, *Mutations* and *Générations* have, by their critical or provocative orientation, disrupted the immunity previously enjoyed by the state. Despite the persistence of censorship and other methods of preventing media freedom, analysis of government activities has become well established.

In the socio-political field, many frameworks of collective action and popular mobilisation can be observed. Political pluralism has spread. Multipartyism has replaced of the monopartyism of the first-generation post-colonial state. The relative institutionalisation of political competition has contributed to the structuring of a competitive political market. Opposition parties have succeeded in making themselves an unavoidable political reality. This diversification and the multiplication of modes of mobilisation are such that effective and total control by the state is now illusive or impossible. This has redefined relations between the centre and the periphery, putting into question the centralised Jacobean state. Decentralisation is progressively being applied, with the aid of local and international funding organisations. However, its social fruition will be achieved only in the long run.

Women's participation in politics is one of the aims of neoliberalism in Cameroon. Politics has been taken up by women who do not wish to play figurehead or marginal roles. Women are more and more present in both formal and informal decision-making. Their representation is low in the executive branch of government, where they occupy positions in ministries responsible for social and women's affairs. But in municipal councils and in Parliament, women's participation is appreciable.

The situation improved largely as a result of the work of women's organisations, which campaigned before different elections to incite women to register on electoral lists, to get into municipal management, to organise electoral campaigns and to invest in their political parties. In political parties, the greater awareness of the female electorate contributed to enlarging women's field of action and to increasing their responsibilities. During elections, political parties did not make much effort to attract women's votes. Women took on various duties of mobilising and organising political parties. Their advance in the public political sphere is significant, and has been supported by cultural and legal organisations and movements. In the public service, as in cultural organisations and political parties, women's organisations have developed, increased and intensified the defence and promotion of their civic, political, economic and social human rights. For example, the Association of Cameroonian Women Lawyers (ACAFEJ) organises legal consultations to inform and advise women on their human rights. Women now use political or social action to defend women's advancement and to question the socio-culturally engendered inequalities between men and women.

Women's political emancipation, developed in the urban milieu, is extending to rural life. Rural women do not express themselves only in the domestic sphere. They have started to become active in the public sphere in order to make themselves heard. Activism and progressive assertiveness is replacing passiveness and docility. This evolution is contributing to a reduction in masculine dominance and is reinforcing female empowerment. The inversion of roles in the home (to women's advantage), the economic devalorisation of cash crops and the valorisation of food crops have legitimised their ambitions.

Parallel to the evolution of neoliberalism in the political context, the economic context has experienced a liberalising evolution. During the last two decades, Cameroon's population has almost doubled, going from seven million in the 1970s to more than fourteen million today. Thirty-eight per cent of the population is urbanised, with the majority being located in the far north, where 80 per cent of the people are agricultural. The most populated provinces are the far north, which has 18 per cent of the total population, the centre with 16 per cent, the littoral and the west, each with 13 per cent. Less populated areas are the south, with only 4 per cent of the population, and the Adamawa and the east, each with 5 per cent. The average population density is 23 inhabitants per square kilometre. But in less populated provinces the density does not exceed ten people per square kilometre.

More than 30 per cent of the population is below the age of ten and 60 per cent is under 20. Demographic pressure creates serious difficulties in the provision of all economic and social services (education, employment and health). In urban areas, a reduction of parental income has reduced the level of children's education. In rural areas, increasing poverty, poor infrastructure and the unemployment of graduates aggravates the diminished role of schooling.

The economic crisis that began in the second half of the 1980s is now continuous and persistent. Cameroon has witnessed the government's disengagement, lay-offs in both public and private sectors, crises in banking, currency devaluation, increased internal and external debt, decreased oil production, collapsed raw material prices, decreased gross national product (GNP), declining imports and exports, increased degradation of living conditions and poverty. From 1988 to 1989, under pressure of international financing institutions (IFIs), the government implemented structural adjustment programmes (SAPs) to reduce the state's role in economic activities, create administrative, institutional and legal frameworks favourable to the private sector and adapt production to the requirements of the global economy. SAPs have had fragile and limited effects on macroeconomic variables, but considerable impact on individuals' behaviour and social systems.

For more than thirty years, economic activities benefited from incentives and varied forms of protection from the state, which was both sponsor and benefactor of the produce-exporting networks (Janin 1996). That protection had three main characteristics: the protection of prices and salaries guaranteed to producers, the protection of customers and the protection of local companies. Prices are payments for products sold and salaries are rewards for work done. Theoretically, in a free market there is a relationship between utilities produced and the returns achieved, between the productivity of the work and the salaries paid. In Cameroon's past, guaranteed prices and salaries lost their rewarding function as contributions to wealth creation and productivity. The state's intervention in economic activities through producer companies (SODECAO, SODECOTON, UCCA and ZAPI) and marketing companies (ONCPB, UCCAO) forced market agents to stand at a distance. State pricing policy enabled agents to become rich without making much effort. Guaranteed prices and salaries allowed the state to become corrupt and to legitimise its domination. The concern with launching a national identity at independence and with fully controlling the public sphere, explains the rapid increase of public expenses and the fixing of rates with no relationship to the market. This conception of the state was magnified in costly regulations based on hereditary redistribution of resources and patronage.

To create a political support and reinforce the power base of the state, there was an appropriation of public wealth and the privatisation of the state by those in power and their relatives. This took place through the secret distribution of economic privileges such as authorisations, contracts and subsidies. Such management of public resources, intended to redistribute revenue rather than create wealth, led to an inefficient allocation of resources and the marginalisation of most of the population.

Public companies were similarly affected. They became arenas for arbitrary authoritarianism and violence, thus explaining difficulties in their functioning. These difficulties included poor productivity due to the number of employees recruited on the basis of patronage and tribal connections rather than for their professional qualifications, and the prominence of ethnic, familial and political criteria in the management of work and production. These practices are incompatible with profit goals, competitiveness, economic production and benefits. The relationship between employer and employees within such companies and between these companies and the state were thus based on protection or submission.

At the beginning of the 1980s, Cameroon found itself with a plethora of public companies, all showing debits. To avoid bankruptcy, the government was compelled to apply international financial institution (IFI) measures, to disengage from commercial life and facilitate the emergence of the private sector. This disengagement initially appeared to be a break-up, demonstrated by the withdrawal of the state from key sectors of the economy (agriculture, commerce, transport, etc.), reductions in subsidies and limits on protectionism. But it revived private investment and reduced state controls and constraints. However, it also brought unfortunate economic consequences, such as performance contracts and staff lay-offs in both the public and private sectors. The neoliberal economy redefined the role of the public sector in socio-economic activities, disrupted communities and led to a questioning of bilateral and multilateral financing because its effect was to increase poverty.

In spite of improved macroeconomic indicators, poverty has clearly grown. In macroeconomic terms, economic revival and the relatively good shape of the economy is indicated. Yet poverty is acute in certain region, and cuts across regional boundaries in its impact on specific social groups and socio-professional categories.

In rural areas, households are severely affected by poverty. The number of people living below the poverty line has increased from 49 to 71 per cent. This considerable spread of poverty has been more extreme for peasants producing export crops, whose loss of income has reached 60 per cent. The price of food crops also fell, causing a 16 per cent diminution of total farming revenues for both export and food crops compared to 1983. The population has grown by 2 per cent per year in rural areas, while per capita income has decreased by 25 per cent. Given this situation, the implementation of strategies to revive rural areas must intensify food crop production and market integration. More than 40 per cent of the active population is today unemployed or has converted to the informal sector or to farming, both of which involve land acquisition or management. These sectors are less regulated or not at all, especially in regard to social protection. A good portion of the population thus lives on a day-to-day basis, subject to an uncertain future, with no formal social assistance.

As a result, social cohesion and stability are highly disturbed. The proliferation of informal activities has declined with the implementation of neoliberal economic development approaches. These neoliberal reforms urge those in informal sectors of the economy to return to former economic roles or to reaffirm their modernity. There is a chaotic reconstruction of social units, accompanied by disorder and social exclusion. But the rise of social activity outside the government sector is a sign of the reconstruction of complex social units, less linked to the state.

Socio-anthropological and Cultural Context

It is also important to outline the socio-anthropological and cultural context of Cameroon. The socio-anthropological context is marked by a diversity of social groups, the breaking up of religious groups, the evolution of women's social status and competition for land.

Cameroon is a land of contrast and diversity. Its territory includes both equatorial and tropical zones, each with particular social groups. These are the so-called centralised social groups predominant in the north and west, and the so-called segmental social groups in the centre, south and east.

The northern, western and littoral regions are heterogeneous, characterised by geographical and human diversity. The northern region consists of the low tropical lands of the Benue basin and the Chad plain, and the Mandara mountains. Its two predominant peoples are the non-Muslim Habes or Kirdis and the Muslim Peulh. In the local collective imagination, the Kirdis are pagan as they have not converted to Islam. In reality the Kirdis are not exclusively pagan, as some are Christian and others Muslim. They are further distinguished by livelihood.

The mountain Kirdis are known as farmers, the plains Kirdis as farmers and stockbreeders, and the Logone riverside Kirdis are farmers, stockbreeders and fishermen. The best-known Kirdis are the Guizigas, the Mafas, the Mundangs and the Tupuris, all stereotyped as pagan, based on their opposition to the Islamic Peulh. The Kirdis are segmental social groups, living in a Muslim-dominated environment. They occupy clearly limited areas in the far north province, where they constitute a demographic majority. The Peulh include the Fulanis, the Hausas and the Choa Arabs. They are found in the three northern provinces of Adamawa, north and far north.

The western region is in the highlands and includes the west and northwest provinces covering the Bamun plateau and the grass fields. Its peoples include the Bamilekes, the Bamun and the 'Anglophones', all of whom are complex and heterogeneous. The Bamileke, for example, include about fifty ethnic groups. And the 'Anglophones', resulting from British colonialism in the northwest and south-west provinces, include about sixty ethnic groups (Sindjoun 1995: 360–68). The western region is densely populated, with demographic growth resulting in intensive land cultivation. Farming, stockbreeding and commerce are the major economic activities and intense competition for land exists among farmers, traders and manufacturers. Occupation and exploitation of the territory is therefore almost total.

The littoral region is located in the Douala basin. Its wide estuaries lie at low altitude on the Atlantic Ocean. It was the first area to be urbanised and, ever since German colonisation, has remained the fastest developing and most populated region of Cameroon because of rural to urban migration. Although cosmopolitan, it is occupied by three major ethnic groups, the Doualas, the Mungos and the Pongos. Agriculture, commerce, industrial production and tourism are the key economic activities. Crop farming is developed, with peasants producing for sale as well as consumption. Agro-industrial and industrial centres are concentrated here. Competition for land is high, between 'indigenous' and 'foreign' populations on the one hand and farmers and manufacturers on the other hand.

Most communities in the northern, western and littoral regions share funda-mental characteristics. They are highly differentiated, with hierarchical social structures, and exhibit religious syncretism. Social life revolves around the cen-tralised traditional chieftancies. At the summit of the hierarchy is a first-grade hereditary chief or king, who holds economic, judicial, political and religious powers. His power over people and property (land and other wealth) is exercised through dignitaries and nobles gathered in councils or sometimes secret societies, as well as through servants of the 'royal court'. Below the king and under his orders are the second-class and third-class chieftains. They are nobles at the head of villages or districts. They are also the managers and tax collectors of land under the chieftainships, including the chiefs' lands, lineage lands, common pasture lands, sacred woods and vacant lands often distributed to young people or new migrants. Land management is according to principles of common law. Talking about the Bamilekes, for example, Emmanuel Ghomsi has written:

> The fon, in so far as he is the holder of the lands of the chieftaincy, responsible for justice, the creator and president of customary societies and the political chief, has a lot of revenue sources: first of all he is a great land owner, and his many lands are cultivated by his wives. After each harvest period, his women give him a portion of the crops. Each time a free land is given to a peasant, the latter has to pay by giving a rent in kind. (Ghomsi 1972: 155–85)

At the bottom of the pyramid are subdued and submissive *fawities*.

This social structure extends beyond the rural areas into urban areas. Hegemonic control of urban areas by the traditional chiefs and the reconstruction of village and tribe in these areas are progressively happening with rural to urban migration. The Bamileke, Bamun and Hausa chieftaincies in the cities of Douala and Yaounde are examples of this tendency (Tchandeu 1985: 72–94).

Segmental social groups exist in the central, southern and eastern regions of Cameroon. The term 'segmental' was coined in the nineteenth century to describe communal social groups. Today it is used to describe social groups in which political relationships are based on familial or parental ties and where power rests on lineage. Segmental societies are therefore decentralised and weak, when differentiated in terms of resources and structures (Hermet 1996: 258–9).

In Cameroon, segmental social groups exist in part of the coastal plain and in the tableland of the centre, the south and the east provinces. Demographic density is generally low, although there are densely populated areas in the south province. The two main social groups are the Pygmies and the Bantu. The Pygmies include the Bagyeli/Bakolas, the Bakas and the Medzan and are considered 'indigenous' as the first forest dwellers. The Bantu are more numerous and include about fifteen ethnic groups.

These communities are relatively autonomous in relation to management of their land. They are ruled by chiefs nominated by the administration on the basis of traditional criteria. Chiefs can be elders or people chosen for their personal moral or political qualities. They regulate social life with the help of a board of nobles.

Dynamism and Fragmentation of the Religious Field

Cameroon is a secular, multi-religious state. Freedom of religion is stipulated in the preamble of the Constitution of 2 June 1972, which was revised and reformed on 18 January 1996. The three dominant religions are Animism, Christianity and Islam. In addition, a multitude of Asian or American sects exists, with a dynamic presence in schools and universities. Religious festivals, both Christian and Islamic, are celebrated.

The social penetration of religion is complex and diversified. The cities of Douala in the littoral province and Yaounde in the central province are in the process of becoming Muslim. Garoua in the northern province, Mokola in the far north province and Ngaoundere in the Adamawa province have considerable Christian populations. However, despite the persistence of some Christian and Islamic centres, different religious movements are evolving throughout the country. Thus, the classic distinctions made, for example, between Animists and Christians in the equatorial zone and Animists and Muslims in the tropical zone, no longer portray the religious dynamism in Cameroon.

However, migration, urbanisation and globalisation are quantitatively and qualitatively transforming religion. The influence of religious movements on cultural, economic, political and social life is now questionable, appearing to be marginal, reduced and superficial.

Evolution of Women's Social Status

Women's social status *vis-à-vis* land is critical to any analysis of women's property rights. Women's social status remains constrained, hindering their real emancipation, their formal recognition and the protection of their economic, political and social rights. The multiplication and diversification of interests around land contributes to reinforcing women's exclusion from formal land rights.

Status is used in law to determine either the rules defining the rights and obligations of an individual or group of individuals; the constituting text of an association, a company; or the judicial rules about the state and its people. Women's status and land rights are thus prescribed by the law for individual women and for women as a group. Outside the law, status indicates an individual's position/rank in society, role, situation and/or social function. Status may be either achieved or ascribed. Ascribed status is received at birth or at different life stages, without having to be deserved or won. Achieved status is acquired by what one does, as a result of one's activity. This present analysis is inspired by the latter conception of status.

It is difficult objectively to assess women's social status in Cameroon. It is complex, raising contradictions and arousing passions. Anthropological and developmental literature imposes stereotyped images of women as being either subdued by men or classified at a low level, always considered as exchange or trade objects (Titi Nwel 1995: 25). In reaction, a Cameroonian sociologist, Henri Ngoa, published a pamphlet with a polemical and provocative title: *No, the African woman was not oppressed* (1975). Ngoa's analysis was based on social reality. However, it did not change the fact that in some social groups, women are exchanged or sold against goods and, like land, handed down as heritage. Is it possible to decide between these contradictory and opposed points of view? Are women poor, subdued, submitted to female genital mutilation, given away in marriage without their consent and exploited in their families and households? Or do they manage our societies?

Women's social status is the expression of multiple realities, influenced by space, time, social groups and organising movements, coupled with the surrounding social and political context. It is therefore necessary to contextualise analysis in relation to tradition and modernity, while bearing in mind the fact that the gap between the two is fluid. Tradition and modernity are not mutually exclusive. Tradition is dynamic and there is an interpenetration between it and modernity.

Women's position in the traditional milieu is ambivalent, complex and controversial. Social norms defining women's roles and social status assign to them a position inferior to that of men. Yet social practices and symbolic representations confer important social roles on women. It is through social institutions and systems of representation that this contradiction is revealed, and it is inherent in the power dynamics of traditional societies (Copet-Rougier 1985: 153). Tradition submits women to a double logic – that of submission and subordination in the public space and of affirmation and power in the domestic or private sphere.

The public sphere contains both the constructive and destructive aspects of the social order. It is the place of exercise of power, of creating and elaborating regulatory norms of social relations. Women are excluded from the public sphere. Their participation in it is marginal, their roles reduced and their influence limited. There are societies where women participate in the public sphere, but they are not many. And, even then, men control power and social activities. This is the case, for example, with the Bagyeli/Bakola and Baka Pygmies and the Bassa in the southern region. Here women (particularly old women) take part in the public sphere, but their participation is peripheral. In general, men withhold and manage public power. They rule, and women submit and obey. Tradition confirms male domination in the public sphere. In the Ewondo clans of the southern region, for instance, the *Mevungu* and *So* rites are institutions for the legitimisation of male power, with the former displaying women's support of male hegemony. They legitimate phallocracy, women's subjection and passive role.

However, the Ewondo clans also assign a politically instrumental role to women. In the politics of the clan, women are a means to acquire influence, a resource. 'The fundamental form of power [with the Betis] is the power to possess women in all the senses of the word: power to acquire them, power to fecundate them' (Laburthé-Tolra 1981: 356). The more wives a man possesses, the more he is honoured. A man's leadership capacity is measured by the number of his wives. This dynamic is valid for all Cameroonian societies – subtle in most segmental communities and rigid in most centralised ones.

However, women do not let themselves be dominated. They develop strategies to circumvent the public sphere and consolidate their control of the domestic or private sphere. This by-passing implies the construction of an exclusively feminine social universe, a 'women's sphere' that goes beyond the domestic space (Droy

1990: 17–20). Women thus express themselves away from the male presence, in domains such as farms, water wells and women's associations.

The domestic or private sphere is where women exercise power. Women have power in their households, inherent in their productive and reproductive roles. Women play a major role in economic production. They are in charge of farming, fishing, and sometimes hunting and small trading. Procreation depends upon them, according to religious justifications. For example, the Fali in the northern region believe that God has given to each woman the role to continue, by uniting with the soil, the creation that he [sic] initiated. Procreation is perceived as a continuation of the divine order, bringing women closer to God. Women also control the process of organising and managing matrimonial ties. They determine the choice of spouses. By so doing, they are responsible for movement of women from household to household (Yana 1997: 38). Finally, women ensure the caretaking and education of their spouses. They take care of their families materially and morally.

In the modern context, the tradition confining women's exercise of power only in the domestic or private spheres is gradually being left behind. Modernity calls into question the content and extent of men's power and offers room for women's power. It is true that conservatism and resistance still exist, perpetuating the domination and marginalisation of women. However, these are being weakened by women's mobilisation. The patriarchal project is in trouble. This is the period of women's emancipation. The global women's mobilisation legitimised by the International Women's Decade from 1975–85, followed by the Cairo Conference in 1994 and the Beijing Conference in 1995 have helped to undermine archaic norms and behaviour and to sensitise women to a consciousness of their rights.

In the political sphere, Cameroonian women occupy more and more space. And in both rural and urban areas, the number of women chiefs continues to increase steadily. Women's representation in political parties, institutions and other decision-making centres is a sign of progression. Women now play the role of flag-bearers in democratic struggles.

In the cultural and economic spheres, Cameroonian women are more devoted to activities that positively affect their social status and reinforce their authority. This is the case, for example, with the mutual aid associations and the *tontines* (mutual savings funds). Some have succeeded in launching credit unions, popular banks and saving banks, which facilitate women's access to credit and loans. The blossoming of women's cultural and economic associations contributes to their political and social emancipation. Women's large and increasing commitment in the formal and informal economy is a strategy of political and social positioning. Concomitantly, the economic weakening of their husbands imposes an inversion of roles in the home, leading to a further change in social status. Women therefore increasingly manage their households. In this way, a profound although silent revolution is taking shape in Cameroon (Sow 1995).

In short, tradition stipulating women's exclusion from and subordination within the public sphere (particularly in the political sphere) still exists. The dominance of men is culturally, politically and socially established and is rooted in institutional infrastructures. However, in spite of this, changes less visible, but profound, are taking place. They can be observed in households, in the circulation of women and in the configuration of social roles and responsibilities. Redefinitions of spheres of power are in the making, although it is difficult to foresee their final outcomes.

Land in Cameroon

Almost everywhere in sub-Saharan Africa, competition for land is intense. Land has many actors, including the state, economic actors and traditional and/or local communities, who all have divergent and multiple interests.

In Cameroon, competition is notably strong between indigenous and 'foreign' populations and between the state and traditional and/or local populations. The latter conflict clearly indicates the divergence between modern land law and customary land law, as the state's policy of land appropriation is opposed to customary systems of land use and management (Bigombe Logo 1996).

The principle underlying Cameroonian land law is set out in Article 1 of Ordinance No. 74-1 of 6 July 1974: 'the State shall be the keeper of all the lands. In that capacity, it can intervene in order to ensure a rational use or in order to take into account the imperative defence of economic options of the nation.' This affirms the state's monopoly over land. It is a principle dating from colonisation, which brought into contact two different concepts of modes of production and ownership of the means of production: the European concept respected individual property rights and the African concept respected collective use and management. The European approach conceives of land as property, and the African approach conceives of land as a common resource. The ordinance cited above embraces the colonial view.

In Cameroon, colonisation favoured the penetration and generalisation of individual property rights. The colonists showed their determination to control land use and management by implementing a policy of native dispossession. They based this dispossession on the automatic appropriation of all land supposedly vacant and without a 'master'. Under German colonisation at the end of the nineteenth century, all vacant lands, except those belonging to chiefs and their communities, became the property of the German Imperial Crown. Under British colonisation, all land, whether occupied or not, belonged to the natives but remained under the control of the British governor, who managed it for the benefit of all. This was stipulated in the Land and Native Ordinance of Northern Nigeria, No. 1 of 1916 and applied to southern Cameroon in 1927, No. 1 of 1929. Under French colonisation, land use, management and ownership remained as under

German colonisation, as stipulated in the French Decree of 12 January 1938. French colonisers carried out massive expropriation of land for the state and developed three major land tenure systems. First, the land tenure system that integrates into the state's private domain 'vacant lands without master', to redistribute them for colonial purposes or individual profit. Second, the land tenure system transforming customary land rights into 'definitive and unquestionable' land titles by registration. And third, the land tenure system establishing customary land rights. The prime objective of generalising individual or private property rights over land was thus coupled with solidifying state monopoly of land (Le Roy 1991: 16–17).

The post-colonial state maintained colonial land tenure systems. The legislative and regulatory texts adopted between 1963 and 1970 preserved the state's monopoly over customary land rights. Decree No. 64-9/COR of 30 June 1964, taken in application of the Decree of 9 January 1963 which established the land tenure system of eastern Cameroon, assigns only user rights over land to customary and/or traditional communities. The subsequent unification of land rights achieved after 1972 transformed land as a collective heritage into state property in two major categories: land previously occupied for a period of ten years; and free unoccupied land. Post-colonial land policy established during the 1974 reforms, and currently in force, instituted land as state property.

This land tenure has become the common law of the land system, confining customary and/or traditional populations to the enjoyment of conditional land rights alone. This was done to realise the political objectives of national integration and economic development. However, the state's ownership of land has taken shape by appropriation. The state is the 'master' of the land, its exclusive owner and manager (Kamto 1996: 90–95). Land now falls into two categories: non-exploited but occupied; and empty and/or 'virgin' lands. Citizens gain access to state land by trying to protect their customary and/or traditional land rights or by acquiring land and registering it. In the first case, communities must establish the land's development by exploitation or occupation. In the second, they must register occupied land (Le Roy 1987: 41–52).

The 1974 reforms instituted only one judicial form of land ownership, that is, land as absolute and exclusive individual and/or private property, and one procedure to exercise that ownership, that is, registration. The attribution of titles to land must be in conformity with the references in the land registers. Titles to land are official testimony of ownership of land as property. Titles can be obtained in many ways: through purchase by mutual agreement; through donations *inter vivos*; through legacies or wills; and through the state's attribution of land with an obligation to develop it.

The formalities and procedures relative to the acquisition of titles to land are set out in Decree No. 76-165 of 24 April 1976. The registration procedure is dependent on an administrative judge, whereas conflicts related to anterior or post-procedures of registration fall within the competence of the judiciary. In practice, although registration is widely practised in urban areas, it is scarce in rural areas. Ignorance of the law, the complexity of the steps to be undertaken and the financial conditions are such that most of farmlands and pastoral lands remain under state control. Yet although the state asserts itself as the owner and exclusive manager of land, its monopoly is resisted by customary law and practice, which tenaciously continue, even in the wake of liberalisation. Although positive law does not recognise them, customary land law and practice still regulate an important part of land, most notably in regard to forest user rights. Customary and/or traditional communities remain linked, by ignorance or by contestation, to their customary land rights. Viewed from the lens of modern legislation, many people appear to be illegally using lands they customarily have user rights to (Kamto 1996: 93).

However, as a study by the Ministry of Environment and Forests reveals, the attitudes of customary and/or traditional communities are not identical in all regions of the country. Nevertheless, customary law and practice sets out identical justifications for questioning positive law on land. These justifications are many and are not legal in nature:

Incorporation of developed and occupied land According to custom, land has been developed and occupied by the ancestors to whom the communities belong. Land belongs to them, serving as a blessed link between ancestral generations and the present. Modern legislation cannot abolish these time-honoured relations.

Notion of free land Free land is land that the Germans stole from the natives and declared 'vacant lands without a master' and therefore 'land of the crown'. Customary and/or traditional communities denounce the notion that these lands were 'vacant' and free for possession by the German colonisers. They belonged to the ancestors, and customary and/or traditional communities consider themselves to be the legitimate owners of these lands.

Preponderance of conflicts of interests The state aims to achieve the general interest, that is, the economic and social development of all citizens, whereas customary and/or traditional communities pursue private interests, seeking to personally exploit, rent or sell land. Thus the state wants to attribute land only to those who will develop it, whereas customary and/or traditional communities wish to keep land as property, whether it is developed or not.

Failure of the 1974 reforms to conceptualise 'communities' Customary and/or traditional communities are indifferent to the 1974 reforms, which they consider useless in rural areas where people continue, as in the past, to occupy and peacefully exploit, without title, land whose limits only the state is questioning. In this sense the 1974 reforms only concern urban areas.

In spite of compulsory land registration, introduced in Cameroon in 1974, the majority of farmlands remains under customary and/or traditional occupation. In 1987, fewer than 30,000 of the 1,145,700 rural farms of Cameroon were on registered lands. There is insecurity in the enjoyment of such land, because the lack of titles does not facilitate the full use of it, and business people or other elites can use the economic crisis affecting peasants to purchase the land, register it and later rent it back to the peasants or evict them from it.

Evidence of land development as a condition of access to land as property Customary and/or traditional communities do not want evidence to take into account the duration of the development.

Various conflicts and tensions are developing between state land law and the customary land law and practice related to rural land status and the use of land for farming. There is a clear increase in land disputes due to illiteracy, opposition to demarcation, migration, overpopulation in some areas (the plains of the far north and the Mandara mountains) and double demarcation.

How can positive law and customary law and practice be reconciled? The question is fundamental and unavoidable.

PART I Land Status of Women in Cameroon

The land status of women has a double reality. It has to do with women's position and roles in land. And it refers back to their status as prescribed by the land acquisition and management process. This analysis attempts to tackle this double reality.

The problem is that of legally improving women's land status. How do, or how might modern and customary law improve women's access to and control over land? Women's land status thus notes the rights that women do and can have with respect to land, as well as the systems to guarantee and manage those rights. Improving women's access to and control over land is different for each normative order. The modern normative order seems to be more liberal and open, whereas the traditional order is authoritarian and rigid.

Women's Land Status in the Modern Land System

The modern land system in Cameroon, considered as positive law relating to the acquisition and the management of land, includes legislative and regulatory texts resulting from the 1974 reforms. These include ordinances of the President of the Republic ratified by the National Assembly, laws voted in the National Assembly and related application decrees.

There are three main ordinances:

- Ordinance No. 74/1/06 of July 1974, determining the land system.
- Ordinance No. 74/2 of 6 July 1974, determining the domain system.
- Ordinance No. 74/3 of 6 July 1974, relative to the expropriation procedure for public utility and to indemnification modalities, modified by Law No. 85/09 of 4 July 1985.

There are also three main laws:

- Law No. 80-22 of 14 July 1980, relative to the repression of land and tenurial offences.
- Law No. 19 of 26 November 1983, relative to the competence of the Consulting Committee and that of the jurisdiction authorities.
- Law No. 94/01 of 20 January 1994, setting the forest, fauna and fishing systems.

Finally, there are four major decrees:

- Decree No. 76/165/ of 27 April 1975, setting the conditions of acquisition of a land title.
- Decree No. 76/166 of 27 April 1975, setting the conditions of management of land as state property.
- Decree No. 76/167 of 27 April 1976, setting the conditions of management of the state's private property.
- Decree No. 84/311 of 22 May setting the conditions for the application of Law No. 80/22 of 14 July 1980, relative to the repression of land and tenurial offences.

These texts are applicable throughout Cameroon (in both the former Anglophone west Cameroon and Francophone east Cameroon). And they are similarly applicable in both urban and rural areas, ignoring the fact that each has its own peculiarities. The texts stipulate the accession to individual property rights over land without forbidding the collective appropriation of land. They provide for the creation of state's domain and for land to be managed by the state in two categories: the first based on land occupied or exploited by individuals and/or customary and/or traditional communities; and the second based on lands yet to be occupied. These unoccupied lands are known as 'vacant without a master'. They suppress the 'usucaption' (prescriptive acquisition) of Article 2265 of the Civil Code, which, before the 1974 reforms, was a way of permanent appropriation, with goodwill, of land occupied or used for ten years. Since the 1974 reforms, registration, conditional on the development of land, has become the unique mode of access to full ownership.

In an analysis of women's land status in Cameroon, the modern land system seems to be more amenable to affirming women's land rights than the traditional land system. It does not differentiate or discriminate between men and women in the process of acquisition and management of lands. However, there are hind-rances to women's benefiting from and fully enjoying these land rights, related to women's comparatively low education and the insufficiencies and the weaknesses of positive law.

Formal non-differentiation and non-discrimination The modern land system is applicable to all citizens, irrespective of race, religion, sex (gender) or social status. There is no formal attempt to subordinate women's land rights.

The Constitution of 2 June 1972, revised on 18 January 1996, stipulates in its preamble that 'the people of Cameroon, declare that the human person, without distinction as to race, religion, sex, or beliefs possesses inalienable and sacred rights'. The liberties and rights enumerated in the preamble of the revised Constitution differ from those in the earlier one by stipulating that 'the nation protects and encourages the woman'. This recognises women's rights and shows that their necessary protection is a constitutional issue. The right to property is one of these rights. The Constitution specifies that all citizens have rights to use and enjoy property and that these rights are guaranteed by law.

Further, legal texts on land and its tenurial aspects do not discriminate between men and women. Law No. 74/1 of 6 July 1974 regulates in a non-categorical way land appropriation by Cameroonians. It stipulates that 'the State guarantees to all the persons physical or moral possessing lands in property, the right to enjoy it and to deal with it freely'. The conditions as well as the procedures for the acquisition of land titles are identical for both men and women, as Decree No. 76/165 of 27 April 1976 confirms when setting the conditions for titles.

However, it is necessary to recognise that the modern land system is deficient when it comes to female succession. Female succession is restricted, hindering women from accessing land as heritage. In addition, women are discriminated against in practice. The complexity and length of land registration procedures hinders them more that it does most men. And cultural and practical barriers continue to make women's access to justice more difficult than men's.

Modalities of women's access to land At the legal level, explicit discrimina-tion against women does not arise. Cameroonian land law recognises and protects women's rights to access land, both as full property and for use. For acquisition as full property with titled land, the owner can sell it to any purchaser of his/her choice.

There should be no more difficulty when the transfer of land occurs through succession, since formal jurisprudence ignores custom and/or tradition with its gender-based inequities, making men the more likely to be validated as heirs of land. However, the situation is different when women wish to acquire full property of land through customary law and practice. In addition to customary possession of land, for example, women could develop the land and decide by virtue of these development efforts to begin the registration procedure. Registration may bring a woman the land title. But custom and/or tradition would ensure her only user rights.

Even at the legal level, women face barriers to acquisition of land in this manner, generally in the form of counterclaims initiated by relatives in order to hamper the women's claims to titles. When customary acquisition occurs through succession, for example, disputes are often raised by the heirs.

Women can, however, exercise separate and non-familial-based land rights in such situations. The most common of these is usufruct, the right to use and enjoyment of property. Under usufruct, land is divided and the owner remains with 'abusus', the right to deal in the property, which is the most profound right, although not the most visible. In conformity with Article 767 of the Civil Code, the spouse in life is granted usufruct on a portion of the land left by the deceased. This right is not always understood or admitted by the beneficiary or the heirs.

Nevertheless, in the modern land system, women have the right to free access to land, titled or not. The law is clear. However, in practice women face difficulties exercising this right because of illiteracy and ignorance.

Hindrances to women's access to land Factors limiting women's access to land are on two levels: the cultural and socio-economic level, and the institutional.

Cultural and socio-economic hindrances to women's access to land are illiteracy and poverty. The level of education is low in rural areas and decreasing in urban areas. It is lower still for girls and women. The number of women with access to education is limited. The modern land system enacted titles to land as the major means of acquiring lands in both rural and urban areas. The rigidity of the conditions demanded, as well as the bureaucratic complexity and slowness of procedures, present obstacles for illiterate women to access land. As Jean-Marie Ela has explained, few peasants can easily get titles from the administrative departments where corruption is greatest. Obtaining a title to land supposes formalities that illiterate peasants cannot fulfil. Most of them get lost in the 'Kafkaesque' bureaucracy (Ela 1982: 97). Cameroonian women are not only illiterate. They are also poor. The cost of the procedures to title land discourages and disempowers women.

The cultural and socio-economic factors are coupled with institutional hindrances. These include the silence of or gaps in positive law on important points relative to women's land status. Positive law has deficiencies relating to women's succession rights in relation to those of men. Women also fear the male-dominated justice system. Most women are incapable of defending their rights in court. Few of them choose a legal solution because they lack confidence in the justice system as a result of corruption. Finally, they fear the retaliation that they are likely to be subjected to in their families or communities following legal action. They therefore adopt attitudes of compromise and/or resignation.

Women's Land Status in the Traditional Land System

Cameroonian customs and/or traditions are generally more rigid in regard to women. Women are marginalized to the benefit of men, who remain the decision-makers, even over decisions directly concerning women. Customarily and/or traditionally, men manage land. Women come to the fore only exceptionally, depending not on custom and/or tradition, but on individual families who try to be reasonable in granting position to their sisters or daughters.

Women are disqualified from the management of land because of the gender-based labour divisions existing in customary and/or traditional communities. Men are the producers of marketable crops such as cocoa, coffee and cotton that provide income or revenue to households. Women specialise in food crops, which are not considered to be income-generating.

In customary and/or traditional communities, women's land rights are limited to user rights. Women are allowed user rights on their fathers' or spouses' land. However, these rights are precarious in that they can be lost in cases of divorce or widowhood. In the Beti region, for example, once a woman is married, she no longer has access to her father's land, except if she breaks her marital ties and only if her father agrees to reinstate her user rights on his land.

Women use land for farming, specifically for food crops. Income- or revenue-generating crops are viewed as signs of land appropriation. If a woman embarks on growing such crops, she automatically becomes the owner of the land.

Custom and/or tradition recognises two modalities for women to access land: acquisition for sustainable use; and acquisition for temporary use. Customary and/or traditional acquisition for long-term use takes the form of donations and inheritance or succession.

Donations cover various aspects of social life. Land can be lent to somebody without the expectation of financial returns. But this is a loan, motivated by filial or parental ties. Donations are generally made between men. They are not accessible to all women. If a donation is made to a woman, it is because she has remained single while having natural male children. The donation is justified because her male children are from 'her' lineage and can inherit.

Customarily and/or traditionally, land used by individuals within communities is inherited. The usual rule is that sons inherit from their father. Inheritance can also be extended to male children born of a girl before her marriage. In such a case, the will of the deceased father will prevail if, while living, he had demanded that the male children of his unmarried daughters be taken into account. In principle, the sharing of land is done by the father. If he dies before having shared his land, the eldest son will do it. Partitioning is in accordance with the number of sons, but unequally so as the eldest is entitled to the largest share. This is justified by the fact that the eldest generally hosts the widow(s) of his late father, as well as his unmarried sisters.

Women, whether in centralised or segmental social groups, do not inherit land, save in exceptional cases. Unmarried girls are taken care of by a family member, normally their eldest brother, until their marriages. They then normally move in with their husbands' families. It is viewed as abnormal for them to own land in their own villages.

However, there are exceptions. A number of women manage their husbands' property, including land. For example, when a widow has male children of a young age, the land left by her late husband enables her to raise them. In such a case the 'real' heirs are the sons and the mother is just a usufructuary. A widow can also inherit land from her husband even if she had no male children. In this case, the land is used for food crops, with land for income- or revenue-generating crops usually going to her husband's brother(s). Finally, a widow can inherit her husband's land even though she has only daughters. In this way, she would be given the means to raise her children. Later, the land would return to her late husband's family.

Customary and/or traditional acquisition for temporary use generally takes the form of a loan. In the forests of the Lekie region, for example, land competition is acute, forcing local communities to move into neighbouring regions and ask for land loans. These land loans are specific allocation. The borrower has to specify what he or she intends to do with the land he or she requests. Food crops are easy to get land loans for, because they grow over a short duration. Women can borrow land for a determined period of time. In this case, it is usually land that is unexploited. The borrower generally has to pay for the land loan, in money or in kind.

Hindrances to the extension of women's traditional rights of use The fluctuating nature of the customary and/or traditional land system, and the orality and non-codification of customs and/or traditions, hinder the extension of women's land rights beyond use.

Instability and variability characterise customary and/or traditional land systems, the law and practice of which vary from one region to another. All customary and/or traditional land systems exclude women from land ownership, but some systems are more rigid than others. For example, according to the Beti land is patrilineal and is transmitted from father to son. If a father has only daughters, the land generally comes back to the deceased family member, that is, to a father or a male relative if he had one, and only exceptionally to a female relative. If a woman has already married, she is not allowed to come and cultivate her own family's land, as she is no longer considered a family member. She may only help her mother if the latter calls upon her.

But custom and/or tradition is variable. Even in the Beti region there are now families that are reacting against custom and/or tradition when they find it inconvenient. Custom and/or tradition is sometimes modified. It is now not unusual to see women inheriting from their fathers. Similarly, in west Cameroon it is not unusual for women to manage their fathers' heritage, although the filiation remains patrilineal.

In addition, customs and/or traditions are characterised by orality and non-codification. There are no written texts about customary and/or traditional land law and practice. Knowledge of them is transmitted orally, from one generation to another.

Finally, women are considered as inferior to men. Because of this they are excluded from decision-making. It is impossible to understand women's status without relating it to that of men and without placing it within the framework of all cultural and social institutions, including eating taboos (Droy 1990: 16). The division of tasks between men and women has been formed from persistent cultural and social models. Women assist men in the fulfilment of tasks necessary for family life (Yana 1997: 42).

Thus, current changes find obstacles among women themselves, who include supporters of both modernity and tradition. They do not agree on how to analyse and improve women's status. Modernists think that women must be treated equally, on the basis of the fundamental principle that all (wo)men are born equal in human rights. But traditionalists think that making such a claim is pointless. Reactions to the Forth World Conference on Women, held in 1995 in Beijing, clearly illustrate this. Many women do not know about the Beijing Declaration and Platform for Action. Modernists want equality with men, but traditionalists ask whether all five fingers on the same hand have the same height, and whether men are equal among themselves. To the traditionalists, modernists are struggling for themselves and not for the feminine gender. They hold that a minority of 'emancipated women' cannot speak in the name of rural women, with whom they have little in common.

Religions and the Construction of Women's Land Status

The revealed religions are more flexible as regards women than traditional religions. This analysis focuses on Christianity, Islam and some traditional religions, and is far from exhaustive.

Christianity is based on the equality of individuals, irrespective of gender. Christianity advocates that all individuals, being created by God, should have the same rights in all domains of life.

This being the case, Christianity acknowledges the same land rights for both men and women. Women have the right to inherit from their fathers, since they are daughters before being wives. For example, in a pastoral message to the Yaounde Archdiocese, the Archbishop said that

women and men in so far as they are descending from a divine creature must communicate everything in the same impulse, for God our father loves his children on equal footing. That's the reason why he wishes that all his children should have a considerable share of his heritage ... We too have to love our children on equal footing and share to them what we have without any difference.

These remarks testify the place that Christianity gives to women as human beings.

Christianity also recognises women's primary contribution to life: they give birth and have a right to places of choice in the society within which they live. They are men's complements rather than subordinates. They are part and parcel of men's being: 'love one another as I loved you'. This love assumes a recognition of the same rights for both men and women, including land rights.

Islam seems rigid with respect to women, because the duties of Muslim women are more talked about than their rights.

Women's status under Islam remains dominated by customary and/or traditional religions. Women suffer the effects of violence more than men (Arkoun 1994: 71). In the customary and/or traditional family, the head of the family has an almost absolute power over his wife and children (Delcambre 1991: 101). Islam sees women as intellectually emancipated. However, women cannot claim the same rights as men. The Qur'an and Hadith are used to explain women's status under Islam. Muslim reformers have pleaded for the improvement of this status; Islamic law is being put into question by changing cultural and social practices.

Islam, as set out in the Qur'an and various Hadith, is different from current cultural and social practices. Islam acknowledges some rights for women, notably the right to inheritance. Women can inherit from their parents (Qur'an, Chapter 4, verse 12). Women have the right to half of men's share. This is justified on the basis that they are taken care of by their husbands.

This right is applicable to all inheritance, including land. Islam therefore recognises women's right to inherit land from their fathers, but not the same amount as their brothers. In practice in Cameroon, this right is flouted to the benefit of custom and/or tradition, so that women are excluded from land ownership and management. According to men, that exclusion is grounded in Sharia law under various Hadith that note women's inferiority and subordination to men.

The traditional religions are Animist. These religions are rigid with regard to women, whose submission to men is required. They do not therefore respect women's right to property, including land.

PART II Evolutionary Tendencies of Women's Land Status in Cameroon

Transformation of Land Systems and Women's Land Status

Women's status is not static. Cameroon is in the process of change and women are involved in that change. This change is attributed to the 1994 CFA franc devaluation that increased prices for cocoa and coffee. In spite of their invisibility and without having acquired the same status as men, women have come to be at the heart of development. It is not difficult to come across women involved in domains formerly reserved for men. For example, since the beginning of the economic crisis women have been involved in the marketing of income- or revenue-generating crops. Most women began doing this to diversify their incomes, to add to their families' decreasing budgets and to emancipate themselves from their husbands' financial guardianship. Their change of occupation is diversely viewed by men. For some, it is a sign of disdain for their husbands or an attempt at independence. For others, it is a help to their husbands.

The transformation of land is also perceptible as a result of the process of commodification of land. Land is no longer a heritage or a resource. It has become a marketable good with monetary value. It can be bought and sold. The market for land in Cameroon has developed. Anyone can now buy land as long as they have money. Women are also now free to buy land and those who have money do so. Women are becoming landowners.

In order to express themselves better and make their abilities known at the local level, women have gathered into associations. There are a multitude of women's associations, including mutual help groups for agriculture and *tontines*. The mutual help groups for agriculture are contributions of (wo)manpower to create large farms and to sell crops once harvested. *Tontines* gather and save money, the financial contributions of members, for use as mutual aid. These associations aim to enable women to supply their own needs and thus free them from male guardianship.

Women's associations at the local level serve as the basis for women's organisations at the national level, which serve as the basis for cooperation between rural and urban women. National women's organisations work in many sectors, including culture, economics, education and health. They help women to access knowledge, enabling them to manage common problems faced and to achieve self-fulfilment.

Customarily and/or traditionally, women cannot become landowners. But with the changes mentioned above, women are freely, with money, acquiring land. Purchasing enables them to counter discrimination and inequality. Women buy land either to farm or build houses, demonstrating that they are capable of taking their lives into their own hands.

Searching for Solutions to Women's Barriers to Accessing Land

Assistance and support to women in need It is imperative to offer support to women in need. An education, development and knowledge transfer process has to be implemented, which will require financial and material support. In addition, some women want to develop microprojects in agriculture. Credit should be extended to such women to assist with purchasing land.

Information and sensitisation of women on their land rights To help women to know their land rights, awareness raising or sensitisation workshops should be held at the local level. Through the media, women's associations and organisations should provide knowledge to women in local languages, so that they can claim their land rights.

Conclusion

Examining women's land status poses problems that have to be solved. Women have an inferior social status to men. There is a link between their social status and their land status, as the former determines the latter. Land thus reflects social relations and the problems that it presents are political. A holistic approach to land, incorporating anthropology, economics, psychology, sociology and law should therefore be adopted, to understand fully women's exclusion from access to and control over land.

Land demonstrates the connection between tradition and modernity, between endogeneity and exogeneity. Customary and/or traditional law and practice predominate in rural areas. Modern positive law and policy do not take this sufficiently into account as regards women's access to and control over land.

Customary and/or traditional land law and practice is rigid with respect to women's access to and control over land. However, it does recognise women's rights of use. Modern positive law is more liberal, establishing women's land rights, but there are hindrances limiting the exercise of those rights. To reduce these hindrances, women's power should be reinforced at all levels. The state should see that its authority is restored and the law respected.

Recommendations

Action to be taken

1. Institutional and legal reforms. At the national level, women's education should be encouraged so that they know and can claim their rights. The law should be made more accessible. The gaps between modern positive law and customary and/or traditional law and practice must be bridged in a conciliatory process.

In this way, modern positive law could serve as a bridgehead to transform customary and/or traditional land law and practice.

2. Customary and/or traditional transformation. At the local level, custom and/or tradition remain an integral part of society, without necessarily contributing to social harmony. Action should therefore be taken to contribute to women's empowerment, enabling women to lobby for the transformation of their cultural and/or traditional social status. Custom and/or tradition must be adapted and modernised. This can occur through the identification and promotion of customary and/or traditional innovations.

Implementation of actions to be undertaken The actions to be implemented should incorporate two strategies.

1. Strategies from the top-down:
- Awareness-raising and sensitisation of policy-makers, including international actors, the state and chiefs.
- Supporting agrarian reforms.

2. Strategies from the bottom-up:
- Building communication and dialogue among women and men.
- Awareness-raising and sensitisation of both women and men.
- Strengthening women's action capacity.
- Supporting micro-projects for the transformation of women's land status so as to secure their access to and control over land.

References

Adjete Kouassigan, G. (ed.) (1982) *Encyclopédie juridique de l'Afrique: droit des biens*, Abidjan: Les nouvelles editions africaines.

'L'Afrique des femmes' (1997), *Politique africaine*, No. 65, March.

Ahanhanzo Glélé, M. (1981) *Religion, culture et politique en africaine noire*, Paris: Présence africaine-Economica.

Albert, I. (1993) 'Des femmes, une terre', in *Une nouvelle dynamique sociale au Bénin*, Paris: L'Harmattan.

Amougou, J.-P. (1985) *La géographie: le Cameroun*, Paris: Armand Colin.

Analyse de la place des femmes: expérience au Sahel (1996) Dakar: ACOPAM-Genre et développement, Programme BIT.

Analyse des conflits et du cadre juridique et institutionnel de l'environnement au Cameroun (1995), Yaoundé: MINEF.

An-Na'im, A., A. Madigan and G. Minkley (1997) 'Cultural transformations and human rights in Africa: a preliminary report', *Emory International Law Review*, Vol. 11, No. 1.

Arkoun, M. (1994) 'La femme en Islam', in Halimi, Gisele (ed.) *Femmes: moitié de la terre, moitié du pouvoir*, Paris: Gallimard.

Bachelet, M. 'Titulaires des droits fonciers coutumiers', in *Encyclopédie juridique de l'Afrique*, Vol. 5.

Barbier, J.-C. (1985) *Femmes du Cameroun: mères pacifiques, femmes rebelles*, Paris: Karthala-Orstom.

Barrière, O. and C. Barriere (1997) *Le foncier-environnement: fondements juridico-institutionnels pour une gestion durable des ressources naturelles renouvelables au Sahel*, Rome: FAO.

Bayart, J.-F. (ed.) (1993) *Religion et modernité politique en Afrique noire: dieu pour tous et chacun pour soi*, Paris: Karthala.

Berhane-Selassie, T. (ed.) (1991) *Gender Issues in Ethiopia*, Addis Ababa: Institute of Ethiopian Studies, Addis Ababa University.

Bigombe Logo, P. (1990) 'Le phénomène du pouvoir dans les sociétés pygmées de l'est-Cameroun: le cas des sociétés Baka du département du Haut-Nyong: mémoire de maîtrise en science politique', Yaoundé: Université de Yaoundé.

— (1996) 'Contestation de l'etat et construction d'une identité spatiale au Cameroun méridional forestier', *Polis: revue Camerounaise de science politique*, Vol. 1, February.

— (1997) 'Changement politique et dynamiques d'instrumentalisation de l'ethnicité Kirdi au Cameroun septemtrional', Yaoundé: GRAPS.

— (1998) *Femmes pygmées: sédentarisation et emancipation*, Yaoundé: GRAPS.

Bigombe Logo, P. and H.-L. Menthong (1996) 'Crise de légitimité et evidence de la continuité politique', *Politique africaine*, No. 62, June.

Binet, J. (1959) *Le statut des femmes au Cameroun forestier*, Paris: ORSTOM.

Bopda, A. (1994) 'De la reproduction sociale à la consolidation de la cellule économique: le rôle de la femme dans la société Beti', in G. Courade (ed.) *Le village Camerounais à l'heure de l'ajustement*, Paris: Karthala.

Butegwa, F. (1998) 'Meditiating culture and human rights in favour of land rights for women in Africa: a framework for community level action', Entebbe: International Conference on Women and Land in Africa.

— (1996) *Le Cameroun dans l'entre-deux*, Paris: Karthala.

Caswell, S. (1998) 'Une force durable: les femmes et la foresterie', *Actualités des forêts tropicales*, Vol. 6, No. 2.

Champaud, J. (1973) *Mom: terroir Bassa (Cameroun)*, Paris: ORSTOM.

Copet-Rougier, E. (1985) 'Contrôle masculin, exclusivité féminine dans une société patrilinéaire', in J.-C. Barbier (ed.) *Femmes du Cameroun: mères pacifiques, femmes rebelles*, Paris: Karthala-Orstom.

Coulibaly, C. (1997) 'Problèmatique foncière et gestion des conflits en Afrique noire', *Stratégies d'avant l'ère démocratique*, Bamako: Editions le cauri d'or.

Courade, G. (ed.) (1994) *Le village Camerounais à l'heure de l'ajustement*, Paris: Karthala.

Creevey, L. E. (1991) 'The impact of Islam on women in Senegal', *Journal of Developing Areas*, Vol. 25, No. 3, April.

Dabtouta, G. (1995) 'Les problèmes fonciers dans les localités de Meskine et de Salak (extrème-nord): mémoire de maîtrise en sciences sociales', Yaoundé: Université Catholique d'Afrique Centrale.

Daou, J. V. and L. Didier (1997) *Les peuples des forêts tropicales: systèmes traditionnels et développement rural en Afrique equatoriale, grande Amazonie et Asie du sud-est*, Bruxelles.

Delcambre, A.-M. (1991) *L'Islam*, Paris: Editions la Découverte.

Delpechin, B. (1983) 'La terre et les femmes: conflits ruraux au Cameroun du sud', *Cahiers de l'ORSTOM: série sciences humaines*, Vol. 19, No. 2.

Diaw, C. M. and J. C. S. Njomkap (1998) *La terre et le droit: une anthropologie institutionnelle de la tenure foncière, de la jurisprudence et du droit fonciers chez les peuples Bantou et Pygmées du Cameroun méridional forestier*, Inades-Formation.

Diaw, C. M., N. Bot Si and Ayong (1997) *Culture itinérante: occupation des sols et droits fonciers au sud-Cameroun*, Londres: ODI.

Doumbé Mulongo, M. (1972) *Les coutumes et le droit au Cameroun*, Yaoundé: Clé.

Droy, I. (1990) *Femmes et développement rural*, Paris: Karthala.

Durkheim, E. (1981) *Les règles de la méthode sociologique*, Paris: Quadrige PUF.

Ebolo, M.-D. (1997) 'Dialectique d'émancipation et d'assujettissement de la société civile et processus de libéralisation au Cameroun: de la société civile mythique à la société civile impure', Yaoundé: GRAPS.

Eboussi Boulaga, F. (1997) *La démocratie de transit au Cameroun*, Paris: L'Harmattan.

Les ecosystèmes de forêts denses et humides d'Afrique centrale: actes de la conférence inaugurale (1996), Brazzaville: UICN, USAID and CIFOR.

Ela, J.-M. (1982) *L'Afrique des villages*, Paris: Karthala.

— (1994) *Afrique: l'irruption des pauvres, société contre ingérence, pouvoir et argent*, Paris: L'Harmattan.

L'encyclopédie de la république unie du Cameroun (1981), Abidjan: NEA.

Etounga Manguelle, D. (1997) *Pour reconstruire et moderniser le Cameroun: on va faire comment? Réflexion pour un programme de réformes*, Yaoundé: Mandara.

Evertzen, A. (1995) *Les villageoises au Bénin: l'acquisition du pouvoir*, Cotonou: SNV.

Ezo'o Bizeme, M. and J.-P. Komon (1996) 'Cameroun: la crise économique continue', *Afrique et développement*, Vol. 21, Nos 2 and 3.

Fall, I. (1994) Conac, G. and A. Amor (eds) *Islam et droits de l'homme*, Paris: Economica.

Fall, R. (1994) 'Femmes et pouvoir dans les sociétés nord sénégambiennes', *Africa Zamani*, No. 2, July.

Faure, A. (1995) *L'appropriation privée en milieu rural: politiques foncières et pratiques locales au Burkina-Faso*, Londres: IIED.

Femme et héritage: propriété foncière et gestion de la terre au Cameroun: rapport d'étude (1997), Yaoundé: NAPMEW and MINASCOF.

'Les femmes et la terre: etude de la tenure foncière au Sénégal' (1995), in *Femmes et la gestion des ressources naturelles en Afrique*, Nairobi: ELCI-CRDI.

La foresterie communautaire: evaluation rapide des droits fonciers et de la propriété de l'arbre et de la forêt (1991), Rome: FAO.

Gasse, V. (1982) *Les régimes fonciers africains et Malgache: evolution depuis l'indépendance de l'Afrique*, NEA.

Genre et développement: une approche nigérienne (1997), Niamey: Coopération suisse-Programme femmes.

Ghomsi, E. (1972) 'Les Bamilékés du Cameroun, essai d'étude historique, des origines à 1920: thèse de doctorat de 3e cycle en histoire', Paris: Sorbonne.

Gianola Gragg, E. C. (1997) 'Apports nouveaux et aspects pratiques de la question foncière Africaine: étude comparée de l'approche civiliste et de celle du common law', *Le Flamboyant*, No. 44, December.

'Grands et larges débats de femmes' (1998), *Mutations*, No. 98, Mars.

Halimi, G. (1994) *Femmes, moitié de la terre, moitié du pouvoir*, Paris: Gallimard.

Hermet, G. (1996) *Dictionnaire de la science politique et des institutions politiques*, Paris: A. Colin.

Hesseling, G. and T. Locoh (1997) 'Femmes, pouvoir, sociétés', *Politique africaine*, No. 65, March.

Huda, S. (ed.) (1995) *Land: A Journal of the Development Practitioners*, Vol. 2, December.

Janin, P. (1996) 'Un planteur sans etat: peut-il encore être un planteur?' *Politique africaine*, No. 62.

Kamto, M. (1986) *Pouvoir et droit en Afrique noire: essai sur les fondements du constitutionnalisme dans les etats d'Afrique noire francophone*, Paris: LGDJ.

— (1996) *Droit de l'environnement en Afrique*, Vanves: EDICEF.

Laburthé-Tolra, P. (1981) *Les seigneurs de la forêt*, Paris: Sorbonne.

— (1985) *Initiations et sociétés secrètes au Cameroun*, Paris: Karthala.

Laburthé-Tolra, P. and J.-P. Warnie (1994) *Ethnologie-anthropologie*, Paris: PUF.

La Clavère, G. (ed.) (1979) *Atlas de la république unie du Cameroun*, Paris: Editions jeune Afrique.

Lavigne Deville, P. (1996) 'Comment gérer le foncier en Afrique de l'ouest?' *Grain de sel*, No. 4, December.

Le Bris, E., E. Le Roy and F. Leimderfer (1982) *Enjeux fonciers en Afrique noire*, Paris: ORSTOM Karthala.

Le Bris, E., E. Le Roy and P. Mathieu (1991) *L'appropriation de la terre en Afrique noire*, Paris: Editions Karthala.

Le Roy, E. (1987) *La réforme du droit de la terre dans certains pays d'Afrique francophone*, Rome: FAO.

— (1995) 'Land use plutôt que land tenure: aux origines de la conception foncière du common law', *Le Flamboyant*, December.

Locoh, T., A. Labourie-Racapé and C. Tichict (eds) (1996) *Genre et développement: des pistes à suivre*, Paris: CEPED.

Losch, B., C. De Fina and J.-C. Deveze (1996) *Les agriculteurs des zones tropicales humides: eléments de réflexion pour l'action*, Paris: Ministère de la coopération.

Malimba-Masuku, V. and N. Hall (1997) 'National Identity in Zimbabwe: Gender and Ethnicity', Cape Town: Conference on National Identity and Democracy.

Mama, T. and Fouda (1996) 'Economie dominante et associations communautaires au Cameroun: le défi de la survie en milieu rural', in *Les stratégies de survie des groupes sociaux victimes de la globalisation de l'économie*, Centre de Recherche sur le Développement, Université de Neuchâtel, EDES.

Mama, T. and J. P. Komon (1997) 'Globalisation de l'économie et viabilité à long terme des changements sociaux au Cameroun', in Honsberger, S. (ed.) *Insertion dans l'économie mondiale et anomie*, Centre de Recherche sur le Développement, Université de Neuchâtel, EDES.

Maugenest, D. and P.-G. Pougoué (1994) *Droits de l'homme en Afrique centrale: colloque de Yaoundé*, Yaoundé: Presses de l'UCAC.

Mbembe, A. (1997) 'The Value of Life and the Price of Death: Persons and Things in African Contemporary Debates on Rights', Cape Town: Conference on Cultural Transformations in Africa.

Meer, S. *Women, Land and Authority: Perspectives from South Africa*, Cape Town: National Land Committee.

Messi Metogo, E. (1997) *Dieu peut-il mourir en Afrique? Essai sur l'indifférence religieuse et l'incroyance en Afrique noire*, Paris: Karthala-UCAC.

Mfochivé, J. (1986) *Les fondements de la foi islamique*, Ydé: Clé.

Minces, J. (1993) 'Femmes en Islam arabe: clés pour l'Islam du religieux au politique, des origines aux enjeux d'aujourd'hui', Bruxelles: GRIP.

Nagel, I. (1987) *La femme au Cameroun et sa participation au développement du pays: une étude sur la promotion féminine*, Yaoundé.

Ngoa, H. (1975) *Non, la femme africaine n'était pas opprimée*, Yaoundé: Clé.

Nguimbog, E. 'Les litiges fonciers freinent le développement agricole', *La voix du paysan*, No. 70.

Nnama, A. (1997) *Crise cacaoyère: inversion des rôles dans les ménages et dégradation de l'environnement dans le sud-Cameroun forestier*, Yaoundé: IITA.

Nzhié Engono, J. (1995) 'Rupture de la modernité ou l'utopisme positiviste,' *Sociétés*, No. 50.

Okani, R.-C. (1998) *Hommes et femmes entre sphéres publique et privée: communication*, Dakar: CODESRIA.

Pamard B., C. Cambrezy and L. Cambrézy (1997) *Terre, terroir, territoire: les tensions foncières*, Paris: ORSTOM.

Papini, R. and V. Buonomo (1995) *Ethique et Développement: l'apport des communautés chrétiennes en Afrique*, Yaoundé: Clé and Institut Jacques Maritain.

Pierre, J.-L. and P. Mathieu (1995) 'Gestion des ressources naturelles: enjeux fonciers et processus sociaux au Burkina Faso', *Bulletin FTPP*, No. 7, March.

Pöli and D. Boursier (1996) *Mémoires d'une femme pygmée: témoignage auto-biographique d'une femme pygmée Baka*, Paris: L'Harmattan.

Pritchard, E. (1971) *La femme dans les sociétés primitives*, Paris: PUF.

'La problématique foncière et la décentralisation au Sahel' (1994), Actes de la conférence de Praia, Cap-vert, Ouagadougou: CILSS.

Propositions pour améliorer la sécurité foncière des jeunes exploitants agricoles dans l'extrême-nord (1995), Maroua: Comité diocésain de développement de Maroua.

Puget, F. (1996) 'Stratégies féminines et développement rural: thèse de doctorat au développement rural', Toulouse: ENFA.

Réseau de savoirs sur les initiatives de la société civile dans le domaine de la réforme agraire et de la sécurité de tenure (1998), Rome: Coalition populaire pour éliminer la faim et la pauvreté.

Riss, M.-D. (1989) *Les femmes africaines en milieu rural: les sénégalaises du Sine Saloum*, Paris: L'Harmattan.

Le rôle des forêts dans le développement des collectivités locales (1998), Rome: FAO.

'Rural Women: Making Gender Equality a Reality' (1997), *Land Update*, No. 61, August.

Saito, K. (1990) *Agricultural Extension for Women Farmers in Africa*, Washington: World Bank.

— (1994) *Agricultural Extension for Women Farmers in Sub-Saharan Africa*, Washington: World Bank.

Schoonmaker Freudenberger, K. (1995) *Droits fonciers et propriétés de l'arbre et de la terre: outils de diagnostic rapide*, Rome: FAO.

Shivji, I. (1995) *Land: The Terrain of Democratic Struggles in Africa*, Dar es Salaam.

— (1997) 'Contradictory Perspectives on Rights and Justice in the Context of Land Tenure Reform in Tanzania', Cape Town: International Conference on Cultural Transformations in Africa.

Sindjoun, L. (1990) 'Le système politique local de la ville de Yaoundé, un modèle d'ethno-bureaucratie gouvernante: thèse de doctorat de 3ème cycle en science politique', Yaoundé: Université de Yaoundé.

— (1994) 'Dynamiques de civilisation de l'état et de production du politique baroque en Afrique noire', Verfassung und Recht in Ubersee.

— (1995) 'Construction et déconstruction locales de l'ordre politique au Cameroun, la sociogénèse de l'état: thèse de doctorat d'etat en science politique', Yaoundé: Université de Yaoundé II.

Situation des forêts du monde (1997), Rome: FAO.

Sow, F. (1995a) *L'analyse de genre et les sciences sociales en Afrique*, Dakar: Université Cheikh Anta Diop.

— (1995b) *Femmes rurales: chefs de famille en Afrique sub-saharienne*, Dakar.

Spécial femmes, No. 80, September.

Spike, P. V. (1996) 'The Politics of Identification in the Context of Globalisation', *Women's Studies International Forum*, Vol. 19, No. 1–2.

Statuts fonciers et politique foncière (1986), Rome: FAO.

Syfia, feux de brousse: l'aventure de la démocratie dans les campagnes africaines (1995), Paris: Syros.

Tchala Abina, F. and Z. Tchanou (1993) *Gestion participative des ressources naturelles en zone tropicale humide au Cameroun*, Yaoundé.

Tchandeu, L. (1985) 'Les chefferies traditionnelles dans la ville de Yaoundé: mémoire de maîtrise en science politique', Yaoundé: Université de Yaoundé.

Tiayon, F. (1998) *Pratiques agricoles et utilisation des terres forestières chez les Ngumba du sud-Cameroun*, Kribi.

Titi Nwel, P. (1995) 'Le statut social de la femme dans les sociétés Bassa du Cameroun', in J.-C. Barbier (ed.) *Femmes: mères pacifiques, femmes rebelles*, Paris: Karthala-Orstom.

Tjouen, A. D. (1982) *Droits domaniaux et techniques foncières en droit Camerounais*, Paris: Economica.

Vidrovitch, C. 'Le régime foncier rural en Afrique noire', *Enjeux fonciers en Afrique noire*.

Wouwer-Leunda, P. V. (1996) *Profil femmes et développement au Cameroun: synthèse*, Yaoundé.

Yana, S. D. (1997) 'Statuts et rôles féminins au Cameroun', *Politique africaine*, No. 65.

TWO

Women and Land Rights in the Third World: The Case of Ethiopia

Zenabaworke Tadesse

PART I The Third World

In the last 20 years, an avalanche of studies on rural women in the Third World has been witnessed. However, relatively few have focused on women's land rights. Reflecting on South Asia, Agarwal argued that 'arable land is the most valued form of property, for its economic, political and symbolic significance. It is a production-creating and livelihood-sustaining asset' (Agarwal 1995: 268). This is true of most agrarian economies and certainly of Ethiopia.

Although most of these studies did not focus on land rights, they have provided valuable insights into the multifarious constraints faced by women in accessing what have been grouped as 'critical resources' (Robertson and Berger 1986: 3–24). This broad classification refers to human, material and social resources. They include women's access to and control of productive resources, information, training and education, employment, social networks and processes of decision-making.

These studies have also convincingly challenged conventional notions of homo-genised households, women and community and similar generalisations such as the rural poor. Of the numerous insights they have provided, including those about household and intra-household relations and the constraints facing the implementation of gender-responsive state policies, the insights related to the gender-based division of labour have been the most helpful.

Revisiting the Household

As will be shown below, most land reform programmes are premised on the use of the household as a unit of allocation. They are based on implicit assumptions about the household as a unitary body and the 'community' as a homogenised and united collection of households. Yet empirical and theoretical works on the house-hold have demonstrated significant inequalities within and between households in the distribution of resources and decision-making (Guyer and Peters 1987; Dwyer and Bruce 1988; Sen 1990; Moore 1994; Hart 1995). These studies, and many others, have demonstrated the fallacy of the unified household with its income pooling and sharing assumptions.

Serious challenges to the unitary model of the household have emerged following the insightful work of Amartya Sen regarding intra-household gender relations. In an earlier work, referring to the Indian experience, he addressed the powerful conflicts of interest that existed within households. He then identified generalised reluctance to face these conflicts as a pattern of 'adopted perception' that entails 'systematic failures to see intrafamilial inequalities and perceiving extraordinary asymmetries as normal and legitimate'. More specifically, he underlined:

> [P]roblems of conflict within the family tend to get hidden by accepted perceptions both of 'mutuality' of interests (going well beyond the actual elements of congruence that do, of course, importantly exist) and of legitimacy and inequalities of treatment. As a result, no policy analysis in this area can be complete without taking up the question of political education and understanding ... This is an area in which social illusions nestle closely to reality, and terrible inequities are cloaked firmly in perceived legitimacy. (Sen 1984: 3)

In another study, Sen suggested that the household is most usefully represented as a case of 'cooperative conflict'. In examples where spouses have different goals and strategies, there are a number of potential solutions that he termed 'collusive agreements'. The solution finally adopted is the result of the bargaining ability of the couple. However, the couples do not come to the bargaining table with equal power (Sen 1990: 126). The cumulative outcome of such critical studies in anthropology, economic and feminist analysis is what Moore has identified as a new consensus on the household. This is synthesised as 'a view of the household which sees it as a locus of competing interests, rights, obligations and resources, where household members are involved in bargaining, negotiation and possibly even conflict' (Moore 1994: 135). But what are the factors that determine negotiating power within the household?

Refining the Bargaining Model

For Sen, differences in the relative bargaining power of members of a household are a function of the fall-back positions available to each member, the extent to which members identify their self-interest with their personal well-being and the perceived significance of their contribution to the household. In addition to self-worth, there are two important factors that determine a person's bargaining power: the actual ability of each member to earn an income or to bring valued resources into the household, and the value given to that contribution by other household members. Sen further argues that women do not define their interests in accordance with 'an objective measure of self-interest' because they lack a perception of 'personal interest combined with concern for family welfare' – a trait 'that helps sustain the traditional inequalities' (Sen 1990: 126).

For her part, Agarwal concurs with Sen's emphasis on notions of legitimacy as determinant of what a person gets, over and above the person's fall-back position. She extends this analysis in some respects. For example, she broadens the notion of legitimacy and applies the bargaining approach to gender relations outside the household. However, she disagrees with Sen's explanation of intra-household gender inequalities. She places much less emphasis than Sen on women's perception of their self-interest and much more on the external constraints to their acting on their interest. To put it another way, what may be needed is less a sharpening of women's sense of self-interest than an improvement in their ability to pursue that interest, including by strengthening their bargaining power (Agarwal 1994: 57). In summary, Agarwal identifies five factors (not always unrelated) that determine a rural person's fall-back position.

• private ownership and control over assets, especially arable land.
• access to employment and other income-earning means.
• access to communal resources such as village commons and forests.
• access to traditional external social support systems.
• access to support from the state or from NGOs (Agarwal 1994: 62).

Such an approach goes beyond intra-household dynamics to consider other arenas of power relations with which women have to contend. In this regard, it has been suggested that when addressing gender relations, our 'reconceptualisation' of the 'household' ought to be in relational terms. This would include adopting 'an analytical as well as empirical focus on the gendered micro-politics of negotiation, cooperation and contestation in different but intersecting institutional arenas' (Hart 1995: 61). In other words, recent literature has identified a large number of institutions beyond the household, which are also gendered. These include communities, labour markets, property institutions, judicial systems and local government (Agarwal 1994; Walker 1998).

Diversity of Households

Yet another insightful contribution to our understanding of households comes from studies that address the diversity of household types. The 'household' is used as a unit of surveys, projects and delivery of services. In these activities, it is often equated with a 'male head'. Numerous studies have identified this conflation of household and male head as one of the major contributory factors to the gross underestimation of women's work and of their access to land, credit, technologies and other services (Staudt 1978; Beneria 1981). Furthermore, these studies revealed that not all households were 'male-headed'. The challenges to headship bias led to the emergence of the concept of 'female-headed households'. These types of households were found to be rapidly increasing due to a variety of socio-economic, cultural and political processes (Evans 1992).

Earlier studies argued that female-headed households were disproportionately disadvantaged relative to other households in that they had lower incomes, less land and fewer other resources. These valuable insights also revealed the problems of 'un-situated concepts in research and policy' and were soon overshadowed by 'several analytical distortions' (Peters 1995: 94). While it is essential to take account of gender and other social differences such as male-headed and female-headed households, the growth of knowledge about female-headed households has resulted in 'the abuse of the concept'.

Although female-headed households are quite heterogeneous, there is a tendency to equate female-headedness with poverty and disadvantage. Yet not all female-headed households are poor and vulnerable. Similarly, there is a tendency to focus disproportionately on household structure as the only dimension that needs to be taken into account when differential advantages and burdens are found between men and women. Moreover, undue focus on female-headed households and a simple opposition between male-headed and female-headed households 'obscures the important role of women in agriculture and other activities within male-headed households' (Peters 1995: 96–8).

There are many conclusions that may be drawn from earlier and more recent reflections on the diversity of households. The characteristics of the household are defined and influenced by relationships outside, because households are embedded in broader intra-household and supra-household social groups, networks and structures and cannot be understood only in terms of their internal dynamics. Similarly, as households and the relations among persons within them change and adapt over time, research and policy need to build a time variable into their method of analysis.

Gendered patterns of family and household organisation, work and income refer not only to relations between men and women as husbands and wives but also to relations between sisters and brothers, co-wives, parents and daughters and others, all of which are mediated in part by gender. Finally, 'too myopic a focus on female-headedness' should not lead to the neglect of analysis of the interaction of gender differentiation with other social differences of age, caste, class, race and ethnicity (Peters 1995: 98–100).

Gender-based Divisions of Labour

The destabilisation of conventional concepts of intra-household relations has also required a fresh look at existing perceptions of intra-household allocations of labour, decision-making and household income. A comprehensive appreciation of intra-household allocation of labour mostly depends on the conceptualisation of the gender division of labour.

A large body of literature has been accumulated on the gender division of labour since the pioneering work of Ester Boserup in 1970. In the initial phase of the debate, feminists challenged the validity of privileging biological factors such as pregnancy, child-bearing and muscular strength as major contributory factors to the historical consideration and perpetuation of the gender division of labour (Beneria 1982; Young 1992).

These studies underscored the need to distinguish between the gender division of labour in both reproductive and productive activities. It was found that, cross-culturally, the gender division of labour in reproductive activities tended to be homogeneous. In most societies, women are responsible for domestic work, household maintenance and child care. However, the gender division of labour in productive activities was found to be quite heterogeneous and responsive to changing material conditions. But the change is complex and accompanied by powerful ideological forces that buttress the established categorisation.

In an earlier study, Roberts noted that

> the sexual division of labour is legitimated and perpetuated by a set of cultural values which assert the gender and kin category of appropriateness of certain tasks. These values have a chameleon-like ability to allocate a gender identity to new tasks and to incorporate this identity within the body of tradition such that culture often acts retrospectively to deny changes in the division of labour. (Roberts 1989: 28)

Gendered division of labour is unlikely to change without a concerted effort to transform the cultural norms which define 'women's work' and 'men's work' in each society.

In terms of intra-household allocation of labour, a large body of literature, particularly that focused on gender relations in sub-Saharan African agriculture, has indicated that women work longer hours than men because of their triple responsibilities – working on their own fields as unremunerated family labour and undertaking domestic labour (Bryceson 1995; Gladwin 1991). As will be shown later, a land reform programme that does not take into account the pre-existing intra-household allocation of labour is likely to increase women's workload without a commensurate increase in women's assets. In some cases, land allocation to male heads of households has tended to increase the practice of polygamy.

General Observations on Land Reform

Land reform is a generic term denoting a wide array of legal and policy-led structural changes, including granting access to land, changing ownership patterns and rights of the state and its subsidiary agents. Land reform is often classified as conservative, revolutionary or liberal depending on the form of property rights adopted, the transformation/maintenance of existing state structures and the process through which the reform was achieved – that is, by purchase or ex-propriation (Putzel 1992, cited in Jacobs 1998). De Janvry, who distinguishes between conservative, liberal, popular and radical land reform according to the overall ideological framework, has made similar observations. These reforms are aimed at maintaining the status quo, advancing national bourgeois revolutions, giving land to the peasants or inducing social change respectively (De Janvry 1988: 272–3).

Latin America

Carmen Diana Deere is a pioneer in the study of women's land rights in Latin America who investigated the gender impact of land reform for almost two decades, as it unfolded in different countries of the region. Having examined land reform programmes that entailed distribution of land to 'the rural poor' and the collectivisation of agriculture into cooperatives, as well as reforms geared towards privatisation and individual legal tenure, Deere observed various 'mechanisms of exclusion' that directly or indirectly inhibited women's land rights (Deere 1987, 1995). These include both explicit and implicit requirements, such as formal educational qualifications and permanent employment in wage labour; cases where one household member is designated as beneficiary; norms and gender ideology.

A good example of gender-neutral legislation and policy, but one that makes implicit assumptions about gender relations and lacks legislation and policy to protect women's rights, is found in the implementation of the agrarian reform of El Salvador. Phases I and III of the 1980s agrarian reform did not stipulate that only men were to be beneficiaries, and nor was land allocated to heads of house-holds. The law stipulated that a beneficiary must be an agricultural producer 16 years or older and a Salvadoran. In principle, the stated beneficiary requirements did not exclude women. However, 'cultural values assume that farmers are men and therefore only men have the right to the land ... when the reforms were implemented, the local committees that decided who were eligible to participate selected few women' (Lastarria-Cornhiel and Delgado do Mejia 1994, cited in Lastarria-Cornhiel 1997: 6).

In land reform programmes that encouraged the collectivisation of agriculture into cooperatives, women comprised a minority of cooperative members. But even those who were members had less control than men over resources, were engaged in marginal activities within the cooperatives, gained the least benefit from their membership and were not found in positions of leadership (Deere 1987: 71–173). Here the 'mechanisms of exclusion' included the designation of undifferentiated beneficiaries such as the 'rural poor' without any consideration of power relations within poor rural households. Consequently, in households where only men belonged to cooperative farms, the benefits of membership were not evenly distributed among household members (Deere 1987: 172).

Land reforms that promoted privatisation and individual legal tenure were based on a number of factors that tended to exclude women from becoming equal beneficiaries. In cases where land was allocated to the head of the household, there tended to be relatively few women beneficiaries. For example, in Honduras, although some land has been allocated to widows and single women, they have generally received low priority and have been awarded plots of very poor-quality land. A gender-disaggregated review of title-holders gaining land through land reform in a number of Latin American countries indicated that women constituted between zero and 25 per cent of the beneficiaries (Deere 1987: 176).

Reforms based on a points system and criteria for qualification tended to exclude women as the requirements included formal educational qualifications, histories of residence in the area concerned, farming experience and good reputations. In most cases, women did not have equal educational opportunities and, even when their agricultural knowledge was extensive, they were culturally perceived as 'helpers rather than experienced farmers in their own rights. Single mothers and other female-headed households failed to meet the good reputation criteria as they did not conform to the patriarchal nuclear family norm' (Deere 1987: 180).

Similarly, laws and policies targeted at household heads tended to undermine women's pre-existing land rights. For example, the Peruvian land reform of 1969 facilitated the distribution of legal tenure to male heads of households. This obliterated the pre-existing formal and informal land access rights held by women in the bilateral inheritance system, as well as the relatively equitable land access under traditional usufruct in most Andean areas (Deere 1987: 180). In addition to undermining the traditional access rights held by women in male-headed households, laws and policies targeting household heads marginalised 'single' women, especially those without dependants, who were thus not viewed as household heads (Deere 1987: 173).

In the majority of cases, land reform programmes in Latin America thus tended to perpetuate, and in some cases to aggravate, gender differentials in access to and control over land. In countries where land reform laws and policies made explicit commitments to women's land rights, as in Cuba and Nicaragua, slightly more positive impacts were observed. However, even in these countries, women, unlike men, are not beneficiaries of mainstream development because their case is relegated to separate units (Deere 1987, 1995).

Asia

Asia is a vast continent and numerous types of land reform programmes have been implemented in various countries. The extant literature on women's land rights appears to have concentrated on the Chinese, Vietnamese and South Asian experiences.

A recent assessment of the Vietnamese experience indicates that women were initially active in land reform and throughout the collectivisation campaigns because these campaigns gave them shares in land. More importantly, the reforms were accompanied by new equality and electoral laws that proclaimed legal sexual equality and female suffrage (Jacobs 1998: 130–31). The collectivisation movement was accompanied by a new marriage law, outlawing child marriage, forced marriage and polygamy.

Subsequently, collectivisation was abandoned and family farms were encouraged. The strengthening of family farms is reconstituting 'patriarchal authority'. The 1993 Land Law seems to allow for the emergence of a land market. Neither of these developments bodes well for rural women, even though women have gained more legal rights through the 1986 Family Law, which provides for joint control of household property, joint consent to economic transactions and equal household domestic responsibility. The law also protects women against divorce during pregnancy and domestic violence. A husband (or wife) convicted of violence may now be imprisoned (Tetreault, cited in Jacobs 1998: 132). Adequate information on the extent to which rural women are benefiting from these newly gained rights is not available. In concluding her synthesis of the Vietnamese experience, Jacobs notes 'the lack of an autonomous feminist movement is likely to have been an important element in the eventual demise of land reform which, for a time, operated in the interests of many peasant women' (Jacobs 1998: 133).

The need for women's independent land rights, the multiple obstacles likely to be encountered in the implementation of such rights and thus the enabling conditions that would facilitate women's participation in land reform programmes, has been extensively documented in the seminal 1994 work of Bina Agarwal. The experience of South Asia dates back to the 1950s, when a number of South Asian countries accepted the principle of women's independent property rights and enacted this in law. However, these rights were limited to inheritance laws governing property in land rather than state-redistributed land (Agarwal 1994: 8). In cases where South Asian women gained land titles through inheritance, their full use and management of the land has been 'barricaded by multiple obstacles'. Women are not deemed fit to control land fully even in matrilineal systems, which tend to grant women relatively higher status. Granting women land rights is perceived as a deliberate and sinister attempt to destroy the family and patrilineage. As a result, in most cases the actual management of a woman's land is undertaken by a man. Moreover, in communities where women have never held land, such rights tend to generate hostility – divorces, accusations of witchcraft, threats, attacks, torture and even murder (Agarwal 1994: 173).

In addition to these obstacles, other factors inhibiting women from claiming land include norms and gender ideologies that enjoin female modesty and seclusion, and emphasise female purity and male sexual honour. Women are thus dependent on male kin, particularly brothers, who can protect them from ill-treatment and violence from spouses and in-laws. Studies on Bangladesh have identified obstacles resulting from Islamic rules of inheritance, which stipulate that daughters receive only half the paternal property given to sons and an eighth of their husband's property where they have children. Women often forgo laying claims to these limited assets for fear of disrupting other kin-ascribed entitlements that guarantee survival and security (Kabeer 1991: 245).

State-redistributed land has the advantage of sidestepping these complex webs of relationships. Indian women have demanded joint titles to state-redistributed land since 1979. In its Sixth Plan of 1985, the Indian Ministry of Agriculture and Rural Development declared that it would 'endeavour' to give joint titles to spouses in programmes involving the distribution of land and home sites. However, this plan has 'remained only a promise on paper' (Agarwal 1994: 5). In addition, in India and other South Asian countries, redistributive land reform programmes

> continued to be modelled on the notion of a unitary male-headed household, with titles being granted only to men where women (typically widows) were clearly the heads. This bias was replicated in resettlement schemes, even in Sri Lanka where customary inheritance systems have been bilateral or matrilineal. (Agarwal 1994: 8–9)

Complex factors explain the persistence of such gender-biased public laws and policies. They include the assumption of gender-congruence in interests within the family, the prevailing view that men are the breadwinners and women the dependants and the belief that land redistribution to women will further decrease farm sizes, lead to fragmentation and in turn decrease farm productivity (Agarwal 1994: 8–9).

However, valuable lessons have been drawn from the Bodghaya movement, the first movement worldwide to secure independent land rights for wives in preference to husbands (Jacobs 1998: 135). The movement was a community-based struggle for land rights in which women played an active role. In addition to claiming land rights for women, the movement also addressed domestic violence and the division of labour in the household. However, when 1,000 hectares of illegally held land was eventually redistributed to the Bodghaya movement, it was decided that it would be allocated to 'landless labourers ... [that is, men], the disabled and widows' (Manimala, cited in Jacobs 1998: 136).

Women protested against this turn of events and noted the increase in authoritarian behaviour as a result of the distribution (Jacobs 1998: 136). In other words, women in Bodghaya 'saw intra-household gender relations being affected not just by their own property-less state, but by their remaining property-less while their husbands become propertied' (Agarwal 1995: 227). In response to women's continued protest, it was decided that, in the future, redistribution of land would be in women's names. In 1982, 10 per cent of land was redistributed in the names of married women and women who were widows, destitutes and even unmarried daughters. In spite of these important gains, however, women found it difficult to cultivate their land: 'Constraints were presented by restrictions on women's use of space, by the patrilocal residence norms and, importantly, by the region-wide taboo on female ploughing' (Jacobs 1998: 136).

Having assessed that these four decades of protracted struggle for women's land rights in South Asia resulted in some gains and numerous obstacles, Agarwal was then able to propose useful conceptual tools and measures that are likely to ensure women's land rights. As noted above, land rights can take a diversity of forms and stem from numerous sources, such as inheritance, community membership, state transfer and tenancy or purchase arrangements. More importantly, land rights are 'claims that are legally and socially recognised and enforceable by an external legitimised authority, be it a village-level institution or some higher-level judicial or executive body of the State' (Agarwal 1994: 19). It is necessary to distinguish between the legal recognition of a claim and its social recognition, and between recognition and enforcement. In other words, unless it is enforced, women's legal right to inherit property may remain only a paper right. Likewise, unless a claim is socially recognised as legitimate and enforced by the community of which the household is a part, women are likely to forfeit their rights in land in favour of other family members – most often brothers.

Another critical distinction is that between ownership of land and its effective control. Legal ownership alone may not include the ability to lease out, sell, mortgage or bequeath land. Furthermore, legal ownership may not provide women with a realistic ability to decide how the land is to be used or how its produce should be disposed of.

The other equally important characteristic of land rights is their temporal and locational dimension. Land rights might be hereditary, or accrue only during a person's lifetime or for a lesser period. Finally, land rights may be made conditional on the person residing where the land is located (Argawal 1994: 9).

To recapitulate, women's independent rights to land mean effective rights – rights not only in law, but in practice. Effective rights imply rights independent of male ownership and control (that is, excluding joint titles with men). Effective land rights make it possible for women to retain their land in cases of marital breakdown, or to escape from marital conflict or violence and to act upon different land-use priorities than those of their husbands (Agarwal 1994: 20).

Sub-Saharan Africa

In sub-Saharan Africa, most land reform programmes have been limited to titling registration of land and settlement schemes. In the recent past, in the context of liberalisation programmes, observers have noted the rapid development of land markets in a large number of sub-Saharan countries. Most of these programmes allocate land titles to male heads of households.

Most customary tenure systems gave women access to land not in their own right, but as their husbands' wives or, in cases of divorce or widowhood, as daughters or sisters of males within their own families. While they may have a right to land through their husbands and other male relatives, they have no right to a particular piece of land and may be forced to move from field to field (Bruce 1993: 46).

Customary tenure systems are heterogeneous and responsive to changing economic and social processes. However, gender is one of the most basic and prevalent factors determining the relations of control and access in customary tenure. Family structures, marriage laws, inheritance practices and religion are the most influential factors in how land is allocated and transferred among households in a community. These same factors decide who has access to and control of land.

In contemporary customary systems, transfer of agricultural land is affected through inheritance, borrowing, gifting and leasing and/or sale. Inheritance is the most common type of transfer. This often implies the transfer of land from 'men of one generation to the men of the next, as female children seldom inherit land' (Lastarria-Cornhiel 1997: 1323).

A major distinction is made between patrilineal and matrilineal societies when discussing inheritance. But in spite of other variations, in both patrilineal and matrilineal customary tenure systems, land is allocated to males and transferred from men to men.

In patrilineal customary tenure systems, both lineage and property are traced through the male line and land is often transferred from father to son. Although men delegate cultivation rights to their wives, daughters and other siblings during their lifetimes, at their deaths only sons and other male relatives assume control of land, with wives and daughters seldom inheriting any land allocated to the households. Widows, and especially widows with young children, usually retain access and cultivation rights to their dead husbands' land as long as they remain in their husbands' community and until their sons are old enough to inherit the land.

In matrilineal customary tenure systems, both lineage and property are traced through the mother's line, but the ownership and control of property remains in the hands of male members of the family – brothers, uncles, nephews, male cousins. Although women are not allocated community land or allowed to inherit such land, daughters tend to have cultivation rights to a parcel of family land even after marriage. Women lose these rights when their fathers die or if they move away from their communities. However, in cases where women received land as gifts from their fathers, they can retain the land. Similarly, women have the option of reclaiming their cultivation rights if they return to their own communities.

Recent changes in customary tenure systems towards individual and private property regimes have led to an erosion of the few rights women had in both matrilineal and patrilineal societies. These changes have not been linear, nor have they have affected all women in the same way. Some men have also lost some of their rights, as what Berry called 'bundles of rights in land' get concentrated in the hands of certain male groups (Berry 1988: 51). Consequently, matrilineal systems become more like patrilineal systems and, over time, only sons inherit land. Women become more dependent on their husbands and their own families for land.

The two key factors that have influenced changes in customary tenure systems in Africa are colonialism and the spread of Islam. The spread of Islam

has had mixed effects on women's land rights. In some societies, the response to Islamic inheritance law has been the provision of land as inheritance to sons and movable property to daughters. In the case of northern Nigeria, daughters do have inheritance rights to land. Not only have women succeeded in having their inheritance rights recognised by their brothers and the community in general, but also women who have moved to another community upon marriage were able to claim their inheritance. However, the existence of purdah forces them to depend on men for cultivation of the land. (Ross, cited in Lastarria-Cornhiel 1997: 1325)

In the context of land concentration and land scarcity, customary tenure systems have come under a multiplicity of pressures for change. Women in a large number of countries are losing their 'invisible' secondary rights to land under customary law and practice. In areas where land markets are emerging, women encounter serious constraints, including lack of property, lack of adequate cash income, minimal political power and a persistent male bias against women owning land. In spite of these obstacles, a small minority of women has been successful in claiming their customary rights to family land, and in accumulating capital and investing in land (Lastarria-Cornhiel 1997).

The above review of the experiences of other countries and other regions illustrates the factors that need to be addressed if women are fully to enjoy their land rights. According to Agarwal, the major factors facilitating women's equal participation in land reform programmes include:

* Existing inheritance laws.
* Women's literacy, including legal literacy (knowledge of their legal rights).
* The social legitimacy of women's claim (whether the claim is considered a valid one in the community of which the women's household is a part).
* Women's access to government officials who administer land-related matters.
* Women's economic and physical access to legal machinery (lawyers and law courts).
* Women's access to economic and social resources for survival outside the support system provided by contending claimants such as brothers or kin.
* Women's ability to organise and form coalitions with other gender-progressive groups (Argarwal 1994).

In her study of the unfolding land reform process in South Africa, Sunde found that women are also constrained by their lack of mobility, their responsibility for child care and the bulk of the domestic labour and their lack of access to technical skills and knowledge. In her view, the key variables enabling women to benefit from land reform include:

- Self-esteem and a sense of autonomy.
- Access to information, economic and social resources.
- A change in gender-role stereotypes.
- A shift in the gender division of labour.
- The ability to obtain additional skills through the planning and delivery process (Sunde 1997).

PART II The Challenge of Ethiopia

In Ethiopia, land rights are among the major development challenges. Land is the most significant livelihood-sustaining asset for the vast majority of the population. Understandably, land rights have been and continue to be one of the most contentious political issues facing the country.

The 1984 national census estimated that the population was 42.6 million people. Presently, the population stands at 58.6 million, of whom slightly over fifty million people reside in rural areas, Ethiopia being one of the least urbanised countries. These figures indicate that the country has a high fertility rate, of about 3 per cent population growth per annum. Ethiopia is multiethnic, multicultural, multilingual and multireligious. Agriculture is the mainstay of the economy, accounting for 51 per cent of total gross domestic product (GDP), 85 per cent of total employment and 85 per cent of exports. The share of the industrial sector in GDP and total exports, including those of small-scale handicraft and other industries, is about 11 per cent and 15 per cent respectively.

The dominant means of livelihood is sedentary agriculture in the form of mixed farming. Crop production complements livestock-rearing and handicrafts. Pastoralism, with different degrees of transhumance, is the predominant means of livelihood in the arid lowlands. Agriculture is based on extensive plough cultivation, with the exception of some areas where there is hoe cultivation. In areas of plough cultivation there is a cultural taboo against women ploughing and sowing. With the exception of these two tasks, however, women participate in every aspect of production, such as weeding, harvesting and post-harvest activities. Similar to the widely documented experience of other African countries, all aspects of hoe-based cultivation depend on extensive female labour. Women also play a significant role in animal husbandry.

Existing records underestimate or completely ignore women's considerable participation in the mixed farming system. For example, both the 1984 and 1994 population and housing censuses are based on gender-biased conceptions of what constitutes an 'economically active' population, and undervalue women's economic activities. Further, as rural households can no longer sustain their livelihoods through agricultural activities alone, men, women and children in rural households engage in a variety of off-farm activities throughout the year. Here, too, women's contributions to total household incomes are by no means negligible. The prevailing notion of the 'male breadwinner', and the extant surveys of rural household incomes, fail to account for or give proper recognition to women's contributions to household finances.

Women's Land Rights Prior to 1991

In Ethiopia, discussions on land tenure could be classified in three periods: pre-1974, 1975–91 and 1991 to the present. Prior to the agrarian reform of 1975, the land tenure system and the concomitant relations of production were heterogeneous. In most parts of the country, peasants gained access to land through inheritance or through corporate groups consisting of individuals tracing their descent from a certain ancestor. A predominant portion of the land in both the south and the north of the country was controlled by political and social elites who had been granted land by the imperial regime, mainly in return for military and administrative services. In this context, the most visible and significant social relationship in most of rural Ethiopia was that of landlord–tenant. In much of northern Ethiopia, women had the right of inheritance. Ruling-class women received land as gifts or were able to purchase land (Hoben 1973; Crummey 1981).

The clarion call of the broad-based political uprising that erupted throughout Ethiopia in 1974 was 'Land to the Tiller'. The land reform launched in 1975 by the military regime known as the Derg promised to end the archaic land system of the imperial regime. It hoped to end the exploitation of the peasants and to improve their economic situation. The broad-based and enthusiastic support that this land reform initially received soon died down, as subsequent laws, policies and practices transformed what was a potentially positive measure into an instrument of rural impoverishment. The land reform, initially perceived as a means of combating poverty and ushering in economic and social justice, ended up accelerating poverty. Students of Ethiopian agricultural transformation argue that smallholder agriculture become microagriculture. Misguided agricultural laws and polices were exacerbated by a costly and drawn-out civil war as well as by recurrent drought and famine.

A gender-aware reading of the Land Reform Proclamation clearly reveals the biased assumptions about women's needs, roles and capabilities in the framing of land reform. Although the proclamation stated that 'without differentiation of the sexes, any person who is willing to personally cultivate land shall be allocated land', in most cases the implementation was discriminatory towards women.

Land was distributed by family size and registered under male heads of households. By using the household as the unit of allocation, the proclamation assumed that households were uniform and failed to take intra-household distributional relations into account. The proclamation also assumed that gender-based divisions of labour in agriculture were immutable and classified women together with persons who, because of age or illness, could not personally cultivate their holding. In other words, the proclamation failed to challenge the cultural taboo against women ploughing and sowing. This effectively reaffirmed the beliefs and practices governing relations between women and men.

Consequently, most women failed to obtain usufructuary rights to land. The situation was worse for women who were in polygamous unions, divorced women and those who came of age after the initial land apportionment. Women in polygamous marriages were negatively affected in that men tended to register just one wife. As a result of numerous socio-economic changes and the widespread practice of early marriage in most rural areas, divorce is frequent and the rate of divorce has accelerated. Although female-headed households are allocated land, often the land titles are of minimal size. Moreover, since women depend on men for a significant proportion of farm labour, they have limited control in deciding land use priorities or type of produce.

Beyond these obvious constraints, other factors severely limited women's rights to land. Land was distributed to peasants who were organised in Peasant Associations and who were entitled to land only as residents of the Kebele. Very often, women who married outside their community 'lost' the shares of land allocated to them in their parental homes. Similarly, divorced women lost their shares of land if they left their marital households (as they usually had to).

However, the degree to which women gained some land rights or were dispossessed depended on the pre-reform practice of female inheritance to land or to its absence pre-reform. In other words, in areas where the practice of women's inheritance existed, this tended to strengthen women's claims to their shares of land in cases of divorce or on returning to their natal communities. Another critical factor was the willingness of the Peasant Associations' leaders and judicial tribunals to accommodate women seeking to acquire rights to land following marital breakdown.

In the context of rapid population growth and land supply limitations, the anticipated land distribution by family size could not be sustained. In the 1980s, landlessness become a glaring reality (Dessalegn 1994). Land shortages, increasing poverty and general social dislocation generated increased marital instability and began to transform the rights and duties formerly assumed to be inherent to marriage and divorce procedures. Often this transformation was to women's detriment. However, existing literature on problems of access to land refers mostly to 'landless male adults'. The size and gravity of female landlessness remains unexplored.

Land reform was accompanied by the establishment of new rural institutions and subsequent reforms such as village resettlement schemes and collectivisation. Each of these processes had a differential impact on men and women. In general terms, women were more disadvantaged. But in spite of monumental difficulties, the various dislocating processes also loosened some customary taboos and offered women limited spaces for the emergence of new identities (Pankhurst 1992).

New Rural Institutions

The most important new rural institution was the Peasant Association (PA). In addition to the management and implementation of the land reform, the PAs controlled the life of the community through the institution of judicial tribunals. These courts had jurisdiction over cases involving land disputes as well as other legal cases. With the exception of female-headed households, most women were excluded from membership in the PAs, since heads of households alone were registered as members. By 1990, it was estimated that women comprised only 12 per cent of PA membership, and were mostly female heads of households or those engaged in small businesses. However, in the early 1990s female membership in PAs was estimated at between 20 and 25 per cent. This growth is most likely due to the death and destabilisation caused by the civil war, resettlement and other calamities (Dessalegn 1994). Moreover, there is no evidence that this increase in female membership translated into active participation.

Similarly, women made up only 7.5 per cent of the membership of producer cooperatives. Hence, most women were, and are, absent from arenas where legal, political and social rules are made and upheld with respect to land.

Promising but Inadequate Land Reform

One of the major opponents of the military regime was the Tigray People's Liberation Front (TPLF), currently Ethiopia's ruling political party. Since its inception in 1976, the TPLF has experimented with various forms of land reform and new rural institutions in the areas under its control. A noteworthy feature of its evolving land distribution system was the granting of usufructuary rights over land to individuals in a household and not to the household as a unit. Until 1987, married status was a prerequisite for the acquisition of land rights. The Land Law promulgated in 1987 abolished this precondition, and land was granted to females and males who had reached the minimum ages of 15 and 22 respectively, with no reference to their marital status or the assets of their parents.

Unfortunately, this land distribution and the attempt to reduce early marriage by females was not accompanied by challenges to the rigid gender-based divisions of labour in agricultural production, including the customary taboos against women ploughing and sowing. Although women joined the TPLF's liberation army and performed what were considered exclusively 'male tasks', including ploughing, the end of the war has meant a return to pre-war beliefs and practices. Therefore, although women have possessory rights to small parcels of land, they continue to depend on male labour for the cultivation of the land (Chiari 1996).

Land Law and Policy Since 1991

Following the demise of the military government in 1991, a transitional government was established which ruled until late 1994. Under the transitional government, Ethiopia became a 'democratic' federal state with eleven regional national states based on ethnicity. On coming to power in 1996, the present government promised that land – perhaps the most contentious political issue in Ethiopia – would be settled through a national referendum. It soon abandoned the idea. Land issues were first addressed under the new Constitution, and subsequently through region-specific land redistribution. To date, land redistribution has taken place only in Region Three, the Amhara region.

During the transitional period, 1991–94, there was a lack of clear legal and policy directives on land ownership. This lack was addressed by the adoption of the Constitution in 1994. The new Constitution retained state ownership of rural and urban land, as well as of all natural resources. The Constitution states that women have equal rights with men with respect to access, use, administration and transfer of land. They shall also enjoy equal treatment in the inheritance of property. The challenge has been how to implement such seemingly egalitarian constitutional provisions. There is no evidence of efforts made by the state to make women aware of their constitutional rights so as to enjoy them.

In March 1977, the Rural Land Redistribution Proclamation of the Amhara National State was promulgated. Article 9 of the proclamation provided for the distribution of land equally to both men and women. However, the redistribution was limited to single women involved in income-generating activities for their livelihoods, and has thus far omitted other categories of women such as divorcees, widows and single adult women who are still dependent on their parents and other family members (Yigrmew 1997).

Securing gender equality in the unfolding land redistribution was overshadowed by the overall ethos of the implementation process. The redistribution of land had a punitive edge as it excluded those it deemed to have been beneficiaries of land and power during the previous two regimes (Teferi 1997). Hence, women whose husbands were members of the previous 'bureaucracy' and women who themselves were members of various committees during the military regime were excluded from the redistribution of land. Given this highly charged context, there was little space to focus on the need for specific attention to be paid to the inequalities suffered by rural women.

Subsequently, the federal government of Ethiopia issued the Federal Rural Land Administration Proclamation that made provision for the enactment of a land administration law by each Regional Council. The proclamation provides for 'free assignment of holding rights both to peasants and nomads, without differentiation of the sexes'. With the exception of Amhara, this proclamation, issued on 7 July 1997, has not been implemented to date. But in addition to granting women legal rights to land, the federal government has set forth principles of equality between men and women in the areas of political, economic, educational and cultural economic rights.

The gap between stated legal and policy goals and their implementation is indicative of the broader problem of developing the rule of law in Ethiopia. Until this larger problem is addressed, it is unlikely that positive law can be the basis of enforceable economic and social rights. Nor will law of itself help to develop adequate institutional and structural support for such rights. The problem is further aggravated by the absence of an autonomous and vibrant civil society whose institutions can advocate women's rights. There are presently only very early signs of an independent women's movement.

Given this background, this analysis of women's land rights in Ethiopia aims to focus on what is meant by independent rights to land for women, and to indicate the multiple and simultaneous points of interventions required to ensure the existence and implementation of such rights. The analysis will evaluate assumptions of current research methodologies and push for the development of more inclusive information to guide development law and policy decisions. The more modest aim is to reduce the marginalisation of gender and women's issues in Ethiopian rural research.

Conceptual Framework

The diversity of forms that land rights can take is underscored. Land rights can be in the form of ownership or usufruct, each with differing degrees of freedom to mortgage, lease out, sell or bequeath (Agarwal 1994). Since the 1974 land reform in Ethiopia, land rights can stem from state transfer. Rights can also stem from inheritance or community membership. These existed in the 'rest' system of northern Ethiopia prior to the 1974 land reform. Land rights may also stem from tenancy arrangements and purchase.

Land rights are 'claims that are legally and socially recognised and enforceable by an external legitimised authority, be it a village-level institution, or some higher level judicial or executive body of the state' (Agarwal 1994). Particularly with women's land rights, it is imperative to examine the difference between the legal and social recognition of land rights as well as between their recognition and enforcement. The lesson from seemingly gender-responsive laws and policies in Ethiopia and elsewhere is that women may have legal rights on paper, but such rights are meaningless unless they are both socially recognised and enforced.

Also important are the temporal and locational dimensions of land rights. Land may be hereditary, or accrue only for a person's lifetime or for a lesser period, and they may be conditional upon the person residing where the land is located. Since the 1974 land reform in Ethiopia, the locational dimension has become critical for women, who very often lose even the minimal rights they might have upon leaving their natal communities for marriage or following marital breakdowns. In rural Ethiopia, residences are part of farms, as they are built very close to cultivation fields. The 1974 land reform did not differentiate between land for residences and land for agricultural activities. Hence, divorced and widowed women have to go back to their parents or reside with other siblings.

There is no blueprint for gender-equitable land reform, as land reform can legitimately take a variety of forms. The important principle is to grant women effective rights, not only in law but also in practice. Independent rights to land provide women with access to the economic and social resources needed for basic survival, and with fall-back positions in cases of domestic violence and marital breakdown. Moreover, women are able to implement their own land right priorities (for example, growing vegetables instead of cereals and controlling the land's produce).

Gender-equitable land reform requires the establishment of structures of governance and local institutions that promote women's active participation in decision-making, and structures of management that challenge long-standing institutional power relations. Making women aware of new land laws and policies and reforming customary laws that discriminate against women is another essential component of ensuring women's land rights (Sunde 1997). For example, promoting family and inheritance laws that guarantee equality in inheritance and recognise the right of women to administer property independent of their husbands and other male kin, are essential components of successful gender-equitable land reform. Such laws are key to creating the social legitimacy of women's claims to land rights. However, they have to be accompanied by context-specific measures that are likely to foster changes in deeply entrenched social attitudes. To be effective, gender-equitable land reform also necessitates the adoption of special measures to advance the interests of rural women, such as ensuring access to credit, information, technical knowledge and markets.

Methodological Concerns

Land reform in Ethiopia followed the international trend of using the household as a unit of allocation, and paid hardly any attention to power relations within the household and the wider social and political environment mediating women and men's effective access to resources. As indicated above, critics of such an approach have demonstrated that household forms vary and are often sites of 'cooperative conflicts', and hence should not be analysed from a set of a priori assumptions. Moreover, a comprehensive appreciation of household dynamics requires an analysis of the complex relations that extend beyond the household, and should include considerations of the community, the market and the state. Understanding the gender aspects of land reform laws and policies as well as their implementation requires an analysis of power relations at each of these different sites of intra-household relations. Current research has solicited data on:

- The legal and social practices that mediate women's access to and control over land (for example, cultural taboos against women ploughing and sowing, customary law regarding marital and inheritance rights).
- Bundles of assets held by households.
- Gender differences in the creation of household assets.
- Strategies of livelihood generation, with emphasis on access to social resources by women and men to ensure household food security and family welfare (access to communal property resources, external support systems, saving groups and other networks that have the potential to provide women with fall-back positions).
- Allocation (differences in male and female perceptions of key economic processes and time allocations for each member of the household).
- Income-generation and expenditure patterns of men and women (understanding the 'perceived contributions' that various members make to household well-being).
- Attempting to assess the actual ability to earn income or to build valued resources into the household and the value given to that contribution by other household members.
- Decision-making power (customary valuations and patterns of labour).
- Possible changes in women's self-esteem and autonomy through an exploration of nuances and shifts within gender relations operating at the level of the household and the community.

Study Sites

The area of study covered two *weredas* (the smallest administrative regions in the context of the current decentralisation) in each of the three different regions of the country, namely the Amhara, the Oromia and Southern regions. The study selected 30 households in each *wereda*. According to the 1994 national census (which has been highly politicised and whose accuracy is contested due to its emphasis on ethnicity), the Oromia region has the largest population, with 18.7 million people or 37.2 per cent of the population. The Amhara region is reported to have a population of 13.8 million people or 27.4 per cent of the population, and the third region, officially known as the Southern Nations, Nationalities and Peoples region (SNNPR), is reported to have a population of 10.4 million or 20.7 per cent of the population.

In view of the fact that most rural households in all three regions have small or micro-landholdings and diversified agricultural systems and livelihood strategies, the study attempted to assess women's access to a broad set of socio-economic resources. The amount of landholdings under one hectare is reported to be 54 per cent in the Amhara region, 53 per cent in the Oromia region and 82 per cent in the Southern region, which has the highest agricultural density in Ethiopia. Those who are reluctant to provide women with independent land rights have used land fragmentation as a justification.

In the Amhara region, the study was conducted in two *weredas* in the zone known as Wello. There were several reasons for the selection of this area. First, land redistribution had been completed recently. Second, it is one of the few exceptional zones where women reportedly were allotted parcels of land equal to their husbands' during the initial land distribution in 1975. This facilitated an exploration of the extent to which customary inheritance rights and the state have made it possible to challenge political and social gender inequities. Third, it is a zone where the two predominant Ethiopian religions, Orthodox Christianity and Islam, are practised, allowing for an exploration of religious factors influencing women's land rights. And fourth, Wello has been, and continues to be, a zone of recurrent drought and famine, providing a case study of changes in gender relations resulting from coping mechanisms, social dislocation and resource management by men and women in a situation of resource scarcity.

The second zone was North Shoa in the Oromia region. Located relatively close to the capital city, Northern Shoa produces cereals and pulses. In the cereal-growing regions, women are believed to participate actively in agricultural production. However, they do not plough or sow. In contrast to the situation in Wello, there is little information on women's land rights prior to and since the 1974 land reform. Using women's land rights as an entry point, the aim was to explore women's roles in this diversified livelihood system.

The third zone studied was Wollaitta, located in the Southern region. Wollaitta is located in the *ensete* (false banana) farming area, which focuses on root crops. However, there are other agro-pastoral activities, including the growing of cereals, cash crops such as coffee and red pepper, and animal husbandry. The root crops are used as sources of food, fodder and fuel. Prior to the 1974 land reform, women in Wollaitta did not enjoy customary inheritance rights. The concern here was to assess the extent to which the 1974 land reform departed from, or reinforced, customary inheritance rights and practices. Further, existing research notes that women do not participate in agricultural work and are mostly involved in the processing of agricultural produce and animal husbandry (Dessalegn 1992;

Sandford and Sandford 1994). Through a compilation of household activity lists, the aim was to assess gender-based divisions of labour and household resource management in Wollaita. The research also hoped to benefit from a collaborative demographic survey of the zone being carried out by the Demographic Training and Research Center (DTRC), the Institute of Development Research (IDR) and Brown University.

In general, the study privileged those areas where a number of studies on land and other rural development issues had already been undertaken. However, attempts were also made to explore the significance of agro-ecology, ethnicity and religion on the nature of gender relations and particularly on women's land rights in Ethiopia.

The methodology used included a lengthy questionnaire assessing:

- Demographic household profiles.
- Household assets (land and animal stock).
- Land redistribution.
- Determinants of men's and women's access to land (including pre-existing and emerging inheritance patterns).
- Dispute settlement mechanisms.
- Divisions of labour in agriculture.
- Animal husbandry and marketing (including the time spent in each activity).
- Household incomes and decision-making thereof.
- Participation in existing social networks.

Attempts were also made to collect administrative and socio-economic data from local government institutions, known as *Wereda* Councils. Focus group discussions were conducted with single, married, divorced and widowed women to solicit qualitative observations of women's various experiences and to check the accuracy of household-generated data that were often given by male household heads. Finally, attempts were made to collect data on the gendered patterns of participation in rural institutions.

Synthesis of Findings

The three regions are composed of very small landholdings, which deepen poverty and necessitate growing attempts by men, women, boys and girls to diversify the livelihood strategies. Of the three zones, only women in Wello have access to what women informants told us were often extremely small (well below the average holding) and marginal land parcels.

In one of the two research sites, Haiq, the population is predominantly Muslim and land seems to be allocated according to Islamic inheritance law and practice. In their natal village, women inherit half that allocated to male siblings. In the other two research sites, in the absence of male siblings, women have limited land rights only when they are widowed. The data for both North Shoa and Wollaita confirm earlier observations by Sandford and Sandford concerning women's land rights in the area known as Moroccho Wollano. Women inherit only if they have no male siblings. Women can exert control over land as long as they are not married, do not have adult sons and are not living with some other adult male (uncle or father). If they are considered part of a household, the man in the household – regardless of who owns the land – makes the ultimate decisions. Women can only exercise control over land when they are not subsumed within a male-headed household (Sandford and Sandford 1994: 196).

In all three regions, female heads of households with adolescent or adult children are relatively less disadvantaged than those who are the only adults or who have only daughters. The former depend on their children for 'male tasks' and do not have to look to relatives or neighbours or enter into sharecropping arrangements. While most female-headed households are indeed poor, especially those who have no grown sons, it would not be accurate to generalise and gloss over the plight of married women who have little or no decision-making power in regard to household assets.

In addition to marital status, another factor determining women's land rights is the type of marriage entered into. The wide prevalence of polygamy in all three regions further constrains women's land rights in the context of growing land shortages. In the Southern region, the DTRC, the IDR and Brown University study found that more than 30 per cent of women in their sample reported that their marriage was polygamous. In a focus group discussion, women confirmed the validity of the findings of the collaborative study, which had noted that 'polygamy has economic implications as a man with several wives can command more resources, produce more food for his household and achieve high status due to the wealth he commands' (DTRC, IDR and Brown University 1998: 95).

In Wello, all the women in the focus group discussions in both research sites opposed polygamy, and appeared to have had some success in reducing the practice. In Wollaita, restrictions on polygamous marriage come from the spread of Protestant Christianity, which prohibits this type of marriage. Informants noted that when a man joins the Protestant church, he is asked to keep only one wife. This has often meant that his other wives are left to fend for themselves and denied access to the resources they accumulated with their former husband. One of our informants, who has been abandoned and who has also converted to Protestant Christianity, had brought her case to the church leaders and was awaiting their response. Judging from the enthusiastic support that other women gave to the woman's narrative of her marital breakdown, shifts in gender ideology are taking place and new perceptions of women's rights by rural women are emerging.

In North Shoa, particularly in Gerera Jarsso, most women had no land rights. In answer to the query, 'do women have land rights?', most male households not only affirmed the absence of such rights, but invariably stated, 'what will she do with it if she has land?' A cause of women's dispossession in this zone is the strongly entrenched practice of early marriage. In this *Wereda* Council district, girls as young as seven years old are given in marriage and can be divorced soon afterwards. During a discussion with one of the newly elected female district councillors, we were informed of a pending divorce case of a seven-year-old girl. The councillors, especially the 20 per cent of them who were female, were sympathetic to the plight of the young girl. But given the widespread nature of the problem in the zone, the case faced lengthy deliberation. It was obvious that the provision in the new Constitution regarding the minimum age for marriage, and other provisions regarding women's rights, are not being implemented. It is doubtful that even the female councillors were aware of the existence of these provisions.

Women's access to land or the benefit they can draw from land, even where they have limited rights, is severely limited because of the gender-based division of labour, particularly the cultural taboos against women ploughing and sowing. Women in all three areas do not plough or sow, but engage in weeding in the two cereal-producing areas and in harvesting in all three areas. In North Shoa, women carry the plough to the field and back to the house, but cannot plough themselves. As women cannot grow cereals on their own, female-headed households without grown children enter into sharecropping arrangements. This limits both their food security and their earning ability. For married women, access to cereals for household consumption or for sale depends entirely on the benevolence of male heads of households.

Gendered time-use patterns The intensity and duration of women's labour input differs considerably from that of their husbands. Undoubtedly, women's labour input is much higher. Tasks such as fetching water and fuel, which are almost exclusively women's tasks, are arduous and time-consuming. Fodder and fuel collection now require much more effort and time than they previously did. This is partly due to the overall underdevelopment of the country, but has been exacerbated by environmental degradation. Similarly, women, with the help of children, undertake other forms of daily 'housework' that also consume considerable amounts of energy and time.

Both women and men participate in animal care, but they tend to specialise in different animals. In rural Ethiopia, livestock are a sign of prestige and wealth. In addition to being a capital asset and a critical source of nutrition, livestock provide other resources, including draught power in agriculture. Livestock in Ethiopia provide over 90 per cent of this draught power. Livestock also provide hides and skins, which are a secondary source of exports. While men mostly use the draught power and control the sales from hides and skins, women control milk and milk products, which are essential sources of nutrition for the household and provide women with some cash income. Another resource drawn from livestock is dung, which is essential for fertilisation and also widely used as building material and household fuel.

The gender-based division of labour varies by region in terms of animal care. In most parts of the country, boys are responsible for herding. Women generally own and care for small animals such as chickens, goats and sheep. They are responsible for the processing and use of dairy and other animal by-products. However, women's productive work in dairying is considered part of their domestic reproductive work rather than an integral part of livestock management. Consequently, women seldom have access to veterinary information and other extension services. An important income-generating activity for women in all three areas is the selling of dairy products. They sell butter and cheese and use the returns to buy other food and non-food items. Milk products are also used as payment in kind for rotating credit programmes and to maintain social networks – women in Wollaita engage in these networks and share labour animals and products through them.

While the gender-based division of labour has generally remained rigid in agricultural production, that rigidity is shifting in the production of new crops, such as vegetables, and in terms of public works. Recurrent drought and ever-shrinking landholdings, particularly in Wello and Wollaita, have resulted in chronic food insecurity for a majority of rural households. In response, multilateral agencies and NGOs have introduced food-for-work programmes consisting of the provision of relief in exchange for people's labour in building wells, constructing roads, planting trees and participating in other environmental conservation projects. A growing number of women enthusiastically participates in these public works to earn cash or food.

Increased but undervalued contribution to household income In all three areas, increasing numbers of women are taking up vegetable growing and marketing. These small, often backyard vegetable gardens provide them with direct access to cash. However, married women also sell household cereals received or stolen from the 'household' granary, which they often use to purchase other condiments or manufactured goods. In addition, women also make food items and brew local drinks for sale. While single, married, divorced or widowed women living with their parents, husbands or other kin make substantial contributions to household livelihoods and incomes, little value is placed on those contributions by other household members. If women had independent land rights even to small plots of land, they would clearly be able to draw more substantial benefits from their activities.

Rural development interventions, by both the state and NGOs, focus almost exclusively on women's practical needs, maintaining or slightly ameliorating women's existing skills such as home management, child care and weaving. In all three regions, there are no attempts to provide technical agricultural information, knowledge, financing or markets. The predominant cultural construction of gender tends to conceal new situations where experience has changed, but gender identities have remained static. Most male respondents and state officials continue to deny the importance of women's work and incomes to family livelihoods, and cling to notions of male breadwinners.

Intra-household allocation of resources In answer to a query regarding household income, all the male respondents emphasised that pooling of resources and joint decision-making govern intra-household resource allocation. However, during group discussions with women in all three areas, the informants denied that resources were pooled and decision-making shared. They asserted that men were taking a more self-centred approach to their own and to family resources and consumption. They particularly lamented men's expenditure on drink and the resultant domestic violence.

Social networks In addition to resources from household production and marketing, both men and women augment household well-being through social resources. Where deepening poverty and land shortages have tended to reduce access to resources from the natal family, social networks are critical resources for rural households. In addition to making contributions in cash and in kind to social networks, rural households invest a lot of time and labour in maintaining social networks. Relative to men's, however, women's lower incomes limit the advantages they can draw from such social networks, including small savings and credit schemes.

A Glimpse of the Future

Socio-economic and political transformation have been the context for increased divorces, male desertions, migrations and mortality. The resulting increase in female-headed households appears to have reduced the customary stigma attached to being unmarried. However, marriage continues to be a highly respected institution.

All three regions have inadequate schools, often located far from most rural households. This reality, the prevailing gender ideology (which perceives women only as housewives), together with women's heavy workload, constrains girls' schooling and educational achievement. In the three regions studied, overall educational attainment is low, and lower still for girls, implying an intergenerational transfer of gender disadvantages and poverty. However, girls who are involved in market activities and in generating income for themselves and their households appeared to be more confident regarding their future prospects.

There are efforts by local party/state structures to organise women into what appear to be savings and credit associations. Given the legacy of the Revolutionary

Ethiopian Women's Association (REWA) of the military regime, these efforts have not generated much enthusiasm among women. Signs of coercion were witnessed, in spite of the official emphasis by Women's Affairs Offices in *Wereda* Councils on the voluntary nature of these emergent associations.

While the access of most women to the public is still mediated through men, more and more women are making self-conscious efforts to appear in public arenas like the *kebele* and *wereda* courts on their own behalf.

The emergence of associations such as EWLA (Ethiopian Women Lawyers' Association) marks significant progress in the struggle for women's rights. However, given the immensity of the problem, there is need for more autonomous associations, committed to promoting women's active participation in challenging power relations within households and within the state.

The experience of this country indicates that for women to be true beneficiaries of land reform, land laws have to be explicitly committed to gender equality and to include mechanisms of public awareness and enforcement. In addition to ensuring implementation of land law, building legitimacy for women's land rights' claims through public education needs to take place.

Women have to be literate and fully aware of their legal rights. They have to have increased access to government administrators of land-related matters and also economic and physical access to legal mechanisms, such as lawyers and law courts. It is imperative that women have a fall-back position, that is, access to economic and social resources for survival outside the support system of contending claimants.

References

ABD Consult (1993) *Impact Assessment of Rural Women and Development Programme. Final Report*, Addis Ababa: Ministry of Agriculture, Agricultural Extension Department, Rural Women's Affairs Division.

Agarwal, B. (1994) *A Field of One's Own: Gender and Land Rights in South Asia*, Cambridge: Cambridge University Press.

— (1995) 'Gender, Poverty, and Land Rights: Bridging a Critical Gap in Economic Analysis and Policy', in Edith Kuiper and Jolande Sap (eds) *Out of the Margins: Feminist Perspectives on Economics*, London and New York: Routledge.

Beneria, L. (1981) 'Conceptualizing the Labour Force: The Under Estimation of Women's Economic Activities', *Journal of Development Studies*, Vol. 17, No. 3.

— (ed.) (1982) *The Sexual Division of Labour in Rural Societies*, New York: Praeger.

Berry, S. (1988) 'Concentration without Privatization? Some Consequences of Changing Patterns of Land Control in Africa', in S. P. Reyna and R. E. Downs (eds) *Land and Society in Contemporary Africa*, Hanover, NH: University Press of New England.

Bruce, J. W. (1993) 'Do Indigenous Tenure Systems Constrain Agricultural Development?', in Thomas J. Bassett and Donald E. Crummey (eds) *Land in African Agrarian Systems*, Wisconsin: University of Wisconsin Press.

Bryceson, D. (ed.) (1995) *Women Wielding the Hoe: Lessons from Rural Africa for Feminist Theory and Development Practice*, Oxford/Washington: Berg.

Chiari, G. P. (1996) 'Land and Democracy in Tigray', in *Occasional Papers Series on Environment and Development in an Age of Transition*, Leeds: University of Leeds, Centre for Development Studies.

Crummey, D. (1981) 'Women and Landed Property in Gondarine Ethiopia', *International Journal of Africa Historical Studies*, Vol. 14, No. 3.

Deere, C. D. (1987) 'Agrarian Reform', in Carmen Diana Deere and Magdalena Leon (eds) *Rural Women and State Policy*, Boulder, Colorado: Westview Press.

— (1995) *Women and Land Rights in the Latin American Counter Reforms*, IAFFE Panel on Property Rights and Women's Empowerment, NGO Forum on Women, UN Fourth World Conference on Women, Beijing, China.

De Janvry, A. (1988) 'The Role of Land Reform in Economic Development: Policies and Politics', in Carl Eicher and John Staatz (eds) *Agricultural Development in the Third World*, Baltimore and London: Johns Hopkins University Press.

Demographic Training and Research Center, Institute of Development Research, Addis Ababa University and Population Studies Training Center, Brown University (1998) *Southern Nations, Nationalities and Peoples Region: Community and Family Survey 1997*, Addis Ababa, Ethiopia: Addis Ababa University.

Dessalegn, R. (1992) *The Dynamics of Rural Poverty: Case Studies from a District in Southern Ethiopia*, Dakar: CODESRIA, Monograph Series 2/92.

— (ed.) (1994) *Land Tenure and Land Policy in Ethiopia After the Derg: Proceedings of the Second Workshop of the Land Tenure Project*, Trondheim: University of Trondheim, Norway Centre for Environment and Development Unit.

Dwyer, D. and J. Bruce (eds) (1988) *A Home Divided: Women and Income in the Third World*, Stanford: Stanford University Press.

Evans, A. (1992) 'Statistics', in Lise Ostergaard (ed.) *Gender and Development: A Practical Guide*, London and New York: Routledge.

Federal Democratic Republic of Ethiopia (1994) *The Constitution of the Federal Republic of Ethiopia*, Addis Ababa: Federal Democratic Republic of Ethiopia.

Gladwin, C. H. (ed.) (1991) *Structural Adjustment and African Women Farmers*, Gainesville: University of Florida Press.

Guyer, J. and P. E. Peters (1987) 'Introduction, Conceptualizing the Household: Issues of Theory and Policy in Africa', Special Issue, *Development and Change*, Vol. 18, No. 2, pp. 197–214.

Hart, G. (1995) 'Gender and Household Dynamics: Recent Theories and Their Implications', in M. G. Quibria (ed.) *Critical Issues in Asian Development: Theories, Experiences, Policies*, Oxford: Oxford University Press.

Hoben, A. (1973) *Land Tenure Among the Amhara of Ethiopia: The Dynamics of Cognatic Descent*, Chicago: University of Chicago Press.

Jacobs, S. (1998) 'The Gendered Politics of Land Reform: Three Comparative Studies', in Vicky Randall and Georgina Waylen (eds) *Gender, Politics and the State*, London and New York: Routledge.

Kabeer, N. (1991) 'Gender, Production and Well-Being: Rethinking the Household Economy', DP 288, Institute of Development Studies at the University of Sussex.

Lastarria-Cornhiel, S. (1997) 'Impact of Privatization on Gender and Property Rights in Africa', *World Development*, Vol. 25, No. 8, pp. 1317–33.

Moore, H. (1994) *A Passion for Difference*, Cambridge: Polity Press.

Pankhurst, H. (1992) *Gender, Development and Identity: an Ethiopian Study*, London: Zed Books.

Peters, P. (1995) 'Uses and Abuses of the Concept of Female-Headed Households in Research on Agrarian Transformation and Policy', in Bryceson, D. (ed.) *Women Wielding the Hoe: Lessons from Rural Africa for Feminist Theory and Development Practice*, Oxford/ Washington: Berg.

Provincial Military Administration Council (1975) 'Proclamation 71/1975: Public Ownership of Rural Lands', *Negarit Gazeta*, Vol. 35, No. 15.

Roberts, P. (1989) 'The Sexual Politics of Labour in Western Nigeria and Hausa Niger', in K. Young (ed.) *Serving Two Masters: Third World Women in Development*, Delhi: Allied Publishers.

Robertson, C. and I. Berger (1986) 'Introduction: Analyzing Class and Gender: Africa Perspectives', in C. Roberston and I. Berger (eds) *Women and Class in Africa*, New York

Sandford, J. and S. Sandford (1994) 'Land Tenure in an Enset Growing Region', in Dessalegn, R. (ed.) *Land Tenure and Land Policy in Ethiopia after the Derg: Proceedings of the Second Workshop of the Land Tenure Project of the Institute of Development Research*, Trondheim: University of Trondheim, Centre for Environment and Development Unit.

Sen, A. K. (1984) *Resources, Values and Development*, Oxford: Basil Blackwell.

— (1990) 'Gender and Co-operative Conflict', in I. Tinker (ed.) *Persistent Inequalities*, Oxford: Oxford University Press.

Staudt, K. (1978) 'Agricultural Productivity Gaps: A Case Study of Male Preference in Government Policy Implementation', *Development and Change*, Vol. 9, pp. 439–57.

Sunde, J. (1997) *Who Benefits? The Gendered Transfer of Development Benefits within the Southern Cape Land Reform Pilot Scheme*, Stellenbosch: Centre for Rural Legal Studies.

Sunde, J. and J. Hamman (1996) *Entitled to What? Gender Land Reform Policy and the Role of the Law*, Durban: Southern African Sociological Association Congress.

Teferi, A. (1997) 'Struggle over Policy Loose Ends: Idioms of Livelihood and the Many Ways of Obtaining and Losing Land in South Wollo, Amhara Region', in *Fourth Workshop of the Land Tenure Project of the Institute of Development Research*, Addis Ababa: Institute of Development Research.

Walker, C. (1998) *Land Reform and Gender in Post-Apartheid South Africa*, Discussion Paper 98, Geneva: United Nations Research Institute for Social Development.

Yigrmew, A. (1997) 'Rural Land Holding. Readjustment and Rural Organisations in West Gojjam, Amhara Region: A Summary Report', in *Fourth Workshop of the Land Tenure Project of the Institute of Development Research*, Addis Ababa: Institute of Development Research.

Young, K. (1992) 'Household Resource Management', in Ostergaard, L. (ed.) *Gender and Development: A Practical Guide*, London and New York: Routledge.

Zenebeworke, T. (1982) 'The Impact of Land Reform on Women: The Case of Ethiopia,' Beneria, L. (ed.) *Women and Development: The Sexual Division of Labour in Rural Societies*, New York: Praetor Special Studies.

THREE
Women's Land Rights in Mozambique: Cultural, Legal and Social Contexts

Liazzat Bonate

§ THIS research attempts to shed the light on the situation of women in regard to land in Mozambique. Its objective is to promote an empirically sound, yet dynamic and visionary understanding of the relationships between religion, human rights and law in the context of cultural transformation in Africa. The research takes a broad view of religion to include indigenous and/or local belief systems, customary law and religious practice. State civil law and enforcement institutions and processes are also examined to envision human rights innovatively as drawing upon cultural and legal norms and institutions as well as on the priorities set by locals.

The fieldwork was conducted in the Nampula province of northern Mozambique, where diverse but relatively homogeneous rural communities are found. An interesting feature of this area, given the gendered approach of this research, is the prevalence of matrilineality.

The impact of the modern state and its institutions on women's situation with regard to land is not readily perceptible. In rural Mozambique, as elsewhere in Africa, women's rights and status are linked to culture and kinship. The primary focus of the research is therefore on women and land within families and communities. The communities selected were from three sites in Nampula province. A pilot study was first conducted at the Muecate administrative post in Muecate district. The research examined women and land among:

- Muslims of the Inguri zone of Angoche city.
- Catholics of the Anchilo administrative post near the provincial capital of Nampula city.
- Adherents of indigenous beliefs of Corrane administrative post in Meconta district.

The religious identity of these communities is, of course, just one identity among the multiple identities held, including ethnic identities. Communities were chosen through initial consultations with local and provincial administrative and religious leaders. However, individual and collective religious identities were later confirmed with the respondents themselves. In all regions, Makua language speakers and Makua ethnic identity predominated, except for Inguri where Koti language and identity prevailed.

The research focused on the cultural, legal and social contexts in which women establish and maintain their access to, and their usage, management and disposal of land, while controlling resources, accessing and using benefits derived from land use and participating in household decision-making. It also assessed the accessibility of, and the extent to which women benefit from, legal norms and cultural, economic, legal and religious women-oriented institutions. The research used numerous primary and secondary data sources, including legal documents promulgated by the Portuguese colonial and independent post-colonial Mozambican states, ethnographic and historical material on customary and religious practices and existing literature and reports of different entities. Primary data collection was undertaken through the study of court records, individual semi-structured interviews with key informants and 50 household questionnaires administered in each of the chosen research sites. Interviews were carried out with court and land registry officials, officers of the Ministry of Agriculture, community chiefs, Christian and Muslim leaders, feminist and human rights activists and members of various non-governmental organisations (NGOs).

Gender issues were also addressed in participatory focus group discussions with homogeneous groups of local women and with mixed groups of local men and women.

Research Sites

According to the second general census of the population, carried out in 1997, the total population of Nampula province is 2.9 million (General Census 1997: 45). The census established that 1.1 million of the population were Muslim, 808,875 were Catholic, and 320,388 were followers of other Christian denominations, including indigenous African churches. Nearly 48,000 were identified as Animists, followers of indigenous African beliefs. The rural population was estimated at 2.2 million.

Inguri zone, Angoche city, Angoche district The district of Angoche has an estimated 114,607 inhabitants (General Census 1997: 4). The population density of the district is relatively high, resulting in conflicts with respect to land and water (District Development Profiles 1997: 4).

The area used by families (the household economy) for agriculture in the district is 66,467 ha, 22 per cent of all land in the district. The main economic activity of the district is agriculture. The basic subsistence crops are beans, cassava roots, groundnuts, maize and rice, and the main cash crops, cashew nuts, coconuts, groundnuts, maize and rice.

The population of the city of Angoche is estimated at 88,716 people (District Development Profiles 1997: 3). Of this population, 23,270 inhabit a quarter called Inguri, where the majority of people come from the Koti islands and claim Koti ethnic identity. According to local officials, more than 80 per cent are Muslim.[1] Although Inguri is an urban area, the population has agricultural fields outside the city and is also involved in fishing. Crafts, industry and trade are in decay as a result of the civil war and International Monetary Fund (IMF) and World Bank economic policies directed at the production of cashew nuts.

Anchilo administrative post near the provincial capital of Nampula city in Meconta district The population of Meconta district is estimated at 123,097 people (General Census 1997: 10). The population density of the district is moderate in comparison to other regions of the province (District Development Profiles 1997: 4). Families (the household economy) occupy 43,306 ha, approximately 11.6 per cent of the district's land (District Development Profiles 1997: 4). The population of the Corrane administrative post is estimated at 42,098 people (General Census 1997: 17). The main economic activity is agriculture. Basic subsistence crops cultivated are beans, cassava, groundnuts, maize, rice and yams. Cash crops are cashew nuts, cotton and groundnuts (District Development Profiles 1997: 5). Cultivation of tobacco is limited and recent. Although there are rivers in the vicinity, fishing is not important, but domestic animals, such as chickens, goats and pigs are kept (District Development Profiles 1997: 6).

Anchilo administrative post, Nampula district The population of Nampula district is estimated at 140,000, yet the population density is not high (District Development Profiles 1997: 3). Families (the household economy) occupy about 40.023 ha (District Development Profiles 1997: 3). The main crops for household consumption are cassava, groundnuts, maize, rice and sorghum. Cashew nuts, cotton and sugar cane are grown for commercial purposes (District Development Profiles 1997: 4–5).

The population of Anchilo administrative post is estimated at 19,449 people. Anchilo is rural, located in the province's interior and subject to influence from the provincial capital 20 km away.

Muecate Administrative Post, Muecate District
(Pilot Research Site)

The population of Muecate administrative post was estimated at 77,906 in 1998 (General Census 1997: 22), and 32,517 ha of land is used for agriculture, mainly by families (the household economy), to produce beans, cassava, groundnuts, maize and rice for household consumption. Cash crops are cashew nuts, cotton and sunflowers.

Socio-demographic Characteristics of the Respondents

A total of 150 households was surveyed in Anchilo, Corrane and Inguri. The age of women respondents ranged from 18 to 87. Literacy among women was low: 50 per cent had never undergone formal schooling and 50 per cent had basic primary education, in many cases not completed. In Inguri, 60 per cent had attended Qur'anic schools. One hundred and four (70 per cent) of respondents were married and 46 (30 per cent) were divorcees or widows. Of these, 24 (16 per cent) were divorced and 22 (14 per cent) were widows.

Among those married, 60 (57 per cent) constituted nuclear families comprised of husband, wives(s) and their own children, while 44 (43 per cent) lived with extended families in the same households. One (4 per cent) divorced woman and three (14 per cent) widows lived on their own, while 23 (96 per cent) divorced women and 19 (86 per cent) widows lived with other family members, including children, children's families, grandchildren, nieces, nephews, uncles, parents, and sometimes relatives of the deceased husbands.

Among the different forms of marriages, de facto unions predominated (47 per cent), where women and men lived together without ceremonies related to marriage. This form of marriage was most common in Anchilo (78 per cent), followed by Corrane (52 per cent) and Inguri (10 per cent). The second most widespread form of marriage was Muslim (32.7 per cent), 90 per cent of which were found in Inguri, followed by Corrane and Anchilo (4 per cent each). Six per cent of marriages were Catholic.

The majority of interviewed people in Inguri (70 per cent) stated that the religion of their partners mattered and thus they preferred marrying Muslims. The majority of those surveyed in Anchilo (100 per cent) and Corrane (96 per cent) said that it did not matter. Out of a total of 104 marriages, 20 (19 per cent) were polygamous. The most frequent number of wives in polygamous marriages was two (92 per cent), followed by three (8 per cent). The average family farmland size was 1.7 ha, ranging from 0.25 ha to 30 ha. The average size among the Koti (2.6 ha) was higher than in Anchilo (1.3 ha) and Corrane (1.2 ha). The largest cash crop lands also belonged to the Koti (two plots of 200 ha and 225 ha).

In Muecate administrative post, the pilot research site, a total of 44 households was surveyed. Among them, 28 (64 per cent) were married couples, seven (16 per cent) were comprised of divorced women and nine (20 per cent) were widows. Four (14 per cent) marriages were polygamous. Of the 28 households of married couples, 21 were composed of parents and their own children. In seven cases, the households included other extended family members. Two widows lived alone.

Ethnographic and Historical Background

Both the Koti and Makua are Bantu. The Koti language is a local variant of Kiswahili (Schadeberg and Mucanheia 2000). Although comprehensive linguistic research has yet to be carried out in Mozambique, the local population claimed that their ancestors came from the Zambezi valley of central Mozambique.[2] This claim is supported by numerous local oral narratives.

The Koti and Makua are matrilineal. According to local oral narratives, people are incorporated into *n'loko* whose members claim common descent from the mythical *erukulo* (uterus) of a female ancestor. Each *n'loko* consists of several smaller *nihimo* (kinship groups). The paramount chief of each *n'loko* is *called mwene n'loko* and the chief of each *nihimo* is called *humu* or *mwene nihimo*.

The dominance of certain *n'loko* or *nihimo* is based on the fact that their members were the firstcomers to the area and are therefore the owners and regulators of land and its distribution. The inheritance patterns of the matrilineal people in Nampula follow, in that the person chosen to replace a maternal aunt or uncle becomes responsible for the funeral rites of the deceased and for the destiny of family lands. Usually this person is a real or putative maternal niece or nephew, a child of the real or putative elder uterine sister of the deceased. In the absence of such an heir, cousins or other family members from the maternal side can inherit, but direct sons and daughters of the deceased cannot.

The Macua *mwene* of Anchilo and Muecate connect the dominance of their *n'loko* to the idea that their ancestors were firstcomers to the land that, they claim, had not been inhabited before. But the Corrane *mwene* encountered people already living there.[3] In Corrane, local oral narratives depict constant battles and contradictions between the newcomers and the *mwene* about who 'came there first'.

Inguri, however, is an urban zone and the Koti there are immigrants from the Angoche islands. The Angoche islands (Ngoja, the old Kiswahili name, was still in use in 1900) were culturally and historically related to the Swahili. According to Swahili oral narratives, the Koti *mwene-inhapakho* (firstcomers) claim Shirazi descent from Kilwa and Zanzibar on the one hand, with the Bantu descending through emigration from the Zambezi valley on the other hand (Lupi 1907).[4]

The Angoche islands were an important trading centre in the network of east African Swahili towns. Similar to other Swahili communities, the Koti are primarily agricultural (Glassman 1995). For mainland people, establishing relations with the Koti was a means to becoming involved in Indian Ocean trading opportunities. In return, the scarcity of land because of the relatively high population density on the Angoche islands encouraged the Koti to seek relations with mainland people as well in order to gain access to new farmlands. The M'Lay and the Sangage were the major givers of kinship relations and land to the Koti. These two ethnic groups were viewed as important vassals of the Angoche Sultanate in Portuguese historical accounts (Lupi 1907). At the beginning of the twentieth century, the

Portuguese transformed the mainland opposite to the Angoche islands and surrounding Paraphato mount into the present urban unit. As a result, the Koti, who had traditionally farmed these lands, were driven further into the mainland in search of land.

From Portuguese pre-colonial and colonial sources emerges a history of permanent fission, fusion, migration and regrouping in Nampula province. Involvement in the international slave trade during the eighteenth and nineteenth centuries, and Portuguese conquest at the end of the nineteenth century, also impacted the positions of the ruling *n'loko* (Amorim 1911; Botelho 1936; Coutinho 1941). However, local oral narratives present local political history as a chain of continuous and uninterrupted events, where the leading *n'loko* and their paramount chiefs owned the land and dominated the local people from time immemorial. But Murphy and Bledsoe underscore that oral reproduction and management of the definitions of pivotal historical events are not random (Murphy and Bledsoe in Kopytoff 1987: 123–47). Rather, accounts of these events are strategically altered and selected to restructure current socio-political relations. Although local chiefs are not currently incorporated into the state's administrative or legal system, their importance and survival has depended on continued use of local oral narratives to define identities and kinship and to establish the boundaries of the lands of kinship groups.

At present, the leadership of women within these kinship groups is difficult to determine, a situation that has led to the belief that women are inherently oppressed even in matrilineal communities (Casimiro et al. 1996). In the course of their conquest, however, the Portuguese had to deal with several female paramount chiefs in Nampula province, among them the 'Queen' Nguema (Coutinho 1941). In Muecate district, local oral narratives note that, before the Portuguese conquest, 'the owner of the Muecate lands was a woman, *apyamwene*, whom the Portuguese called *rainha* (queen). At that time, *apyamwene* was the owner of all these lands. Although there were always enough men, the land was distributed instead among responsible women.'[5]

The Mussa Quanto, the legendary nineteenth-century *wazir* (military leader) of the Angoche Sultanate, could not rest until he recovered his beloved sister Mahera from Portuguese captivity (Lupi 1907). The Portuguese explained his unrest in terms of his deep emotional attachment to the beautiful and intelligent Mahera. But affections aside, the captivity of Mahera probably would have had important socio-political consequences for the Mussa Quanto kinship group because she was their *apyamwene*. The Portuguese themselves recognised that she was an influential and respected person (Lupi 1907).

In matrilineal kinship groups, an *apyamwene* accompanied each *mwene*. An *apyamwene* is usually an elder uterine sister of the *mwene*. The current *apyamwene* identifies a niece with promising characteristics, then educates and raises the girl to prepare to replace her on her death. In Mozambique, some of the local *mwene*, feminists, historians and state officials frequently downplay the cultural and socio-political influence of the *apyamwene*, often depicting her as being solely responsible for female initiation rituals. While this role is important, the *apyamwene* is in fact the spiritual leader of the community, whose powers to communicate with ancestral spirits and the land help to solve major community crises. In local oral narratives, the *apyamwene* is seen as a living carrier of the ancestor spirits of those who emigrated from their birth lands and those who clean new lands of their malevolent spirits before people can settle there. In Bantu farming communities, the *apyamwene* has powers to heal the land and to oversee its fertility, and the fertility of the community, through female initiation rites and other healing practices (Vansina 1990; Schoenbrun 1998). Thus the *apyamwene* is crucial to the well-being of the land and its people.

It is believed that the Portuguese envisioned the transformation of matrilineality into patrilineality and associated patriarchy. Although this idea is generally accurate in terms of the consequences of colonisation and the development/modernisation projects of the Portuguese, it cannot be proved true with respect to law (Pitcher 1996: 81–112). Article 117 of the 1933 Law on Overseas Administration Reform permitted the investiture of a woman for the post of local chief within the new colonial administrative system in cases where having a female chief was '… quando essa for a tradiçao local' (a local tradition) and 'the attributes and duties of a female chief were similar to those of a male chief' (Decreto-Lei No. 23: 229 1933). This gender specificity is, however, absent from the 1961 Law on Overseas Administration Reform, where local chiefs are addressed by male gender alone (Decreto-Lei No. 43: 896 1961).

After independence, FRELIMO (Front for the Liberation of Mozambique) declared the end of traditional exploitative and oppressive structures and their related mentality. *Apyamwene*, like other traditional structures, began to be considered obsolete. Women's issues had now to be addressed by the new government, through participation in Organizaçao da Mulher Moçambicana (OMM), the Mozambican Women's Organisation. However, despite persecution, *apyamwene* continue to play important roles in rural communities today.

Legal Background

The research sites were conquered by the Portuguese at the end of the nineteenth and the beginning of the twentieth centuries. Therefore, only colonial legislation from the beginning of the twentieth century will be considered.

The Portuguese divided the population of Portuguese colonies into indigenous and non-indigenous (Article 7, Decreto-Lei No. 23: 229 1933). Indigenous people were subject to their own 'traditions and customs' and local chiefs were maintained within the Portuguese colonial administrative system (Article 7, Decreto-Lei No. 23: 229 1933; Decreto-Lei No. 39: 666 1954; and Decreto-Leis No. 43: 893–7 1961).

The non-indigenous population included the Portuguese, as well as other European and Asian immigrants who were considered citizens of their respective states and subject to the laws of those states. Despite several attempts, the Portuguese were not able to codify the local 'traditions and customs' (Da Silva Cunha 1953).[6] But according to the Portuguese, legal pluralism prevailed in their overseas territories.

After independence, Article 4 of the 1975 Constitution of Mozambique declared the end of legal pluralism by eliminating 'traditional oppression and exploitation structures and their related mentality'. But Law Number 12/1978 established a dual judicial system, consisting of Judicial Courts led by professional judges and Popular Courts led by non-professional judges, who were elected locally and who arbitrated according to common sense and good will. However, the main purpose of this measure was to endorse hierarchical uniformity and guarantee the application of formal law at all levels (Raynal in *Revista Jurídica* 1997: 19). In practice, despite the persecution of traditional authorities and other actions of the centralised state, the majority of Mozambicans continued to follow local beliefs and culture.

Since 1990, the legal system has become more accommodating of legal pluralism. Articles 200 and 203 of the 1990 Constitution endorse 'all other norms of the legal order' and continue to uphold laws that do not coincide with the Constitution. This allowance was followed by the 1992 reform of the legal system, in which Community Courts replaced Popular Courts. The difference is that Popular Courts had to consult people through popular assemblies to hear their views with regard to legal decisions of the court, but Community Courts' final legal decisions rested with elected judges. However, their competencies and human and material resources remain limited. Thus, while Community Courts are legally part of the official legal system, they are practically 'left to themselves without national or legal coordination' (Casimiro 1992: 4). The competencies of Community Courts are limited to cases referred to as social cases, which include small-scale conflicts and cases not involving criminal offences or large sums of money. Although Community Courts consult official legal documents such as the Penal Code for their decisions, they rely on informal methods of settling disputes.

At independence, the state nationalised land, although land previously the property of the Portuguese was not redistributed to peasants. The First Land Bill of independent Mozambique, approved in 1979, declared all land state property, and formerly private farms became state farms or socialist cooperatives. Small-holding rural families could have 0.5 ha of wetland and one hectare of dryland per family member.

With the liberalisation of structural adjustment programmes beginning in 1987, land reform again came to the fore. The new Land Law 19/97 was approved by Parliament in 1997. Article 3 of this law maintains that land is the property of the state and cannot be sold, or in any other form be alienated, mortgaged or encumbered. However, Articles 7 and 9 of the law also recognise the right of 'local communities' to use and benefit by occupation, in accordance with 'customary norms and practices', if such norms do not contradict the Constitution. Such rights can be proved by testimonial proof presented by members of local communities (Article 15, 1997 Land Law), who are also entitled to participate in the management of natural resources, conflict resolution and identifying and defining the boundaries of 'community lands' (Article 24, 1997 Land Law). Rural communities were expected to be empowered through this law. However, the term 'local community' is ambiguous and lacks precedent. The law therefore recommends that Parliament approve additional laws to specify the meaning and responsibilities of 'local communities' as well as mechanisms to identify their representatives with respect to land (Article 27, 1997 Land Law; and Kloeck-Jensen 1997: 6). One step forward in this direction was the approval by the Ministerial Council in August 2000 of the decree recognising 'traditional authority'.

Women and Land in Nampula Province

Generally, rural Mozambicans live outside the influence and scope of legal norms. During the prolonged civil war that ended in 1992, the presence of the state was not strongly felt in Nampula province. New state laws are inclined to follow the Portuguese example with respect to local customs and traditions. At the same time, as local cultural and religious practices have not been codified, it is impossible to determine the extent to which they can be identified as laws or norms and how rights can be defined and established (Ranger in Hobsbawm and Ranger 1983: 211–62).

According to local cultural perceptions, *n'loko* and *nihimo* lands are owned collectively by members of kinship groups and cannot be alienated. Thus an individual may only hold land on the basis of usufruct – he or she can occupy and use it, but cannot own it. In all research sites, these perceptions were still strong.

Article 21 of the 1997 Land Law attempted to maintain these cultural perceptions by stating that rural communities shall manage natural resources and conflict resolution by relying on 'customary laws and practices'. Within the land tenure system of Nampula province, the *n'loko* or *nihimo* ensures access to land to all members of the group without gender differentiation. Everyone is allocated land by the paramount chief, through consultation with lesser chiefs. This was incorporated into Article 7 of the 1997 Land Law.

Besides kinship lands, there are virgin lands that can be acquired by individual effort through their clearance and cultivation. But such lands cannot be turned into self-acquired property, because they are usually under the control of kinship groups. However, they can be inherited by direct descendants or can become a bequest by the will of the deceased.

Trees are owned individually, irrespective of whose land they are planted on. As such, they can be alienated or turned into a bequest. By buying or inheriting a tree, a person who is not a member of the kinship group where the tree is located can gain access to its lands. In Nampula province, this practice became a widespread way of bypassing both local cultural perceptions and state laws prohibiting the sale of land and occupation, without prior consultation with the local community (Article 9, 1997 Land Law).

Although all populations in the research sites were matrilineal, women's situation with respect to land varied from place to place and from household to household. The assumption of some historians is that matrilineality is more favourable to women than patrilineality (Casimiro et al. 1992). Another assumption is that the predominant pattern of residence among matrilineal communities is uxorilocal. Feminists seek to show how women are oppressed. Thus it has been concluded in some studies that the *atata* (maternal uncle) controls women in the same way that older males control women in patrilineal communities (Casimiro et al. 1992). Another conclusion is that Christianity and Islam transformed matrilineality into patrilineality and introduced patriarchy. However, the results of fieldwork for this study revealed that the impact of Christianity and Islam with respect to land is minimal.

The official titling of land is provided for by Article 10 of the 1997 Land Law. The process is slow and the number of women with title deeds is much less than that of men. In the research sites, between 1991 and 2000, six women and six men in Angoche, one woman and three men from Anchilo and one woman and seven men from Corrane applied for land titling. In Anchilo, where Catholicism predominates, the Diocesan Commission for Land is promoting the collective land titling rights of local communities, also enshrined in Article 10 of the 1997 Land Law.[7] The 1997 Land Law is therefore better known in Anchilo than in the other research sites, as the Diocesan Commission for Land actively campaigned for the elaboration and promulgation of the law.

Access to Kinship Lands

The first question addressed with respect to women's access to kinship lands was whether a woman could become the main heir of these lands. After the 1961 administrative reform, women could not legally be a *regulo* (paramount chief in Portuguese, *inhapakho* in the local language) recognised by the colonial government. But a woman could still be a *humu* within smaller kinship units in the traditional cultural sense of being an owner and regulator of kinship lands without holding any specific title.

Male and female opinions diverged. In Muecate, both genders were inclined to permit this possibility.[8] In Anchilo and Corrane, both women and men thought that it was impossible.[9] However, the local oral narratives of the Umbuechiua kinship group, who claim to be among the firstcomers to Anchilo, note that *mwene* and *apyamwene* performed the initial distribution of land together.[10]

Although the reasons for this territorial divergence are not clear, the closeness of Anchilo to the provincial capital, Nampula City, and the greater involvement of Corrane in cotton production since colonial times, could probably offer an explanation. Also, perhaps the constant battles of the Mucapera and Napita dominant kinship groups against firstcomers could shed light on the roots of gender discrimination against women in Corrane. The firstcomers, who were eventually expelled to neighbouring areas, continued to pose a threat for the inhabitants of Corrane. The threat of attack probably led to militarisation of the men and marginalisation of the women.

The Koti's kinship lands are mostly situated on the Angoche islands. Nevertheless, they had control over kinship lands and revenues.[11] According to local oral narratives, the Koti's *inhapakho* were always men. However, within smaller kinship groups, women could become the main heirs.[12] One of the interviewed women maintained that she had inherited land from her maternal uncle, who had appointed her as the main heir.[13] When the uncle died, first, as a good Muslim, she paid all his debts. She then distributed land among her kin, including the deceased uncle's children, and had been overseeing its use ever since.

Unless totally excluded from kinship, which is an almost impossible occurrence, anybody can claim a parcel of kinship lands at any time of his or her life. Inheritance of kinship lands is matrilineal. However, people do not actually inherit kinship lands, because they cannot be turned into private property or bequeathed. Land rights are merely usufruct, with the main heir controlling use of the land. Forty-nine per cent of men and 50 per cent of women claimed they inherited kinship lands from putative or real maternal uncles: 23 per cent of men and 16 per cent of women from their maternal grandfathers and 15 per cent of men and 16 per cent of women from their mothers. Only 8 per cent of men and 7 per cent of women inherited from their fathers. In Muecate, the pilot research revealed that 26 women (59 per cent) inherited lands from their kin, having obtained it from their mother's line. Six women (14 per cent) were using their kinship land from their maternal side and expected to inherit it later. The rest had no access to their kinship lands, either because they had never claimed it or because they were living too far away. In only two cases were women reluctant to claim their lands, due to conflicts with other kin.

Thus people living within their own communities had relatively easy access to and use of their kinship lands. Some outsiders, including those married to local people, also had access to their ancestral kinship lands in other areas, or at least some control over the revenues. For example, none of the Koti in Inguri actually lived on their kinship lands, because these lands were situated on the Angoche islands. Nevertheless, they had access to those lands and could indicate where their individual shares was located. However, due to the scarcity of land for farming, their shares were frequently expressed in coconut tree numbers, from which they received relatively regular revenues.

Theoretically, nobody could be denied access to kinship lands based on gender.

The question was therefore whether or not it could happen in practice. In Inguri, all the Koti and non-Koti respondents had access to their kinship lands independently of the gender variable. Only one husband, originally from Mozambique island, did not have access to his kinship lands, because of distance. A similar situation prevailed in Anchilo, where only three women had no access to their kinship lands.

Conversely, in Corrane, both males and females underscored that the inheritance would usually would go to male members of the kinship group to the detriment of female members. Two interviewed *regulos* stated that 'our culture always despised women ... a woman cannot stand in front of a man or be equal to him'.[14] In Corrane, a total of 18 women (36 per cent) out of 50 had no access to their kinship lands.

In the Muecate pilot research, 59 per cent of women inherited lands from their maternal line, while 14 per cent were using those lands, but had not yet inherited them. Of two non-local widows, only one had access to her deceased husband's kinship lands.

Access to Self-acquired Lands

Those interviewed indicated that people could acquire land by clearing virgin lands or forests. One motive for self-acquiring lands was to secure the future of the children by leaving them land independent of kinship. Another motive was to increase land available for family subsistence purposes. An additional reason was to cultivate cash crops to generate income that would remain either under the control of an individual or his immediate family, and beyond the reach of extended kin. Finally, and most importantly, acquiring land by clearing was the way outsiders usually access land for farming. It was possible to ask for land from the state (mainly the former private property of the colonisers), but doing so was relatively rare. Only one woman and one man in the sample acquired land in this manner.

The most common way of acquiring lands was therefore cultural. Anybody who wished to acquire independent lands must first certify its availability with the local *mwene*. The *mwene* would become a witness in case a conflict arose later. The newly acquired land was then cleared and worked. In order to enable the direct descendants of the new landowner to access this land after his death, an agreement would have to be reached with the *mwene*. If such an agreement is not reached, then the self-acquired land could still be disputed matter by the direct descendants and local kingship groups, or, if the land was located within the limits of the greater *n'loko*, between heirs indicated by the deceased as beneficiaries and maternal relatives.

In focus group discussions, women in Anchilo, Corrane and Muecate revealed that because of their limited labour and monetary resources and the absence of machinery, they felt unable to self-acquire lands through clearing. This was done by their husbands, whom they joined in working the lands after clearing. However, women who were able to barter for labour with small amounts of cash, oil, soap and second-hand cloth, could hire people to clear for them. This practice was particularly noticeable among Koti women, who are good saleswomen and traditionally exchange fish for labour on the mainland.

The self-acquired lands of the Koti consist of those in Inguri and lands acquired through negotiations with mainland people. As immigrants to the mainland, the Koti cannot claim it as their kinship lands. In Inguri, some Koti had established themselves before the Portuguese arrived. But the Portuguese delineated and distributed these lands to the Koti. These lands are divided into small plots, on which the residences of the Koti are constructed. Previously considered state lands, these properties are gradually being turned into real estate, which can be inherited by any male or female descendant of the owner, or become a bequest.[15] In Inguri, only three respondents had their farmlands near their residences, within the borders of the city.

As the Angoche islands are difficult to access on a daily basis and as land is scarce there anyway, the Koti of Inguri farm in the surrounding Angoche city regions of the mainland. It takes them between one hour and 30 minutes and six hours to reach their farmlands. In order to gain access to these lands, the Koti have to establish a good rapport as well as mutually beneficial agreements with the local populations.[16] The best way to do so is by establishing kinship relations through marriage, which Koti have succeeded in doing. The lands are rented for a pre-determined period of time, usually a year. Each year, the terms of the agreement are reconsidered and the Koti have to pay an established amount of money. The Koti also request local *mwene* for virgin lands, which they clear and often attempt to turn into self-acquired property. Another way for the Koti to access land is through first buying trees, then fully appropriating the land where the trees stand.

All of these ways of acquiring land by the Koti are both culturally abhorrent and illegal under Article 13 of the 1997 Land Law. But appropriating land on the mainland is the only way for the Inguri Koti to guarantee the land for their families. Women play an active part in these processes, although male relatives execute actual accord and payment with local people. Of a total of 47 Inguri respondents using lands in the mainland, ten (21.3 per cent) claimed that they bought their lands, of which six (60 per cent) were women and four (40 per cent) were men.

In Corrane, most local people indicated that they cleared land primarily for cotton production to obtain cash. No local married woman claimed that she bought or cleared land. Among local couples, both husbands and wives participated in clearing virgin land consequently used for cotton production. Another local used her husband's inherited kinship land for family subsistence, but her husband cleared additional land for cotton. Two unmarried local women, one divorced and one widowed, were deprived of access to their kinship lands and to their former husbands' lands, so were forced to clear land to survive. Among the non-native residents of Corrane, one man and one woman married to locals maintained that they bought land from locals by purchasing cashew nut trees, with posterior appropriation of the land.

In Anchilo, the most attractive means to acquire cash was to purchase cashew trees and produce peanuts on self-acquired lands. Here as well the purchase of trees was often followed by attempts to appropriate the land beneath them. Two local couples claimed they had bought cashew nut trees jointly, while two other local couples indicated that they had jointly cleared virgin lands to produce peanuts for cash, in addition to using household farmlands obtained through kinship. One local husband maintained that he cleared virgin lands for himself to grow peanuts. One non-local wife claimed she bought the land from the locals to grow peanuts for cash. Among married women in Anchilo, there were no cases of buying or clearing lands on their own.

Access to Rented Lands

According to culture in Nampula province, both women and men have the possibility of either renting land or sharecropping with the owner. Sharecropping is the usual way in which people with no land rights, and who are not local, can gain access to land. There are many different types of contracts in use between foreigners and locals, but monetary compensation is still rare for land use, except among the Koti of Inguri.

Newcomers are generally forbidden to plant trees, in particular, cashew nut, coconut and fruit trees. The reason for this is that trees are owned individually, so that trees planted by foreigners would become their private property, not belonging to the kinship group that owns the land. As mentioned above, planting or buying a tree is frequently used as a means to appropriate the land under it. Tree-related land disputes are particularly acute in Anchilo and Corrane, where local women, during focus group discussions, revealed that most newcomers dispute the ownership of land where they have already planted cashew nut trees.

As previously pointed out, the principal way of gaining access to land on the mainland among the Koti of Inguri is by renting. Each Koti pays an established sum to the local kinship group or *mwene* for renting land. The agreement is annual and the Koti frequently change lands, if a dispute or other inconvenience arises. Also, locals take advantage of the Koti by renting them virgin lands, which after being cleared and used are offered the following year to another person for a higher sum. The competition for land among the Koti themselves is as fierce as that between the Koti and the locals. Forty-seven respondents (94 per cent) of the total of 50 in Inguri had been renting land from the surrounding Angoche city. In 81 per cent of cases women rented lands, and in only 8 per cent of cases did men rent. Four couples indicated that they rented jointly.

Conversely, in Corrane, women rarely rented lands by themselves. They also avoided participating in cotton production, to the desperation of agricultural and women's NGOs and cotton companies.[17] Women's main responsibility is culturally defined as farming for household subsistence. Thus they cannot spare time for participating in cotton production. The land under cotton production is usually cleared and prepared by cotton companies, which also provide machinery and pesticides. However, the cost of this assistance is discounted from the price of the produce sold back to the cotton companies. Often, producers do not make money and even become indebted. In addition, cotton prices decreased significantly in the last few years, so that not only women, but also men, are steadily losing interest in it. Nevertheless, there was one widow, considered to be among the leading cotton producers, who was making a considerable amount of cash per year according to local standards.

Making cash is culturally perceived as the husband's responsibility. Nevertheless, most wives and husbands claimed that they jointly rented lands for cash crops. These were often lands additional to the kinship lands reserved for family subsistence. A total of five such local married couples (out of 22) were found to rent separate plots of land. Ten couples, consisting of local wives and foreign husbands, also jointly rented lands, independent of whether the wives had access to kinship lands or not. Only two husbands rented land in their own names, while their wives had no access to lands. No married woman rented land in her own name, but one divorced woman and two widows rented land for cash crops, specifically cashew nuts. But these women technically rented trees rather than land. Two non-local couples, of whom the wives (a nurse and a teacher) were assigned by the state to work in Corrane; although their non-native husbands accompanied them, it was their duty to find lands and negotiate the renting of these lands with the locals.

Urban people from Nampula city, the nearby provincial capital, frequently seek to rent lands in Anchilo. Paid by waged labour and having access to cheap goods, urban Nampula women often manage to strike good deals with the locals. There is also a significant presence of Maconde people, who remained in Anchilo after the independence war, although many of them are divorced or widowed women. From general observation and interviews, these Maconde women were also renting lands successfully.

Of 36 married households, 17 comprised local spouses on both sides. In six of these local couples, husbands and wives rented land jointly. In six other households where one of the spouses was non-native, husbands and their local wives also rented land jointly. Two non-local divorcees and two non-local widows rented lands on their own. Most rented lands were used for family subsistence. However, Anchilo people value cashew nut trees and sought to buy them whenever they could. In some cases, they claimed they rented trees rather than land. In other cases, they bought trees but then appropriated the land. The Nampula urban population also used this strategy to access lands.

Use, Management and Disposal of Land

Article 9 (A and B) of the 1997 Land Law provides individual persons with the right of land use and benefit 'in accordance with customary norms and practices', or if a person has been using the land for at least ten years in good faith. However, 'in accordance with customary norms and practices', kinship land use rights are not transferable either to or from spouses or their children. This prohibition is against the provisions of Article 13 of the 1997 Land Law, which states that 'the right to land and benefit may be transferred by succession, without distinction by sex'.

It is generally culturally perceived that the kinship land where a couple resides or farms for household subsistence, whether it comes from the wife's or the husband's side, is the domain of the wife. Thus the married woman's right to use this land is safeguarded. However, the destiny of this land upon divorce or widowhood depends on the residence of the couple. Although all the respondents in this study were matrilineal, residency was diverse. If the marriage was uxorilocal, upon divorce or widowhood the man lost his right to use household land, while the woman's right remained unchallenged. If the marriage was virilocal, upon divorce or widowhood the woman frequently lost this right.

Out of the total of 104 married households, 34 per cent resided uxorilocally, 45 per virilocally and 21 per cent lived on independent lands. The majority of the virilocal residencies were registered in Inguri (67 per cent) and Anchilo (47 per cent). In the Muecate pilot research, eight (29 per cent) of the total 44 households resided virilocally and three (ten per cent) on independent lands, which belong neither to the wife's nor to the husband's side of the family. The rest of the residences (61 per cent) were uxorilocal. Muecate women, even young ones, always have access to kinship lands and marriage is not a condition to start using them.

If the woman is local and moves back in with her own kinship group after divorce or widowhood, she can request a parcel of kinship lands. However, if she is not local and is either not willing or too elderly to move back, she is frequently denied the right to access the kinship lands of her former husband by his extended family. This is also true for women born and raised locally whose mothers were not local. As the land belongs to her father's extended maternal kin, she must seek land from her mother's side, where she would frequently not know anybody. In these instances, while men manage to negotiate their access to land with other men, women often suffer denial and stigmatisation. Article 10 determines that 'individual persons, men and women, who are members of a local community may request an individual title upon partition of the particular land parcel from the area of the community'. However, the definition of who is a member of the local community may be understood differently by the local community and the law. Although even newcomers can access the land locally through self-clearing or renting, upon divorce or widowhood such land might become a matter of dispute.

While an immigrant from another community who is married to a local man can be considered a member of the local community, he or she will continue to be a stranger with respect to land, even after a long period of time. To illustrate this point, three examples from Muecate are given below. But this situation is common among all communities of Nampula province.

In Muecate, three immigrant women, two elderly widows and one married woman, were interviewed. All of them had kinship lands in their places of birth, but had lost access to them and contact with their relatives due to long distances and war. The widows were left without any land from their husbands, because the family of the deceased had appropriated it although they had lived in the community for 30 to 40 years. Being elderly and having no other means of survival, they had to beg for land from the locals. Both managed to rent small parcels of land and were poor. The third woman, married, was born and raised in Muecate, so was practically a community member from early infancy. After the death of her father, who was from Muecate, his land was taken away by his maternal family, while her mother, who was an immigrant, could not leave her any land.

With respect to self-acquired land, often a married woman uses it together with her husband, independent of whether the land was cleared by the husband, or at the request and by the efforts of the wife. Moreover, she may routinely take as active a part as her husband in the clearing of virgin land and the working of it. However, upon divorce, the husband frequently continues using this land while the wife loses access to it. And upon widowhood, the woman often loses this right in favour of the deceased husband's matrilineal family.

As stated above, the access of the Koti to their kinship lands on the Angoche islands did not differ according to gender. But the lands on the mainland have been rented mostly by women. Therefore, even though the majority resided virilocally, this did not alter women's situation with regard to the use of land, even after divorce or widowhood. Among the Koti of Inguri, agriculture is the responsibility of the woman, while the man is involved in income-generating activities unrelated to land. This means that negotiating the renting of land and controlling family subsistence agriculture is in the hands of a wife. But the lands were considered common to the couple in 78 per cent of cases, and household rented lands were not divided into the wife's or husband's part.

In principle, anybody, whether female or male, can rent kinship lands to a third party. But the *mwene* and other extended kin should be consulted. According to those interviewed, a Koti woman, like a Koti man, is entitled to rent her own parcel of kinship lands on Angoche islands, but she first needs to communicate this to other kin. In particular, her maternal uncle has to be consulted and must also witness the transaction, so that in case of her death, the renting person cannot appropriate the land. Of the respondents, 63 per cent maintained that the decision about renting kinship lands rests with the woman herself and 38 per cent claimed that she needs to consult her extended family.

When the land was bought, some Koti claimed that the disposal of this land rests with the one in the name of whom it was bought, female or male. This included the *mahari* (dowry), which was mostly given in cash, but previously could also be conveyed in land and trees, particularly among the Koti. Of the Koti women in Inguri, 24 per cent considered land or trees could be given to a woman as *mahari* and 72 per cent considered that land and trees could not be given as *mahari*. Also, 82 per cent of women in Inguri responded that *mahari* belonged to a woman alone, while 14 per cent said it belonged to the woman's extended kin. Only one woman believed that it belonged to her husband. This situation denotes that although the influence of Islam is significant here, in practice Koti cultural perceptions took precedence. Of Inguri women, 38 per cent owned their own trees, including cashew nut, coconut and fruit trees. To the majority (21 per cent) of married respondents, these trees belonged to the wife alone, while 15 per cent were willing to share them with their husbands. Only 6 per cent considered them to be under their husbands' control. Women alone could decide on the sale of these trees, but 26 per cent of wives would at least show the resulting money to their husbands.

In Anchilo, 37 women respondents had their own inherited lands. Of these, 33 indicated that they could not dispose of these lands freely without consulting with the *mwene* or extended kin. The trees were owned privately and could be freely disposed of individually. However, the majority preferred not to sell trees, but rather to keep them for their children's security. In Anchilo, trees were frequently inherited from other kin, together with land. The value attributed to cashew nut trees by the locals was difficult to overestimate. Twenty-one women had their own trees, of whom only seven considered selling them. On such sales, ten women would opt to consult with extended kin, while ten other women indicated that the trees represented their children's security and could not be sold.

In Anchilo, of the 36 married couples in the sample, eleven (30 per cent) resided uxorilocally, 16 (47 per cent) patrilocally and eight (19 per cent) lived on independent lands. One couple alternated between the wife's and husband's sides. Six respondents (12 per cent) were divorcees and eight (16 per cent) were widows. Among these, one foreign woman was divorced and another foreign woman was a widow. None had access to or control of her own kinship lands in other areas. Thirty-seven women had their own inherited kinship lands. Thirty-three of them responded that they could not dispose freely of their land. Only three felt free to dispose of it as they wished. One woman said she would not consult anybody, three said they would consult their maternal uncle and one her maternal grandfather. Two women indicated they would consult the *regulo* and the rest their extended family.

In Anchilo, as elsewhere, a married couple tended to have access to and benefit from land jointly, irrespective of whether it was from the woman's or the man's side, was rented or self-acquired by one of the spouses. Only nine couples (25 per cent) indicated that household land and farmlands belonged either to the husband or the wife. Of these, in eight households both spouses were local and had inherited their kinship lands. In six of the nine cases, cash crops were grown on both sides, while in two cases cash crops were grown only on the wife's side. One non-local wife claimed that she bought the land locally, while her local husband inherited from his kinship group, and both grew cash crops. However, upon divorce or widowhood, a woman loses the right to use cleared and thus self-acquired land that the couple previously used jointly, and this right passes either to her former husband or to his maternal kin. Among the six divorced women interviewed, none had access to her former husband's land, while among the eight widows, only one still used her husband's land, but only through his previous consent.

Three such cases were raised during focus group discussions with local women.[18] In the first case, a woman, together with her husband, cleared land to grow cashew nuts trees to leave to their children. Unfortunately, the husband died early. His maternal nephew came and occupied the cleared land, barring the widow's access to it. Despite repeated efforts to recover the land through local *mwene* and her own uncle, she did not succeed.

In the second case, a husband took a second wife without the knowledge of his first wife. A conflict between the spouses ensued and the first wife was expelled from the couple's residence. The first wife's brother and the wife herself presented the case to the police and the Community Court, but this led to nothing. The husband barred his former wife from access to the children, residence and land.

In Anchilo, widows frequently marry their deceased husband's brother to stay within his kinship group and safeguard their access to household possessions and land. In the third case, a widow married her deceased husband's brother. The new husband moved into her house. After a full year of cohabitation, during which he did not assist the widow or her offspring in any way, the new husband left for Nampula city. To her dismay, the widow found herself homeless, because the new husband had sold it without her knowledge. At the same time, the maternal kin of the deceased first husband began to occupy the lands he had previously cleared and acquired. This widow presented her case to the police and the *regulo*, but nothing has been done so far. She now lives with her mother.

In Corrane, decision-making about kinship lands rests with male relatives. A woman's opinion is only considered when she is divorced or widowed, and without the means to survive other than through the land in question. All women respondents using kinship lands indicated that they could not freely dispose of them. Cultural perceptions of trees were similar to those in Anchilo. Locals tended to increase the number of trees and took advantage of any opportunities to buy or plant trees. Eighteen women among the respondents had their own trees, of whom 17 owned cashew nut trees and one a coconut tree. Twelve women said that they would decide about the sale of the trees themselves, two would consult their husbands and four would speak with their maternal uncles.

In Corrane, of the sample of 35 married couples, twelve (34 per cent) resided virilocally, 13 (37 per cent) uxorilocally and ten (29 per cent) resided on independent land. These lands could be rented if the couple was not local or if one of the local spouses (usually the wife) was denied access to his or her kinship lands. Because of culturally based patriarchal attitudes towards women, men also opted for residence on independent lands, to safeguard the subsistence of children or of the wife against the extended family in case of their own deaths.

The extended family appeared to be aggressive with respect to divorcees and widows. Usually, if the divorce or death of the husband occurred in the middle of the agricultural year, the husband or extended family would wait until the crop was harvested. The produce is then divided either between the divorcing spouses or between the widow and the husband's kinship group. In practice, this rarely happened. In focus group discussions, both men and women revealed that if a widow insisted on dividing a couple's belongings or produce despite the unwillingness of the deceased's kinship group, then it was concluded that she had killed her husband by witchcraft for the purpose of owning these things.

In Corrane, as noted before, the majority of couples rented or cleared lands jointly. Only two men did this in their own names. Of a total of 35 couples, four had land comprised of two halves, one belonging to the husband and the other to the wife. In three cases, both local spouses inherited land. In one of these cases, both kinship lands were reserved for family subsistence, and land rented jointly was used for cash crops such as cotton and rice. In the second case, cash crops were cultivated on the husband's side and the wife's land was reserved for subsistence. And in the third case, both inherited lands were used for cash crops. In another case, a foreign husband used rented land as well as his local wife's inherited kinship land for rice. Thus the general tendency for spouses to cooperate in consideration of the family's well-being predominated.

This changed upon divorce or widowhood, when the extended kin came into the picture. Of eight divorced women, only one still used her former husband's land. And of seven widows in the sample in Corrane, only one still used the land of her deceased husband.

In one divorce case, the first wife was originally from Lichinga in Nyassa.[19] Her local husband took a second wife and expelled the first wife from the couple's residence. Although the conflict took place in the middle of the agricultural year, the husband refused to wait until the harvest to divide the crops with the first wife. The two wives began battering each other. The intervention of the extended family did not improve the situation. The case is pending with the police, with the husband claiming that the first wife was adulterous and a witch.

Access to and Control Over Benefits from Land

This section focuses on gendered perceptions of control over decision-making and benefits at the household levels, by concentrating on access and control over land and benefits from land. These benefits are crops and cash from the sale of crops. Household benefits result from land benefits and additional work within the household such as the production of traditional beverages, embroidery and weaving for sale. Among the Koti, in contrast to the Makua from other surveyed areas, the influence of Islam in shaping perceptions about benefits is considerable.

In all research sites, in establishing wealth rankings within local communities, women and men maintained that most rich people were men and most poor were women, in particular elderly widows with no local land rights. Wealthy men were those who had access to cash, particularly the owners of bars, clubs, shops and other enterprises. Wealthy men in Corrane also included successful male members of agricultural associations working on cotton production. Overall, women were less wealthy than men.

Control Over Benefits: Household Decision-making

A woman has a certain autonomy over benefits resulting from her own economic activities, while the couple jointly controls benefits resulting from the couple's land. On divorce, when the residence is virilocal, a wife often loses her right to the couple's family belongings (such as the house and domestic utensils) and kinship lands. She can also be deprived of her share of the harvest by her husband on divorce, and by the matrilineal family of the deceased on widowhood.

Control over household food was mostly in the hands of women, because they control lands for household subsistence. In the Muecate pilot research, it was revealed that the wife controlled food in 84 per cent of cases, while 8 per cent responded that husbands controlled it. In Corrane, 100 per cent of women and 97 per cent of men responded that women controlled food in households, while 3 per cent of men considered that both wife and husband controlled it. In Anchilo, 78 per cent of wives and 87.5 per cent of husbands revealed that wives controlled food. None of the respondents thought that husbands controlled food on the household level, while 22 per cent of wives and 3 per cent of husbands considered that they controlled food together. Among the Koti of Inguri, 68 per cent responded that wives, 8 per cent that husbands control it and 6 per cent that the couple jointly controls food.

The Koti of Inguri differed from the rest surveyed, because they were culturally closer to the Swahili than to the Macua in perceptions of family relations between husbands and wives. Among the Koti interviewed, marriage follows Islamic laws of the *shaf'i madhhab* (school of law).[20] This means that it is the husband's obligation to provide for his wife or wives and children, while the wife's or wives' obligation is to be obedient to him. In practice, women continued to be responsible for family food production, while husbands had to earn cash. The Koti man controls benefits from his land and his own economic activities, but the benefits should be spent to fulfil his religious duty to provide for his wives and children. According to members of the Brazanji female *qasida* singing group, it is their husbands' prerogative to decide about the sale of, for example, rice crops, and they also keep the money. However, 46 per cent responded that the wife decides about the sale, 36 per cent that the husband does, 14 per cent that the couple jointly does and 4 per cent that other people do.

A Koti woman controls her own land and economic activities and the resulting cash and purchases. Forty-three per cent felt that benefits from her own land belong to the woman herself, 25 per cent that they belong to her husband, 18 per cent that they belong to the couple jointly and 14 per cent that they belong to other family members.

Control over cash within the family varied according to the respondents' gender. Culturally, cash should be provided and controlled by the husband. It is perceived to be humiliating for a man not to be able to provide cash for his family. While men are welcome to produce cash crops and take waged labour, women are expected to take care of household members and their alimentation. It is not culturally repugnant for a man to embroider and sew even women's clothing. However, it is perceived to be shameful when a man sells produce from lands allocated for family subsistence that are controlled by the wife. Even if there is a surplus from family farming, it is desirable that it is sold by the woman herself or by junior members of the family, such as children and teenagers. Only when the household land's size is significant and its surplus considerable, can a man respectably involve himself in it. As it is generally understood that cash crop production is a male domain and subsistence farming a female domain, there are also some kinds of produce the selling of which is considered to be shameful for men.

These cultural trends are, of course, being eroded with economic transformation, literacy and modernisation. In Inguri, 27 per cent of respondents indicated there were products that should be sold only by women. In Anchilo, 29 per cent of women and 7 per cent of men and, in Corrane, 34 per cent of women and 32 per cent of men considered such sales shameful.

Cash brought by a husband into the family is expected to be mostly controlled by the wife unless there are major purchases to be made, in which case they are decided by the husband or together by the couple. Husbands had higher literacy levels and interactions with development/modernisation and derived products and services from them. Wives were too busy with family caretaking and farming. However, this also varied among the research sites. In Muecate, 40 per cent of wives said they themselves controlled cash and 52 per cent indicated that their husbands did. Only 8 per cent indicated that couples controlled money together. In Corrane, 54 per cent of wives and 57 per cent of husbands indicated that wives controlled cash. Fifteen per cent of wives and 9 per cent of the husbands indicated that they controlled money together. In Anchilo, 72 per cent of wives and 58 per cent of husbands indicated that wives controlled cash, while 14 per cent of wives and 29 per cent of husbands said that husbands controlled it. Fourteen per cent of wives and 13 per cent of husbands considered that they controlled cash together.

Decision-making about spending money within the household or on purchases was culturally perceived to be the domain of the wife, except for important or major expenditures and purchases. In Muecate, in 52 per cent of cases, the husband made such decisions alone; in 40 per cent of cases, the wife did so alone; while in 8 per cent of cases they were made jointly. An actual purchase was performed by the husband alone in 24 per cent of cases, by the wife alone in 40 per cent of cases and jointly in 24 per cent of cases. In Inguri, 60 per cent of couples made decisions jointly, while in 31 per cent of couples, husbands made them alone. In Anchilo, 71 per cent of husbands and 58 per cent of wives indicated that wives made such decisions alone, while 22 per cent of wives and 17 per cent of husbands indicated husbands made such decisions alone. The rest indicated that such decisions were made jointly.

Dispute Settlement

In Mozambique, there are both formal and informal dispute-settlement mechanisms. Formal mechanisms include the Community and Judicial Courts, while informal mechanisms were created by Article 21b of the 1997 Land Law, that requires the participation of 'local communities' in the resolution of conflicts by relying 'upon customary norms and practices'.

As stated before, rural Mozambicans generally operate outside the scope of formal norms and legal institutions. The majority of cases in the research sites were resolved by the efforts of local community leaders and thus went unregistered. The *mwene* is expected to look after land, regulate its use and settle disputes related to land.[21] This is equally true with respect to the *apyamwene*, whose functions are to mediate between human and spiritual life and to oversee the fertility of the land and of its people. The 1997 Land Law acknowledges the role of a 'traditional authority' in solving land disputes.

According to local oral narratives, land was divided between clans and lineages in ancient times. Each *mwene* knows boundaries and limits of the families and clans to whom lands were allocated. Inside families, each member delineates his or her own land and each can use the land as the members agree.

The involvement of the Judicial Courts in resolving land disputes in the research sites was minimal. In each site, judges and other officials of the Judicial Courts were interviewed and court reports were examined. The impact of Community Courts was more significant than that of Judicial Courts. All research sites had a Community Court and a District Judicial Court. The Community Court of Angoche city is comprised of five elected judges, including one woman. They were elected in 1985 by a popular assembly and since then have never been re-elected. Neither did they have an established mandate. They receive about 150 cases annually.

No court existed in the Koti's Angoche islands before 1999, when the Judicial Commission was established. The islanders, according to the City Central Community Court judges, never bring cases to the court. Instead, they resolve problems among themselves. But if cases involve significant amounts of money or serious crimes, they are taken to the Community Court in Aube. Otherwise, the secretary of the Dynamising Groups intervenes. But the *inhapakhos* are still influential in solving disputes.

Before 1994, there were no Community Courts in Corrane.[22] Between 1982 and 1986, the Department of Social Affairs of the Communal Village was responsible for settling disputes. The Department functioned until 1994, when the Community Courts were established. There are currently five Community Courts in Corrane. In the Community Court of the administrative post itself, there are five judges, including one woman. They were elected at a general meeting of local dignitaries and are traditional or government officials.

Anchilo Community Court is comprised of five elected judges, including two women. All male judges were elected in general assembly, while the female judges were elected by the Community Court in Rapale, which is the district's central court. Women are expected to deal with the cases involving women. They have to analyse the injuries on the bodies of female victims and verify women's evidence by visiting their families and homes.

In Muecate district there are eight Community Courts, including one in the administrative post itself.[23] There are up to six judges elected by the local population and usually one young literate man as a scribe in each of the Community Courts. None of the members of the Community Courts receives monetary support or a salary from the state. They are primarily farmers. Revenues from cases are deposited in the bank account of the Public Administration Section.

Fifty-eight per cent of respondents indicated that the administration and government have authority within their communities, while for 37 per cent authority was viewed as resting with the 'traditional authority'. In Inguri, for 3 per cent of respondents, authority was viewed as resting with the shaykhs (Muslim religious leaders). Fifty-six per cent indicated that the government is responsible for land and related disputes, while 37 per cent indicated that the 'traditional authority' is responsible. In Inguri, 4 per cent believed that this responsibility rested with the shaykhs.

Land Disputes

Land is abundant in Nampula, so disputes are rare. Land disputes in the research sites involved conflicts between family and lineage members, between individuals and the local community, and between the local community and private enterprises. No cases involving women were found. Most cases were solved by local communities and were not registered.

The only case at the Corrane Community Court, although unregistered, involved Agosto Vicente and one of the judges of the court. The judge lent a parcel of his family land to Agosto Vicente, who later claimed that the land was his own. The case was taken to District Judicial Court. The Judicial Court presented the case to members of the District Agricultural and Community Development Unit, who consulted with the local community and learned that the judge's claim was correct. After consultation with both parties, the land was divided between them. Agosto Vicente accepted that he was borrowing land for agriculture from the judge, whose family was the true owner.

In Inguri, within urban areas, land disputes emerged between neighbours about the limits of each other's land.[24] But as land was delineated by the state, it was relatively easy to solve the conflict by consulting the appropriate documentation. Land conflicts are also frequent between the Koti and owners of land in the interior.[25] The most cited reason is that local people give the Koti abandoned or virgin land for agriculture. After the Koti clear and cultivate it for up to three years, the owners then rent it to someone else for a higher price. But there were also cases where the Koti had occupied the land of local communities. Between 1997 and 2000, five or six cases of this kind came up.[26]

In the Angoche Community Court, there was only one registered case involving an inhabitant of Inguri land and a local person from Munari zone (Mario Ossufo vs. Augusto João, May/2000). Augusto João occupied land that, according to him, was vacant. Later, Mario Ossufo claimed that the land belonged to his ancestors. After failed attempts by the local community to settle the dispute, the case was transferred to the City Community Court. The *mwene* and elders of the local community were called to give oral evidence following the provisions of Article 12b of the 1997 Land Law. The dispute was settled in favour of Mario Ossufo. However, Augusto João was compensated for his labour in clearing and working the land.

In the Angoche District Judicial Court, there was also only one registered case (Agostinho Assane vs. Momade Assane, 1995). Both parties were inhabitants of Inguri and disputed land in the interior Boila region. In 1991, Agostinho Assane solicited a governor of the province to use land with cashew nut trees on it. This was authorised in 1995. However, there were also coconut trees on the land belonging to a third party, Omar Chale, who sold those trees to Momade Assane. Agostinho Assane attempted buy the coconut trees from Momade Assane, but failed. Although the owner of the land was Agostinho Assane, Momade Assane collected his coconuts from the same land. In Agostinho Assane's understanding, Momade Assane was infringing his property rights. After failed negotiations, Agostinho Assane presented the case to the District Judicial Court. The verdict was that because Agostinho Assane was authorised by the state to occupy the land, Momade Assane should accept payment for his coconut trees from Agostinho Assane and withdraw from the land. In this case, it is evident that the state violated both customary and state law.

Sister Maria do Jesus from the Anchilo Catechetic Centre said that there were several land disputes involving the local population and private enterprises, resulting from the latter's occupation of land abandoned by the owners during the civil war. When the owners returned, the disputes emerged. But all such conflicts were successfully solved due to the intervention of the local traditional authority, the Agriculture Sector and the Diocesan Commission for Land.

Only one case was taken to the police in Anchilo. A person bought cashew nut trees from a local inhabitant. But after buying the trees, this person also started using the land where they were planted. The kinship group with rights to use this land opposed the move. The case was solved by oral evidence given by the local *mwene*, favouring the local kinship group. The person who sold the trees had to pay back the money to the buyer.

According to Pedro Antonio Sacuro, head of agriculture in Anchilo, there are more conflicts involving individuals than individuals and private enterprises. These disputes are related to the boundaries or limits of individual land. In cases where agricultural officials are asked to intervene, they demarcate the boundaries together with the local *mwene*. This kind of dispute is new and rare in rural Nampula because land is plentiful. But the Catholic Diocesan Committee, with its centre in Anchilo, became so involved in the elaboration and promotion of the 1997 Land Law that they were anxious to delineate individual and community lands. This anxiety was due to the perceived threat from large private enterprises, who occupy land by force or illegally. This preoccupation was noticed only in Anchilo. There were some disputes involving individual or collective household lands and private entrepreneurs. One such case between locals and Filipe Muianga was still pending, because of his unwillingness to appear.

Family Disputes: The Accessibility and Importance of Institutions to Women

During focus group discussions with local women in Anchilo and Corrane, the importance of social institutions, such as hospitals and schools, surpassed the importance of formal and informal justice or legal institutions. This, of course, is due to the prevailing poverty and malfunction of social institutions. Also, hospitals and schools are less accessible to women, because most women do not have cash to pay for their services and to buy medicine and school materials. Traditional healers were thus understood to be more accessible and important to women than hospitals.

As mentioned above, land disputes involving women were not apparent in any of the research sites. The relevance of the 'traditional authority' (the local *mwene*) therefore appeared less important for women. Women did not trust the police and the Community Courts, because they were thought to be openly corrupt. The Community Court was considered more corrupt, perhaps understandably as its members do not receive any wages. Local women also preferred going to the police because they had weapons and prisons, and could scare men and their maternal families (sanction measures). In the understanding of local women, the fact that there were women in the Community Courts and the police had no effect on the overall disadvantageous position of women with respect to their rights.

Women also mentioned that religious institutions did not care about women, particularly with respect to settling disputes involving divorcees and widows and their former husbands and/or extended families. In Anchilo, predominantly Catholic women criticised local representatives of the Catholic Church. However, the Catholic community, comprised of ordinary local women, provided networks of solidarity and support for women.

Among the Koti in Inguri, Islamic and Swahili culture determined relations between the private (domestic) domain and the public domain (religious institutions). It is culturally objectionable for a woman to bring private (family) matters into the public domain. Female shaykhs and the *shawriyya* of the Sufi orders were expected to educate younger women and give advice to elder ones, but they were reluctant to talk about family matters with married women. Coastal women introduced the notion of *sidiq* (*chittik* in southern Mozambique), where women collectively contribute cash that each woman can use in rotation. This was a common practice among Muslim Inguri women.

In all the research sites, conflicts related to family matters, such as polygamous marriages, contested divorces, access to family belongings and land upon divorce and widowhood, were often not taken to official justice institutions. They were instead arbitrated by the family or clan *mwenes* and, in acute cases, taken to the police. In Anchilo and Corrane, women insisting on their rights within families were frequently accused of adultery and witchcraft and suffered from social stigmatisation. Widows contending for their rights were often accused of murdering their husbands for the purpose of obtaining the family belongings.[27]

Women's organisations, such as the Association of Rural Women (AMR) and OMM, and the *apyamwene*, were considered by local women to be powerless to resolve conflicts involving women within families. Corrane women asked how women could ameliorate their situation if even men of the traditional and government institutions could not do so.

Conclusion

This research attempted to explore women's situation with respect to land in Mozambique. The fieldwork was conducted in Nampula province in the diverse but relatively homogeneous, religious rural communities of Inguri in Angoche city, of Macua in Corrane and Anchilo and of Macua in Muecate, where the pilot research was conducted. Women's situation was examined through the prism of local cultural and religious perceptions, because the impact of the state and of state laws is minimal. The research focused on the socio-cultural and legal contexts in which women establish and maintain their access to, usage, management and disposal of land, and how they control its resources and access and use its benefits. It also focused on women's participation in household decision-making.

According to local cultural perceptions, *n'loko* and *nihimo* lands are owned collectively by members of kinship groups and cannot be alienated. Thus an individual may only hold land on the basis of usufruct. He or she cannot truly own it. In all the research sites, these perceptions were still strong. Besides kinship lands, there are virgin lands that can be acquired by individual effort through clearance and cultivation. Trees are owned individually, independent of the land on which they are planted.

Although all the populations of the research sites are matrilineal, women's situation with respect to access to land varied from household to household and from place to place. The impact of Christianity and Islam on land practices is not discernible. Because of the prevalence of a customary/traditional system of land allocation that does not discriminate according to gender, women have equal access to land. Only in Corrane are discriminatory attitudes towards women manifested.

Inheritance of kinship lands is matrilineal. But people do not literally inherit land, because it cannot be turned into a bequest or privatised. Family members are merely given a share of land on which to exercise usufruct rights by the main heir, who controls the family's use of the land. The majority of those interviewed received their land from the maternal side of the family. This allows women to maintain a certain degree of independence from their husbands. In Nampula, both women and men also have the possibility to rent land or to sharecrop with the owner. Women have limited means to self-acquire lands through clearing or renting in Anchilo, Corrane and Muecate, but were actively involved in such processes in Inguri. Newcomers are forbidden to plant trees, particularly cashew nut, coconut and fruit trees. However, in practice, buying or planting trees was a vehicle for the appropriation of land by both women and men.

Generally, the kinship land, where a couple resides or farms for household subsistence, whether from the wife's or husband's side, is the domain of the wife. A married woman's right to use this land is therefore safeguarded. However, when she becomes divorced or widowed, her former husband or his extended kin usually denies her access to those lands. This is particularly problematic if a woman is not native to the community.

With respect to self-acquired land, often a married woman uses this land jointly with her husband. But upon divorce, the husband frequently continues using this land while the wife loses access. Upon widowhood, the woman often loses this right in favour of the deceased husband's matrilineal family.

Women are autonomous in the management and use of their own lands and trees, but often opted to consult with their extended family. Decision-making within the household reflected cooperation between the spouses rather than gendered conflict. Only in Corrane is more power attributed to males. But in practice, a woman has autonomy over the benefits resulting from her own economic activities, while the couple jointly controls benefits resulting from the couple's land. Upon divorce, when the residence is virilocal, the wife often loses her right to the couple's family belongings (the house and domestic utensils) and kinship land. She can also be deprived of her share of the harvest by her husband if divorced, or by the matrilineal family of her husband if widowed.

Control over household food is in the hands of women, because they also control land used for household subsistence. Control over household cash varied according to the respondents' gender. Culturally, cash should be provided and controlled by the husband. It is perceived as humiliating for a man not to be able to provide cash for his family. Decision-making about purchases and spending money within the household is perceived to be the domain of the wife, except for major purchases and expenditures. The wife controls cash brought into the family by a husband, unless there are major purchases to be made, which are decided on by the husband or by the couple.

While men are welcome to produce cash crops and take waged labour, women are expected to take care of household members and their health. It is not humiliating for a man to embroider and sew, or even to make women's clothing. However, it is shameful for a man to sell produce from land allocated for family subsistence, which is controlled by the wife. As cash crop production is male and subsistence farming is female, the selling of some kinds of produce is also shameful for men.

Land is abundant in Nampula so disputes are rare. Land disputes in the research sites involve conflicts between family and lineage members, between individuals and the local community and between the local community and private enterprises. No case was found involving women. Most cases are solved by the local community and are not registered. Most grievances of local women are related to conflicts between divorced or widowed women and former husbands and their extended families. However, it is objectionable for a woman to bring family matters into the public domain. In all the research sites, conflicts related to family matters, such as polygamous marriages, contested divorces and access to family belongings and land upon divorce and widowhood, are often not taken to official justice or legal institutions. They are arbitrated by the family or clan *mwenes* and, in acute cases, are taken to the police.

Women's organisations such as AMR and OMM and the institution of *apyam-wene* were considered by local women to be powerless to resolve conflicts involving family matters. Corrane women wondered how women could ameliorate their situation if even men of traditional and government institutions could not do so.

Interviews

Inguri, Angoche

Estevão Amisse, Director, Autarchic administrative unit, Mossurir, Aiyyuba Demeia, *regulo* Mutulema, Namukulio zone of Namaponda Velha

Amina Hasan, member, Conselho Islâmico

Adamji Karhila, shaykh and member, Conselho Islâmico

Bramgi Mamade, shawriyya Shadhuliyya Yashrutiyya

Amarale Muhilole, *regulo* Mipaco, Namaponda Sede

Chamsi Ossufo, shawriyya, Brazanji group and khalifa Shadhuliyya Madaniyya

Chale Quesso, khalifa Qadiriyya, Namaponda Sede

Echtar Shurtiyya, khalifa Shadhuliyya Yashrutiyya

Ali Ussene, shaykh and District Delegate, Congresso Islâmico

Mamade Abdallah, shaykh and member, Conselho Islâmico

Hasan Bashir, ruling *inhapakho*

Hasan Ali 'Côncaco', shaykh and member, Conselho Islâmico

Jamaldin Elembwe, shaykh and member, Ahl al-Sunna (Andar al-Sunna)

Mohammad Hamid, responsible for Unit Two, Inguri zone, Angoche city

Sayyid Hasan, khalifa Rufa'iyya, Qatamoyo island

João John, District Delegate of the Instituto Par Assistencia Juridica

Zainab Swalehe 'Macandinha', khalifa Shadhuliyya Yashrutiyya

Julio Abakar Muhamade, Secretary, Autarchic administrative unit, Inguri

Sayyid Khaled 'Nakapa', healer

Haji Fatima Namuali, khalifa, Sufi order and teacher at the madrassa

Relogio Nikaka, judge, Community Court, Namaponda Sede

Mussa Ibrahimo Siraj, shaykh and member, Ahl al-Sunna (Ansar al-Sunna)

Shale Abdallah Yussufo, *regulo* Licuaro, Inguri

Anchilo

Manuel Amos, head, Land Cadastre, Direção Provincial de Agricultura, Nampula

Francisco Buana, head, administrative post

Pedro José Calisto, scribe, Judicial Court, Meconta

Maria Joana Cardoso, president, Fiscal Council, Rural Women's Association

Maria Fernando, member, Rural Women's Association

Sister Maria de Jesus, Cathechetic Centre

Maria da Luz, member, Rural Women's Association

Alfredo Capetine Machaieie, District Director, Agriculture and Rural Development, Nampula

Sabina Nhamanha, member, Rural Women's Association

Antonio Riare, resident

Pedro Antonio Sacuro, head, Agriculture

Lius Ernesto Umbuechiua, *regulo* Unbechiua

Corrane

Fernando Abel, *regulo* Mucapera
Laurinda Artur, 18, Armando Miguel's new wife
Artur Baltazar, supervisor, CLUSAC
Arnaldo Manuel Jamal, Ministry of Agriculture
Fatima José, 48, wife of Armando Miguel
Adolfo Madruga, judge and president, Meconta Sede Community Court
Father Fernão Magalães, Mission Nossa Senhora da Conceição
Momade Manuel, head secretary
Julio Arão Maquina, agricultural extension worker
Armando Miguel, 48, husband of Fatima José
Adolfo Jose Murihiwa, judge and president, Meconta Sede Community Court
Paulo Nantombe, technical assistant, SODAN
José Parrinha, associate representative, Sattar-Agrico
Arlindo Suanheia, technical assistant, Associação Yussuf Nurmamade
Andrè Trato, *regulo* Napita
Jacinta Unromora, Mucapera *apyamwene*

Muecate

Afonso Chicoche, *regulo* Rainha
Manuel Nauacha Palhota, District Director, Agriculture and Rural Development,
    Meconta
First Secretary, FRELIMO Party
Shaykh, local mosque
Focus group discussions

Inguri, Angoche

Female members of Brazanji *qasida* singing group, Association 'Nur Islamo'
Female members of the Ahl al-Sunna (Ansar al-Sunna):
Muizala Ma'aruf
Maimuna Mussa Piloto
Amina Mussa Ussene
Female shaykhas of the turuq (Sufi Orders):
Fatima Abdallah, *naquibo* Shadhuliyya Yashrutiyya
Muantimo Chamo, shawriyya Shadhuliyya Yashrutiuua
Faida Husein, khalifa Shadhuliyya Madaniyya
Mwaneima Mandiha, khalifa Shadhuliyya Bagdade
Muaisha Yussufo, shawriyya Shadhuliyya Madaniyya
Male khalifas of the turuq (Sufi Orders):
Sayyid Hasan Abakar, Shadhuliyya Madaniyya
Mussa Piloto, Shadhuliyya Madaniyya
Ussene Suleiman, Shadhuliyya Yashrutiyya
Amade Swaleh, Shadhuliyya Yashrutiyya

Sharifo Terno, Shadhuliyya Yashrutiyya

Community Court of Angoche city
Fatima Amusse, elected judge
Raúl Cardoso, elected judge
Jamal Chale, elected judge
Florêncio Manuel, elected judge and president
Alberto Uhanhoboa, scribe

Anchilo

Women, regulado de *Umbuechiua:*
Flora Almeide, 29, divorced
Halda Amisse, married (second wife in a polygamous marriage)
Fatima Calavete, 23, married
Maria de Luis, 53, widow
Gracinda Martins, 29, divorced
Maria Muamigo, 45, married
Clara Pires, 34, divorced
Eminda Sabado, 55, married
Joana Satavi, 34, divorced

Women and men
Twelve people (names not registered), consisting of seven women and five men

Community Court
Mali Amade, judge
Constantino Artur Amisse, scribe
Ismela Hassane, judge
Armando João, judge
Cecilia Augusto José, judge
Cecilia Lopes, judge
José Macurere, scribe
Fernando Notas, judge and president

Corrane

Women, regulado *Mucapera*
Florinda Alberta, 30, married
Rita Fernando Chave, 25, married
Marta Jorge Dieja, 30, married
Lucia Fernando, 25, married
Angelina Francisco, 23, married (second wife in a polygamous marriage)
Madalena Malissa, 40, married
Quiteria Miranda, 22, married (second wife in a polygamous second marriage),
  one child

Luciana Muacigarro, 60, married
Inacia Pacota, 35, married
Josefa Samuli, 45, married
Petira Teteha, 70, married
Joaquina Vitorina, 21, married (second wife in a polygamous marriage)

Women and men (married)
Ana Agostinho, 27
Cecilia Armando, 32
Silvestre Capuquia, 45
Rosa Charahane, 33
Ernesto João, 40
Jose Mucussete, 32
Ernesto Namurque, 60
Cesar Prame, 45
Elsira Sabonete, 45

Shaykhs
Jamal Assane, Qadiriyya Sa'adat, imam, local mosque and member, Congresso Islâmico
Salimo Colete, owner, mosque and member, Conselho Islâmico
Justino Dale, muride Qadiriyya and member, Congresso Islâmico
Habimo Ismail, member, Conselho Islâmico
Salimo Mussa, owner, mosque and member, Conselho Islâmico
Paulo Venhane, khalifa Qadiriyya Saadat and member, Congresso Islâmico

Community Court
Anabela Assane, judge
Fernando Chapule, scribe
Arlindo Andrade Daudo, judge and president, Jabire Jojo
Arlindo Lola, judge
Zito Luciano Martinho, judge
José Sabonete, judge and president
Afonço Sale, judge
Ricardo Francisco Wate, assistant

Muecate
Women (names were not registered)
1. Age 22, divorced, Catholic
2. Age 20, married, Catholic
3. Age 27, divorced, Catholic
4. Age 18, married, Muslim
5. Age 25, married, Catholic
6. Age 25, married (first of three wives in a polygamous marriage), Catholic

7. Age 20, divorced, Catholic
8. Age 42, widowed, Muslim
9. Age 37, divorced, Catholic
10. Age 26, married (second wife in a polygamous marriage), Catholic
11. Age 60, married (first wife in a polygamous marriage), Muslim
12. Age 48, divorced, no religion
13. Age 25, married (second wife in a polygamous marriage), Muslim

Notes

1. Interview with Mohammad Hamid, responsible for Unit Two, Inguri.

2. Interviews with Fernando Abel, *regulo* (permanent chief) Mucapera, Corrane; Afonço Chichoche, *regulo* Rainha, Muecate; André Trato, *regulo* Napita; and Luis Ernesto Umbechuia, *regulo* Umbechuia, Anchilo.

3. Interview with *regulo* Mucapera.

4. Interview with Hasan Bashir, ruling *inhapakho*.

5. Interview with Afonco Chicoche, *regulo*, Muecate administrative post.

6. *Estatuto dos Indigenas* (indigenous status) was approved by Decreto Lei No. 39: 666 in 1954, but revoked by Decreto-Lei No. 43: 893–7 in 1961, which recognised legal pluralism with respect to the indigenous populations of the colonies.

7. Interviews with Manuel Amos, head, Provincial Land Cadastre, and Sister Maria de Jesus.

8. Interview with Afonco Chicoche, *regulo* Rainha and focus group discussions.

9. Interview with *regulo* Umbuechiua.

10. Interview with *regulo* Umbuechiua.

11. Interview with Hasan Bashir, current *inhapakho*, Angoche islands.

12. Interview with Sayyid Khaled Nacapa, healer.

13. Interview with Chamsi Ossufo, influential Sufi woman.

14. Interviews with Fernando Abel, *regulo* Mukapera and Andre Trato, *regulo* Napita.

15. Interview with shaykh Mamade Abdallah, Inguri.

16. Interviews with Aiyuba Demeia, *regulo* Mutulema, Namaponda Sede and Amarale Muhilole, *regulo* Mipaco.

17. Interviews with Artur Baltazar, supervisor, Clusa Association, Paulo Nantombe, technical assistant, SODAN; José Parrinha, Association Sattar-Agrico; and Arlindo Suanheia, technical assistant, Yussuf Nurmamade Association.

18. Interviews with Flora Amede, Clara Pires Beja and Filomena Joao Vieira and focus group discussions with local women.

19. Interviews with all involved in the conflict: Laurinda Artur, second wife; Fatima Jose, first wife; and Armando Miguel, husband.

20. Interviews with female and male religious dignitaries, and focus group discussions with members of the Brazanji female *qasida* singing group.

21. All interviewed *regulos* were unanimous in this respect.

22. Interview with Jose Sabonete, judge and president of the Community Court.

23. Interview with Alde Abudo Pasarera, judge, District Judicial Court, Muecate.

24. Interviews with shaykh Mamade Abdallah and Sayyid Khaled Nakapa.

25. Interviews with Relogio Nikaka, judge, Community Court; Namaponda Sede and Shale Abdallah Yussufo; and *regulo* Licuaro, Inguri.

26. Interview with Joao John, local delegate, IPAJ.

27. Focus group discussions.

References

Amorim, Pedro Massano de (1911) *Relatório sobre a occupaçao de Angoche*, Laurenço Marques: Imprensa Nacional.

Armstrong, A. (ed.) (1987) *Women and Law in Southern Africa*, Harare: Zimbabwe Publishing House.

Benda-Beckman, K. et al. (eds) (1997) *Rights of Women to the Natural Resources: Land and Water*, The Hague: NEDA.

Botelho, J. J. T. (1936) *História militar e política dos Portugueses em Moçambique, de 1833 aos nossos dias*, Lisbon: Centro Tip Colonial.

Branquinho, J. A. G. M. (1969) *Prospecçaõ das forças tradicionais: distrito de Moçambique*, Relatorio: Portugal, Provincia de Moçambique, SCCI.

Carrilho, J. (1990) *Accesso e uso da terra para agricultura (2nd edn): 20 seminario sobre o estudo do sector agrario*, Maputo: CDA.

Casas, M. I. et al. (eds) (1997) *Circulos de trabalho e discussão: relatorio de debates acerca de autoridade tradicional*, Maputo: African-American Institute.

— (1998) *Gender Profile of Nampula Province: Final Report*, Maputo-Nampula: Embassy of the Kingdom of the Netherlands.

Casimiro, I. et al. (1992) 'Maintenance Rights and Women in Mozambique: Case Studies in the Southern Region', in *Women and Law in Southern Africa Project*, Maputo: Department of Women and Gender Studies, Centre for African Studies, Eduardo Mondlane University.

— (1996) 'Rights to Succession and Inheritance', in *Women and Law in Southern Africa Research Project*, Maputo: Department of Women and Gender Studies, Centre for African Studies, Eduardo Mondlane University.

Coutinho, Joao de Azevedo (1941) *Memórias de um velho marinheiro e soldado de Africa*, Lisbon: Livraria Bertrand.

Da Silva Cunha, J. M. (1953) *O sistema Portugues da política inígena: subsidio para o seu estudo*, Coimbra: Editora Lda.

— (1990) 'FAO and Women in Agricultural Development: paper prepared for the second joint donor WID meeting', Maputo: UNDP.

Decreto-Lei No. 23: 229 Ministério das Colónias da República Portuguesa aprova a Reforma Administrativa Ultramarina, in *Boletim Oficial da Colónia de Moçambique*, I Serie-No. 51, Lourenço Marques, 28 December 1933.

Decreto-Lei No. 43: 896, Ministério do Ultramar, República Portuguesa, in *Boletim Oficial de Moçambique*, I Serie, No. 36. Lourenço Marques, 14 September 1961.

District Development Profiles (1997), UNHCR/UNDP.

General Census (1997), Government of Mozambique.

Glassman, J. (1995) *Feasts and Riot: Revelry, Rebellion and Popular Consciousness on the Swahili Coast, 1856–1888*, Portsmouth: Heinemann; London: James Currey; Nairobi: EAEP; Dar es Salaam: Mkuki na Nyota.

Green, R. H. (1992) 'Women's Land Use Rights in SSA: Modernisation as Marginalisation, What is to be Done?' Ontario: 12th symposium on law and development, University of Windsor.

Hobsbawm, E. and Ranger, T. (eds) (1983) *The Invention of Tradition*, Cambridge: Cambridge University Press.

Kloeck-Jenson, S. (1997) 'Analysis of the Parliamentary Debate and New National Land Law in Mozambique', Maputo: Land Tenure Centre Project, Eduardo Mondlane University.

Kopytoff, I. (ed) (1987) *The African Frontier: The Reproduction of Traditional African Societies*, Bloomington and Indianapolis: Indiana University Press.

Lingen, A. et al. (1997) *Gender Assessment Studies: A Manual for Gender Consultants*, The Hague: NEDA.

Lundin, I. B. and Machava, F. J. (eds) (1995) *Autoridade e poder tradicional, Vol. I*, Maputo: Ministério da Administração Estatal. Núcleo de Desenvolvimento Administrativo.

Lupi, E. C. (1907) *Angoche: breve memoria sobre uma das capitanias-móres*, Lisbon: Ministério dos Negocios da Marinha e Ultramar.

Machado, A. J. M. (1970) *Entre os macuas de Angoche: historiando Moçambique*. Lisbon: Prelo Editora.

Martin, D. M. and Hashi F. O. (1992a) *Law as an Institutional Barrier to the Economic Empowerment of Women: Working Paper Number 2*, Washington, DC: Poverty and Social Policy Unit, Technical Department, Africa Region, World Bank.

— (1992b) *Gender, the Evolution of Legal Institutions and Economic Development in Sub-Saharan Africa: Working Paper Number 3*, Washington, DC: Poverty and Social Policy Unit, Technical Department, Africa Region, World Bank.

— (1992c) *Women in Development: The Legal Issues in Sub-Saharan Africa Today, Working Paper Number 4*, Washington, DC: Poverty and Social Policy Unit, Technical Department, Africa Region, World Bank.

Martins, O. (1992) 'Direito consuetudinario: a propriedade e a sucessão entre os Macuas, 1890–1930', unpublished paper, Eduardo Mondlane University.

Negrão, J. et al. (1999) *Advisory Project of Nampula's Strategic Programme: Year One Report*, Maputo-Nampula: Cruzeio do Sul Trust Fund.

Palmer, I. (1985) *The Impact of Agrarian Reform on Women: Women's Role and Gender Differences in Development*, West Hartford: Kumaria Press.

Pitcher, A. (1996) 'Conflict and Cooperation: Gendered Roles and Responsibilities within Cotton Households in Northern Mozambique', *African Studies Review*, No. 39, November.

Quadros, M. C. et al. (1999) *Relatorio de avalião do projecto: ORAM Nampula*, Nampula: ORAM.

Ranger, T. O. and Kimambo, I. N. (eds) (1972) *The Historical Study of African Religions*, London: Heinemann.

Revista Jurídica Dezembro (1997), Vol. 3, Maputo: Faculdade de Direito, Universidade Eduardo Mondlane.

Schadeberg, T. C. and Mucanheia, F. U. (2000) *Ekoti: The Maka or Swahili of Angoche*, Koln: Rodiger Koppe Verlag.

Schoenbrun, D. L. (1998) *A Green Place, A Good Place: Agrarian Change, Gender, and Social Identity in the Great Lakes Region to the 15th Century*, Portsmouth: Heinemann; Kampala: Fountain; Nairobi: EAEP; Oxford: James Currey.

Tique, C. (1997) 'Peasant Perceptions of Land Degradation and Conservation in Mozambique: The Case of Namialo, Nampula Province', unpublished PhD thesis, University of Illinois.

Tique, C. et al. (1998) *Relatorio do seminario sobre genero e desenvolvimento*, Maputo: ORAM.

Vansina, J. (1990) *Paths in the Rainforests: Towards a History of Political Tradition in Equatorial Africa*, Madison: University of Wisconsin Press.

Welch, G. H. et al. (1988) *Women and Law in Zimbabwe, Mozambique and Tanzania: Working Papers on Women and Law, Number 20*, Oslo: Institute of Women's Law, Department of Public Law, University of Oslo.

Women and Law in Southern Africa Project (1992), Maputo: Department of Women and Gender Studies, Centre for African Studies, Eduardo Mondlane University.

Women and Law in Southern Africa Research Project (1996), Maputo: Department of Women and Gender Studies, Centre for African Studies, Eduardo Mondlane University.

FOUR

Women and Land in Northern Nigeria: The Need for Independent Ownership Rights

Hussaina J. Abdullah and Ibrahim Hamza[1]

By independent rights ... I mean rights independent of male ownership or control (that is, excluding joint titles with men). Independent rights would be preferable to joint titles with husbands for several reasons: one, with joint titles it could prove difficult for women to gain control over their share in case of marital break-up. Two, women would also be less in a position to escape from a situation of marital conflict or violence ... Three, wives may have different land-use priorities from husbands which they would be in a better position to act upon with independent land rights. Four, women with independent rights would be better able to control the produce. Five, with joint titles the question of how the land would subsequently be inherited could prove a contentious one. This is not to deny that having joint titles with husbands would be better for women than having no land rights at all; but many of the advantages of having land would not accrue to women by joint titles alone. (Agarwal 1994: 20)

§ USING this as our point of departure, we argue that ownership without independent rights is, in the final analysis, no ownership at all, and we therefore make the case for independent land rights for women. We argue that independent land rights are necessary for Maguzawa and Muslim women who already enjoy (nominal) rights to own land, to enable them to make decisions on the acquisition, use and disposal of this resource. For non-Muslims without ownership rights, we argue that demands for ownership have to go hand in hand with independent rights on matters of usage and disposal (that is, control).

Land is one of the most important resources in Africa. It is one of the resources most contested on the continent, pitting individuals and groups against one another and against the state. Wrapped up in the land question are not just economic concerns, but also cultural, historical, political and social (class and non-class) claims. Not surprisingly, disputes over land are among the most bitter forms of conflict in Africa. Although various aspects of the land question in Africa have been studied, only recently has there emerged increasing activist and intellectual concern with the gender dimensions of land, with particular reference to women's right to independent access to, and control over, this critical resource (Davison 1988; SAFERE 1995; Meer 1997). This concern has gathered steam against the background that although in most parts of Africa women are active farmers, their right to ownership and control of land is circumscribed by custom, religion, law or a combination of all three. How this plays out differs from one part of the continent to the other. Even within the same country, there are different practices in existence.

This study is therefore intended to contribute to an understanding of land as it relates to women and as viewed from the human rights paradigm. The main objective is to undertake a critical, empirical study of women's land rights in northern Nigeria, and the manner in which these rights are shaped by religion, tradition and law. The purpose is not only to examine women's rights of access to, ownership of and control over land, including women's inheritance rights, but also to study how religion (canonical and Sharia), tradition and law (customary and non-customary) act and interact to condition the definition and practice of women's land rights. The primary focus is a review of historical practice and an analysis of empirical data on three categories of women (married, divorced and widowed). Marriage is used as a determining variable in women's land rights because it is the major means by which women and men access land in Africa. However, whereas women's land rights are dependent on their relations with men, men's land rights are not dependent on their relations with women. Moreover, women are threatened with dispossession if divorced or widowed (Small 1997: 46).

In northern Nigeria, where marriage is fluid (especially among the Hausa and the Maguzawa), the strategies that women have employed to secure their land rights will be discussed. For it must not be assumed that, in the face of religion, tradition and the law, women are simply the passive victims of discriminatory practices. The study has therefore also been interested in capturing and under-standing the ways in which women use tradition, religion and natural justice to assert and/or defend their land rights. Furthermore, since there is contestation over what constitutes custom/tradition, as well as differences over doctrinal in-terpretation among different Christian and Muslim groups, the study examines the extent to which this plays out in favour of or against women's land rights. The study assumes that religion and tradition are not static and that the extent to which their practice works against women is empirical and cannot be answered or settled *ab initio* on the basis of prevailing pathologies. The study thus tries to capture actual practice on the ground with regard to women's land rights.

Origin and History of Northern Nigeria

The geographical area known as northern Nigeria comprises the federal capital territory of Abuja and 19 of the 36 states of Nigeria's federation. It is 720 miles wide, 410 miles long and about 300,000 square miles in size. It is bordered by Benin, Cameroon and Niger. Based on the provisional figures of the 1991 census, it contains about 55 per cent of Nigeria's population. Of this number, slightly over half are women. Most of the area is Hausa land, made up of several Hausa-speaking emirates and states. Although much of the area was incorporated into the Sokoto Caliphate after Uthman Dan Fodio's 1804 jihad, not all its inhabitants are Muslim. There are also Christians and adherents of indigenous religions. Despite being predominantly Muslim, northern Nigeria is a multi-religious area.

The formal incorporation of the area into the international capitalist system began on 1 January 1900, after three years of negotiation and struggle between the British government, the Royal Niger Company (RNC) and local rulers. The RNC was keen to protect its economic and political interests in the area, having established a commercial presence before the formal onset of direct colonial rule. The RNC, successor to the National African Company (NAC), had through the manoeuvrings of its owner, Sir George Goldie, won a royal charter in 1886 to advance British commercial and other interests in the area. This charter gave the RNC absolute power in the area, including the 'power to administer, make treaties, levy customs and trade in all territories in the basin of the Niger and its effluents' (Elias 1971: 3).

There was already some contact between agents of the British government and representatives of the Caliphate before the onset of direct colonial rule in the area. Aside from various expeditions undertaken by British explorers, the British government and the Caliphate had their first contact in 1885, one year before the royal charter was granted to the RNC. This was followed with a second contact in 1893. The first led to the signing of a treaty that conferred some recognition on the RNC (then NAC). This treaty gave the RNC trading rights on the rivers Benue and Niger. As a result of the second contact, the RNC was given jurisdiction over foreigners in the area.

However, the RNC's power over the area was short-lived, as it was unable to contain local resistance to its trade monopoly, ward off competition from French capital and suppress the internal traffic in slaves in the north. The British government, not wanting to loose its grip on the area, delegated Sir Frederick Lugard, its Commissioner in the area, to take over the administrative functions of the RNC. The RNC's royal charter was revoked and the protectorate of northern Nigeria was declared (Elias 1971: 3). The subjugation of northern Nigeria, which started in 1900, was completed in 1903 with the defeat of the Caliphate's army by the British army and the imposition of British colonial rule over the area.

As part of the negotiated agreement between the RNC and the British colonial government, the RNC agreed to retain its

> commercial rights and privileges, surrendered its other rights and interests, including all the land hitherto acquired by means of various agreements with local chiefs and princes, to the Crown for the lump sum of 865,000 pounds, subject, however, to the payment to the Company of 50 per cent of mining royalties for a period of ninety-nine years. (Elias 1971: 4)

To mark the end of the Caliphate's rule and the beginning of British colonial rule in northern Nigeria, Lugard noted triumphantly that

> the Fulani in old times under Dan Fodio conquered this country. They took the right to rule over it, to levy taxes, to depose kings and to create kings. They in turn have by defeat lost their rule, which has come into the hands of the British. All these things which I have said the Fulani by conquest took the right to do, now pass on to the British. (Appendix iii, Northern Nigeria Annual Report 1902: 164)

Despite this proclamation, the British colonial government did not abrogate the laws of the Caliphate. Rather, through a policy of indirect rule, it super-imposed its own laws upon existing ones. For Islam and Islamic law were already rooted in the political structures of the area. For example, by the time the area was subjugated, nearly every emirate had a judicial court presided over by an *alkali* (judge). But despite the dominance of Islam, non-Islamic courts existed side by side with Muslim ones. These courts served non-Muslims who had agreed to co-exist with Muslims. They were thus accorded *dhimmi* (tributary) status within the Muslim domain.

Traditional African Religion in Northern Nigeria: The Case of the Maguzawa

Since the practice of traditional African religion is based on the distinctive cultural and social characteristics of a given ethnic group, it is not possible to present a uniform overview of the traditional African religions of northern Nigeria. The area has more than a hundred ethnic groups. But despite differing practices, adherents of traditional African religions have four fundamental beliefs. These are the belief in the Supreme Being (God), belief in the deities or lesser gods, belief in spirits (including ancestral spirits and others) and belief in the power of magic and medicine (Kayode and Adelowo 1985: 235). These can be illustrated further with the example of the Maguzawa, one of the ethnic groups in this study.

The term Maguzawa is said to have originated from the Arabic word *majus*, used to describe non-Muslims living peacefully under the protection of a Muslim state. The Maguzawa are therefore the non-Muslim Hausa. They are found in several *unguwoyi* (small rural communities) around the Muslim Hausa states and the emirates of Bauchi, Daura, Jigawa, Kano, Katsina, Sokoto and Zaria. They are predominantly agriculturists (Naniya 1990).

In Kano state, the Maguzawa are located mainly in the Gaya Rogo, Tudun Wada and Wudil local governments. They are the largest non-Muslim group in Kano state. According to Meek, they are descendants of the original inhabitants of Kano, dating to before the *Habe* (Hausa) invasions of the eleventh century (Kan/Prof His/5/1936). A Bamaguje is only recognised as such provided he [sic] follows the traditional religion of his people. 'To be a Bamaguje is to fit a distinct non-Muslim stereotype that distinguishes you from both a Muslim and a mere "pagan"' (Last 1993: 269). The Maguzawa are the only Hausa sub-group that is identified by its religion. On conversion to Islam, a Bamaguje becomes a Ba-Kano (Kan/Prof/His/5/1936).

The Maguzawa were deemed good citizens because they paid protection tax to the state and fought alongside their Muslim protectors (Last 1979). The Maguzawa 'have survived because they have maintained a posture of defencelessness and have always migrated to the geographical fringes of Hausa land' (Ibrahim 1997: 31).

According to their religion, the world is divided into two parts – inhabited and uninhabited. In addition, there is the ancestors' spiritual world and the world of *Iska* (demons and spirits) (Krusuis 1915: 6). The latter is made up of two spirits, the white and the black, which are friendly and unkind respectively. The leader of the white spirits is *Kure* (male hyena) and is recognised as the patron of the Maguzawa spirits. *Kure* is sacred to all Maguzawa. It may not be killed and its meat may not be eaten. It is believed that *Kure* protects its adherents and supplies them with all their needs (Krusuis 1915: 10). The Maguzawa communicate with the spiritual world through the *Yan Bori* (the Bori people), male and female, who act as mediums between them and the spiritual realm (Krusuis 1915: 18).

Islam in Northern Nigeria

Islam spread into northern Nigeria from the Kanem Borno empire, one of the first areas in West Africa to come in contact with the new religion. Although Islam was introduced into northern Nigeria in the twelfth century, its impact was felt only in the fourteenth century through the proselytising efforts of the Wanwagara merchants. The process of Islamisation was taken a step further by al-Maghili, an Islamic scholar who wrote a treatise on Islamic governance for Muhammadu Rumfa, the first Muslim King of Kano, in the second half of the fourteenth century. Despite the acceptance of the treatise in Kano and other parts of Hausa land, Islam did not root itself into society because the Hausa rulers, whose duty it was to propagate the religion's practice, were lax in their attitudes towards Islam. Most rulers combined Islamic rituals with non-Islamic practices and did not insist on the conversion of their subjects. 'Pre-Jihad northern Nigeria was irreligious ... the so-called religious leaders were either pagans or syncretists who took what they wanted from Islam and combined it with local religions and culture' (Kukah and Falola 1996: 30).

The ambiguous attitude of the rulers towards Islam, coupled with corruption, economic decline, excessive taxation and the political marginalisation of the poor, antagonised the Fulani Muslim settlers in Hausa land. For them, being Muslim meant strict adherence to the religion. They were uncomfortable with the Hausa way of practising Islam and sought to purify the religion through 'a return to the pure and primitive [sic] faith of Islam purged of heresies and accretions' (Trimingham 1968: 199–200).

In 1804, Shehu Uthman Dan Fodio, a Fulani scholar, began the task of purifying Islam. By 1812, the Sokoto Caliphate, a new political dispensation based on the Sharia (Islamic law), had been established to replace the non-Islamic rule of the Hausa Kings. This conquest led to the imposition of Sharia on the existing legal system and the adoption of Islam by the general populace. In establishing an Islamic state, Dan Fodio adopted the Maliki doctrine, as opposed to the other three doctrines – Hanafi, Hanbali and Shafi'i. This was because the Maliki doctrine was already in existence in the area and in West Africa in general.

> The Sharia ... became the most common and official legal system. Every Emir must establish and administer the Sharia. Each town had its judge, and every emirate its Court of Appeal. To the Jihadists, the only legitimate code of law must derive from the Sharia. It was through the implementation of the Sharia that the reforms of the Jihad were to be carried out, as they affected the poor, property and commercial interactions. Thus, law was to be the supreme instrument of change. (Kukah and Falola 1996: 38)

Governance in the Caliphate was based on the obedience of the emirs (the heads of the emirates) to the Sultan (the head of the Caliphate). Each emirate was to be governed according to 'Islamic laws, repair mosques, convert pagans and promote Islamic education' (Kukah and Falola 1996: 36).

Although the Sharia is the principal legal statute in northern Nigeria, especially in civil matters (marriage and inheritance), it has not completely replaced customary laws. Despite the influence of Christianity and Islam, the customary laws of various ethnic groups in northern Nigeria, particularly with respect to civil matters, have for most part remained unchanged.

Christianity in Northern Nigeria

Christianity has a more recent history than Islam in Nigeria. It was introduced only in the second half of the nineteenth century and gained a foothold in southern Nigeria, but its spread in northern Nigeria was slow. Christian penetration of northern Nigeria began in 1857 with the opening of the Niger mission by Samuel Ajayi Crowther. The aim of the mission was to serve 'all the peoples of the Niger River from its delta northwards up to and including all the northern states of present day Nigeria' (Clarke 1986: 65). As part of his efforts to evangelise in northern Nigeria, Crowther got the emirs of Bida, Gwandu and Ilorin and the Sultan of Sokoto to receive Arabic versions of the Bible from the Church Missionary Society (Ayandele 1966: 118).

The conversion of northern Nigerian Muslims was the primary objective of Crowther and his successors, because to them 'no one became a Muslim for sound intellectual and religious reasons' (Clarke 1986: 108). Further, the idealised picture painted by various European explorers, especially Barth, of the area and its peoples as civilised, industrious, prosperous and eager for European manufactured goods made it enticing to the missionaries (Ayandele 1966).

But despite their conviction and efforts, the missionaries were unable to make inroads into the Muslim areas of northern Nigeria because of the entrenchment of Islam, the clash between Islam and Christianity and the unwillingness of the British colonial government to allow them to evangelise in the Muslim areas. This does not mean that the British colonial government was anti-missionary. Rather, it wanted to maintain the relationship it had developed with the Caliphate and it was not going to allow the missionaries to jeopardise this. For example, objecting to the missionaries' desire to evangelise in the area, H. H. Middleton, the District Officer in Hadejia emirate in Kano province, stated:

> It has been considered inadvisable and inexpedient in the past to permit missionary activity amongst Moslem states during normal times, [and] to do so now would, in my opinion, constitute an act of treachery and ingratitude unworthy of our best traditions. I make no apology for the use of somewhat strong terms as I think that the occasion demands the fullest expression of our views in a matter where our honour is at stake. For the last three years the Moslem chiefs of the Northern Provinces have stood by us with a loyalty, fidelity, and devotion that will not lightly be forgotten by those who have worked with them during this period ... missionary activity would be construed by the natives to be an unwarrantable interference with their religion and a breach of faith that they could neither forget or forgive. (AHK/15246)

Although the Christian missionaries failed in their attempt to convert northern Nigerian Muslims, they had some successes among the non-Muslims of the area. The process of converting the non-Muslims of northern Nigeria can be divided into two phases – pre- and post-1945.

Pre-1945, the conversion rate among non-Muslims was similar to that among Muslims. For example, in the Birom village of Forum in the present Plateau state, there were only three converts in an eleven-year period (1910 to 1921). This was attributed to the missionaries' policy of excluding polygamous men and beer drinkers from worship, as well as lack of indigenous leadership in the churches and the reluctance of the local population to accept Christianity. To become a Christian meant losing economic, political and social status as well as social networks (Clarke 1986).

Post-1945, there was an increase in the number of converts and a proliferation of churches in the area. This was due to a number of factors, including changes in the strategies of the missionaries (the training of local evangelists and pastors), the introduction of education and health care in their pastoral work and the undermining of local institutions by the British colonial government. However, despite these changes, the number of Christian converts was still negligible in proportion to the population of northern Nigeria (Clarke 1986: 113).

Research Sites

The research for this study was carried out in three different sites in northern Nigeria, to reflect the diverse cultural, religious and social characteristics of the area.

Muslim areas of Kano and Sokoto states The first research site was the predominantly Muslim areas of Kano and Sokoto. Both are among the biggest population centres in Nigeria. They are also among the oldest centres of Islam in West Africa. But Kano, the foremost commercial centre in northern Nigeria, is the seat of the populist-radical Tijaniyya brotherhood, while Sokoto, the seat of the old Caliphate and the home of the Sultan, is dominated by the more conservative Quadriyya brotherhood. Studying the experiences of Muslim Hausa women in the two centres afforded the opportunity to observe the differential effects (if any) that the radical and conservative variants of Islam, as practised in Kano and Sokoto respectively, have on women's land rights.

What is presently known as Kano state came into being in May 1967 with the creation of twelve states from the three regions (east, north and west) that made up the Nigerian federation at independence in 1960. Kano is the second most industrialised and populous state in Nigeria's present 36-state federation. Kano occupies an important place in Nigeria in general, and in northern Nigeria in particular. In addition to being one of the earliest sites of Islam in northern Nigeria, Kano is the economic capital of the area and the home of populist and radical politics (Olukoshi 1985: 53).

The city of Kano was founded in the seventh century. Wangawara traders from Mali introduced Islam to the city in the second half of the fourteenth century (Kano Chronicle). Islam in present-day Kano includes various sects – the Shiites, the brotherhoods or the Sufis, the Sunnis and the Yan Tatsine (Zakaria 1997: 29). The most prominent of these sects is the Sufis, made up of the Tijaniyya and the Quadriyya brotherhoods. Migrant Senegalese traders introduced the Tijaniyya brotherhood in Kano, while the Quadriyya brotherhood, with its origins in Iraq, might have been introduced by Fezan Arabs from Morocco (Zakaria 1997: 29). The Quadriyya brotherhood's early status in Kano and northern Nigeria as a whole was enhanced because the leaders of the Jihad belonged to this brotherhood (Callaway 1987: 96). It dominated Kano's religious landscape from the fifteenth century up to World War I, when Sarki (emir) Abbas, the then Sarki of Kano (1903–19) converted to the Tijaniyya brotherhood. However, it was during the reign of Sarki Muhammadu Sanusi (1953–63) that the Tijaniyya brotherhood gained wide prominence in Kano. Sarki Sanusi used his position to increase the authority and status of the Tijaniyya brotherhood until it became the dominant sect in the area (Callaway 1987: 96).

Kano took its place as a bastion of populist and radical politics in the early 1950s. Under the aegis of his political party, the Northern Elements Progressive Union (NEPU), Mallam Aminu Kano, a young schoolteacher learned in Islamic law, launched an attack on the Northern People's Congress (NPC), the dominant party in the area, and its allies in the emirate's political structure. He accused the NPC of betraying the ideals of Islamic governance (equity and justice) outlined by the jihadists. His party's declared objective was the institution of a democratic system based on Islamic governance ideals in which the interests of the *talakawa* (oppressed) would be represented. Hence, accountability and social justice became the themes of his party (the People's Redemption Party, PRP) through his political career. 'NEPU/PRP rhetoric was phrased in terms of Islamic reform. Campaign themes centred around notions of equality, knowledge, literacy, political reform and modernisation. Equality was extended to include women, but only in so far as Qur'anic interpretations allowed. NEPU's advocacy of education and political emancipation for women did not imply support for Western feminist concepts' (Callaway 1987: 98). Although Mallam and his colleagues did not advocate fundamental restructuring of gender relations, by raising issues that affect Muslim women's status (the right to education and to participate in public life, child marriage and polygamy), they expanded political debate in the area. Although limited, these demands were radical in Muslim northern Nigeria, where women do not enjoy most of the rights stipulated in the Qur'an.

The study on women's land rights in Kano was conducted in Dawakin Tofa local government area, located within the Kano closed-settled zone, 20 kilometres west of Kano city. The area was chosen for its close proximity to Kano city and because of the rural nature of its economy. Although located close to the state capital, it is not affected by the rapid urbanisation taking place in the state. Dawakin Tofa town and district have the largest number of villages in Kano emirate, 98 in all.

Migrants from Mali established the town in the sixteenth century. It is known for its pottery, mostly produced by women. The principal occupation in Dawakin Tofa is farming, characterised by peasant landholdings, and crafts, notably pot-making.

Sokoto state, the religious capital of northern Nigerian Muslims, was one of the seven states created in 1976 to establish the then 19-state federation. It was a war camp during the jihad. After the jihad, it became the headquarters of the Caliphate (1809–1903). It was the capital of Sokoto province under the British colonial government.

While Kano and his associates championed the rights of women and criticised their exclusion from public life, the NPC under the leadership of Sir Ahmadu Bello, a Sokoto prince and the premier of the then northern region, opposed these principles. Waziri Ibrahim, a minister in the NPC government, defended his party's position and criticised the regional governments in the east and west of the country for granting suffrage to women. According to Ibrahim, 'we in the north are perfectly happy. Our women are happy about their condition and I appeal to other members of the Republic to please leave us in peace. There is not a single northern woman who has told anybody that she is unhappy. We know what is right for women and our men know what is right for themselves' (Callaway 1987: 99). In the same vein, Bello noted that 'female suffrage is inimical to the customs and feelings of the great part of the men of this region' (Callaway 1987: 99).

Even though the NPC and its successor, the National Party of Nigeria (NPN), were against granting women a proactive role, they did not ignore them in their quest for political dominance. Women were seen and used as objects of political entertainment – chanting, singing and dancing at rallies. The women who performed these functions were mostly *karuwai* (prostitutes).

Yabo, the local government area studied in Sokoto state, was part of the pre-jihad Hausa city state of Kebbi. The town, 48 kilometres from Sokoto town, was established by a group of migrant Fulani from Daura. Present-day Yabo is made up of 14 villages. The town has a close relationship with the Sultanate, as it was one of the earliest towns to support the jihad. Yabo is well integrated into Sokoto's rural economy, with farming being the principal occupation of its inhabitants.

The Tijaniyya's emphasis on social justice and the promotion of women's rights has not translated into fundamental differences in the status of women in Dawakin Tofa. In many respects, the social status of Kanawa women is no different from that of women in Sokoto, a centre of Quadriyya Islam. This is due, in part, to the fact that the NEPU/PRP political machine that dominated politics in Kano saw the declaration of support for the promotion of women's rights as electorally beneficial. But this political rhetoric of NEPU/PRP activists did not transcend religious teachings on the place of women. The Tijaniyya and Quadriyya brotherhoods do not have separate laws or interpretations over issues such as inheritance. Both use the Qu'ran, Hadith (sayings of the Prophet) and Ijma (consensus opinion of the Ulama) as the basis of political and religious discourse.

Maguzawa areas of Kano state The second research site was in the part of

Kano state inhabited by the Maguzawa. The research was undertaken in Tudun Wada local government area, in the villages of Barangwaje, Jarkaya, Karefa, Tanigel and Tuku. As noted earlier, the Maguzawa of Kano are a Hausa-speaking ethnic group listed among the earliest settlers in the area, who are followers of indigenous religion. For almost two centuries, they have resisted efforts aimed first at Islamising and then Christianising them. As a consequence, they have been marginalised from the economic and political mainstream of contemporary Nigeria. The Maguzawa have no independent political authority, because of their subservience to Muslim Hausa authority. The role of the *sarkin arna* (pagan king) or *mai unguwa* (hamlet or ward head) was tax collection and general mediation (in community conflicts and in marriages). 'The Maguzawa always tried to limit their contact with Muslim officialdom, hence the strategy of retreat and attempts to settle their problems internally' (Ibrahim 1997: 32).

The traditional life of the Maguzawa differs from that of Muslim Hausa. It centred on beer drinking, 'the major traditional form of recreation and the symbol of conviviality, generosity and humanity' (Ibrahim 1997: 32). This has changed because of inroads made by both Islam and Christianity. Muslim converts have had to restructure their lives and Christian converts have also made changes. The Evangelical Churches of West Africa (ECWA), the major Christian denomination in the area, forbids the consumption of alcoholic beverages and smoking and encourages monogamy and Christian marriages.

Recent statistical evidence suggests that in the context of the economic crisis afflicting the country, which has ravaged the livelihoods of the Maguzawa, this tribal group has succumbed to pressure exerted by missionaries for their conversion. Out of about 76,381 Maguzawa living in Kano state, 33,843 have converted to Christianity and 16,533 to Islam, while the remaining 26,005 have tried to stay true to indigenous religion (Ibrahim 1997: 25). Although the Maguzawa are close to the Muslim Hausa, they have not converted en masse to Islam as predicted by Greenberg (1946) or Barkow (1970). In fact, they seem, by and large, to have maintained their resistance to Islam. Thus the Maguzawa provide the opportunity to grasp the ways in which women's land rights are handled, in a setting where indigenous religion is practised.

Unlike their Muslim counterparts, Maguzawa women are not secluded. Nor are they treated as legal and social minors.

> Maguzawa women are both more free and more encumbered than their Muslim village sisters. They are not in seclusion and may frequent the village market. They are not expected to veil themselves or comport themselves with exceptional modesty ... But Maguzawa women work hard and instead of devoting themselves to their crafts must devote themselves to raising food for their families. (Barkow 1970: 94)

Last observed that Maguzawa women participate fully in economic and social life. They are autonomous and control their sexuality. One indication of their autonomy is that they alone have the right to decide whether they are too sick to do the work expected of them. Maguzawa women do a lot of agricultural production and farming. They are responsible for feeding their families most of the year (November to June), while their men feed their families during the raining season and generate money for tax, clothing and farming implements (Last, quoted in Ibrahim 1997: 32). Money from farming belongs to them and they have the right to dispose of it as they deem fit. As a result of their economic independence, they are relatively more prosperous than Muslim Hausa women. However, despite their relative autonomy, Maguzawa women remain one of the most oppressed groups of women in Nigeria because they are almost wholly responsible for social provisioning in the household. 'Apart from the responsibility of women in feeding the family, they are also expected to provide basic necessities such as medicine, soap, pomade and clothing for themselves and their children' (Ibrahim 1997: 33).

Christian areas of southern Zaria emirate   The last research site, southern Kaduna, lies between Hausa land, the Benue-Niger valley and the northeastern part of the Jos Plateau. Southern Kaduna is the geographical area south of Zaria emirate in the former Zaria province. In the pre-colonial period, some parts of this area were under the Caliphate. But during the colonial period, the whole area was subordinated to Hausa-Fulani rule in Zaria and Jema'a (Turaki 1982: 12).

Southern Kaduna is a belt of northern Nigeria where Christianity serves as a common thread binding together various minority ethnic groups. The peoples of southern Kaduna were among the first to convert to Christianity in northern Nigeria, following the onset of colonial rule. Today, the area is dotted with many churches from different Christian denominations. The churches are not merely institutions that minister to religious needs. They are also, to an extent, the focal point around which social life is organised. Studying southern Kaduna afforded the opportunity to see how Christianity has affected women's land rights in an area where women play prominent roles in farming activities and where customary inheritance practices do not allow women to inherit land.

The field survey in southern Kaduna was carried out in Kamurun Ikulu village in Zango Kataf local government area. The Ikulus are found mainly in Anchuna, Kamurun Ikulu and Padan Ikulu villages. Before the Ikulus were transferred to Zango Kataf in 1925, the three villages were distinct entities with recognised traditional rulers (Meek 1931: 85).

Land Administration and Tenure

Land administration and tenure were established in the Sokoto Caliphate long before the imposition of British colonial rule.

The Caliphate developed a theory of land tenure intended to establish Sokoto's primacy over the emirates and to maintain the political and social cohesion of the Caliphate as a whole (Jumare 1994: 64). The Caliphate also focused its attention on land tenure and administration to prevent the emerging aristocracy in the area from appropriating land needed to resettle people displaced during the jihad (Jumare 1994: 67). The Caliphate's land tenure policy was based on the Qur'an, Hadith and Ijma, and vested control of all mineral lands in the state. Inheritance and selling of land were forbidden. However, usufructory rights were granted to worthy individuals to exploit land. The objectives of the Caliphate's land policy were population settlement, generating revenue for the state (through the taxation of non-Muslim lands and royalties from mining), exempting *waqf* (conquered land) from taxation, increasing land under cultivation, developing agricultural production and increasing the fertility and productivity of the soil (Last 1977: 77).

The Caliphate's land policy governed both Muslims and non-Muslims within its jurisdiction. In the Muslim areas, lands were declared *waqf* and thus exempted from financial and labour exploitation but the payment of *zakkat* (one-tenth of produce after harvest) was made compulsory. The emirates paid annual land tax or tributes to the Caliphate. In addition to being administered through customary laws, non-Muslims also paid land tax for protection. This granted them both proprietary and usufructory rights (Jumare 1994: 111).

Land in the Caliphate was administered on the basis on which it was acquired. Thus, land was classified into four categories. The first is *waqf*, land captured after a jihad. Such land can neither be sold nor given out as a gift. It is held in trust for all Muslims. The second category is *suhr* (non-Muslim land) that is based on the recognition by non-Muslims of the suzerainty of Muslims. Non-Muslims residing on this land are protected but in return they pay stipulated amounts for the protection received. They are allowed to observe their customs and religion and they have the right to bequeath, lease out or sell their land. The third category of land is that which belongs to non-Muslims who converted voluntarily to Islam. Occupants of such lands can only be dispossessed of land if they revert back to indigenous religions. The fourth category is *ushr*, abandoned land acquired by Muslims from non-Muslims. It is state land that can be disposed of by the leader of the Muslim community (NAK/KanoProf5/1/10591; Jumare 1994: 74).

All different categories of land had clearly specified conditions of tenure. *Zakkat* was to be paid for all categories of land. Land tax was not required for cultivating *waqf* land and usufructory rights could be claimed by reviving it through building or cultivation. Proprietary rights in the other three categories could be obtained through the same procedures (Jumare 1994: 74).

The Caliphate's discourse on land centred on the categorisation of tenure practices into three – *al-hima* (protected lands), *iqta* (virgin lands) and *mawat* (dead lands). Protected lands were reserved under certain conditions by the imam (religious leader of the community) for the purposes of grazing animals used for the jihad or belonging to the poor and for charity (Jumare 1994: 80). Jurisdiction over lands was vested in the imam, who granted ownership to individuals. However, the imam's authority was not absolute. He was not allowed to grant permanent ownership on land acquired by compulsion or treaty because possession renders it *waqf* (Dan-Fodio quoted in Jumare 1994: 72). To forestall confusion over which land the imam had the right to dispose of, the Shehu divided the lands in the Caliphate into five categories:

> Land acquired by compulsion (*anwantan*) which cannot be sold or given away but is to be retained for the benefit of the Muslims; land taken by peace treaty which is kept by its owners who can do what they like with it; land whose people embraced Islam while it was in their possession and which belongs entirely to those people; land whose people (owners) fled abandoning it and this belongs to the Imam who can deal with [it] according to his discretion; land whose owners have not accepted Islam and have not made peace either and this the Imam can grant to whoever he wishes. (Dan Fodio, quoted in Jumare 1994: 82)

Virgin or unoccupied lands were those appropriated from non-Muslims to which they have no inheritance rights. Non-Muslims could only possess proprietary rights over virgin lands if they were located in a distant area. In addition, such lands should not contain the immovable property of non-Muslims. Ownership of virgin lands can be acquired:

> By the act of cultivating it, or by virtue of it being adjacent to a virgin land which has been thus cultivated, or by the Imam giving it to someone as a grant or by making it a hima [protected] ... to cultivate virgin land is subject to the Imam's consent, but a dhimmi [non-Muslim] cannot cultivate such land at all. On the other hand, a virgin land far from inhabited areas can be cultivated even by a dhimmi without seeking the Imam's consent ... whoever cultivates a virgin land has the rights of ownership over it, together with *harim* [reserve]. (Shehu Dan Fodio, Kitab al-Fark quoted in Jumare 1994: 84)

Land designated as dead is that which has not been cultivated or reclaimed. It can be fallow, pasture or vacant land. In principle, tenure over dead land can be established through cultivation of the land and its reserved spaces, by grants from the ruler and by official reservation.

Land administration and tenure in contemporary Nigeria is based on three sources of law – native law and custom, statutory law and received English law (Yakubu 1985: 6). Native law and custom embodies both customary and Islamic laws.

Customary law Under customary law, land is seen as inalienable property belonging to the whole community. It is seen as a gift from God, to be enjoyed and used by all those entitled to it. Ownership is through a grant from the head of the family or community. Alienation of land to non-members of the community is restricted and can only be effected with permission from the head of the family, the community and committee of elders. The principles of land ownership are built on the assumption

> that the entire family has proprietary rights in the land ... the individual grantee is held to possess usufructuary rights over land granted him [sic]. It should however be added that individuals may acquire absolute rights in land through gifts among living persons (*inter vivos*), pioneer clearing of virgin forests or through partition of family landed property. Rights acquired in any of these ways become proprietary rights, the owner being free to dispose of such rights without consultations with anyone else. (Famoriyo 1987: 103)

Islamic law Land tenure and land law in northern Nigeria was based on three factors: Sharia, local custom and politics and the discretionary power of the ruler (Meek 1957: 163). In Sharia, land is considered as 'indispensable to individual and social life just like water, air, light and fire and no person will have an exclusive power of control over it except for the part he [sic] uses' (Yakubu 1985: 8). Land is a gift from Allah (God) and everybody has usufructory rights to it (Yakubu 1988: 8). Furthermore, land ownership is not limited by time.

Land in Sharia is administered legally under three categories. The first, occupied land, refers to land that is under use. Acquisition of land in this group can be through a grant from the emir, inheritance, clearing, cultivation and fencing. Once occupancy is established, the occupier assumes complete ownership as he or she can bequeath, pledge, loan, rent or sell the land.

The second category, unoccupied land, is divided into two – town land and land outside town. The former refers to all vacant land in and around the town. Authority of occupation is vested in the emir. Once the land is allocated, the allottee gains complete ownership. This type of land cannot be alienated to strangers without the approval of the emir. On the other hand, lands far away from the town, or bush land, do not need the permission of the emir for occupation. They can be occupied through clearing, cultivation or fencing.

The third and final category is what is referred to as *waqf* (common land). Historically, this included land acquired through warfare or treaty. Nowadays, land can only be declared as *waqf* by the emir after due consultations with elders. Land in this category is used for praying grounds, markets or grazing.

Statutory law Statutory land law in northern Nigeria came into being with the defeat of the Caliphate by the British colonial government. Lugard, then British

High Commissioner in the area, stated that 'the Government will, in future, hold the rights in land which the Fulani took by conquest from the people and if Government requires land, it will take it for any purpose' (Shaw 1905: 451).

To back up these words, the British colonial government sought to establish its right to control the land of northern Nigeria with the Land Proclamation Act of 1902. Under this Act, all land in northern Nigeria was classified into two categories, Crown and Public land (Yakubu 1985: 16). Crown land referred to all land purchased by the British colonial government from the RNC. The British colonial government had the power to dispose (lease, rent or sell) this land without recourse to anyone. In addition, trespass was forbidden. Public land was that acquired from the Caliphate and non-Muslims who were not conquered by jihadists. This land was left to local people to enjoy and use according to native custom and law. However, local people were not allowed to alienate the land to non-indigenous people without the consent of the British High Commissioner (Yakubu 1985: 17).

The Land Proclamation Act was later amended by Lugard's successor, Sir Percy Girouard. The amended law, the Land and Native Rights Proclamation of 1910, was in use until 1962, two years after Nigeria's independence, when the Land Tenure Law was adopted. The 1910 law reduced the rights enjoyed by both chiefs and their subjects under native custom and law:

> All native lands and all rights over the same are hereby declared to be under the control and subject to the disposition of the government and shall be held and administered for the use and common benefit of the natives and no title to the occupation and use of such lands shall be valid without the consent of the Governor. (quoted in Yakubu 1985: 19)

Although the Land Tenure Law of 1962 (which later became the Land Use Act of 1978, adopted for use in all of Nigeria) replicated the principles of the 1910 law, it distinguished between two rights of occupancy – customary and statutory.

Customary rights covered all tenure systems administered by communities or their leaders since pre-colonial times, under which the majority of holdings were held under rights of inheritance derived from community membership. Such rights are defensible in local Sharia courts. However, there is no documentary record of them, except for the Native Authority Revenue Survey of the home districts of Kano emirate, discontinued in 1957. Otherwise, claims to customary rights are incapable of legal defence above the level of local Sharia courts and cannot be used as security for loans.

Statutory rights are registered in the Lands Division of the state administration. Their acquisition follows a costly and lengthy process of application and approval. They are restricted to urban and government land. The statutory Certificate of Occupancy confers leasehold rights for periods of up to 99 years, is renewable and is acceptable by banks for purposes of loans and mortgages. The administration of lands by the State Ministries of Lands and Survey is restricted to lands held under statutory occupancy and is subject to a series of rules and amplifications laid down in the 1960s by the Northern Region Ministry of Land and Survey (Mortimore 1987: 16–17).

On 29 March 1978, the federal military government of General Olusegun Obasanjo promulgated the Land Use Act. This Act, the land law presently governing the whole of Nigeria, was enacted because of an increase in population, industrialisation and urbanisation, but, most importantly, to ease the problems encountered by the federal government in acquiring land for public purposes. In the context of northern Nigeria, land scarcity became evident as result of five factors:

1. Rapid urbanisation fuelled by the petrodollars from the oil boom.
2. Demand for land by the federal government for large-scale irrigation schemes.
3. The extension of World Bank-funded integrated rural development schemes.
4. The disappearance of grazing lands.
5. Growing ecological menaces such as soil erosion, drought, desertification and woodland degradation which combined to increase the pressure for land. (Mortimore 1987: 15–16)

Land Use Act of 1978 The Land Use Act of 1978 'redefined the rights and obligations of the government and those of the cultivators and others with interests in land' (Ega 1987: 41). The Act vested all titles to land in each state government. As such, no right of occupancy and use of land is valid without the consent of the governor (Yakubu 1985: 200). It further divided the lands into two categories – urban and other land. The former is under the jurisdiction and management of the governor, while the latter is managed by the local government authority in which it is located. The Act, however, did not define urban and other land. That task was assigned to the governor. In addition, as noted earlier, the Act recognises two rights of occupancy: customary, bestowed by the local government and statutory, granted by the governor. The right of occupancy, which is backed by a certificate, is dependent on the payment of rents that are part of the agreement but not inconsistent with the Act. Existing title-holders apply for a certificate as proof of occupancy. However, if the land is undeveloped, the holder can retain only one plot of up to half a hectare. Any excess goes back to the state and will be administered in accordance with the Act.

The broad objectives of this Act are to:

• Permit all Nigerians to enjoy and use land and the natural fruits thereof in sufficient quantity for the sustenance of themselves and their families.
• Permit the federal, state and local governments to acquire land cheaply and easily for public purposes.
• Prohibit land speculation and escalation of land prices. (Yakubu 1985: 209)

The Act has been subjected to critical analysis by land tenure scholars (Famoriyo 1987; Yakubu 1985; Ega 1987). But its disadvantages from women's point of view have not been discussed. Yet it is clear that the Act was formulated on the false premise of gender equality, as it granted every Nigerian equal access to land. First, in granting equal access in a situation of gender inequality, the Act reinforces existing stereotypes of men as breadwinners and women as dependants. Second, the Act does not recognise *de facto* land ownership, the situation in which most women find themselves. Third, the registration of customary rights of occupancy threatens the rights of women who have mainly secondary rights, especially as these cannot be converted to ownership rights.

Received English law Received English law (the body of general laws applied in Nigeria) is based on English common law, the doctrines of equity and the statutes of general application in force in England on 1 January 1900. Although developed primarily for the purpose of legal action affecting foreigners and indigenous litigants under the British colonial government, it has become the main legal instrument in the country. It is different from both customary and Islamic laws in that it is administered principally in higher courts.

The adoption of received English laws in Nigeria has led, in certain cases, to the direct application of English land law in the country. For example, courts in Nigeria hold that a person can lose his or her rights under the rule of prescription (long ownership). In addition, the following English statutes are applicable in Nigeria: the Fraudulent Conveyancing Act 1571; the Statute of Distribution 1670; the Real Property Limitation Act 1833; the Wills Act 1837; the Conveyancing Act 1833; and the Land Transfer Act 1897 (Yakubu 1985: 22).

Inheritance and Women's Land Rights

With the exception of Hamza (1994) and Jumare (1994), most recent studies on land tenure in northern Nigeria have ignored the issues of gender relations and women. The exclusion of women has been attributed to the widely held view that women do not own or have access to or control over land (as in the non-Muslim areas), and to the practice of *kulle* (female seclusion) which restricts women's use and management of land (Jumare 1994: 262). These have led to women's rights being subsumed under those of men.

As part of the process of developing a land policy in northern Nigeria, the British colonial government instituted a judicial enquiry, the Northern Nigeria Lands Committee, to investigate tenurial practices existing at that time. One of the issues investigated was the disparity in land ownership between women and men. The committee found that in Muslim areas, judicial corruption influenced both women's and men's land rights, while in non-Muslim areas, gender inequality in inheritance was responsible for the disparity in land ownership between the sexes.

This attempt was followed by the work of British colonial ethnographers and sociologists like Meek and Nadel. Meek observed in his study of land tenure practices in northern Nigeria that women did not exercise land rights, took no part in primary agricultural production in some communities, assumed minor roles in others and were responsible for major farming activities in some others (Jumare 1994). According to Nadel, land tenure among the Nupe was dominated by men, reflecting the culture and tradition of that community, even though the emirate was part of the Caliphate.

Although women's right to inherit land was established in Muslim northern Nigeria by the jihadists, it was not applied uniformly in the area. Women's inheritance rights in relation to land were recognised in Sokoto province, but the practice in Kano, Niger, Yola and Zaria provinces deviated from the Maliki code. For example, C. W. Cole, a senior district officer in Zaria emirate, reported that rights to economic trees replaced women's rights to land: 'Maliki law would not prevent the deceased's daughters entering into possession but in practice the custom prevails. The female heirs however have in local custom and in law an absolute right to the fruits of the economic trees' (quoted in Jumare 1994: 8).

In addition to recognising women's inheritance rights, the practice in pre-colonial and colonial Sokoto was that land belonging to under-age children and women was not to be sold, because it undermined the security of family land. However, women (especially the elderly) were granted access to their land if they so desired. But as the British colonial economy developed and land became expensive, women's inheritance rights were threatened. Some judges refused to recognise women's inheritance rights, while others ruled that women (excluding the wives of the deceased) could inherit farmlands (Jumare 1994:·7). This practice continued until the British colonial government, in consultation with jurists, directed all judges to recognise women's inheritance rights because both Islamic and English laws acknowledge such rights.

The Rowlings land report on Kano outlined eight means by which land is acquired or transferred. These are: allocation of uncleared bush or an abandoned farm by the village head; purchase (*saye*); gift by an existing holder (*kyauta*); inheritance (*gado*); acceptance of a pledge (*jingina*); loan (*aro*), lease (*aro*); and sharecropping (*kashi* or *nomamuraba*) (NAK/KanoProf/6508/52: 18).

On inheritance in Kano, the Rowlings report also noted the following:

> Inheritance is straightforward in the case of resident male heirs: they arrange among themselves. Females are not accorded any right of succession to either farmland or houses, the reason being that they go, or should go, to live with their male relatives or, in due course, with a second husband and would, therefore, tend merely to take over rights in order to sell them. The Emir may instruct that a woman who has no other support be left in occupation of a farm or house but this is an act ex-gratia, not of right. Property of a man who

dies without heirs escheats to the treasury. A farm will be left with the village head for realloting [sic]: a house given to someone else or, in the city, retained by the Emir as a 'gidan sarauta' (house of the aristocracy) to be used as he sees fit. (NAK/KanoProf/6508/52: 26)

This practice, observed in the 1940s, is a Hausa custom legitimised by the ruling of Sarki Usman bin Abdullahi bin Dabo in 1923 when he decreed that:

> Whoever come across this Declaration (*al Barawah*) that the Emir of Kano Usman bin Abdullahi, the son of Sultan Kano Dabo, has made an absolute rule that women should not be entitled to the inheritance of farmland (*al-Bustam*) from this date Saturday 1st Zul Qaidah 1314 A H equivalent to 14th June 1923 C E, the same rule applies to housing ... this was done after investigating the problem in the margin of sharha Aqrab Masqlikh and after consultation with the ulama. (Hamza 1994: Appendix 1c, 146).

On 7 March 1924 (Friday 1 Sha'aban 1324 A H), a new declaration stating conditions on which women's rights to inherit houses were to be recognised was made:

> I would like to inform you from this day henceforth whoever dies and left his inheritance and his house and he has no heirs but women and the house belonged to him and is not part of the land of the emirate, that house should be lumped together with the rest of his property and be divided among them (women heirs). And each of them would take her share and whatever remains from that should be deposited with Bait el-Mal. This is what we intend to do God, the Almighty willing in order to ward off unnecessary litigation and vengeance. (Hamza 1994: Appendix 2c, 149)

Women's non-inheritance of farmlands was reinforced in the same declaration, and their rights to inherit houses where there are male heirs were not recognised:

> Then if the deceased left a house belonging to him and left property and he has both male and female heirs, then the property should be divided among them all, and then the house should be left to the male heirs alone, in the same manner with the farmland, for females have no right to that. Likewise whoever acquire from the Emir a desolate land or undeveloped land as a gift then he developed it with his own money and he then died, and did not leave behind a male relation, then that house should be sold and the money divided among the heirs and the remaining would be deposited with Bait el-Mal. (Hamza 1994: 149)

Some scholars (Tahir, quoted in Hamza 1994) have attempted to explain the state's action with a view to showing that it was not anti-women. According to Tahir, the state had to disinherit women in order to stem the increase in social vices such as prostitution, which, according to him, was becoming rampant in the society. 'The immediate cause was provided by a woman of Unguwan Makama

... Though pre-menopausal, she had refused to marry and had converted the house she inherited into an assignation for unfaithful married women, young girls and vagrant wives' (Tahir, quoted in Hamza 1994: 149).

Hamza, on the other hand, argued that to understand the state's action, the history of Kano before the 1920s should be studied. He noted that the declaration prohibiting women from inheriting land was based on the application of the concept of conquered land and *urf* (custom). In Islamic jurisprudence, conquered land is land acquired through a jihad. All pre-existing laws found among the conquered peoples should continue to operate, provided they do not contradict the Sharia. In Maliki law, conquered land should not be purchased, sold, hired or given out as a free gift without a *fatwa* (religious sanction). Conquered land is designated state property and placed under the custodian of the emir, or any head of the Muslim community. When the jihadists conquered Kano in 1804, all its laws and customs that contravened the Sharia were not only abolished, but Kano was also declared an Islamic state. Thus all land in Kano was treated as conquered and became part of the Sokoto Caliphate.

The declaration of all land in Kano as conquered was in line with existing practice between Muslim conquerors and a non-Muslim community and vice versa. In the case of the former, the conquered community must operate in accordance with Islamic laws and values, or accept the condition of *amanah* (trusteeship) and pay the *jizya* tax. The reverse operates in the defeat of a Muslim community by non-Muslims. Any law promulgated by the conqueror that affects the social lives of Muslims must be adhered to until Muslims are able to liberate themselves. Based on the above, it was easy for the British colonial government to take over and treat all land in Kano as conquered.

Like the concept of conquered land, all customary practices in existence in a conquered society that are not contradictory to the Sharia are accepted as part of Islamic law. When the jihadists conquered Kano, they established an Islamic state and abolished all non-Islamic practices. With an Islamic state in place, women's rights to inherit land and landed property were established and recognised. However, this was not the case in practice, as the concept of *ahafu dharayn* (choosing a lesser evil) was applied to these rights. This concept is applied when a Muslim community is confronted with a thorny issue. The lesser evil is chosen in order to preserve societal equilibrium. *Ahafu dharayn* was applied to women's rights to inherit land and landed property because it was believed that the application of the Islamic injunction on women's inheritance rights would lead to economic disintegration (having too many heirs and heiresses to share the property) and social disintegration (quarrels between brothers and sisters). Women, who were not allowed to inherit land under Hausa customs and traditions, would under Islam claim those rights and assert their independence *vis-à-vis* their male kin. In other words, the establishment of women's rights to own property would reduce male authority, power and wealth and thus diminish patriarchy.

Rather than critique the state for its anti-women stance, Tahir and Hamza unwittingly justified the decree. How can the disinheritance of an entire gender by a single individual be explained away? Whatever inconvenience the establishment and/or recognition of women's inheritance rights might have caused their male relatives, Kano would not have disintegrated and therefore the application of *ahafu dharayan* was unwarranted.

The annulment of women's inheritance rights was a deliberate action by the emir and was supported by the British colonial government. In his report to the Acting Resident in Kano, the district officer stated that:

> the court has decided that it will not award farms or houses to women by inheritance in the future. To do so the Waziri and Mallams say is contrary to custom and law. This issue cropped up for reasons unknown in Emir Abbas' time and was dropped on the advice of the Mallams. To prevent it cropping up again, the Emir wishes therefore to have it duly recorded for reference and to prevent disputes. (NAK/KanoProf 5/1/5579A)

The Acting Resident gave his support: 'Yes, I see no reason to forbid the enactment of custom and law. Women will own houses and have the right of occupancy of farms (to purchase). It is merely the question of inheritance which is affected' (NAK/KanoProf 5/1/5579A).

Based on the conspiratorial way in which women were denied their inheritance rights, the assertion that 'inheritance of farmland is one aspect of the land question which manifests the gender problem' encapsulates the land problem in colonial northern Nigeria (Jumare 1994: 6).

On 1 April 1954, Sarki Sanusi, the emir who popularised the Tijaniyya doctrine in Kano, annulled the ruling disinheriting women. It is said that emir Sanusi's counter-declaration was based on a complaint brought to him by a woman who was humiliated and barred from her brother's house (which he had inherited under the previous inheritance law) by his wives. After consultation with the ulama that confirmed that there is no doctrine in the Sharia prohibiting women from inheriting farmland, houses or both, the emir then reinstated women's inheritance rights. This incident notwithstanding, emir Sanusi would have taken this action because he was an Islamist and well versed in Qur'anic teachings. Furthermore, according to the 1954 Kano Province Annual Report, the resident officer noted that Sarki Sanusi has upon his ascendancy promised reforms in three areas. 'Public sessions of his own court and a root and branch change in its membership. Limitation of the high offices to be held by members of his own family, reorganisation and retrenchment of his personal household and land registration and reform in Kano city' (NAK/KanoProf Annual Report, Kano Province 1954: 1).

Sarki Sanusi's action redressed the injustice done to women. According to Islamic jurisprudence, the *radd al-Mazahlim* (redressing of injustice) is applied to restore either individual or group rights that have been violated by previous regimes. It is applied when there has been a general miscarriage of justice or in times of chaos or war: 'In Islamic tradition, the *Mazalim* jurisdiction was exercised by Moslem sovereigns to provide their subjects with an avenue of complaint against unjust acts or decisions on the part of officials or judges appointed by the rulers' (Christelow 1994: 81).

The *radd al-Mazahlim* has been applied only twice in the history of Kano. The first was during the reign of Sarki Abbas (1903–19) to restore the property rights of victims of the Kano civil war of 1892–94. The second time was in 1980, when the PRP government set up a committee to restore the rights of victims of the anti-NEPU policy of the NPC in the first republic (1960–66). This attempt failed, as the NPN-backed successor of the NPC federal government sponsored a civil riot that led to the burning and looting of public buildings, such as the Ministry of Lands and Survey and Radio Kano, and the killing of innocent people.

What this means is that Sarki Sanusi's re-establishment of women's rights was not backed by the *radd al-Mazahlim*. What is not clear is whether a law not backed by the *radd al-Mazahlim* can be revoked. But since the declaration and his ouster in 1954, there has not been a counter-declaration. With the reintroduction of women's rights to inherit land and landed properties, it is reported that the courts in the state became inundated with various claims. Some of the claims dated as far back as the nineteenth century and generated a response in which male relatives became less sympathetic to the problems of their female kin (Hamza 1994: 111).

From the literature consulted and the research findings, women's land rights appear to be determined and influenced both by culture and religion. In general, inheritance in northern Nigeria is based on Islamic law and customary intestacy. In Muslim areas, land is accorded to women based on Sharia. Where errors are made, they are redressed through the same channel. A good example is the revocation of the colonial law and ordinance in 1926 with regard to women's rights to inherit farmland and houses in Kano.

In most non-Muslim areas, inheritance is patrilineal. Under this form of inheritance, male children inherit their father's property. Those who are entitled to inherit include male children of the deceased, his brothers, his brother's male children, parents and grandparents. Wives, daughters, sisters, aunts and all female relations are excluded (Yakubu 1985: 134). However, patrilineal female relations, such as sisters related through the father or aunts through the paternal grandfather, are considered as possible inheritors. But women in most non-Muslim communities still cannot inherit land, because of the belief that when married, women will pass their land rights to their children who are members of different lineages (their husbands'). However, as a result of the secular Land Use Act, they can now purchase land and develop it.

This discussion of women's land rights was undertaken from a human rights perspective, albeit cognisant of the fact that conventional human rights are still inadequate to address and advocate women's rights, because of the tendency to separate civil and political rights on one hand and economic, social and cultural rights on the other, with the former given priority over the latter. From women's point of view, both sets of rights have to be treated in an integrated manner.

Despite this shortcoming, human rights are still worth using, because they provide the only international framework to determine norms, procedures and standards, and 'provide concepts and strategies, formal and informal, that women can shape in the light of [their] diverse needs and contexts to challenge abuses, promote positive programmes and, at the most fundamental level, to empower women in (their) daily lives' (International Human Rights Law Group 1993: 1).

In using the human rights framework, 'we stress the need for an expansive approach that considers the economic conditions under which rights are constructed, violated, or pursued' (Fried 1994: 55). Hence the use of Agarwal's analysis, developed in her study of women's land rights in South Asia. According to her:

> Rights are defined as claims that are legally and socially recognised and enforceable by an external legitimate authority. Rights in land can be in the form of usufruct (that is rights of use), associated with differing degrees of freedom to lease out, mortgage, bequeath or sell. Land rights can stem from inheritance (individual or joint family basis), community membership, transfers from the state, tenancy arrangements, etc. Rights in land have temporal and sometimes locational dimension: they may be hereditary, accrue only for a person's lifetime (or lesser period) and may be conditional on the person residing where the land is located. (Agarwal 1994: 19)

Agarwal further identified four elements and the constraint/social reality an individual and/or group might face in demanding recognition of their land rights. These are the distinction 'between legal recognition of a claim and its social recognition and between recognition and enforcement; between ownership and control; between ownership and use rights; and rights conferred by inheritance and those conferred by the state' (Agarwal 1994: 19).

In addition to human rights, women's access to and control over land must be examined. Women's land rights are closely associated with access to land. Access is different from rights, as it does not allow for the disposal or perpetual use of the land. Women's access to land, in many cases, is determined on the basis of rights (usufruct, loan, lease and ownership) and through informal networks (friendship and goodwill) on which no rights can be claimed. For example, the general practice in most of northern Nigeria is for a man to allot a piece of land to his wife to farm, but she cannot claim it as a right. On the other hand, rights bestow security on the owner because she can sell, bequeath and use the land in perpetuity. Thus, in our study we shall distinguish between law and practice, and between women's rights and access to and control over land.

Inheritance in Muslim Areas of Kano and Sokoto States

The position of women in Muslim Hausa communities is that:

> Women were jural minors, subject to numerous incapacities in relations with their agnatic guardians and husbands alike. However, by Muslim law, women may demand divorce, recover debts from their husbands or other and hold property in their name. By contrast, Hausa custom denied women the right to inherit valuable capital goods (*dukiya*) such as land, farms or compounds, except when widows acted as trustees for their sons. Women, could, however, inherit slaves, cattle … but pastoral Fulani oppose female inheritance of cattle, their major capital goods. (Smith 1997: 36)

Women are recognised as legal entities under Islamic law. They can acquire and retain their own property, inherit and be inherited from. Women can inherit from their deceased parents, husbands, brothers, sisters, daughters and other relations. However, women's inheritance is less than that of male heirs. Based on Qur'anic injunctions, women inherit one-half of the male share. Daughters are entitled to half the share of their brothers and wives to one-eighth if there are children and one-fourth if there are none. Where a daughter survives the deceased, she is entitled to half the net estate, while an only son gets the entire estate. Although this inheritance practice is biased against Muslim women, if adhered to, it can be argued that Muslim women's inheritance (and land) rights are secured because they are based on a religious injunction to be obeyed by all concerned. In the Maliki tradition, a married woman cannot give out more than one-third of her property without her husband's consent.

Under Islamic law, women can acquire or inherit land in six ways:

> Firstly, a woman as a mother has a right to inherit from a share of her off-spring's land. Secondly, a woman as a wife is eligible to a share of her deceased husband's land. Thirdly, women were eligible for inheritance of their deceased parents' and other maternal and paternal relations' land. Fourthly, women also inherited from their siblings. Fifthly, women who owned male or female slaves had the right to inherit their property including land. The sixth source can be divided into two: gift and purchase. (Jumare 1994: 269)

> Zulaihat, a 50-year-old divorcee, is in her fifth marriage. She did not inherit from her parents, as they had no farmland or house. Since she is childless, she cannot have access to any of her former husbands' property, and neither can she lay claim to their property in spite of the fact that she was once married to them and might have contributed to acquiring the wealth.

A divorced Muslim woman is entitled to take all her personal property, including land and landed property. This includes all her dowry and any gifts she received during the marriage. If the dowry was not paid in full at marriage, the husband must complete payment before the divorce. It is said that the divorced woman is entitled to a parting gift from the husband as a consolation (Uzodike 1993: 309). However, she loses her inheritance rights upon divorce, but she is not required to pay back her dowry and her children do not lose their inheritance rights.

In spite of the religious injunction against women's rights to inherit property, the general belief among men in the research sites is that such rights are unwarranted, because women allegedly have no need for land as they are usually married and are catered for by their husbands. Even when divorced, according to the men interviewed in Dawakin Tofa and Yabo, women are looked after by their male guardians. Furthermore, they claimed that women rarely engage in farming activities. Rather, under the supervision of their husbands, they hire labour to cultivate the land. They maintained that because women engage in household chores and petty commodity production, they do not have time to take on the arduous task of farming and therefore have no need for independent land ownership rights.

Inheritance in Maguzawa Areas of Kano State

Inheritance among non-Muslims is based on the customs and traditions of each ethnic group. Although there may be variations in matters of detail, the general principle is the same. Inheritance is through male descent and those entitled to inherit are male children of the deceased, his brothers, his brother's male children, parents and grandparents. Wives, sisters, aunts and all other female kindred are excluded from inheritance (Yakubu 1985: 134). In the event that there are no relations to inherit, land goes back to the community. However, if that happens among the Jaba of southern Kaduna, female relations are allowed to inherit the land.

Women are in most cases, therefore, not entitled to inherit or to have personal rights to land. 'They have nothing to be inherited and don't inherit as well' (Yakubu 1985: 138). Women's land rights are thus only through family or marriage. The right they derive from either is usufructory and they therefore cannot alienate the land. On the death of their husbands, they are (sometimes) allowed to continue using land allocated to them by their deceased husbands, on the condition that they remarry a member of the family or stay as part of the family. If they opt out, they lose the land. If, because of old age, they stay with their children, they retain their right to use the land. Women using family land do not have the right to alienate such land either.

According to colonial historiography (NAK/KanoProf His/5/1936) and inheritance practices among the Maguzawa are patrilineal. The district officer in Kano noted that 'the estate of the deceased passes on to the eldest son who also inherits his father's wives ... No woman inherits farm land' (NAK/KanoProf His/5/1936). On the other hand, Naniya notes that 'Both male and female heirs are given equal share of the deceased property, with the younger ones or minors taking the lion share while female heirs are excluded from the farmland. The wives of the deceased are also given a share of the property. The method of distribution is strictly guided by equity' (Naniya 1990: 31).

The research findings reveal that Maguzawa women can now inherit farm-lands from their deceased parents, but not on an equal basis with men. Unlike Islam, which has an inheritance-sharing formula, the Maguzawa's customary law has none. It was not possible to establish when this practice came into being. However, Tasalla Mazadu, a 75-year-old widow, did not inherit from her parents, but her daughters inherited farmlands from her husband's estate when he died about 30 years ago.[2] Maguzawa women are not allowed to sell the land they inherit, and if they marry away from their family home they either rent out the land or ask their brothers to farm it. While their children are not entitled to inherit the land, their brothers' children are. In other words, when a Bamuje woman dies, the farmland inherited from her parents reverts back to the family. But in spite of the fact that women's right to inherit land is now recognised among the Maguzawa, brothers frequently refuse to acknowledge this right.

Although Tarana's brothers refused to give her land from the farms left by their deceased father, she has through hard work acquired four farms valued at about 90,000 naira. The farms were bought with proceeds from the sale of local beer. Even though she is not desperately in need of her family land, she wants to take her brothers to court to seek justice.

Tsakani, also disinherited by her brothers, is not as fortunate as Tarana. She was given two plots of farmland as her share of their deceased father's estate. The brothers later took back the two plots without any explanation. She has not bought any land and does not plan to go to court as she has no money. She farms on a plot given to her by her husband.

The inheritance rights of divorcees and widows are precarious and depend on the benevolence of family heads.

Under Maguzawa tradition, a divorced woman is required to return the bride-price to her husband's family and loses all matrimonial rights (residential and land). Her children also lose their right to inherit from their father's estate. But she is entitled to whatever landed property she may have acquired during the marriage. Divorced women who did not acquire land during their marriages hope that their families will accept them back and provide them with land. If their families do not provide them with land, they have to work as labourers on other people's farms.

> Takorau, 46, was married to Barau for 16 years. On his death, she did not inherit his farms because they had no children. She was asked by his family to leave the residential home. She did not return to her parental home, as she had bought farmlands in her husband's village. Her brothers' children, and not her sisters', will inherit the farms she bought, because according to Maguzawa culture her sisters' children belong to other families.

The situation of widows is determined by their fertility and their willingness to remarry. A menopausal widow with children who chooses not to remarry will, because of her children, continue to have right of abode and usufructory rights to land. A pre-menopausal widow who opts not to marry, but to stay and look after her children, will have access to both her home and the land because of the children. But if the widow is pre-menopausal, she is usually expected to marry someone from her dead husband's family to continue the lineage. If she obliges, she will be allowed to stay in her home and will have continued usage of the land allotted her. However, if she marries outside of her husband's family, she loses all rights to her home and land. The situation is different for a childless widow. The number of years in marriage notwithstanding, she is expected to return to her ancestral home on the death of her husband. However, if the husband's family displays a sense of responsibility, the widow is allowed to use land given to her by the deceased.

> Lange, 65, was married to her deceased husband for 45 years. They had no children. Rather than send her away, as was the custom, her husband's family gave her two farms to enable her to earn a living, as she had no one else to provide for her.

According to informants in Kamurun Ikulu in southern Kaduna province, women have no inheritance rights. In the past, the women were inherited on the death of their husbands because it was believed they needed to be taken care of. Widow inheritance was considered to be necessary for family cohesion. If no suitable members of the deceased husbands' families could be found to inherit them, they are considered part of the families and provided with farms. But this only happens if the widows have female children and no males.

Haushi stated that according to Ikulu custom women cannot inherit their fathers' or husbands' property. They are only entitled to inherit their mothers' personal property (clothing, cooking utensils and furniture). On the death of her husband, if a woman has male children they will inherit their father's property. If there are no male heirs, the houses and lands of the deceased pass on to his relatives. A divorced or widowed woman in need of farmland has to ask her male relatives to allot land for her to use during her lifetime. If granted, she can use the land for as long as her male relatives wish. On her death, however, the land reverts to its owner.

However, polygamy and widow inheritance are disappearing because of Christianity, which has placed restrictions on the number of wives its adherents can have. Divorced women and childless widows have no place when they become single.

Mama Kwanya, a widow aged 70, said that Ladi, a childless widow now residing in Kaduna town, the capital of the state, refused to be inherited by her husband's brother. Because of that, her deceased husband's family rejected her request for land. Her brothers also refused to give her land to cultivate. She left for Kaduna, as she felt no attachment to the village.

Inheritance among the Ikulu is patrilineal. When a man dies, his property goes to his male child(ren). Wives and daughters are excluded. If the children are young, the property is held in trust either by the mother or by a male relative of the deceased. However, male relatives are not always trustworthy although it is expected that a male relative of the deceased will help in caring for the family. If the deceased has no male child(ren), his property is shared among his male relatives, including his father. A widow with male child(ren) has unlimited access to landed property and land and may be allowed some control over such resources, subject to the longevity of the male child(ren). If she survives her children, such rights cease.

Lami had three sons and four daughters with her late husband. On his death, the three sons inherited the three farms left by their father. Because the children were young, Lami held the property in trust for them. The land was located in the government grazing reserve for the Fulani. In establishing the reserve area, the government stated that persons with proof of continuous cultivation of twelve years and more would be issued with a certificate of occupancy on registered agricultural land. The farms of Lami's children and two other persons were not taken over by the government, as they met the requirement.

When Lami was informed of the issuance of the three certificates of occupancy, she went to the project office to collect them. On getting there, she was informed by the project officer that her brother-in-law had collected one of the certificates. Lami herself was given only one of the remaining certificates. The third certificate is with the project officer for safekeeping. All efforts by the village head and Lami to collect the certificate from her brother-in-law have been unsuccessful. The brother-in-law has leased out part of the land and is farming on the other part.

Lami has, however, kept the issue alive by telling her children of their uncle's illegal action.

Inheritance in Christian Areas of Southern Zaria Emirate

Inheritance under a Christian marriage in which the man dies intestate is not as clear-cut as it might appear to be. This is because the legal status of Christian marriage in Nigeria is ambiguous. Case law (Cole vs. Cole 1898) established that when a person who married under Christianity dies intestate, inheritance rules of received English law should apply. But recent judgments have set aside this decision, by applying customary inheritance rules. For example, the presiding judge in the case of Obiekwe vs. Obiekwe noted that:

A good deal has been said about 'church marriage'. So far as the law of Nigeria is concerned, there is only one form of monogamous marriage and that is marriage under the Act. Legally, a marriage in a church (of any denomination) is either a marriage under the Act or it is nothing. In this case, if the parties had not been validly married under the Act, then, either they are married under the native law or custom or they are not married at all ... In either case, the ceremony in the church would have made not a scrap of difference to their legal status. (Yakubu 1985: 158)

Thus, women contracting monogamous Christian marriages without a marriage certificate based on the Marriage Act of 1914, whose spouses die intestate, will not inherit their husbands' estates, including land. For a church marriage to be legal, a licensed certificate issued by the Registrar of Marriages should back it. Most churches are licensed to perform marriage ceremonies and provide marriage certificates to make the ceremonies legal. A woman married within the church should therefore be entitled to inherit her husband's estate. She will inherit a quarter of her husband's estate if she has children and half if she has no children (discussion with Professor Jadesola Akande). Where a church is not licensed to perform marriage ceremonies, marriages contracted by it are not legal.

Christian marriages are common in southern Kaduna, one of the research sites.

Research Findings

The empirical data for this study were generated through interviews and questionnaires administered to households selected to represent a balanced mix of married, divorced and widowed women in the research sites. The 100 women are from the three research sites, with 50 coming from the Muslim areas of Kano and Sokoto states and 25 each from the Maguzawa and southern Kaduna sites.

The data in Tables 4.1 to 4.5 provide background information (age, marital status, number of marriages) and information on the land rights of respondents. Apart from Maguzawa women who bought and rented land in their own names, the data show that women's land rights are principally determined by their relationships to men, either as wives or as daughters, and hardly ever as individuals entitled to own/control land in their own right. The data confirms the belief that women will be married throughout their life cycle and that their husbands will cater for their everyday needs.

Table 4.1 shows that 48 per cent of the respondents were married, 31 per cent were divorced and 21 per cent were widowed. It also reveals that 26, 35 and 39 per cent of our respondents were aged between 20–30, 31–40 and 41+ respectively.

Table 4.1 Respondents classified by age and marital status

Location	Marital status			Age		
	Married	Widowed	Divorced	20–30	31–40	41+
Kano	12	6	7	3	6	16
Sokoto	10	7	8	5	8	12
Maguzawa	8	3	14	6	12	7
Southern Kaduna	18	5	2	12	9	4
Total	48	21	31	26	35	39

Maguzawa women accounted for 46 per cent of the divorced population, almost half the sample size. This was followed by 26 per cent from Sokoto, 22 per cent from Kano and 6 per cent from southern Kaduna. Southern Kaduna accounted for more than one-third of the married women's sample, followed by the Muslim areas of Kano and Sokoto and Maguzawa respectively.

The data presented in Table 4.2 show the fluidity of marriage in the research sites. Almost two-thirds of the sample have been married more than once, with 32, 22 and 7 per cent in their second, third and fourth marriages respectively. When the data are disaggregated, it is obvious that marriage is most fluid among Hausa and Maguzawa women.

Considering that marriage is the main source through which women access land and gain economic and social security, how is the high divorce rate in the research sites explained? Do Hausa and Maguzawa women not care about security? Or do these women use divorce as a strategy to gain/retain their access to land?

The divorce rates in this study can be attributed to various factors, including women's right to inherit land. In southern Kaduna, women's land rights depend on their marital status. Given the predominance of Christian marriage, which forbids divorce, divorce is almost non-existent. In the other sites, divorce is common because women's land rights do not depend on their being married. Irrespective

Table 4.2 Respondents classified by number of marriages

Location	Number of marriages				Total
	1	2	3	4	
Kano	8	14	2	1	25
Sokoto	7	10	8	0	25
Maguzawa	3	4	12	6	25
Southern Kaduna	21	4	0	0	25
Total	39	32	22	7	100

Table 4.3 Respondents classified by access to and control over land (ownership)

Location	Yes	No
Kano	20	5
Sokoto	18	7
Maguzawa	22	3
Southern Kaduna	22	3
Total	82	18

of their marital status, women in both sites can and do inherit their fathers' land. Further, marriage is fluid, due to the fact that Hausa husbands have the right to *talaq* (unilateral divorce) and Hausa wives can escape oppressive or unhappy marriages by running away or demanding divorce. Among the Maguzawa, as will be argued later (p. 169, divorce is common because of the rejection of Christian marriage by both sexes. As a result, women who can afford to return their bride-price move in and out of marriage when they are unhappy with their marital situations.

The data presented in Table 4.3 on land ownership show that 82 per cent of women have access to land, while 18 per cent do not. From Table 4.4, it is evident that 31.8 per cent inherited land from their parents, 21.5 per cent from their husbands, 29.5 per cent were granted user rights by their husbands, 12.5 per cent purchased land (this includes three married women who had user rights on their husband's land), 3.4 per cent rented land (this includes a woman with usufructory rights on her husband's land) and 1.1 per cent received land as a gift.

It had been expected that, with the fluidity of marriage in two of the research sites, women would have cleared or rented land to secure their livelihoods. This

Table 4.4 Respondents classified by source of ownership

	Parent	Husband[1]	Husband[2]	Purchase	Rent	Gift
Location						
Kano	13	7	0	0	0	0
Sokoto	10	8	0	0	0	0
Maguzawa	5	2	8	11[3]	3[4]	0
Southern Kaduna	0	2	18	0	1	1
Total	28	19	26	11	4	1

Notes: [1] Inheritance from husbands. [2] User rights from husbands. [3] Includes three women with user rights from husbands. [4] Includes one woman with user rights from husbands.

Table 4.5 Respondents classified by ownership structure

Location	Independent	Non-independent
Kano	0	20
Sokoto	0	18
Maguzawa	11	18
Southern Kaduna	0	22
Total	11	78

did not happen, because there was no vacant land for clearing in both of the research sites and because women's inheritance rights are recognised in these sites. Even though Hausa women can inherit land by four other ways, no respondents got land through those ways. According to Table 4.5, only 12.5 per cent of respondents had independent land rights (the right to dispose of land without interference from external sources). These right were, however, limited as respondents' maternal nieces and nephews cannot inherit the land.

In Dawakin Tofa and Yabo, although Islam recognises women as legal entities, none of the Muslim women in the sample enjoyed independent land rights. When asked why this was so, almost invariably the answers given reflected the dominant male perspective that women have no need for independent land rights since their fathers, husbands, male relatives or in-laws were there to provide for them. The response of Hajiya Safiya Siriddaw, one of the respondents, was representative of the answers received:

> A woman has rights over her personal effects. Her husband has rights over her property also. This is due to the fact that a woman must consult her husband about every activity she undertakes in his house. She cannot engage in any activity (business, trade etc) without his instruction, consent or approval. A woman's property is under the control of her husband. She cannot dispose of it without his consent. If a husband wants to use any part of his wife's property, she cannot object. This code is enshrined by both tradition and religion that a woman is under the guidance of her parents or husband. A woman can have independent thinking only when she is divorced and does not have surviving parents or male kin. Under this condition she can decide for herself what is best for her. This is only for well-disciplined women. (Authors' field survey 1998)

Callaway and Jumare observed this practice in their studies of Kano and Sokoto respectively. However, Callaway questioned this practice, while Jumare did not. 'Women do have specific property rights through inheritance, but this is not the same as actual control ... While women have access to property in that they inherit and technically own it and in that they can keep and spend or invest any income they might generate, in Kano actual managerial rights (particularly to land and real estate) usually belong to fathers, brothers and husbands' (Callaway 1987: 27). Similarly,

> in Sokoto, where propertied women spent most of their lives in purdah, management of their land and estates usually remained with one of their male relations ... This did not in any way affect women's right to own land. Men are more visible in land matters because of their direct connection with agricultural production, livestock grazing and construction of houses. (Jumare 1994: 275)

Jumare argued that this male control does not affect women's right to land tenure. This may be true, but as women have no direct contact with the outside world, they might be cheated by their male managers. For example, their properties might be sold without their knowledge and/or consent. Where they consent to the sale, proper accounts might not be rendered (Jumare 1994: 10). When this happens, women go to court to seek redress. Of what use is land ownership to women if they do not have the independent right to take decisions about the land?

Although inheritance and ownership rights of Muslim Hausa and Maguzawa women are recognised, they do not have full control over such lands. Muslim Hausa women can bequeath the land to their children or to any other person, but they cannot sell, lease or mortgage the land without recourse to a male guardian. Maguzawa women cannot bequeath, sell or mortgage such land because of social constraints. But they do have control over land purchased with their own money. However, their sisters' children cannot inherit such land, as they are seen to be members of a different lineage. For divorcees, childless widows and widows without male child(ren), among the Maguzawa and in southern Kaduna where women are not allowed to inherit land, women can, through the benevolence of the village head or a male relative/male in-law, be given user rights to land. Such land can be used for as long as the benefactor wishes, but it cannot be claimed as the women's property.

Custom, Religion and Law

This research not only focused on the ways in which women's land rights are shaped by custom, religion and law, but looked at how custom, religion and law have acted and interacted to define and put into practice women's land rights. By doing this, it revealed the impact of Christianity and Islam on gender relations and women's inheritance rights, and the various strategies women have used to establish and/or safeguard their land rights.

Only Maguzawa women established and/or defended their land rights. However, the non-involvement of women in the two other sites does not mean that historical (Kano and Sokoto) data should be ignored or that parallels (Igbo women and women in southern Kaduna) should not be drawn.

Kubura, a widow, lives in her deceased husband's house. In addition to the house, she inherited land, cultivated by her sons. She and her four sisters have refused to lay claim to their father's house, which is now controlled by their nephew (their only brother's son) because he died over sixty years ago and they do not want the house to be divided (sold and the money shared among them) according to Islamic rules of inheritance, so they have allowed the nephew to keep the property.

Below are presented cases of women who have used the law to establish and/ or secure their land rights. Some Muslim respondents noted that there was no reason for them to use the law to establish their inheritance rights, because their siblings and/or co-wives recognised their rights. Others refused to use the law to establish their rights because they did not want to cause disaffection in their families. Southern Kaduna women did not engage in any struggles, because 'you cannot go to court or participate in any action to establish/demand justice for a non-existent right'.

Muslim areas of Kano and Sokoto states Christelow (1991) and Jumare (1994), in their historical studies of Kano and Sokoto respectively, illustrate how women have used the law successfully to demand and defend their land rights. Christelow's study of judicial records from twentieth-century Kano points out the successes achieved by widows in claiming their children's land rights. In granting trusteeship of the land to the widows, the Emir ruled that the lands should not be sold, loaned out, pawned or donated to a third party (Christelow 1991: 138).

From Yabo's court records in Sokoto (access to court records in Dawakin Tofa was denied), it was found that women went to court not only to defend their rights against their husbands' relations, but also against co-wives and stepsons.

Case Number 1 272/73 (Muinna vs. Maidamma)

Date: 17 July 1973

Muinna, a widow, went to the Alkali court demanding that it grant her children their share of her deceased husband's property. She took a case against Maid-amma, her husband's first son, because of his refusal to divide the estate. Her husband, Maiyara of Ruggar Magaji village, had had two wives, ten sons and three daughters. The husband's estate comprised a house and five farms (three large bush farms and two cultivable grain farms).

The court granted her request. The property was valued, sold and the proceeds divided among the wives and the children. The property was divided into eight parts. The wives were given one share. The remaining seven parts were divided into 13 shares, with each male child taking two shares and each female child one share.

Case Number 2 461/72 (Magna vs. Liege)

Date: 30 October 1972

This case centred on Liege's (the accused) refusal to give her co-wife Magna her share of their deceased husband's property (three farms). Liege refused to give Magna and her children their share on the grounds that the defendant had been away for three years and had not helped till the land.

The court requested that the farms be shared according to Sharia. The widows got one eighth of the three farms. The three sons got two shares each while the two daughters got one share each of the remaining seven parts.

Case Number 3 253/67 (Ayashe Sasseda vs. Sanda Sasseda)
Date: 8 July 1967

Ayashe, a housewife, took Sanda, her brother-in-law, to court because he had illegally acquired her husband's two farms. According to Ayashe, her husband abandoned her with five children. Since she had no other source of livelihood, she wanted the court to request Sanda to return the farms to her and the children. The presiding judge asked Sanda if Ayashe's case against him was valid. He replied in the affirmative, but insisted that the farms should be left with him as he had already started cultivating them.

The court ruled in favour of Ayashe and her children. The judge noted that Ayashe's husband was still alive and should be responsible for his children. But since he was not around to fulfil his familial obligations, his wife was entitled to whatever property he owned.

Non-Muslim areas of the Maguzawa in Kano state In a unanimous judgment by the Federal Court of Appeal in Enugu, the Nnewi inheritance practice, similar to that of southern Kaduna, was described as 'repugnant to natural justice, equity and good conscience'. In his lead judgment in the case of Augustine Nwafor Mojekwu and Caroline Mgbafor Okechukwu Mojekwu, Justice Niki Tobi said:

> We need not travel all the way to Beijing to know that some of our customs, including the Nnewi Oli-Ekpe custom ... are not consistent with our civilised world today, including the appellant ... All human beings, male or female, are born into a free world and are expected to participate freely, without any inhibitions on grounds of sex and that is constitutional. Any form of social discrimination on grounds of sex, apart from being unconstitutional, is an antithesis to a society built on the tenets of democracy which we have freely chosen as a people. I am unable to come to the conclusion that this appeal has merit. On the contrary, I come to the conclusion that the appeal has no merit and it is hereby dismissed. I award N2,000 costs in favour of the respondent (Caroline). (*Guardian*, 19 September 1997)

From the field data, only the Maguzawa women established or defended their land rights. Two strategies – the rejection of Christian marriage and legal redress – were used.

To understand the rejection of Christian marriage, an explanation is necessary. Maguzawa women are hardworking and are responsible for social provisioning in households. Christianity is pivotal to the everyday lives of converts. It is a religious doctrine that governs the daily lives of its followers. Maguzawa Christians are expected to do away with all customs and traditions (beer drinking, polygamy and divorce, among others) and imbibe Christian values not only by conversion but by practice (baptism and monogamy).

This fact is used by both women and men for different reasons. Maguzawa men reject Christian marriage because it forbids polygamy, meaning they can have access to only one woman's labour and resources, whereas customary/ traditional marriages allow an unlimited number of wives and access to more labour and resources. Maguzawa women, on the other hand, view Christian marriage as restrictive as it forbids divorce, used by women to opt out of abusive and exploitative relationships.[3] It is therefore not surprising that there is a high rate of divorce among the Maguzawa.

> Giya, 40, is in her third marriage. She initiated the two divorces because her previous husbands were exploitative and did not contribute to the family's upkeep. She says that if she becomes dissatisfied with her present marriage, she will leave to contract another or stay on her own. According to her, 'if I had a Christian marriage, I cannot leave because the church forbids it. The pastor and the church elders will prevail on me to stay in an unhappy relationship.'

Only one respondent used legal redress as a strategy, because it is cumbersome, expensive and takes too long.

Other strategies to secure women's land rights, such as land registration or group formation, did not feature in the research sites. Although land registration provides women with security of tenure and gives them the right to bequeath land to whomever they wish, women have not registered their land because the process is as expensive and tedious as seeking legal redress. Group formation has not been effective in the research sites, because these efforts were not women's own initiatives. They were part of the government's top-down approach to women's development. Furthermore, socio-cultural constraints governing land and the seclusion of women in Muslim areas of Kano and Sokoto states made this impossible.

> Ande Binni took her two brothers to court because they refused to honour her inheritance rights. The case took three years and she had to sell one of the farmlands to offset the debt of N12,000 she used in prosecuting the case. She now owns two farmlands.

Conclusion: The Case for Women's Independent Land Rights

The effects of Christianity and Islam on women's inheritance rights in northern Nigeria are both positive and negative. In the Muslim areas of Kano and Sokoto states, the introduction of Islam was positive, as it established women's rights to inherit compounds, farms and land, which was not possible under Hausa custom. On the other hand, although conversion to Islam would enable Maguzawa women to pass on their inheritance to their children or sisters' children, it would also mean they could no longer participate in activities in the public domain because of the practice of purdah (female seclusion).

Rather than build upon Maguzawa norms and improve the status of women, Christian organisations have adopted a conservative Christian doctrine on women's status. According to a pastor, 'women are like sheep, they have to be organised by men' (Ibrahim 1997: 21). Furthermore, by ruling out divorce in Christian marriage, the church is unwittingly condoning the abuse and exploitation of women and promoting male domination, while taking away the only weapon women have to escape unhappy marriages. The monogamy that the church promotes is not based on equal partnership but on the subservience of women to men. Thus Maguzawa women have opted for traditional marriage (with polygamy) rather than for Christian marriage (monogamous).

Unlike Maguzawa Christians, Christian marriage was the dominant form of matrimony among southern Kaduna Christians. A widow's inheritance rights are guaranteed under a church marriage if a marriage certificate is issued by the Registrar of Marriages. The certificate makes the marriage recognisable under the Marriage Act of 1914 and the Matrimonial Clauses Act of 1970. A widow can inherit under testate succession, based on the provisions made for her by her deceased husband, and under intestate succession, her inheritance is based on rules of distribution as outlined under the Administration of Estates Law, as follows:

1. Where the deceased leaves no parent, sibling or issue, the entire estate is held in trust for the surviving wife.
2. Where the deceased leaves a wife and issue (whether or not there are other relatives):
- The widow inherits all personal effects.
- A sum of money equivalent to the value of one-third of the estate is paid to the surviving spouse with interest at the rate of 2.5 per cent from the date of death until the money is paid.
- Subject to providing for that sum and the interest thereon, one-third of the residuary estate is held in trust for the surviving spouse during her life and then in statutory trust for the children.
- Two-thirds of the residuary estate is held in trust for the children.

(Quoted in Okagbue 1997: 85–6)

Even though Christian marriages in southern Kaduna are recognised under the Marriage and Matrimonial Clauses Act, the inheritance rights of widows and daughters are still governed by custom. As a result, the liberating effect that church marriages should have on women's inheritance rights is not felt. From discussions with respondents and some male informants, church marriage is viewed as a blessing, as it neither stops polygamy nor establishes women's inheritance rights. In order words, the church's vision of Christianity as a governing principle for the daily lives of its adherents is not extended to women's inheritance rights in southern Kaduna.

Thus this research has focused on the need for women's independent land rights both for those with nominal rights and those without rights. Ownership without independent land rights is no ownership at all. Independent land rights would enable women to secure access to and exercise control over land. Women's land security means 'rights to a piece of land on a continuous basis, free from imposition or interference from outside sources, as well as [the] ability to reap the benefits of labour and capital investments in land either in its use or upon its alienation' (Lawry et al. 1992: 3).

Independent land rights are necessary for women as they would lead to their autonomy (their ability to make and take decisions on their fertility, sexuality and incomes) and would enhance their status. In addition, independent land rights would empower women to challenge existing gender inequalities and ultimately lead to a reordering of gender relations.

The achievement of independent land rights cannot happen in a vacuum. A gender-responsive law and policy reform programme aimed at restructuring gender relations with respect to land is needed. In arguing for women's independent land rights, the role of culture/tradition and religion in the continued denial of women's inheritance rights cannot be ignored. The reform programme should therefore include the following recommendations:

- Customary/traditional land allocation practices should include women more centrally as independent entities.
- Gender equality in inheritance and the issuance of title deeds should be established.
- Land rights through occupancy should be recognised with or without title deeds so that women cannot be dispossessed at divorce or widowhood.
- Uniform inheritance laws should be established.
- The programme should be situated within the wider development programme of the state to ensure increased income for women.

The programme should be accompanied by educational campaigns undertaken by community-based and non-governmental organisations, including environmental, human rights, legal and women's organisations. Traditional and religious institutions, as well as relevant government bureaucracies, should be targeted. For 'law reform to protect the human rights of women must be accompanied by educational measures to foster social change and economic and political initiatives to advance women's status if it is to have a significant impact on women's de facto rights' (Sullivan 1992: 854).

Notes

1. The authors would like to thank Drs Jibrin Ibrahim and Reverend Father Mathew Kukah for their help in the Maguzawa and southern Kaduna research sites.

2. Emir Sanusi's ruling re-establishing Muslim Hausa women's inheritance rights may have influenced the Maguzawa.

3. It had been expected that Maguzawa women would prefer Christian marriage to traditional marriage as the former guarantees monogamy.

References

Agarwal, B. (1994) *A Field of One's Own: Gender and Land Rights in South Asia*, Cambridge: Cambridge University Press.

Ayandele, A. E. (1966) *The Missionary Impact on Modern Nigeria 1842–1914: A Political and Social Analysis*, London: Longman.

Barkow, J. H. (1970) 'The Hausa and the Maguzawa: Process of Group Differentiation in a Rural Area in North Central State, Nigeria', unpublished PhD thesis, Michigan State University.

Berger, I. and C. Robertson (eds) (1986) *Women and Class in Africa*, London: Africana Publishers.

Callaway, B. (1987) *Muslim Hausa Women: Tradition and Change*, Syracuse, NY: Syracuse University Press.

Chretien, J.-P. et al. (eds) (1993) *L'invention religieuse en Afrique*, Paris: Karthala.

Christelow, A. (1991) 'Women and the Law in Early Twentieth Century Kano', in C. Coles, and B. Mack (eds) (1991).

— (1994) *Thus Ruled Emir Abbas: Selected Cases of the Emir of Kano's Judicial Council*, East Lansing: Michigan State University Press.

Clarke, P. B. (1986) *West Africa and Christianity*, London: Edward Arnold.

Coles, C. and B. Mack (eds) (1991) *Hausa Women in the Twentieth Century*, Madison: University of Wisconsin Press.

Davison, J. (1988) *Agriculture, Women and Land: The African Experience*, Boulder, CO: Westview Press.

Ega, L. A. (1987) 'The Need to Redefine Rights under Customary Land Tenure in Northern Nigeria', in M. Mortimore et al. (1987).

Elias, T. O. (1971) *Nigerian Land Law*, London: Sweet & Maxwell.

Famoriyo, O. A. (1985) 'Administration of Land Allocation in Nigeria', *Land Use Policy*, Vol. 1 No. 3.

— (1987) 'Acquisition of Land and Compensation in Nigeria', in M. Mortimore et al. (1987).

Fried, S. (1994) 'Summary of Lectures on Women's Economic and Social Rights', *The Indivisibility of Women's Human Rights: Continuing Dialogue*, New York: Centre for Women's Global Leadership, Rutgers University.

Greenberg, J. (1946) *The Influence of Islam on a Sudanese Religion*, New York: J. J. Augustin.

Hamza, I. (1994) 'Dorayi: A History of Economic and Social Transformations in the Nineteenth and Twentieth Centuries in Kano Emirate', unpublished MA thesis, Usuman Dan-Fodio University.

Hill, P. (1977) *Population Prosperity and Poverty in Rural Kano 1900–1970*, Cambridge: Cambridge University Press.

Ibrahim, J. (1997) *Structural Adjustment and Social Provisioning Among a Marginalised Minority: The Maguzawa of Kano*, Lagos: Mimeo.

Ikime, O. (ed.) *Groundwork of Nigerian History*, Ibadan: Heinemann Books.

International Human Rights Law Group (1993) *Token Gestures: Women's Human Rights and UN Reporting*, Washington, DC: Women in the Law Project of the IHRLG.

Jumare, I. (1994) 'Gender, Class and Land Tenure in the Sokoto Sultanate of Nigeria', unpublished paper, Toronto: African Studies Association.

Kayode, J. O. and E. D. Adelowo (1985) 'Religions in Nigeria', in R. Olaniyan (1985).

Krusuis, P. (1915) 'Die Maguzawa', *Archiv fur Anthropologie*, Vol. 14.

Kukah, M. H. and T. Falola (1957) *Land Tenure and Administration in Nigeria and the Cameroons*, London: HMSO.

— (1996) *Religious Militancy and Self-Assertion*, Aldershot: Ashgate.

Last, M. (1977) *The Sokoto Caliphate*, London: Longman.

— (1979) 'Some Economic Aspects of Conversion in Hausa Land (Nigeria)', in N. Levtzion, *Conversion to Islam*, New York: Holmes and Meier.

— (1993) 'History as Religion: De-constructing the Magians Maguzawa of Nigerian Hausa Land', in J.-P. Chretien et al. (1993).

Lawry, S., M. Roth and K. Wiebe (1992) 'Land Tenure and Agrarian Structure: Implications for Technology Adoption', working paper, Madison: LTC.

Levtzion, N. (1979) *Conversion to Islam*, New York: Holmes & Meier.

Meek, C. K. (1931) *Tribal Studies in Northern Nigeria*, Vol. 11, London: HMSO.

— (1957) *Land Tenure and Administration in Nigeria and the Cameroons*, London: HMSO.

Meer, S. (ed.) (1997) *Women, Land and Authority: Perspectives from South Africa*, London: Oxfam.

Mortimore, M. (1987) 'The Lands in Northern Nigeria: Some Urgent Issues', in M. Mortimore et al. (1987).

Mortimore, M., E. A. Olofin, R. A. Cline-Cole and A. Abdulkadir (eds) (1987) *Perspectives on Land Administration in Northern Nigeria*, Kano: Department of Geography, Bayero University.

Naniya, T. M. (1990) 'The Transformation of Justice in Kano Emirate', unpublished PhD thesis, Bayero University.

Northern Nigeria Annual Report (1902).

Obilade, A. O. (ed.) (1993) *Women in Law*, Lagos: Southern University Law Centre and Faculty of Law, University of Lagos.

Okagbue, I. (1997), 'The Legal Rights of Widows in Nigeria', in B. Owasanoye and B. Ahonsi (eds) *Widowhood in Nigeria: Issues, Problems and Prospects*, Lagos: Friedrich Ebert Foundation and Human Development Initiatives.

Olaniyan, R. (ed.) (1985) *Nigerian History and Culture*, Ibadan: Longman.

Olorunfemi, A. (1985) 'The Fulani Jihad and the Sokoto Caliphate in the Nineteenth Century', in R. Olaniyan (1985).

Olukoshi, A. O. (1985) 'Some Remarks on the Role of the Levantine Bourgeoisie in the Capitalist Industrialisation of Kano', *Nigerian Journal of Political Science*, Vol. 4, Nos 1 and 2.

Orr, C. (1965) *The Making of Northern Nigeria*, London: Frank Cass.

Paden, J. (1973) *Religion and Political Culture in Kano*, Berkeley: University of California Press.

Pittin, R. (1979) 'Marriage and Alternative Strategies: Career Patterns of Hausa Women in Katsina City', unpublished PhD thesis, University of London.

SAFERE, (1995) Vol. 1 No. 1. Special Issue on Women and Land in Southern Africa.

Shaw, Flora (1905) *A Tropical Dependency: An Outline of the Ancient History of the Western Sudan with an Account of the Modern Settlement of Northern Nigeria*, London: James Nisbet.

Small, J. (1997) 'Women's Land Rights: A Case Study from the Northern Transvaal', in S. Meer (1997).

Smith, M. G. (1997) *Government in Kano 1350–1950*, Boulder, CO: Westview Press.

Sullivan, D. J. (1992) 'Gender Equality and Religious Freedom: Towards a Framework for Conflict Resolution', *Journal of International Law and Politics*, Vol. 24, No. 2.

Trimingham, J. S. (1968) *Islam in West Africa*, London: Oxford University Press.

Turaki, Y. (1982) 'The Institutionalisation of the Inferiority Status and Socio-Political Role of the Non-Muslim Groups in the Colonial Hierarchical Structure of the Northern Region of Nigeria: A Socio-ethical Analysis of the Colonial Legacy', unpublished PhD thesis, Boston University.

Uzodike, E. N. U. (1993) 'Women's Rights in Law and Practice: Property Rights', in A. O. Obilade (1993).

Yakubu, M. G. (1985) *Nigerian Land Law*, London: Macmillan.

Zakaria, Y. (1997) *The Cultural Context of Business: A Study of Firms in a Northern Nigerian Society*, Uppsala: ACTA Universitatis Upsaliensis.

Archival Sources

AHK[1]/15246: Missionary Enterprise in Moslem Districts of Northern Province.

AHK/16032: Rights of Non-Mohammedans Before Mohammedan Courts.

Kan/Prof/His/5/1936: Pagan Communities in Kano Province: Reports on the Maguzawa, Batawa and other groups by various officers.

NAK[2]/KanoProf[3] 5/1/5579: Inheritance of Farm and House Property in Kano Province.

NAK/KanoProf 5/1/4042: Islamic Law of Inheritance: application to Christian converts 1939–1940.

NAK/KanoProf 2/31/LAN 32-11: Land Tenure in Northern Provinces.

NAK/KanoProf 5/1/10591: Notes on Muhammedan Law in Northern Province 1933–1949.

NAK/KanoProf 512038: Recognition of Marriage Between Moslems and Non-Moslems, 1933–1948.

NAK/KanoProf 5/1/5579A: Ruling as to Farm and House Inheritance by Women.

NAK/KanoProf 2/31/LAN 32: Rural Land Tenure.

NAK/KanoProf Annual Report, Kano Province 1954.

NAK/Kan Prof/6508/52/1947 Notes from the Rowling Report 'Land Tenure in Kano Province'.

[1] Arewa House, Kaduna

[2] National Archives, Kaduna

[3] Kano Provincial Office

FIVE

Culture, Practice and Law: Women's Access to Land in Rwanda

Jennie E. Burnet and the Rwanda Initiative for Sustainable Development

Women constitute the majority of the Rwandan population and labour force, particularly in agriculture, but have faced substantial constraints on their participation in the economy and society. The discriminatory laws and practices in education, employment, inheritance and finance have marginalized women. Consequently, the majority of women in Rwanda remain poor and vulnerable. (Rwanda Development Indicators, Ministry of Finance and Planning, 1999)

§ AS in other African states, women in Rwanda face numerous cultural, 'customary', economic, legal and social constraints to their access to land and ownership of property in general. The above quotation summarises what is generally accepted to be the status of women's rights in Rwanda. As for their rights to land, 'the discriminatory laws and practices' have an even greater impact on women and on female-headed households because of the scarcity of land. Rwanda has an average population density of over 300 people per square kilometre and more than 91 per cent of the population depend on agriculture for their livelihoods. Therefore, access to and control over land is crucial for all Rwandans, but especially for women, since the number of women- and child-headed households (the majority of these 'children' being girls) has greatly increased as a result of the war and genocide of 1994, the 1996–99 insurgency in the northwest and the HIV/ AIDS epidemic.

The post-conflict and post-genocide context has thrown into conflict several cultural and legal assumptions previously controlling women's access to land. Furthermore, Rwandan women have been forced into new roles in the family and society because many men were killed in the 1994 genocide and massacres and many others have been imprisoned. Other recent developments in Rwanda have transformed the ways in which decisions about land are made. For example, the government of Rwanda (GOR) has implemented a new rural settlement policy that requires the population to build their homes in grouped settlements or villages (known as *imidugudu*[1] in Kinyarwanda). In the past, Rwandans lived scattered over the hills and not in villages as in other parts of Africa. The intent of the new policy is to increase the amount of land available for agricultural activities and encourage a shift towards large landholdings and commercial agriculture, but so far its negative impact on Rwandans and their ways of life has outweighed the positive development (Hilhorst and van Leeuwen 1999; Musahara 1999; RISD 1999a, 1999b).

The Rwanda Initiative for Sustainable Development (RISD) carried out this research to establish what rights in practice Rwandan women have to access and own land. The study began from a broad notion of rights, considering what is due to a person according to culture, custom, Rwandan statutory law and international human rights law.

The specific objectives of this RISD study were to establish the main forces influencing women's access to and control over land; to understand how ordinary citizens as well as decision-makers (such as government authorities) at the local and national level conceive of women's land rights; and to delineate the vectors that protect or guarantee women's control of land. Of particular interest were the influences of cultural values, customary norms and laws, religious institutions and norms, statutory law and national policies in relation to the actual reality on the ground. Particular attention was paid to cultural ideas regarding women and their capacity to control land, the two major customary systems (*ubukonde* and *igikingi*) controlling land tenure in Rwanda, statutory law controlling land tenure in Rwanda (in particular the new inheritance law promulgated in 1999), recent national policies impacting land tenure (in particular the villagisation policy implemented since 1994), the mechanisms by which disputes over land are resolved and the impact of women's associations and cooperatives on women's access to land.

Research Design and Methodology

This RISD study was based on the complete model approach. The research design was developed to include as much field research and grassroots input as possible, in addition to standard literature reviews and national policy analysis. To account for substantive regional differences in terms of cultural and family norms, customary land practices, economic activities based on different ecological zones and implementation of national policies influencing land distribution, research was carried out in communes in four regions of the country.

The first region was Kinigi commune in Ruhengeri prefecture. Customary land tenure in northwestern Rwanda (*ubukonde*) differs substantially from other regions. This region is also known for a 'traditional' acceptance of polygamy due, in part, to intense cultivation of the especially fertile soil. Kinigi commune was in the thick of the insurgency crisis from 1996–99 because it borders the Birunga National Park, which was the operational base for rebel forces trying to destabilise the Rwandan government. Insecurity from the insurgency significantly influenced implementation of the villagisation policy here.

The second region was Mugina commune in Gitarama prefecture. This commune was chosen because it falls in the central region of Rwanda, controlled by *igikingi* customary land tenure. In addition, Mugina has known two different national land policies, the *paysannat* system of the First Republic, and the villagisation policy of the post-genocide government. Finally, RISD has a long-term sustainable development project in the commune and wanted to build up its knowledge base of local land issues.

The third region was Kahi commune in Umutara prefecture. Kahi is a new commune created following the 1994 genocide and war. It is a semi-arid region, largely settled by old-caseload refugees[2] from Uganda and dominated by pastoral activities, although there is also some agriculture. Prior to 1994, most of Kahi commune was part of the Akagera National Park.

The fourth and final region was Kigarama commune in Kibungo prefecture. This commune reflects the particularities of Kibungo prefecture, which has been almost completely 'villagised' according to the national villagisation policy. The installation of large numbers of old-caseload refugees, as well as the return of new-caseload[3] refugees, required land sharing and redistribution that have affected virtually the entire population.

Women's rights in these different cultural, ecological and socio-economic settings were studied in the context of family and community norms, with a view to establishing the nature of women's rights to access and/or control land and how these rights have been influenced by custom, religion and statutory law. The study also focused on whether initiatives to raise awareness about family property laws have influenced opinions on these issues, and what the level of women's participation has been in land policy formulation and the land reform process.

Primary data collection for the study was conducted at the grassroots level in the four communes using participatory rural appraisal (PRA) techniques. The field research teams used direct observation, open-ended interviews, semi-structured focus group sessions, mapping, diagramming and other PRA exercises to gather data from local residents, community elders, communal officials, elected members of grassroots structures, church members and leaders, agricultural cooperatives, members and leaders of local women's associations and other organisations.

Literature reviews were conducted to study the evolution of land law and land policy in Rwanda from pre-colonial days through the colonial and post-colonial periods. These reviews included published statutory law, government studies and reports, non-governmental and intergovernmental organisation reports and studies, academic research, National University of Rwanda student theses and other materials.

At the national level, semi-structured interviews (SSI) were conducted with staff of relevant GOR ministries and other GOR institutions and commissions concerned with land, legal matters, women's affairs and human rights. SSIs were also carried out with representatives of international and national non-governmental organisations, UN agencies and other key informants knowledgeable about land, statutory law, customary practices, women's affairs, human rights and advocacy on land issues.

Following the field research, RISD conducted a focus group to seek input from representatives of selected government ministries and commissions, human rights and women's organisations and key informants knowledgeable about customary and statutory law, life in rural Rwanda and Rwandan history.

An initial version of this report was presented at a workshop on women and land held by RISD from 24–25 April 2001. This final study includes pertinent information gathered during that workshop, as well as the final recommendations and action plan endorsed by workshop participants.

A comment should be made about the research methodology *vis-à-vis* gender. Some participants in the workshop on women and land took offence at the idea that the workshop discussed women's access to and control over land to the exclusion of men. However, this study is based on a gender approach that neither privileges women over men nor excludes men from the picture. A gender approach looks at a person's position in society, in the family, in the economy and so on in relation to power. A gender approach includes the biological sex of a person (male versus female) combined with issues related to age, stage in life and even sexual orientation. For instance, with the division of labour in Rwandan society, children (*abana*) under the age of six years are assigned light tasks without much distinction between boys and girls. However, at a later stage in life, girls start doing household tasks like fetching water, and boys start looking after livestock and other energy-demanding tasks. In Rwandan society, women (*abategarugori*) can be said to have a different gendered position from widows (*abapfakazi*) although they share the same biological sex.

History of Land Tenure in Rwanda

Pre-colonial period: *ubukonde* and *igikingi* On the arrival of Europeans at the beginning of the twentieth century, two principal systems controlled land tenure in Rwanda: *ubukonde* in the north and northwest (currently Byumba, Gisenyi and Ruhengeri prefectures) and *igikingi* in central, eastern and southern Rwanda (Andre 1998: 142; Cyiza 2000). These systems were different, but shared notions of collective ownership of land among members of patrilineages (*imiryango*).

In the *ubukonde* system, people gained rights to large tracts of land by being the first to clear and valorise the land (known as *gukonda*). In this system, a lineage held rights to land corporately and major decisions about managing landholdings were taken by the lineage chef (*umutware w'umuryango* or, in speaking of land specifically, *umukonde*). The *abakonde* lineages held economic and political power over their *ubukonde* and could grant rights to others to use land in their territory through a form of clientship known as *ubugererwa* (Cyiza 2000). Clients were required to make payments to their patrons, most often in the form of a portion of the harvests or in manual labour in the patron's fields or enclosure (Newbury 1988: 79).

There were three specific types of *ubukonde*, including *ubukonde bw'inzogera* (hunting grounds), *ubukonde bw'inka* (grazing lands) and *ubukonde bw'isuka* (agricultural lands). In all three types, the *umukonde* (*ubukonde* owner) allowed others access to these lands in exchange for gifts and/or labour.

In the early nineteenth century, under the reign of Mwami Yuhi Gahindiro, another form of land tenure was introduced called *igikingi* (Newbury 1988: 81). When the colonialists arrived in Rwanda at the end of the nineteenth century, *igikingi* was the most common land tenure system in central and southern Rwanda. An *igikingi* was land distributed by the *mwami*[4] or his chiefs (*abatware b'umukenke*) on the approval of the *mwami* to either heroes (*intwari*) from war or other individuals commanding respect in society. *Ibikingi* were vast tracts of land designed for grazing cattle. During the pre-colonial period, these domains were especially under the control of important Tutsi pastoralists in the central and southern part of the kingdom. If the holder of an *igikingi* lost favour with the chief or lost his cattle through disease, mismanagement, or raiding, the chief seized his *igikingi* from him and gave it to someone else who had cattle (Cyiza 2000).

The recipient of an *igikingi* was expected to make regular gifts to the chief or *mwami* who had bestowed the *igikingi* on him. If his *igikingi* was transferred to another region, he would go and introduce himself to the new leader (called *gukeza*) and bring gifts. He also gave the new chief a cow, called *inka y'indabukirano*, to show him respect. Seasonal gifts (like pots of honey, milk and so on) were maintained in this relationship between patron and client. These obligations were fulfilled to stay on good terms with the chief, and included sending labourers to work at the home of the chief who had given the *igikingi*.

The holders of *ibikingi* had full control over the land and thus could partition it and allot plots (*amasambu*) to others in order to cultivate. These cultivators became clients and owed seasonal gifts and servitude to continue benefiting from the land bestowed on them. Following the harvest, the *igikingi* owner had the right to graze his herds in the fields before his client, even if the client had cattle (Cyiza 2000; Gasasira 1995: 38).

In the regions controlled by the *igikingi* land tenure system, land reserved for hunting was known as *ubukonde bw'inzogera*, as in the *ubukonde* system. The right to hunt on this land was granted by the *mwami* or a chief under his authority.

Colonial period In the colonial period, statutory laws regarding land ownership were introduced to institute land titles, but these laws only applied to foreigners, while the 'natives' still relied on customary law. Titled properties (*parcelles cadastrées*) were limited to the colonisers and the few Africans who could prove that they were 'civilized' (*civilisé*).[5] No Rwandan, not even the *mwami*, met the *civilisé* standard and thus Rwandans remained governed by customary law and could not receive land titles. Furthermore, the *mwami* would not accept a title to land he already considered to be his.[6] The majority of landowners according to statutory law during the colonial period were religious institutions, especially the Catholic and Protestant churches, a few colonists and the so-called Bahindi who had immigrated as traders from East Africa.

Transformations occurred in the customary systems of land tenure due to shifts in political power under colonial rule. In the early part of the twentieth century, with the added military backing of first German and then Belgian colonisers, the Mwami Yuhi Musinga consolidated the central court's domination of the formerly independent chiefs in the northwest. The *ubukonde* system transformed because of the greater political control of chiefs (*abatware b'abanyabutaka*) under the authority of the *mwami* and the central kingdom. As political control increased, the means of gaining *ubukonde* rights changed. In the early part of this evolution, land was still gained through *gukonda*, but the meaning of the term changed. Chiefs began granting *ubukonde* based on how far the lineage chief could shoot an arrow (*ubukonde bw'umuheto*) or their capacity to clear the bush using a machete (*ubukonde bw'umupanga*),[7] rather than on who cleared and claimed land independently. During this period, lineages began making gifts to political chiefs in the form of cattle and agricultural products, in order to be considered for land allocation. Over time, the *ubukonde* system continued to evolve. Eventually, chiefs partitioned (*gukebera*) the virgin land, which was often referred to as *igisagara*, and the beneficiaries of this scheme would then be called *abakonde*.[8]

In the 1930s, the *ubukonde* system of the northwest was officially replaced by the *igikingi* system, on orders of Mwami Yuhi Musinga (Andre 1998: 144). Yet many former *abakonde* in the northwest did not recognize the new official owners of the land, all of whom were chiefs (*abashefu n'abasusehfu* or *ibirongozi*) sent from the central court to ensure the incorporation of the northwest into the central kingdom. Conflict between the former and new landowners was great, but people bided their time, waiting for an opportunity to reclaim their lands (Cyiza 2000).

Under the *igikingi* system of land tenure, patrons became more and more demanding of clients, thanks to additional backing from the monarchical regime and the colonisers. With increasingly scarce land, people living under particularly stringent patrons could no longer 'vote with their feet', move to another region and become the client of a different patron (Andre 1998; Uvin 1998; Newbury 1988).

The consolidation of the *mwami* and the central court's power during the colonial period resulted in the loss of common lands, whether they were *ubukonde* or *igikingi*.

In addition, it transformed notions away from corporate lineage groups to nuclear family units. By introducing the head tax (charged to male heads of household), reinforcing local indigenous authorities' ability to require *corvée* labour for road building and land clearing and encouraging the cultivation of cash crops such as coffee and tea, the colonial government vested the responsibilities of the lineage group in individual adult men. Colonialism eroded the remaining institutions that gave women access to resources, and intensified the development of institutions where women's labour was appropriated by the rulers and by the state. By the end of the colonial period, the vast majority of Rwandans relied primarily on women's labour and women's activities to support households (Jefremovas 1991: 382).

Between 1952 and 1954, Mwami Mutara Rudahigwa abolished the *ubukonde* system of land tenure and required all abakonde (*ubukonde* owners) to share their land with the clients exploiting it. At the same time, the *mwami* abolished the *ubuhake* system of cattle clientship, but the *igikingi* system of land tenure and clientship remained more or less intact (Newbury 1988: 145–6).

In 1959, a movement against the monarchy and colonialism began. Up until the installation of the First Republic in 1962, Rwandan politics was punctuated by violence. In certain regions of the country, instances of ethnically motivated violence broke out. In most cases, it took the form of threats, beatings and the burning of houses, but in some cases (such as Bugesera) there were massacres. During the period 1959–62, many former *abakonde* in the northwest took advantage of the instability to evict the newer (and unrecognised) chiefs who had been installed by Mwami Yuhi Musinga (Cyiza 2000).

With the transformations in land systems throughout the colonial period and the introduction of a monetary economy, Rwandan notions about family and land began to change as well (van Hoyweghen 1999: 358). Yet the legal individualisation of land rights occurred late in the colonial period, during the transition from colonial to indigenous rule. First, in 1960, an administrative decree suspended the *igikingi* land tenure system and vested decisions over pasture lands first in the hands of the *sous-chefferie* and later in the hands of communal authorities. This suspension became a total suppression over time (Gasasira 1995: 38). An edict of 26 May 1961 officially abolished the *ubukonde* land tenure system and gave clients ownership rights over their land. In practice, however, cliental relationships still existed between patron and client. The client was still expected to pay rent or dues on an annual basis to the patron, but the edict restricted the prerogatives of excessive patrons and protected the clients' rights to remain on the land (Gasasira 1995: 37–8). The long-term result of these two laws was the parcelling-out of lands held corporately into individually held agricultural plots. With the end of colonialism, there was an attempt to register land with communal authorities through ministerial instructions (No. 66/ORG of 26 April 1961) from the Interior Ministry. This attempt failed because the circular was never published. Thus these instructions were unknown by local authorities or by citizens (Gasasira 1995: 6).

First and Second Republics From about 1960 onwards, the colonial administration and then the independent Rwandan government introduced the *paysannat* system in some areas. This system had first been attempted in the early 1950s, when the government called on people to live in *insisiro*, which were agglomerations of people originating from one ancestor. This system did not become popular, as there were no financial or other incentives for people to move. Under the *paysannat* system, the government distributed plots of land to nuclear families. In most instances, recipients were young men who did not have sufficient land of their own to establish households. In the *paysannat*, houses were built in rows along a road and were surrounded by the families' fields. Families received a certificate 'guaranteeing' their rights to use the land as long as they met certain requirements, which varied from region to region. These *paysannats* usually had individual agricultural holdings as well as communal fields where cash crops were cultivated by the entire settlement (Olson 1994).

The *paysannat* system was limited to regions where the population was not dense and to uninhabited tracts of land. For example, the majority of Mugina commune was a royal hunting ground (*ubukonde bw'inzogera*) until the end of colonialism and thus uninhabited. In the 1960s, land in Mugina commune was distributed to peasants in the *paysannat* system. Each household was required to cultivate a certain number of hectares of coffee, and they were required to keep the land intact as a single parcel. In the Mugina *paysannats*, unmarried daughters and widows were allowed to inherit the house and land, but married daughters were required to live from their husbands' land.[9] Today in Mugina commune, recipients of *paysannat* landholdings still retain the rights to use and exploit this land. Many people even have the original certificates they received to guarantee their rights to exploit the land. Yet, in contravention of these original agreements, many *paysannat* recipients have divided the land among children or sold portions of their plots to others.

The *paysannat* system was carried out as a pilot project financed by the Belgian government. For several reasons, the Rwandan government did not implement it in all regions of the country. First, it was politically difficult to implement in regions that had already been settled as this would require the redistribution of land. Second, the financing for *paysannats* eventually evaporated because other financiers were not interested.

With increasing land scarcity due to the population explosion, the 1970s saw growing out-migration from Gikongoro, Gisenyi, Kibuye and Ruhengeri to the east and central parts of Rwanda. In the 1980s, this migration from the highlands to the foothills continued and began spilling over into the savannah areas of the east. Because the soil quality and rainfall were lower in the savannah, agricultural productivity was lower (Bart 1993; Olson 1994). Historically, the eastern savannah areas of Bugesera, Kibungo and Umutara have known numerous famines. Today these areas remain particularly vulnerable to food insecurity.

Post-conflict and Post-genocide Context

The political crisis of 1959–61 led to the flight of thousands of Rwandan refugees, who left behind their property and land. Subsequent political crises, especially in 1964 and 1973, forced other Rwandans to follow suit. The return of these refugees became an important political question for the Habyarimana regime in the 1980s. Negotiations for the return of these refugees failed (Hilhorst and van Leeuwen 1999: 6), and Habyarimana maintained the position that their return was impossible because of land scarcity.

Beginning in October 1990, the Rwandan Patriotic Front (RPF) waged a war against Habyarimana's regime to unseat his government and to guarantee refugees' right of return to Rwanda. Around the same time, a multiparty system was instituted inside Rwanda, allowing the political opposition to take to the public stage. In 1993, the Rwandan government, opposition political parties and the RPF reached a peace agreement and signed the Arusha Accords. These Accords were not implemented, as foreseen, because of stalling on the side of Habyarimana's government and the increasing power of hardliners in the government who did not want to share power with the opposition or the RPF.

This crisis culminated in the 1994 genocide and war. These upheavals brought about the almost total destruction of Rwanda's physical and administrative infrastructure. The genocide ended when the RPF took control of most Rwandan territory in July 1994. About two million Rwandans fled the RPF forces and went into exile, along with the genocide planners and killers (Hilhorst and van Leeuwen 1999: 6). They stayed in refugee camps in Tanzania and Zaire.

The new Rwandan government, known as the government of national unity, called all Rwandans to return from exile. Between 1994–96, approximately 800,000 Rwandan refugees flowed in from neighbouring countries (Hilhorst and van Leeuwen 1999: 6). Most of them had spent many years in exile and some had never seen Rwanda. Upon return, most returnees were initially obliged to occupy properties abandoned by those who had fled in 1994. Eventually, many of these exiles were settled in *imidugudu* (villages) constructed by the United Nations High Commission for Refugees (UNHCR) and international non-governmental organisations (NGOs).

In late 1996 and early 1997, the new-caseload refugees returned en masse from the camps in Tanzania (an estimated 480,000) and Zaire (an estimated 720,000) (Hilhorst and van Leeuwen 1999: 6). At the time, the GOR promised to respect these new returnees' entitlements to property abandoned in 1994. This resulted in an immediate need for housing that was answered by the *imidugudu* settlement policy (Hilhorst and van Leeuwen 1999: 6).

The 1993 Arusha Accords had provided for the return of Rwandan exiles by creating a villagisation programme, known as *imidugudu*, as a means to resettle Rwandans who were willing to come back to Rwanda. This programme resembled the *paysannat* system and had some of the same intentions: to group the population in the hopes of intensifying and modernising traditional agriculture, and to provide services more easily to a grouped population. An added aim was to reduce conflicts over land. The 1993 Arusha Accords stipulated, in Article 4 of the chapter relative to the repatriation of refugees, that refugees returning after more than ten years should not reclaim their lost property but instead be resettled in unoccupied land with government assistance.

Following the end of the war in 1994, the new Rwandan government began to plan *imidugudu* sites with the support of UNHCR (Hilhorst and van Leeuwen 1999: 8), but as there was no urgent housing need, progress was slow. Finally in December 1996, the Cabinet passed a resolution making *imidugudu* the only form of rural settlement allowed. The subsequent ministerial directive (MINITRAPE 01/97) explicitly stated that 'building on a plot other than MUDUGUDU is hereby prohibited' (as quoted in RISD 1999a: 4). While the original conception of *imidugudu* in the 1993 Arusha Accords created grouped settlements in uninhabited lands, in 1996 the aim of national policy became to regroup the entire population in villages over time (Hilhorst and van Leeuwen 1999: 8). This new goal required the redistribution of land, but no policy was in place to handle such a redistribution. To date, the Rwandan government has not yet put into place a national land policy, although it is in the process of drafting one.

The problems and controversies of the *imidugudu* policy are well documented elsewhere (Hilhorst and van Leeuwen 1999; Human Rights Watch 2001; Laurent and Bugnion 2000; Musahara 1999; RISD 1999a, 1999b). In the context of this study, RISD looked at this policy's implications for women's access to and control over land. Although RISD found problems with the policy in general, only its relevance to women's access to and control over land will be discussed.

Beneficiaries of the *imidugudu* housing programmes include shelterless people of all categories: old- and new-caseload returnees, genocide survivors afraid to return to the site of their homes before the war, those on whose land the *imidugudu* were constructed and young people seeking to set up homes apart from their parents (RISD 1999a: 8). For the most part, *imidugudu* have provided housing to female-headed households without discrimination. In many cases, genocide survivors, single mothers, widows and female-headed households were given preferential treatment in housing assistance through *imidugudu* resettlement. In some *imidugudu*, female-headed households far outnumber male-headed households. Some respondents in all regions complained that not enough housing assistance was provided to vulnerable groups such as the disabled, the elderly and widows. In Kinigi commune, some respondents complained that they were still living in grass shelters or tents with sheeting, because they were unable to build houses on their own. Widows find it particularly difficult to build houses when there are no programmes for the provision of labour or metal roofing.

Both those who have benefited from land redistribution and those who have given up land have objected at certain points. In certain instances, there has been injustice in land sharing, which has impacted women as well as men. Land belonging to influential people in the Rwandan government was not tampered with and some powerful individuals among the returnees got larger shares of land than others.[10] RISD found that the *imidugudu* policy did not result in widespread discrimination against women in terms of allocation of land, but in certain instances (especially in Kinigi commune), the elderly, widows and child-headed households (most of which are headed by girls) did not have the means to construct adequate housing for themselves and have not yet received any assistance to do so.

Use or Ownership?

The current Rwandan land tenure system is two-fold, consisting of customary and statutory land tenure systems. Gasasira (1995) links this duality of legal settlements to 'the discrimination established by the colonial authorities between native populations and foreigners. Foreigners' lands were submitted to statute law whereas those belonging to natives were governed by customs' (Gasasira 1995: 7). Gasasira's accurate analysis leaves Rwanda with a difficult legacy to manage, especially in the post-genocide context.

In the comprehension of most Rwandans, they own the land that they occupy and use. This is land that they have inherited, bought or taken possession of through government-sponsored land distribution (or redistribution) such as the *paysannat* system or the newer *imidugudu* policy. Yet according to the 1976 Decree Number 09/76, all land in Rwanda belongs to the state (aside from cadastral properties) and citizens retain only usufruct rights. This same decree prohibits any Rwandan from buying or selling customary rights to land without authorisation from the Ministry of Land. Nevertheless, Rwandans have regularly sold and bought these rights without asking for such authorisation, and conceive of themselves as the owners of such land. The government-sponsored land distribution programmes (the *paysannat* and *imidugudu* systems) are not governed by any specific Rwandan legislation, but rather reside on government policy, general understanding and occasionally contracts between local government bodies and individual landholders (Gasasira 1995).

As will be demonstrated, the fundamental contradiction between popular conceptions and state practices is at the root of many land disputes today. Rwandans familiar with statutory laws and the court system and with economic means may exploit the current situation to take land away from someone with a customary or traditional claim to it. Women are particularly vulnerable in this situation, especially when they do not have a legal (civil) marriage to protect their rights. With the further complications arising from the 1994 genocide and war, the massive displacement of the population and the new villagisation policy, land conflicts arise more and more frequently, because there are more legitimate disputes over property and because certain opportunists want to manipulate the situation in their favour.

Neither colonial statutory law nor post-colonial statutory law specifically protected women's rights to land. In virtually all instances, it was assumed that the men associated with women, whether fathers, brothers or husbands, would protect their rights. In many instances, statutory law specifically limited women's rights. The laws on commerce stated that women could not engage in commercial activities or in paid labour or enter into a contract without the express consent of their spouses (Article 4 of Law No. 2/08/1913). In 1998, this law was modified slightly (Number 42/1998) to allow women to open a bank account without their husbands' consent (United Nations Fund for Children 1988), but women still did not have the right to enter into contractual agreement or work without their husbands' consent.

While these statutory limitations to women's rights to own property or control financial resources were technically eliminated by the 1999 inheritance law (Number 22/99), it is unclear whether limitations still exist for married women in the community of property regime.

Women's Access to and Control over Land

According to Rwandan custom, women's land rights are guaranteed by men because they are dependent upon the men in their families; they are 'managed' but also protected by their fathers, then their husbands and finally by their male children. In general, land was inherited patrilineally from father to sons (Gasasira 1995). Although land was held commonly by the lineage, each male descendant was allocated a plot for constructing a house and fields for cultivation. Forests and grazing land remained the common holding of the lineage, and the lineage chief (*umutware w'umuryango*) managed this common holding. This practice maintained the family's legacy intact, but also guaranteed the sons' rights to marry and procreate. In turn, women were guaranteed access to land through their husbands' families.

When a woman was married, she automatically gained access to her husband's fields to cultivate for her husband, their children and herself. If, or when, her husband died, a widow remained on the husband's land, holding it in trust for her male children. If the widow was still within her reproductive years, levirate marriage (a brother of the deceased husband marrying the widow) was often practised. Through levirate marriage, the brother-in-law became responsible for the two separate households, but he produced children in place of his brother (the sons he produced with his brother's wife were considered his brother's sons and not his own). Yet levirate marriage sometimes caused conflicts between the different children's competing interests. If there were no children, a widow most often returned to her own family in the hopes of marrying again. Thus, according to

Rwandan customary practices, a widow possessed usufruct rights over the land of the deceased husband until her sons were mature enough to manage the family property. These usufruct rights were conditional on a widow's 'good conduct', that is to say, they lasted as long as she remained faithful to her husband's lineage either through sexual abstinence or levirate marriage.

There were other provisions by which women could gain access to land. In many regions of Rwanda, a woman could receive outright gifts of land from her father or use of land from her father's family. For example, before the genocide, a woman, married or not, could at times receive land 'as a gift (*urwibutso*) from her elderly father. The gesture [wa]s denoted by the verb *kuraga*' (Pottier 1997: 17). In Ruhengeri, a newly wed girl could receive a gift of land known as *intekeshwa* from her parents when they came to help her 'get used to her new home' (*gutekesha*) following her wedding ceremony.[11] Similarly, a married woman in Ruhengeri would often receive a gift of land known as *inkuri* when she presented a newborn baby to her father's family.[12] Both of these land gifts remained the outright property of the woman and were inherited by her sons. In other regions of Rwanda, gifts made on these occasions were most often made in the form of cattle, so did not have the same implications for land access and ownership as in the northwest.

Other forms of access to land existed for women in the form of temporary user rights over land held by their fathers' patrilineage. For example, a daughter rejected by her husband or his family (known as *indushyi*) could be given a portion of land (called *ingarigari* in the centre and south or *ingaragaza* in the northwest) from lands held in reserve by the patrilineage for such emergencies (Andre 1998; de Lame 1996; Pottier 1997).[13] Similarly, a woman who never married and did not bear children (*uwagumiwe*) could also receive an allocation of land from the lineage's holdings.[14] The *ingarigari* land was controlled by the lineage chief (*umutware w'umuryango*) who was supposed to permit access to it in the interests of the entire lineage. According to Pottier, a woman 'would have access to it for as long as she was deemed in need, if necessary, for life. After her death however, the land would be reclaimed by her late husband's nearest patrikin' (Pottier 1997: 17). Yet, according to RISD field research, the *ingarigari* land reverted to the woman's brothers when she no longer needed it (in the case that she remarried or was reconciled with the husband who had rejected her.)[15]

Even before the genocide, these cultural protections for women's access to land were under attack. In general, Rwandan customary norms and practices allocated plots to women and other secondary right holders only as long as this land was not needed by the household. If a man or his family found themselves in need of land, a woman's field (allocated under the customary systems delineated above) could be taken from her for reallocation. Constraints on women's access to land were heightened when land became increasingly scarce, and men's landholdings came under pressure.

Conceptions of Women's Land Rights Today

Custom plays a major role in determining land claims today in rural Rwanda. Among rural respondents, both men and women held a strong conviction that the family land and property belong to the head of the family (*umutware w'urugo*), who is often a man, but in certain circumstances can be a woman.[16] This is a significant shift from earlier ideas that land belonged to the lineage and was controlled by the lineage chief.

Today, in most regions, land is considered to be family property and is used by either men or women in the best interests of the family. In an ideal situation, decisions about land are made through mutual understanding between husband and wife. Yet many male and female respondents declared that a woman could never be equal to a man in terms of knowing how best to manage family resources. They backed this argument by citing Genesis 2: 18, 20–23:

> *Kandi uwiteka Imana iravuga ati 'si byiza ko uyu muntu aba wenyine; reka muremere umufasha umukwiriye' … Uwiteka Imana isinziriza uwo muntu ubuticura, arasinzira: imukuramo urubavu rumwe, ihasubiza inyama: urwo rubavu Uwiteka Imana yakuye mure uwo muntu, iruhindura umugore imushyira uwo muntu. Aravuga ati 'uyu ni igufwa ryo mu magufwa yanjye, N'akara ko mu mara yanjye. Azitwa Umugore kuko yakuwe mu mugabo.'*[17]

> The Lord God said 'it is not good for the man to be alone; I will make a helper suitable for him' … So the Lord caused the man to fall into a sleep; and while the man was sleeping, He took one of the man's ribs and closed up the place with flesh. Then the Lord God made a woman from the rib He had taken out of the man. The man said 'this is now bone of my bone and flesh of my flesh; she shall be called "woman" for she was taken out of man.' (Genesis 2: 18, 20–23)

Thus for many Rwandans, Christianity (and in particular Roman Catholicism) has been synthesised with traditional notions to justify the belief that women should act as a companion or a helper whose duty is to assist men in effecting their duties.

Although many Rwandan women accept the notion that women should be less than equal partners in marriage, they insist that land and property are held in common by a husband and his wife and that decisions about it should be taken together. Yet most male respondents argued that men have greater rights over land as land has 'always belonged to men'. Men used several Rwandan proverbs to justify their arguments:

> *Umugore abyara umuryango w'ahandi.*
> A woman gives birth to an outside lineage (and thus cannot herself own land in that lineage).

> *Umugore ntagira ubwoko, afata ubw'umugabo.*
> A woman does not have an identity, she takes her husband's.

Nta mugore ugabana iz'iwabo, azihabwamo.
A woman does not inherit from her family, it is given to her.[18]

In general, men believe that women cannot be landowners because they cannot go to war to become heroes (*intwari*).[19] In men's conception, women have no legitimate claims to land ownership or control – they have access to land only through their relationships to men. A few respondents did, however, cite two historical exceptions. In one case, Nyirakigwene, a woman in Gitarama, inherited cattle, *igikingi* and power upon the death of her husband. While her husband was still alive, Nyirakigwene had shown her capacity to 'be a man'[20] and exploit resources effectively. In the second case, from Kibungo, Nyirakabuga had influence because she had once been the wife of Mwami Yuhi Musinga.

In Kahi commune, Umutara prefecture, research respondents, especially men, were outspoken about women's lesser rights to family property. They asserted that men and women could only have equal rights to land as brothers and sisters inheriting their father's land. Yet in marriage, women could not hold equal claim over the home or land, because 'it is men who toil to secure the needs of the home', while women come and find everything in situ 'except for a few domestic utensils such as plates, saucepans and her clothing'. Their conclusion was that men own everything and have the right to own it.[21]

The proverbs used by respondents, as well as their generalisations about women and land, point to the risk for Rwandan women *vis-à-vis* land: their access to land depends on their good relations with men, whether they are their fathers, their husbands, their husbands' families or their brothers. While women accept that it is 'good enough' to use their husbands' lands, they recognise that their rights are guaranteed only if they have loving husbands who respect them. Furthermore, the former customs through which women gained land independently have largely passed away, due to the problems of land scarcity and population pressures. Before the genocide, in the early 1990s, *ingarigari* land was still given to daughters, but their brothers were likely to pressure them into giving the land up early (Pottier 1997: 17). Since the genocide, however, women and girls are unlikely to have access to their own lineage's land except in cases where everyone else in the lineage was killed.[22]

Vulnerable Populations

A traditional notion in Rwanda is that of protecting 'vulnerable' individuals, including girls rejected by their husbands (*indushyi*), widows and orphans. Rwandan culture respected provisions to guarantee land, and therefore survival, to these individuals. This notion still exists today. In ranking exercises performed in Kahi and Kinigi communes, respondents indicated that widows with children should have the highest priority in receiving land.[23] Yet the realities of the post-genocide context have challenged this notion in practice. Today, widows, orphans and women whose husbands are in prison constitute the vast majority of family heads of households. The intensity of need is such that families and communities are not capable of assisting all those in need. Thus, in some cases, widows, orphans and other vulnerable individuals are denied their cultural and statutory rights to land and other resources.

The GOR, the United Nations, other inter-governmental organisations and international NGOs have tried to take into account the special needs of vulnerable individuals. For example, in many instances, implementation of the *umudugudu* policy attempted to assist vulnerable individuals. In the communes involved in the study, women-headed households received equal consideration for land grants with male-headed households under the *umudugudu* policy.[24] In Kigarama commune, Kibungo prefecture, certain vulnerable individuals were given special treatment in consideration for land grants. Single women considered 'too old for marriage', widows, genocide survivors and other female-headed households received land grants (between 4,800 and 1,000 square metres) equal to those received by male-headed households. Despite this 'equal treatment' *vis-à-vis* land redistribution in Kibungo, many former landholders in this region believe that their rights to land have been violated. The study was unable to establish whether women or other vulnerable individuals were unfairly treated in the redistribution of land they owned before implementation of the *imidugudu* policy.

One ethnic group of the population historically vulnerable to landlessness is the Batwa. In most regions of Rwanda, Batwa historically lived on the edges of natural forests, which they exploited for their survival through hunting and gathering. Over time, the natural forests have been reduced and most Batwa do not have sufficient land to sustain themselves through agricultural activities. They make their living from menial day labour and, in some places, pottery making. Batwa suffer from social marginalisation. For example, most other Rwandans will not share food or drink with them during festivities. Batwa also tend to live separate from others. To date, most of the land redistribution policies in Rwanda have ignored the Batwa. In Kinigi commune, RISD found that the Batwa have small plots with only enough space for a small grass shelter or house. They do not have land to cultivate.

The study also found that women who had not had a legally recognised marriage were the most vulnerable to losing their access to or control over land. The difficulties of these women are discussed below.

The Marriage Problem

Today, marriage is a multi-step process requiring three different ceremonies: a customary marriage ceremony, a civil marriage ceremony and a religious marriage ceremony. To be considered a 'real' marriage by most Rwandans, any of these three steps can be followed. Yet Rwandan law gives legal recognition only to civil marriages held before government authorities. Few marriages in the countryside today receive legal recognition, because few people go through the legal marriage process. Before the Rwandan Constitution of 1979, all three forms of marriage were legally recognised and protected.[25]

A customary marriage ceremony consists of a set of rituals culminating in the transfer of a cow or other property from the husband's family to the bride's family. Often, this part of the marriage ceremony is respected by Rwandans either in the regular exchange of bridewealth before other stages of the marriage ceremony, or, in instances of 'forced marriage', the exchange of cattle or other goods after the fact. The majority of marriages in the countryside today meet this minimum requirement of marriage in the social sense. However, marriages based on this exchange of bridewealth are not recognised by the Rwandan state. Thus in the event of divorce or other rupture, women's rights to land and property are not protected by law. Children born in such an arrangement have legal rights over their father's land or property only if they can prove their paternity, or if the father or his family accept paternity. In such marriage arrangements, women gain usufruct rights to their husbands' land. These rights depend upon the goodwill of her husband or his family, or eventually on her children's inheritance rights to such property.

A civil marriage ceremony consists of going to the commune office and taking an oath on the Rwandan national flag in the presence of local government officials. The marriage documents require the reporting of the amount of bridewealth paid by the husband's family to the woman's family.[26] In Rwanda today, few newly married couples are legally married. For example, in Kigarama commune, Kibungo prefecture, fewer than 60 per cent of women are legally married, according to communal authorities.[27] Numerous reasons were cited for the low number of legal marriages. The most frequently cited was the expense involved in a legal marriage. Such a marriage requires not only the bridewealth of the traditional marriage, but also commune fees for marriage certificates and the other identity papers required. Although not regularly enforced today, in the pre-genocide period young men had to prove that they had a house and plot in order to marry legally. In addition, married couples have the social obligation of throwing parties for both the customary and civil marriage ceremonies. This sort of money is out of the reach of the vast majority of rural Rwandans today. Other reasons cited were cultural or social. For example, in the case of recently repatriated Rwandans (old-caseload refugees) living in Kahi commune, Umutara prefecture, legal marriage was felt to be 'too legalistic'. Respondents said that going to the commune and 'swearing on the national flag' did not have any relevance to marriage.[28] The vast majority of these returnees came from Uganda, where common law and traditional marriages are legally recognised.

Polygamous marriage exists to a limited extent. In the northwest, it was fairly common and traditionally accepted. The fertile land and need for agricultural labour made polygamous marriage useful for men with large tracts of land or enough wealth to procure additional land. In other regions of the country, polygamous marriage was less common, but not unknown. Prior to the genocide, each wife in a polygamous marriage generally had a house and fields for her and her children. This form of marriage was limited to wealthy men, as other men could not afford to buy sufficient land to maintain several households.

Rwandan law does not allow for polygamous marriage and requires all legal marriages to be monogamous. This has the effect that all additional wives remain in informal marriage arrangements that are not legally recognised. Second and third wives, as well as their children, are particularly vulnerable to losing access to land in cases of rupture with or death of the husband. In many instances, legal wives take advantage of their situation and attempt to take property and land away from additional wives. The only legal recourse in this instance is for the children of additional wives to secure legal recognition of their paternity. The new inheritance law has complicated this issue, because the legal wife must also agree to the paternity of these other children. Even if these 'illegitimate children' of polygamous marriages manage to secure legal paternity ties with their fathers, their claims to his property in inheritance disputes are much more limited than the children of legally recognised marriages.

Two cases from Kigarama commune in Kibungo prefecture illustrate the difficulties of polygamous marriages and the inconsistency in adjudicating conflicts over land arising from such marriages. In one case, decided by the Canton Court, Mukandoli was legally married to her husband and had children with him. Later, her husband married a second woman, Uwamahoro, who shared the family property with Mukandoli. Upon the husband's death, Mukandoli attempted to take all of the husband's land and property, leaving nothing for the second wife and her child. The court decided that the two women must share the land, holding it in trust for their children, who were the rightful heirs with equal rights. In a second case, Munyangoga and his wife Mukankusi migrated from another region to settle in Kigarama commune. On their arrival, they secured a piece of land and began exploiting it. Later, Munyangoga married a second wife and brought her to occupy the same land as his first wife. The first wife, Mukankusi, filed a complaint and brought the case before the Canton Court. This time the court ruled in favour of the first wife and forced the second woman to leave and find another property, whether or not her husband could help her.[29]

Rwandan law does not allow for common law marriage, nor does it protect women's rights in cohabitation or in informal marriage arrangements. Yet the majority of Rwandan women are now or have in the past been 'married' in a social sense. They do not receive the legal protections afforded by a civil (and thus legal) marriage. Accordingly, the majority of Rwandan women are left vulnerable to the goodwill of their husbands and their husbands' families to ensure their access to land. Numerous conflicts over land adjudicated by the courts and local government officials concern women or children who have lost their usufruct rights to land as a result of informal marriage situations. According to the president of the Canton Court in Kinigi commune, 200 cases have been received so far by the court, among which 190 are related to land and 30 per cent involve women claiming their rights over land.

In a recent case heard by the Butare Court of First Instance, a woman had been married and cohabitating with a man for 18 years, but they had never legalised the marriage at the commune office. The woman already had a child from a previous liaison with another man. This girl lived with her mother, her mother's husband and their children. The man died in exile in Zaire in 1996. Upon return to Rwanda with their children, the woman went back to their house and land. In 1998, her husband's brothers forced her and the children to leave the fields, and asked the woman to leave the house along with the girl who was not from the same father. The brothers-in-law said that they would take their brother's children and raise them, but they no longer wanted the woman to use the house or fields. The woman first went to local officials, who adjudicated the case through *gacaca*.[30] The *gacaca* process found in favour of the woman and children and the brothers were ordered to allow them to return to the fields and stay in the house. The brothers never complied with the decision, so the woman took her case to the legal court system. So far, the tribunal has not yet decided the case. Women living in informal marriages are particularly vulnerable to losing their access to land.

New Inheritance Law

After a long battle by children's and women's rights groups and the Ministry of Gender and Women in Development, the Rwandan Transitional National Assembly promulgated a new law to give equal inheritance rights to male and female children with respect to inheriting their parents' land and property. It supplemented the civil code and was published in the *Official Gazette* of the Republic of Rwanda in November 1999, thus becoming law (Rwanda 1999). This new law created three different property regimes within legal marriage to replace the previous system.

In the previous system, all property was held as community property within marriage, and both spouses were meant to take decisions about resources in the interest of the family. But in many cases, the husband alone managed the financial resources and property of the family. In general, women were happy with the arrangement, relieved that they did not have the responsibility and believing that their husbands acted in their and their children's best interests. In some instances, however, men abused this right and used family resources to maintain mistresses or second wives, or tried to take over resources gained through the wife's commercial ventures for other purposes (Jefremovas 1991).

The 1999 inheritance law established three different property regimes in marriage: community property, separation of property and limited community property. A couple must choose a property regime at the time of their civil marriage ceremony before communal authorities. In community property, all property of either spouse becomes the community property of the household. In separation of property, each spouse manages his or her property separately and contributes to the household proportionally according to his or her means. In the limited community property regime, each spouse inventories his or her contribution to the community property of the marriage. This community property falls under the laws for community property regime, while other assets remain as individual property adjudicated according to the laws for separation of property.

The major change in this law comes in the areas of inheritance, where male and female children are given equal rights to inherit property. According to Rwandan customary practice, only male children inherit, because female children are expected to benefit from their husbands' land and property. The equality between the sexes guaranteed by the new law includes bequests made prior to the death of the parents (Article 42) and the division of property upon the death of a parent (Article 50).

The law attempts to preserve an important aspect of Rwandan tradition *vis-à-vis* inheritance of land. According to customary practice, a father divides his property before his death and allocates land to each of his sons, so that each son can build his house and marry.[31] The father retains a portion of the legacy to maintain himself, his wife and minor children. This portion of the land is then divided on his death and the sons are expected to support their mother. Article 43 of the new law preserves this practice, but includes girl children in the division of property. The Article states that 'all children, without distinction between girls and boys, alive or where deceased before parents their descendants, excluding those banished due to misconduct or ingratitude, have a right to the partition made by their ascendants'.

A major weakness of the new law is that it only governs instances of legal marriage, whereas a significant majority of marriages in Rwanda today are not legal. A second weakness is that it guarantees the inheritance rights only of legitimate children, as stated in Article 50: 'all legitimate children of the "de cujus", in accordance with civil laws, inherit in equal parts without any discrimination between male and female children'. In instances where a man had more than one wife, with only one legal wife, the 'illegitimate children' (the children of the non-legal marriages) do not have legally protected inheritance rights.

The study's field research found that Rwandans, particularly rural Rwandans, were confused by the new inheritance law and its motivations. Most respondents had heard about the new law on the radio, but they had no detailed information. Their general understanding was that it gave male and female children equal rights to inherit the family property, but they did not know about the three different marriage regimes or other details of the law. Ownership and inheritance of land is not treated under the new inheritance law, as Rwandan law states that all land is the property of the Rwandan state. Although rural Rwandans' main concern is land, the new inheritance law does not address this issue. Because of these problems, most rural respondents felt that the new inheritance law is applicable only to urban Rwandans.

There are many cultural and customary impediments to implementation of this law for the reason that most rural Rwandans do not understand its underlying motivations. While both women and men believe that children should be treated equally in matters concerning the sharing of family property, they worry about the problems caused by land scarcity and small landholdings within a family. If a family has small landholdings and must include female children in the division of these properties, the resulting portions of land will be too small to sustain families. In general, men believe that the law should not be applied, because there is not enough land to be distributed among all children. Furthermore, they believe that the law is unfair because women will have two different shares of land (one from their parents and one through their husbands), while a man will have only the share inherited from his parents. Significantly, men generally do not believe that women, on their own, have the capacity to exploit land and property effectively.[32]

One case in Kigarama commune illustrates that men do not believe that their male children should inherit equally, much less their female children. Aloys Nyiringabo, 76 years old, has been married to Agnace Uzamukunda for over 44 years and they have nine children (four boys and five girls). Nyiringabo had already distributed plots to each of his sons so that they could build their houses and marry. He recently made a will giving all his remaining property (his own house and fields) to his first-born son. He made this bequest because he expects his son to take care of his sisters and mother.[33] If he and his wife are legally married, they fall within the community property regime, the only property regime that existed prior to the 1999 inheritance law. As long has Nyiringabo's will meets the requirements set forth in the 1999 inheritance law, his bequest should be respected by the courts.

In general, women agree that girls should use their husbands' lands and should not inherit from their own families' lands. Female respondents explained that only women who fail to marry, or rejected women (*indushyi*), should claim their customary portions of family lands. Most female respondents believe that women should not have equal shares of family lands as long as they are still married. However, women emphasised that they have a right to claim and use family lands if they do not have husbands or are rejected by their husbands. Male respondents, on the other hand, did not mention this customary right in the context of the new inheritance law. Rural women said that the inheritance law can only work in urban areas where both men and women work, or for wealthy families with large landholdings.

RISD found virtually no cases where the new inheritance law has played a role in adjudicating disputes over land. One case in Kinigi commune, Ruhengeri prefecture, involved the new inheritance law. The Canton Court made a judgment attempting to apply the new law, but it is unclear whether the law was appropriately applied since it is not retroactive. In the case, a man had two wives, one who produced only girls and the second who produced one son. On the death of the parents, the son inherited all the family land without giving any portion to the half-sisters. After the introduction of the new inheritance law, one of the half-sisters claimed her mother's share of the land, arguing that she was the rightful heir to her mother's land, even after a period of 20 years. Although local officials and the family elders decided that the girl should not have a portion of the land, the Canton Court gave a small portion of the land to the half-sister and left the rest for the brother, with the provision that he would have to share more of it if his sister was in need. It is unclear why the new inheritance law had any bearing on the decision of the case, as the death of the parents occurred well before this law came into effect.[34]

In general, the new inheritance law faces resistance, because of its collision with prevailing customs in terms of conceptions of marriage and inheritance. The question of the three property regimes poses problems for young couples planning to marry. In most cases, men do not bring up the question with their fiancées and assume that women will accept the community property regime since it is the 'custom'. Women often assume that the men will manage the family's financial resources in the best interests of everyone, so they do not bring up the question before marriage either. If women do have concerns about the property regime, they are often afraid to bring it up because they feel 'lucky' that they have fiancés and do not want to anger them.[35] Even where fiancés receive pre-marital counselling (for example, in the Catholic Church), they are reluctant to discuss the issue of property regimes, either through fear of creating conflict before the wedding ceremonies or because they assume that they will never have conflicts or problems over financial resources.[36]

Researchers found that the vast majority of respondents were ill-informed about the new inheritance laws and the three different property regimes available. Girls and women in particular are ignorant of the rights guaranteed them by the new inheritance law. The law does not address the problems of women who are not in legalised marriages, nor does it protect the rights of women involved in or children born of polygamous marriages.

Resolution of Conflicts over Land

As the land tenure system in Rwanda amalgamates customary practices and statutory law, there are several mechanisms for resolving land disputes. These include appealing to family councils and *gacaca*, to local authorities or to courts.

Rwandans often begin by appealing to one body and continue appealing to another, more official, body if they are not satisfied with the outcome.

Most disputes are initially tabled in family councils (*imiryango*) where they are often resolved through *gacaca*. However, this type of *gacaca* should not be confused with the legalised *gacaca* currently being put into place by the GOR to hear the cases of the more than 100,000 people currently imprisoned and accused of genocide. *Gacaca* as customary conflict resolution involves calling together the family elders and other wise people from the hills. Everyone involved in the case gathers in the backyard of the family enclosure where *agacaca*, a short grass, used to grow (hence the name *gacaca*). The group then listens to testimony from the two sides of the case and calls other witnesses as necessary. In general, everyone is given the chance to speak, and the group then comes to a consensual decision about how to resolve the conflict. While still widely practised today, this customary *gacaca* has no legal basis. The decisions are not legally binding and thus depend on the goodwill of those involved in the conflict to back up the group's decisions.

For cases not resolved by *gacaca*, or where one of the parties is not happy with the decision, people often seek redress from local authorities. The cases are forwarded gradually from the *nyumbakumi*,[37] to the *responsable* at the cell level, to the *conseiller* at the sector level, and finally to the burgomaster at the commune level. It is not uncommon during this process for people to try to influence the decision or outcomes by courting the favour of people at each level. The field research found that local authorities rely on customary law as well as statutory law to resolve land disputes. While allowing for fluidity in decision-making, this practice also invites partiality into the system.

If an individual decides to pursue the case in the legal system, he or she first files a complaint with the Canton Court. If the Canton Court is not operating, or if the case involves claims related to the genocide, it is forwarded immediately to the Court of First Instance. Decisions of the Canton Court can be appealed within a certain amount of time to the Court of First Instance. Decisions of the Court of First Instance can, in turn, be appealed to the Appellate Courts. Decisions made at the courts rely on statutory law in most cases, but recourse is made to customary law when the statutory law does not cover the dispute at hand.

Women's Strategies for Accessing Land

Beyond challenging the loss of land in the courts, women have adopted many other strategies to increase their access to land. Female genocide survivors often return to their own families' land. They feel safer living among the people they grew up with, where their surviving brothers can protect them. This strategy works well for genocide survivors who do not have many people left in their families, since land is abundant. In many instances, they are not capable of exploiting all the land available to them because they lack the necessary inputs in terms of labour, seed or other materials.

Another strategy adopted by many women is that of joining farming co-operatives or women's associations. Many of these organisations access land by renting fields with the money raised through contributions and membership dues. Alternatively, they are allocated state-owned fields by communal agricultural technicians and local authorities. Some of the organisations interviewed by RISD had initially planned to raise money to buy land. These aspirations have not been met, owning to low agricultural yields and lack of income from agricultural activities. Members also expressed fears over the conflicts that could arise if their organisations bought land.

Women in Kinigi commune explained that they prefer women's associations because often men are dishonest and want to dominate female membership. They said that often men are merely 'thieves', hoping to benefit from aid or credit programmes targeting women. Such men often steal whatever money or other inputs come from the programmes, leaving the women to explain or repay the loans on their own.

Another advantage of belonging to women's associations is assistance (especially agricultural inputs) from national and international NGOs. In the communes visited during the study's field research, women mentioned Asoferwa, Care International, Communal Development Fund (CDF), the Dutch Government, Ingabo, International Rescue Committee (IRC), Lutheran World Federation (LWF), the Ministry of Gender and Women in Development, Women in Transition (WIT) and World Vision.

Women mentioned numerous benefits of belonging to women's associations:

- Associations are a source of group counselling and education.
- Associations encourage women to be self-reliant by engaging them in income-generating activities and reducing men's responsibility to buying everything at home, and thus lead to women's increased status within the family.
- Through participation in the day-to-day planning and organisation of association, women improve their decision-making capacities.
- Women gain access to land for cultivation through membership.
- Cooperatives improve food security and lead to improved welfare of family members.
- Cooperatives are a source of short-term credit and savings to cope with family emergencies or large expenses.

Despite these advantages, women's associations still face challenges. In some instances, men do not want their wives to participate in cooperatives because they feel that they are a waste of time. Many women are discouraged from joining if their husbands are not supportive. Women sometimes face exploitation by men involved in the cooperatives. Because the associations' fields are located far from main roads, they have difficulty getting their produce to markets. They are forced to sell to middlemen at low prices because transportation is not available.

For poor women, it is often difficult to join associations because they cannot raise the necessary membership fees. Similarly, many women's cooperatives cannot find the required registration fee to pay at the commune office. This lack of registration puts them at a disadvantage, because the association is then denied access to communal land. In addition, agricultural inputs and other assistance coming from aid and credit organisations are channelled to officially registered cooperatives.

Land scarcity also affects women's associations. In Kinigi commune, one woman's association had lost its fields because an *umudugudu* was built on them. To date, the association has not received replacement fields.[38] In other regions, all communal land is already under cultivation and associations cannot find the capital necessary to rent fields from other people.

Relying on Men: Conclusions

Although a great deal has changed, in daily life Rwandan women still rely on their relationships with men to gain access to land for their own and their children's survival. While this situation is tenable for women in legally recognised marriages with men who respect their needs and rights, in most cases women's rights to land rely on men who are not there. According to the 1996 socio-demographic study, 34 per cent of households nationwide are female headed (ONAPO 1998: 44), and in Butare prefecture this rises to 43 per cent (ONAPO 1998: 44). While these are the most reliable statistics available, they are now outdated given the changes that have occurred since.

The number of female-headed households is higher today if the influx of new-caseload refugees in late 1996 and early 1997 is taken into account. Many women returned from the camps without their husbands or as widows. Many others saw their husbands imprisoned on return. These women, although not technically widows, live like widows in most senses. Another factor leading to the rising numbers of female-headed households is the 1996–99 insurgency. This uprising in the northwest resulted in many more widows and child-headed households. And finally, the HIV/AIDS epidemic is beginning to leave in its wake child-headed households where both parents have succumbed to the disease.

Women in informal marriages (especially those in polygamous marriages) and widows are among the women most vulnerable to losing their access to land in Rwanda. In many instances, widows find their land rights challenged by brothers-in-law who want to live in the house or exploit the fields. Widows who have children following the death of their husbands are particularly vulnerable to losing these battles. Women in polygamous marriages face similar problems on the death of their husbands, although their challenger is often a legally recognized co-wife.

Women in informal or polygamous marriages are often chased off their husbands' land when a dispute arises with their husbands or if the husband dies. Furthermore, since all land belongs to the state according to Rwandan statutory law, the 1999 inheritance law does not include land. Rwandan women therefore remain marginalised in terms of land ownership.

In addition to these gender-specific disadvantages, Rwandan women face the same problems of land scarcity and poverty as men. Since the 1980s, there has been a trend towards the buying up of small landholdings in the countryside by wealthy employed Rwandans, especially civil servants and state agents (Uvin 1998). In several cases cited by Uvin (1998), poor rural Rwandans sold their land under economic distress and then found their situation worsen. RISD's research for this study found instances of the distribution of larger landholdings to influential people in the government in the implementation of the *imidugudu* policy, confirming other research (Hilhorst and van Leeuwen 1999; RISD 1999a, 1999b). Access to land for poor rural Rwandans remains difficult and must be addressed by the national land policy and land bill currently under development.

While significant steps have been made in levelling the disparity between men's and women's rights in Rwanda, more work is needed. The promulgation of the new inheritance law was a step in the right direction, but more needs to be done to protect the rights of 'illegitimate' children and of women involved in informal marriages, including polygamous marriages.

Recommendations

Based on the recommendations initially proposed by RISD, workshop proceedings and breakout sessions, participants at the women and land workshop unanimously adopted the following recommendations and action plan on 25 April 2001:

On the marriage problem

1. The Rwandan National Assembly should revise family law regarding marriage to recognise marriages according to the four marriage practices in Rwanda:
- Civil marriage through local authorities.
- Religious marriage (through the church, mosque or other recognised religious institution).
- Traditional marriage through agreement between the two families.
- Common law marriage based on length of cohabitation.

2. In order to increase the percentage of legally recognised marriages in Rwanda:
- Raise awareness about the legal marriage process.
- Simplify the legal marriage process.
- Raise awareness about the issue of the bride-price.
- Simplify customary marriage by reducing the costs involved.

3. In order to decrease the frequency of polygamous marriages, which are illegal according to Rwandan statutory law:

- Raise awareness among young girls about marriage.
- Raise awareness about the issue of polygamy, especially among men.
- Encourage women to take legal action against their husbands in instances of polygamy (polygamy will die by itself due to economic hardship).

4. More research is needed on the issues raised around legally recognised marriages.

On the new inheritance law

5. The GOR and international, national and local NGOs should undertake an intensive education programme to help Rwandans understand the new inheritance law. This programme should:

- Focus on all groups (children, women, men and so on).
- Be broad-based and inclusive (address multiple issues and subjects, include other laws).
- Work at different levels through different means (churches, government and so on).
- Use varied media explaining the law in simple language (meetings and seminars in rural areas, theatre, brochures and posters, the press including the Kinyarwanda newpapers, radio and so on).

6. At the local level, committees should be set up to deal with inheritance issues.

7. The Rwandan National Assembly should revise the family law to:

- Expand it and be more specific in terms of defining key terms.
- Include 'illegitimate' children and increase their rights to inheritance.
- Reduce fees for legal marriage and to give grace to the poor.
- Empower local authorities to implement the law.

On land scarcity and population growth

8. The GOR and international, national and local NGOs should:

- Expand the school curriculum (include gender and legal education).
- Give increased attention to universal, basic education.
- Provide free and universal primary school education for all Rwandan children, regardless of sex.
- Give increased access to secondary education for Rwandan children.
- Provide education and literacy programmes for adults.
- Provide opportunities to women for higher education.
- Improve the population's knowledge about the law and the legal system.
- Provide effective economic assistance for the poor.

9. The GOR should put into place universal access to family planning in order to control population growth, with the National Population Office, in collaboration with the Ministries of Education and Health, becoming responsible.

10. The GOR should promote income-generating and employment activities outside of agriculture by:

- Reviewing the education system in general.
- Creating apprentice and technical training centres all over the country.
- Diversifying professions and trades.
- Professionalising Rwandans.

On the land policy and bill

11. The GOR should formulate a sustainable national land policy and bill giving every Rwandan (regardless of sex) equal rights to land ownership.

12. The national land policy and bill should reaffirm every Rwandan's right to access and own land, as did the 1993 Arusha Accords. Furthermore, the new land policy and bill should specifically address women's rights to access, own and control land. Every Rwandan needs a piece of land to live, but they do not all need to be farmers. Access to land does not necessarily constitute control over land. Therefore, land is a cultural as well as a judicial issue.

13. The Ministry of Gender and Women in Development must take a leadership role in the development and drafting of the national land policy and bill to ensure that women's rights to access and control land are effective and to raise awareness among women of their rights.

14. Any further implementation of the *imidugudu* resettlement policy should be done with care so as to avoid the mistakes witnessed to date. Where possible, mistakes should be corrected.

15. As land has a greater cultural than economic value in the minds of Rwandans, they must be educated about the value of land as a means of production.

On the environment

16. The education of women on environmental issues will have a positive impact on sustainable production, as well as on children's education. It should:

- Raise awareness of women about environmental issues.
- Target women farmers for agricultural extension and education.

On discrimination

17. The Rwandan National Assembly should appoint a subcommittee to review and revise all bodies of Rwandan law to ensure that no Rwandan (regardless of age, ethnicity, religion, sex or any other characteristic) is discriminated against. It should aim to:

- Raise awareness among illegally or unofficially abandoned women so that they know and understand their rights and how to use the legal system to reclaim those rights.

- Raise awareness in the rest of the population about individuals' rights and how to respect them.

- In order to protect the rights of vulnerable individuals and their ability to access land, the GOR should offer special intervention and protection programmes.

Notes

1. *Imidugudu* is plural and *umudugudu* is singular.

2. 'Old-caseload refugees' is the term commonly used to refer to Rwandans returning to Rwanda between 1994 and 1996 who had been in exile from 1959–90.

3. 'New-caseload refugees' is the term commonly applied to Rwandans who fled the country in 1994 and returned from 1996–97.

4. The *mwami* was the political and spiritual leader of the central Rwandan kingdom. At the beginning of the twentieth century, the kingdom was in the midst of an expansion (through warfare) into bordering regions (present-day Kibungo and Cyangugu) of Kinyarwanda speakers.

5. *Civilisé* was legally defined by the colonial administration as any non-European who lived in a Western-style house, wore Western clothes, ate Western food with Western utensils, and so on. Anyone seeking classification as *civilisé* was subject to inspection at any moment by colonial administrators (interview with key informant, Kigali Town, January 2001).

6. Interview with key informant, Kigali Town, January 2001.

7. Interviews with key informants and community elders, Kinigi commune, Ruhengeri prefecture, November 2000.

8. Ibid.

9. Interviews with key informants, Mugina commune, Gitarama prefecture, November 2000.

10. Interviews with key informants, Kahi commune, Umutara prefecture; Kigarama commune, Kibungo prefecture, December 2000.

11. Interviews with key informants and community elders, Kinigi commune, Ruhengeri prefecture, November 2000.

12. Ibid.

13. Interviews in Kinigi commune, Ruhengeri prefecture, November 2000; and in Kigarama commune, Kibungo prefecture, December 2000.

14. Interviews in Kinigi commune, Ruhengeri prefecture, November 2000.

15. Key informant interviews, Kinigi commune, Ruhengeri prefecture, November 2000; and Kigali, January 2001.

16. The most common instance is that of a widow holding her husband's land in trust for her male children. The next most common is that of child- or girl-headed households.

17. Two important variants in translation are interesting to note. First, the word for 'man' in English is translated as *umuntu* in the Kinyarwanda. The word *umuntu* designates a person without indicating their sex. The word in Kinyarwanda most commonly used for man is *umugabo*, a word that necessarily implies the notion of marriage and is thus not

possible in this Bible verse, where the man is not yet married. Another interesting note about the Kinyarwanda translation is the word 'helper' of verse 18 in the English version, which is translated to an equivalent word, *umufasha*. In common parlance, Rwandan men often refer to their wives as *umufasha wanjye* or 'my helper', since the literal term *umugore*, meaning both wife and woman, has a negative connotation.

18. Informant interviews, Kinigi commune, Ruhengeri prefecture, November 2000; Mugina commune, Gitarama prefecture, November 2000; Kahi commune, Umutara prefecture, November 2000; and Kigarama commune, Kibungo prefecture, December 2000.

19. Land (*ikigingi*) under one of the traditional land tenure systems in Rwanda was awarded to heroes, defined either by heroism in battle or by political preference.

20. Even today in Kinyarwanda, one tells a woman that she is a man (*uri umugabo*) to convey that she is worthy of respect and has accomplished something remarkable.

21. Informant interviews, Kahi commune, Umutara prefecture, December 2000.

22. Informant interviews, Kigarama commune, Kibungo prefecture, December 2000 and Kinigi commune, Ruhengeri prefecture, November 2000.

23. Informant interviews Kahi commune, Umutara prefecture, December 2000 and Kinigi commune, Ruhengeri prefecture, November 2000.

24. Informant interviews, Kinigi commune, Ruhengeri prefecture, November 2000; Mugina commune, Gitarama prefecture, November 2000; Kahi commune, Umutara prefecture, November 2000 and Kigarama commune, Kibungo prefecture, December 2000.

25. Women and Land Workshop proceedings, Kigali Town, April 2001.

26. Although unknown by many rural Rwandans, the bridewealth can be a 'gift to be named later' in cases of poverty.

27. Interviews with local officials, Kigarama commune, Kibungo prefecture, December 2000.

28. Interviews with residents, Kahi commune, Umutara prefecture, December 2000.

29. Interview with Canton Court president, Kigarama commune, Kibungo prefecture, December 2000.

30. *Gacaca* is a traditional system of conflict resolution in which elders from the community and concerned parties call witnesses to explain the situation. The elders then make a recommendation to resolve the conflict and the group decides by consensus what the final decision will be.

31. The correlation in Kinyarwanda between building a house and marriage is close. For example, the phrase *yubatse inzu*, he built a house, is a euphemism meaning 'he is married'.

32. Interviews with local residents, Kigarama commune, Kibungo prefecture; Kahi commune, Umutara prefecture; Mugina commune, Gitarama prefecture; Kinigi commune, Ruhengeri prefecture, November–December 2000.

33. Interviews with residents, Kigarama commune, Kibungo prefecture, December 2000.

34. Interviews with Canton Court officials, Kinigi commune, Ruhengeri prefecture, November 2000.

35. Since the 1994 genocide and war, there are far fewer single men than women of marriageable age. The socio-demographic study conducted by the National Population Office shows that the overall sex ratio (number of males per 100 females) for the Rwandan population is 86, but in the 20–24 age group it drops to 71 and in the 25–29 age group it is only 69 (ONAPO 1998: 18).

36. Interview with a pre-marital counsellor in the Catholic Church, Gikondo, Kigali, November 2000.

37. *Nyumbakumi* is the administrator of ten houses, the smallest administrative grouping in Rwanda.

38. Informant interview in Kinigi commune, Ruhengeri prefecture, November 2000.

References

Andre, Catherine (ed.) (1998) 'Terre Rwandaise: acces, politique et reforme foncieres', *L'Afrique des Grands Lacs Annuaire*, 1997–98, Paris: L'Harmattan.

Bart, François (1993) 'Montagnes d'Afrique, Terres Paysannes: le cas du Rwanda', *Espaces Tropicaux*, Vol. 7, Bordeaux: Presses Universitaires de Bordeaux.

Cyiza, Augustin (2000) 'Land Use in Rwanda', Kigali: Rwanda Initiative for Sustainable Development.

de Lame, Danielle (1996) 'Une Colline Entre Mille ou Le Calme Avant La Tempête: transformations et blocages du Rwanda rural', Annales *Sciences Humaines*, Vol. 154, Tervuren: Musée Royal de L'Afrique Centrale.

Gasasira, Ephrem (1995) *The Land Issue After the War*, Kigali: MINAGRI/UNDP.

Hilhorst, Dorothea and Mathijs van Leeuwen (1999) 'Imidugudu: Villagisation in Rwanda; a Case of Emergency Development', *Disaster Sites*, No. 2.

Human Rights Watch (2001) *Uprooting the Rural Poor in Rwanda*, New York: Human Rights Watch.

Jacob, Irenee (1984) *Dictionnaire Rwandais–Francais*. Vol. I (A–H), Kigali: Imprimerie Scolaire.

Jefremovas, Villia (1991) *Loose Women, Virtuous Wives and Timid Virgins: Gender and Control of Resources in Rwanda*, CJAS.

Laurent, Chantal and Christian Bugnion (2000) *External Evaluation of the UNHCR Shelter Programme in Rwanda 1994–1999*, Geneva: Reintegration and Local Settlement Section, UNHCR.

Musahara, Herman (1999) 'Villagisation and Land Use in the Context of the Rwandan Economy', paper presented at a workshop, Kigali.

Newbury, Catharine (1988) *The Cohesion of Oppression*, New York: Columbia University Press.

Olson, Jennifer M. (1994) *Demographic Responses to Resource Constraints in Rwanda*, East Lansing: Michigan State University.

ONAPO (1998) *Final Report: Socio-demographic Survey 1996*, Kigali: Ministry of Finance and Planning.

Pottier, Johan (1997) 'Social Dynamics of Land and Land Reform in Rwanda: Past, Present and Future', paper presented at conference on 'Understanding the Crisis in Africa's Great Lakes Region'.

RISD (Rwanda Institute for Sustainable Development) (1999a) 'Land Use and Villagisation in Rwanda', Kigali.

— (1999b) 'Land Use and Villagisation: Workshop Report', Kigali.

Rwanda, Republic of (1999) 'Law to Supplement Book One of the Civil Code and to Institute Part Five Regarding Matrimonial Regimes, Liberalities and Successions', Kigali: Official Gazette of the Republic of Rwanda 38(22).

UNICEF (1988) *Situation Analysis of Children and Women in Rwanda*, Kigali: UNICEF.

Uvin, Peter (1998) *Aiding Violence: The Development Enterprise in Rwanda*, Connecticut: Kumarian Press.

van Hoyweghen, Saskia (1999) 'The Urgency of Land and Agrarian Reform in Rwanda', *African Affairs*, No. 98.

SIX
Women and Land in Africa: A Case Study from Senegal

Ngoné Diop Tine and Mohamadou Sy

§ IN Senegal, as in other African states, land is considered an important resource. This is a consequence of the place that agriculture occupies in the Senegalese economy. Land provides its owner with an essential means of survival. Land is therefore one of Senegal's most complex issues. If it is not the explicit cause of fratricidal conflicts which Senegal has experienced,[1] it is their implicit cause. Bloody ethnic conflicts have often been witnessed over land – those opposing the Peul herdsmen and the Serer farmers, as well as those opposing members of the same family, who may go as far as to take up arms against one another.

In view of its importance and its complexity, land has been the subject of numerous studies carried out by intergovernmental organisations (IGOs such as the Food and Agriculture Organisation, the International Monetary Fund and the World Bank). In addition, studies on land have been sponsored by African states themselves. However, it must be emphasised that only recently have studies relative to land integrated gender analyses. This shows the secondary level of interest thus far in female dimensions of land issues.

And yet, it must be admitted that African woman in general and Senegalese women in this instance, represent the labour force on land. An FAO report in 1985 found that 70 per cent of agricultural produce, whether to feed Senegalese families or to export, is produced by women, who none the less have no rights of ownership over land. Women constitute 75 per cent of the Senegalese rural population and carry out 81 per cent of agricultural work. They cultivate about 70 per cent of subsistence crops but are also responsible for the whole food chain from production to consumption, including transformation.[2]

The socio-cultural factors inherent in custom (tradition) and religion define and govern the human rights of Senegalese women, of which the right to own land is considered unimportant. In fact, tradition and religion strictly define the status of women, granting them explicit duties and/or obligations and treating with disdain even the most elementary rights. Depending on whether a woman is married, divorced or a widow, she is assigned the duty and even the obligation to cultivate the land belonging to her husband or his family. Yet she is denied the right of possession. Statutory law institutionalises the way in which custom and religion define and govern women's rights to own land.

The main objective of this study is therefore to analyse how tradition, religion and law interact to define and govern women's rights to own land in Senegal, within a human rights paradigm. Three groups of Senegalese women – married women, divorced women and widows – will be identified. And since custom and religion differ from one community to another, three communities will be examined: the Wolof, the Serer and the Peul communities. These communities were chosen because of the diversity in their customs and religions, as well as in their links binding women to land.

The Serer community functions on a matriarchal basis, the basic principle of which is that inheritance is through the maternal line of descent. It must be noted, however, that even though Serer tradition grants importance to the maternal line, Serer women do not have the right to own land. If they inherit their uncles' lands, for example, these should pass to their male children. In addition, the advent of Catholicism has brought about significant modifications in the practice of Serer traditions. Women can now own small patches of land, but they can cultivate it only after having completed tasks assigned to them on lands belonging to their families or husbands.

The Peul community is patriarchal and rigidly organised into a hierarchy, with the nobility at the top and the casted at the bottom. Even though it is entirely composed of Muslims, the application of custom is still important when it comes to land. Here, land belongs to men. In terms of land distribution and ownership, women belonging to the nobility are in the same boat as casted men.

Finally, the study examines the Wolof community, which is 95 per cent Muslim.

The divergence of views on what constitutes custom or tradition must be noted. Similarly, religion is subject to controversial and varying interpretations, often by men, to the detriment of women. Therefore, the study will examine how this situation may work in favour of women. In other words, how can women interpret and/or use tradition and religion to defend their rights to land?

The study is not limited to critical analysis. Its other objective is to open perspectives for the promotion of women's rights to own land. It has therefore been conducted in a three-stage process:

- Carrying out empirical and theoretical research on land ownership of Senegalese women.
- Making concrete proposals for the promotion of Senegalese women's rights to own land and the evaluation and dissemination of these proposals through

non-governmental organisations (NGOs) and the Ministry of Women, Children and Family Affairs.

- Incorporating comments and suggestions emanating from this evaluation into the original proposals and communicating these proposals to NGOs and government policy-makers with a view to their eventual implementation.

Status of Senegalese Women

Senegal is a Sahelian state situated in West Africa and was, during French colonisation, the capital of French West Africa (FWA). With a surface area of about 250,000 square kilometres, Senegal is bordered in the east by Mali, in the west by the Atlantic Ocean, in the north by Mauritania and in the south by Guinea Bissau and Guinea Conakry. The Senegalese population, estimated at 8.3 million in 1995, is characterised by the significant demographic weight of women (52 per cent), the predominance of young people under the age of 20 (58 per cent) and rapid demographic growth (an annual rate of 3 per cent).

Despite progress in education and health, the fertility index remains high at six children per woman. The health situation of women is still a cause for concern, explained by negative socio-cultural behaviour, the insufficiency of health services and the feminisation of poverty. The demographic and health survey conducted in 1992–93 gives a rate of 510 maternal deaths for 100,000 successful deliveries.

In 1995, the illiteracy rate among women was estimated at 78 per cent, as against 53 per cent for men. The full-time education rate for girls is still insignificant, decreasing as they progress through the educational system. Statistics from the Ministry of National Education in 1995 revealed that girls represent 46 per cent of pupils enrolled in primary schools, 33.7 per cent of high school enrolments and only 26.7 per cent of those enrolled at the higher education level. The poor education of Senegalese women is largely responsible for their limited access to wage-earning jobs. Even though women represent 70 per cent of the active population, female wage-earners make up only 7.4 per cent of the female population. These wage-earners are concentrated in the primary sector, agriculture (75 per cent) as well as in the informal sector.

The work of women remains invisible and depreciated. The aggravation of poverty because economic, political and social development programmes completely ignore women is attested to by Isabelle Droy:

> identified in the statements, forgotten in the statistics, classified as family workers, dumb in the programmes, women are marginalised in the new institutional (training, access to credit) and legal (land allocation) or organisational mechanisms. Women as 'instruments' for the physical reproduction of the group, for the creation of basic social relations, for agricultural productions are classified at the same level as 'things' ... they disappear behind men, be they father, brother or husband.[3]

At the legal and political levels, Senegalese women are in an unenviable position. Even though the Senegalese Constitution entitles women to vote and to stand for Parliament, and despite the ratification in 1985 of the Convention on the Elimination of All Forms of Discrimination Against Women, women represent only 10 per cent of members of the current Parliament. Women's access to decision-making organs is thus limited.

PART I Senegalese Women's Land Rights

It is important to define, first of all, the notion of 'ownership'. For the purposes of this study, ownership relates to three rights:

- The right to use land (usus).
- The right to enjoy land (fructus).
- The right to exploit land (abusus).

Thus the right of possession (ownership and control) of land should not be confused with the right of access. The right of access is restrictive because it is limited to use. The right of possession of land cannot be violated, except for public benefit and then only following fair and prior compensation. Within this study, land refers to land used for agriculture or similar purposes.

Sampling and Data Collecting Techniques

This study prioritised women in three ethnic groups – the Wolof, the Peul and the Serer – that make up Senegal's population. Islam and Christianity are the two major religions, with 98 per cent of Senegal's population following Islam. Only one Serer and Christian research site, Joal-Fadiouth, was used. The other two essentially Muslim research sites included the rural Wolof community of Medina Sabakh, at the heart of the groundnut basin in the arrondissement of Medina Sabakh, Department of Nioro du Rip, Region of Kaolack, and the rural Peul community of Medina Ndiathbe in the arrondissement of Cascas, Department of Podor, Region of Saint-Louis.

In each of the three research sites, discussions were held with the following:

- Married women, divorcees and widows, who constituted the target of the study, with emphasis being placed on the status of category to understand better the way in which tradition, religion and law treats them.
- Administrative authorities, particularly sub-prefects and heads of the Multi-functional Centre for Rural Extension (CERP), who are responsible for ensuring that laws are implemented and for providing technical support to rural councillors.
- Locally elected representatives who represent the population in rural councils and are competent to allocate and revoke land.

- Religious authorities such as marabous and priests to ascertain religious opinions and views on women's land rights in a country in which almost everybody is a believer.
- Traditional authorities who are the custodians of tradition, exercise customary law and ensure social balance.

In addition:

- At least one woman leader of a women's association was met. Other women included both members and non-members of women's associations.
- At least two administrative authorities were interviewed, including sub-prefects and their deputies or heads of CERP.
- In regard to locally elected representatives, at least the first vice-president of the Rural Council responsible for state-owned land and a female rural councillor were interviewed. In Joal-Fadiouth commune, meetings were also held with members of the Rural Interest Group (RIG), which includes both rural and municipal councillors.
- With respect to religious authorities, priority was given to specialists in Islamic law rather than marabouts in general.
- With respect to traditional authorities, each village chief was met, and in the Joal-Fadiouth commune discussions were held with the deputy mayor.

Data collection was facilitated by a documentary review relative to women and on land in Senegal in particular, and in Africa in general; and field surveys with the help of guides instead of questionnaires, owing to the nature of the study, which required a qualitative approach, and to the fact that the targets were mostly illiterate.

Finally, the data collected were analysed according to a systematic approach.

Table 6.1 Distribution per target and per ethnic group

Target Groups	Wolof		Peul		Serer		Total
	No.	%	No.	%	No.	%	
Women	28	65.11	25	67.57	25	63.41	78
Administrative authorities	2	6.66	2	5.41	3	7.31	7
Locally elected representatives	5	17.85	5	13.51	5	12.20	15
Religious authorities	3	9.77	3	8.10	2	4.88	8
Traditional authorities	5	17.85	2	5.41	5	12.20	12
Total	43	100	37	100	40	100	120

Source: Ngoné Diop Tine and Mouhamadou Sy

Women's Traditional Land Rights

Among the Wolof, customary law on land is of two kinds. The first and most important is the 'right obtained by virtue of fire', detained by the *lamane* (the descendant of the person who first burnt down the forest to demarcate territory with a fire lasting between three and six days). The second, which some do not consider a real right, is the 'right obtained by virtue of the axe', which corresponds to concessions made by a *lamane*, on his own land, to a farmer to clear it in return for payment of symbolic rent (a sheaf of millet).

Traditionally, women do not own land. According to the imam of the Medina Sabakh mosque:

> it is the status of the woman which explains why she is not often associated in the sharing of land since she is expected to remarry and to often leave her village. She thus prefers to be under the authority of her brothers. This is what explains why the land is confiscated by men.

In Wolof tradition a woman, whether married, divorced or widowed, cannot own land. She is entitled only to the right to use land. Thus all land belonged to husbands, who could redistribute some fields of land for their wives' use. These fields were, in general, used to cultivate groundnuts. Big fields belonging to husbands were reserved for growing millet.

Serer customary laws on land are similar. Landowners obtain land rights by virtue both of fire and the axe. The relationship between land and the producer occupies a predominant place among the Serer, as they are a rural ethnic group. And land has also maintained its esoteric and mysterious aspects. Paul Pelissier, author of important work on Senegalese farmers, justifies the almost religious power of the *lamane*:

> the unquestionable nature of his rights lie, above all, on the initial agreement which he entered into with the spirits of the forest, consolidated by ancestors whose work and fervour have fertilised the soil and who continue to live 'on the spot' in the kingdom of the dead. The *lamane* is, besides, one of the priests of the religion of the land, who, by his sacrifices, his offerings, his rites, obtains for the living the favours of the Pangol, which are indispensable for the fertility of the fields as well as for the prosperity of the flocks.

Finally, succession grants importance to inheritance by virtue of kinship on the mother's side. This is why only women can inherit their mothers' rice paddy-fields, because women devote themselves to rice farming. Similarly, nephews inherit their uncles' properties because men cultivate millet.

However, the break with tradition resulting from the modernism of the early 1960s has sanctioned paternal lineage. Today, men no longer inherit from their uncles but from their fathers.

Customary laws among the Peul differ from those of the Wolof and the Serer in distinct ways. First, the Peul do not traditionally recognise the supremacy of the right obtained by virtue of fire over the right obtained by virtue of the axe. Both are recognised as traditional methods of land acquisition. And second, as a result of its mystical character, land is not an individual affair but a family or community affair. On this basis, all men and all women are entitled only to the right to use land.

The land of each family is, in general, managed by a patriarch who is responsible for distributing it to various members of the family, giving more priority to men according to the principle of gerontocracy. Women are in the same boat as casted members of the community, and their access to land depends on the amount of water available. For example, when land is discussed among the Peul, the comparison is made between land in the Walo area, which is liable to flooding, and land of the *dieri*, which is the object of little envy. In periods of food scarcity, tenant farming is different from *taile* among the Wolof and the Serer, in which cases the tenants pawning land still benefit from the use of the land given as sureties as long as their debts remain unpaid.

Women's Religious Land Rights

Women's right to own land is recognised by Islam without any reservations. Inheritance applies to the totality of the father's or husband's property. Women have the right to inherit property from their fathers on the principle of one share for women and two shares for men. Wives are entitled to one-eighth of the property of their husbands when the deceased husbands have children and to one-fourth if they are childless. This discrimination, favourable for men, is justified by the fact that men are responsible for households.

There is, however, widespread belief that women cannot inherit land under Islamic law because of the Islamic recommendation that women stay at home to take care of household chores. According to this erroneous opinion, women should not work on the land and consequently cannot own land.

Finally, Islam has a conception of public land. If an outsider exploits farming land, openly and publicly, for ten years without its real owner complaining, the land then becomes owned by the outsider. If a family member exploits farming land belonging to this same family, the land becomes his after 40 years.

Christianity does not admit any ambiguity with respect to women's land rights. According to Christianity, men and women are equal and, as such, have the same rights. Therefore, women can own land in the same way as men. According to Christian religious authorities interviewed, Christianity aims for family welfare and therefore encourages all initiatives relative to the development of women.

Women's Statutory Land Rights

The National Law 64-46 of 17 June 1964 is the main legal reference as far as land is concerned in Senegal. In his statement on 1 May 1964, former President Leopold Sedar Senghor indicated that 'the object of the law was to move from Roman law to Negro-African law, from the bourgeoisie conception of land ownership to the socialist conception of traditional black Africa in order to counteract the landlord mentality which had developed'. The law was voted into being in a context marked, in the rural areas, by a traditional land system that benefited only a minority – the large landowners or *lamanes* whose land transactions were detrimental to farmers without land.

The law covers 95 per cent of Senegalese land and, in principle, all land, with the exception of certain categories, falls under it. By virtue of Article 1 of the law:

> considered as national domain [is], by right, all land which is unclassified, unregistered or the ownership of which has not been transcribed in the land registry at the date of entry into force of the present law. Not considered as part of the national domain [is], by right, all land which, at that date is not subject to a registration procedure on behalf of a party other than the State.

Land belonging to the national domain is classified into four areas, according to urban and rural needs as well as national development and environmental concerns. They are urban areas, local areas, pioneer areas and classified areas.

For the purpose of this study, local areas are particularly interesting because urban areas fall under the competence of the communes, pioneer areas are reserved for large agricultural development companies (to conduct joint management programmes with farmers for development) and classified areas are forested areas. However, it should be noted that some pioneer areas end up in the local areas. The local areas include land falling under the authority of indigenous populations through their locally elected representatives. In Articles 7 and 8, for example, the law provides that:

> the local area corresponds to land which is regularly exploited for rural settlement, farming or animal rearing. The land belonging to the local zone is allocated to members of the rural community who ensure that they are developed and exploited under the control of the State and in accordance with laws and regulations.

Management of land falls within the competence of the state, development and planning bodies and rural communities on the basis of certain criteria, including equity and profitability. The underlying principle is that land should be given to those who will exploit it favourably for agriculture. The relevant authority's role is to ensure that legislative and regulatory provisions relative to the national domain are implemented in an efficient manner; to represent the state before local communities; to exercise control over management actions taken by Rural Councils and to prevent conflicts over land.

Apart from the law establishing the national domain, there is a law establishing rural communities. By Law 72-25 of 19 April 1972, the state established rural communities whose role is to promote community development at the grassroots through farmers' participation. Under this law, 'the Rural Community is composed of a certain number of villages belonging to the same locality, bound by solidarity due, particularly, to proximity, having common interests and able to find the resources necessary for their development'. The Rural Council is an essential organ of the rural community and the only organ competent as far as land allocation and revocation are concerned. However, in accordance with Article 336 of the Local Authority Code, decisions of the Rural Council are enforceable only after approval by the sub-prefect. There are three conditions of land allocation. First, the possibility of using land should be granted first to inhabitants of the rural community. Second, land is allocated to an individual only providing that he or she develops it. Finally, the allocation of land belonging to the national domain is for an unspecified duration, but the only causes for its revocation are the absence of development and its reintegration into state-owned land.

The decision to carry out this study in the research site of Mbodiene Village in Nguenienne Rural Community required getting acquainted with the Rural Interest Group (RIG), the only body authorised to manage farming land under the jurisdiction of the Nguenienne Rural Community and, to a lesser degree, under the Commune of Joal-Fadiouth. Created by Decree 80-1105 of 4 November 1980, the RIG is an original mechanism for the joint management of farming land by two neighbouring administrative entities. The RIG of the Nguenienne Rural Community and of the Commune of Joal-Fadiouth is a unique example in Senegal and, if only for this reason, it deserves particular attention. Elsewhere in the state (in Mbour and Pout, for example), similar mechanisms could be initiated to resolve conflicts over land.

Traditionally, the populations of the two administrative entities shared the same farming land. However, under the administrative division issuing from Law 72-25, the population of Joal-Fadiouth Commune saw their local areas transferred to the neighbouring Nguenienne Rural Community. Since the population of Joal-Fadiouth drew most of its revenues from agriculture rather than fishing, which is practised by outsiders, it was obliged to turn to the Nguenienne Rural Community to dispose of farming land. Frustration was created on both sides. To redress this frustration, the RIG was set up.

Article 17 of the decree specified that

> the attributions entrusted to the Rural Council and to its Chairman with regard to the management of land falling within the national domain situated in the Nguenienne Rural Community are exercised by the Chairman of the Rural Interest Council.

Later on, Article 17 continues:

> the allocation can be pronounced in favour of either a member of the Rural Community or of several members assembled in an association or cooperative, or to persons living in the Commune of Joal-Fadiouth but who are engaged in agricultural and pastoral activities mainly in the Nguenienne Rural Community.

The RIG is composed of six members, including three rural councillors of the Nguenienne Rural Community and three municipal councillors of Joal-Fadiouth Commune. Four out of the six councillors are elected by universal suffrage and the remaining two represent associations of an economic or social nature. The chairmanship of the RIG rotates between the chair of the Nguenienne Rural Community and the mayor of the Joal-Fadiouth Commune.

PART II State of Women's Land Ownership

Women of all marital status unanimously expressed their land needs among the Wolof, the Serer and the Peul.

Women's Land Ownership Among the Wolof

Among the Wolof in the Medina Sabakh Rural Community, women's land owner-ship and the manner of its acquisition is set out in Table 6.2.

Of the 28 women interviewed, only 12 (42.85 per cent) own land. Women landowners are, in general, married women, followed by widows and divorcées. The most common manner of acquisition is through the Rural Council delibera-tions, followed by succession. It should be noted that women who own land mostly belong to women's associations. Almost all women admit having the right to use land and to use it as required by men (by husbands and brothers).

The Rural Council deliberations have benefited members of women's associ-ations. However, allocations of land to women are limited because of the scarcity

Table 6.2 Land ownership and manner of acquisition (Wolof)

Marital status	Manner of acquisition				Total	
	Inheritance	Acquisition	RC deliberations	Gifts	No.	%
Married women	1	1	4	1	7	58.33
Divorced women	0	0	1	0	1	8.34
Widowed women	2	1	1	0	4	33.33
Total	3	2	6	1	12	100

Source: Ngoné Diop Tine and Mouhamadou Sy

of land. Existing land belongs to *lamanes*, who, because they cannot exploit it themselves, lend the land to farmers in exchange for annual royalties. Members of women's associations who need land either turn to the village chief or negotiate with the landowner and, later on, request that it be allocated to them by the Rural Council. At this point, the Rural Council only confirms, through its deliberations, the contract concluded between the women's association and the *lamane*. The rural councillors are sensitive to collective requests, especially when they are supported by the CERP head or the sub-prefect. The presence of women (who are 25 per cent of rural councillors) has not brought about significant change to women's land ownership because the Rural Council no longer has land to distribute.

In most cases, Islamic succession laws have been complied with among the Wolof, providing widows and orphans with the opportunity to inherit an eighth and a quarter respectively, depending on whether the property came from the woman's father or her husband. Land is considered as property.

In cases where Islamic succession law has not been respected, customary law was given priority. This priority is established by arguing, in cases of a father's death, that a woman is expected to marry and her brothers will allow her use of land as needed; and in cases of a husband's death, that the woman is expected to remarry and leave her marital community. Customarily, the inheritance of land has always been a male affair. Men are entitled to redistribute family land to members of the family (including women) who request it. Thus women's access to land depends on the will of either their fathers, their brothers or their husbands.

Although traditionally land was considered an inalienable and sacred property, over the years, the commercialisation of the economy, demographic growth and the arrival of new land-hungry migrants have resulted in the institution of transactions over land. The sale of land is practised especially by large landowners such as *lamanes*, who are reluctant to apply the law relative to the national domain. Since land can be bought, any wealthy woman can now buy it. Although the buying of land by women has not been widespread, this limitation is justified not by the application of the law relative to the national domain but by the fact that some land is seen as belonging to the community.

Factors Limiting Women's Land Ownership Among the Wolof

Shortage of land constitutes a major, objective constraint to women's land owner-ship in the entire groundnut basin. Gender-based constraints to women's land ownership are compounded by the absence of fallow land and the salinisation of land. All those interviewed were of the view that it is now almost impossible to obtain land in the Medina Sabakh Rural Community, explaining the migration towards the south of Senegal. However, according to the vice-chairman of the Rural Council, responsible for state-owned land, the rural council has about a hundred hectares of reserved land situated ten kilometres away from Medina

Sabakh Rural Community. Unfortunately, this land has become solidified and its exploitation would require substantial investment.

The way in which women are viewed socially has not changed to a great degree. Prejudices and stereotypes attached to women endure, with many men still seeing them as inferior. Furthermore, some women appear not to resent these prejudices and stereotypes. In fear and respect of tradition, they are satisfied with what men let them have, hoping that change will occur some day. For this socio-cultural reason, all the women interviewed accept their marginalisation. Even when decisions affecting them directly are made, their participation remains ineffectual.

Women suffer from the absence of strong female leadership. The chairs of women's associations have limited powers. They are incapable of influencing decisions taken by men, let alone exercising coercive authority over men.

Deficiencies in education and training affect both women and the rural councillors. Even though women are aware of the existence of Law 64-46, their knowledge of its content is still superficial. For example, none of the women talked to knew that the law entitled them to attend Rural Council deliberations, since over 80 per cent of them were illiterate.

Women are not aware of the importance of the Rural Council or of its numerous prerogatives, especially within the framework of regionalisation. It is perhaps for this reason that the Rural Council is not considered by women to be an important organ. They justify their low representation in this decision-making organ on the basis that it is monopolised by men. But the women interviewed did not take any action to ensure better representation within the Rural Council, or to see to implementation of law relative to the national domain. Why? They do not want to disrupt tradition.

The rural councillors also suffer from this lack of education and training. Many of them are illiterate and, as such, their implementation of laws written in French is not feasible. The function of rural councillors is viewed to be that of social and political promotion. This is evident in the fact that awareness-raising sessions organised for rural councillors are often transformed into political platforms.

The weight of tradition is such that religious and legal provisions granting women land rights have lost their meaning, because they are not implemented. Tradition serves as a reference both for inheritance and for implementing the law relative to the national domain.

It remains difficult to implement the law in general and that on the national domain in particular because of the existence of strong customary law. Abdoul Aziz Diagne's observation is that 'the law relative to the national domain continues to pose problems, nearly thirty years after its promulgation. Its aim was, however, to create and develop rural communities which progressively take over responsibility for their economic and social development. Its implementation is far from being perfect.' The sub-prefect of Medina Sabakh Rural Community also admits that the provisions of the law relative to the national domain are not applied, except in two cases. The first is when the Rural Council agrees to allocate land when it has been proven that it does not belong to anybody. But either the land allocated is not of good quality, or it is situated far from the village. And the second is when there are conflicts over land and the sub-prefect resolves the conflicts by referring to the provisions of the law on the national domain. But such conflicts are, in general, brought first before traditional and religious authorities. Turning to administrative authorities is a last resort.

There are several cases certifying the non-implementation of the law on the national domain. *Lamanes* still endure in Medina Sabakh Rural Community. The scope of land speculations, and the allegiance of farmers without land, ensure that the law on the national domain does not achieve its major objectives. Almost thirty-three years after its adoption, it continues to be denounced, and as far as land is concerned Senegal remains the same. For example, as the rainy season approaches, the *lamanes* engage in land transactions. They lend land to the needy in exchange for royalties, which vary between CFA15,000 and CFA25,000 per hectare.

Administrative authorities and locally elected representatives are witnesses to such illegal transactions, but point either to socio-cultural inertia or legal incompetence to justify such criminal transactions. These justifications are insufficient, however. For political reasons, rural councillors are careful not to upset their constituents. As a result, they are sometimes not preoccupied with implementing the law on the national domain. In fact, land ownership is often monopolised with the complicity of the chairs of rural communities.

Women's Land Ownership Among the Serer

Of the 25 women interviewed among the Serer, 88.46 per cent own land. Women's land ownership is a reality, particularly in comparison with the Wolof and the Peul. Married women are the major landowners at 52.17 per cent, followed by widows and divorcees respectively. However, women's land ownership should not be understood in a Western sense.

Inheritance is the main means of acquiring land, followed by allocations by the Rural Council. Serer women occupy privileged positions, explained by the vice-chair of the Rural Council as follows: 'women inherit land in the same capacity as men. However, since paddy fields are the business of women, only girls inherit from their mothers.' This allegation was confirmed both in Fadiouth and in Mbodiene, where women engage in rice farming in the dregs as well as in rain-fed sugar-cane cultivation. Men, in general, grow millet and the limits of their land are precise.

The Rural Council has not revoked land, again because of what was referred to as socio-cultural inertia.

Of a total of 33 members of the Rural Council, eight are women. The Rural Council thus treats applications emanating from women's associations favourably and makes efforts to find land for them, including making arrangements with large landowners. All opportunities offered to the RIG are made use of in the population's interests.

Many members of the Rural Council of Nguenienne are literate, with experience in management. It is the best-organised Rural Council of the three research sites and the most perceptive of the population's needs. The procedures guiding applications for land are clear and well known by the population. Applications for land are addressed to the chair of the RIG between January and April each year. If for land for agricultural programmes and projects, they have to be accompanied by feasibility studies and technical reports from the CERP.

Christianity is not a constraint to women's land ownership. Neither has it, at least so far, interfered with inheritance. A woman's access to land depends on her wish to have such access. Moreover, land among the Serer cannot be subject to transactions, nor can it constitute gifts.

Factors Limiting Women's Land Ownership Among the Serer

Shortage of land, particularly of farming land, is a reality as a result of demographic pressure, salinisation and 'tannification'. Since the land that can be cultivated is limited, the population tends to look for new land. Even the paths used by livestock in search of pasture are sometimes utilised for agricultural purposes. This can lead to conflicts between farmers and animal breeders. As a result of land shortages, the RIG is not well thought of by the rural councillors of Nguenienne, who see it as a means of expropriating land from their constituents. The area has only one reserve – the 4,000 hectares of the classified forests of Ngazobil.

Another factor limiting women's land ownership concerns the demarcation fees of CFA5,000 per hectare, which have to be paid to the Rural Council to obtain land. Women's associations that need land are required to pay large fees.

Table 6.3 Land ownership and manner of acquisition (Serer)

Marital status	Manner of acquisition					Total	
	Inheritance	Acquisition	RC[1] deliberations	Gifts	RIV	No.	%
Married women	8	0	4	0	0	12	52.17
Divorced women	2	0	1	0	0	3	13.04
Widowed women	6	0	2	0	0	8	34.79
Total	16	0	7	0	0	23	100

Note: [1] Rural Council
Source: Ngoné Diop Tine and Mouhamadou Sy

The Rural Councillors are reluctant to allocate large areas of land and therefore ensure that any programme or project requiring land will have a socio-economic impact. In addition, the RIG does not give out title deeds, except for arboriculture projects. Instead, it gives out exploitation permits, valid for one or two years. The reasons given to justify this are that the distribution of title deeds might exhaust distributable land, mortgaging the future of generations to come. In addition, holders of title deeds might be tempted to sell their lands.

Women's Land Ownership Among the Peul

Of a total of 25 women, only eight (32 per cent) own land. In other words, fewer than one woman in three is a landowner. This low rate is partly due to the fact that land is not given as a gift, nor inherited or bought among the Peul. The female landowners are married or widowed. None of the divorced women interviewed owns land. Among the Peul, divorced women have status close to that of young girls and live, in general, with their fathers or elder brothers.

In northern Senegal, women's fate is far from enviable. Despite the penetration of Islam into Peul culture, tradition remains predominant. Women's land ownership is not linked to the provisions of the law on the national domain nor to interpretations of Islamic law. It is based on customary law. Among the Peul, land is considered sacred and cannot be owned by an individual, whether that person is a man or a woman. Neither men nor women are entitled to own land. Land belongs to whole families and is communally owned. There are, however, a few exceptions in which land has been shared out among family members but continues to be managed by the patriarch of the family.

Although almost all the women interviewed know that Islam entitles them to land, religious law is not implemented and women lose the opportunity to take up their succession rights. Besides, erroneous interpretations of Islam make people

Table 6.4 Land ownership and manner of acquisition (Peul)

Marital status	Manner of acquisition					Total	
	Inheritance	Acquisition	RC[1] deliberations	Gifts	PIV	No.	%
Married women	0	0	3	0	3	6	75
Divorced women	0	0	0	0	0	0	0
Widowed women	0	0	1	0	1	2	25
Total	0	0	4	0	4	8	100

Note: [1] Rural Council
Source: Ngoné Diop Tine and Mouhamadou Sy

believe that Islam has no consideration for women. Men sometimes deliberately confuse customary law and Islamic law so as to strengthen such prejudices and perpetuate male domination.

But both traditional and religious authorities unanimously admitted that Islam gives women the right to own land. The law on the national domain also recognises the woman's right to own land. In the face of such unanimity, how is the non-compliance with the provisions of Sharia law explained? How is the exclusion of women from land ownership explained? To these questions, a specialist in Islamic law on Amorphil Island provided the following reply:

> The Sharia is not implemented in issues of inheritance because the tradition predominates and as long as the latter makes it possible for order to prevail, so much the better. The woman has the right to own land but very often she makes no claims because she can win her case before her brothers.

With regards to the right to use land, women are better off. They can exploit land in decline in the same way as men, although men are given priority. Underlying this is the idea that men, as heads of households, should have access to the means of production. However, many women are also heads of households, because this area has seen large-scale male migration. But paradoxically, even when they are absent, Peul men have more rights over land than the women left behind to cultivate them.

The Rural Council of Medina Ndiathbe has immense land reserves and both the local population and other Senegalese, including potential agro-businessmen, apply for their use. However, because of the communal nature of land ownership, the Rural Council allocates it only to individuals who have the consent of other members of their families. This implies that the Rural Council refers less to statutory law and more to customary law in its decisions.

When women's associations need land, they refer first to their village leaders (traditional chiefs) and then to their rural councillors. In some cases, the traditional chiefs allow women to exploit some of the land. If the village chiefs are reticent, the request is addressed to the Rural Council. No legal appeals are made. This situation is precarious, as women do not obtain any proof of allocation from the Rural Council and it is not possible for them to make investments on land that does not belong to them. The case of the Cascas Association for the Promotion of Women illustrates this. Members of this women's association, created in 1974, have been exploiting a 22-hectare irrigated zone in the village (Périmètre Irrigué Villageois, or PIV) lent to them by men of the village, thanks to the support of the NGO Union for Solidarity and Mutual Aid (USE).

Within the framework of development programmes or projects, certain pioneer areas managed by the Company for the Development and Exploitation of the Delta Lands (SAED) are subject to PIV. These areas are afterwards retroceded to the population. Such retrocession applies to both men and women, making it possible for many men to acquire personal plots of about 0.20 hectares. This form of land ownership reduces inequalities between the sexes and embraces attendant socio-economic realities. Women are among the major economic agents of the Senegal Valley and, for that reason, they should be able to use, benefit from and dispose of as they wish the means of production, the most fundamental of which is land. Almost everywhere in the Senegal Valley, on plots of land funded by bilateral agencies or NGOs, women's associations are exploiting land. They grow market gardens, cultivated with the help of power-driven pumps installed at the bank of the Senegal river.

Factors Limiting Women's Land Ownership Among the Peul

Although land exists in abundance, this area is conservative and resistant to change. Women justify their silence and the lethargy of women's associations on the basis of tradition. This explains the non-compliance with statutory and Islamic law as well as the marginalisation of women by decision-making bodies.

Men's views of women's land ownership are not homogeneous. In the view of some men interviewed, women deserve to own land, in recognition of their new economic roles and their contributions to the upkeep of families. Other men, however, expressed the view that women's land ownership should not be encouraged. As one such man explained, 'women have become very ambitious. They want to take the place of men. The NGOs and projects support women a lot to our detriment. Women's access to land is going to lead to the loss of men's power.' Several other men shared this view. For the economic breakthrough of Peul women over the past 20 years has instilled doubts in some men. Some villages, for example, refuse to allocate land to women's associations for no apparent or valid reason.

Another constraint to women's land ownership is the lack of organisation of the Rural Council. The Medina Ndiathbe Rural Council faces many difficulties. The geographic boundaries of some traditional areas are difficult to define because the Rural Council is supposed to be composed of a given number of villages. The land register and the rural cadastre are non-existent. There is no follow-up on applications for land. And applicants for land are required to pay CFA6,000 per hectare to the Rural Council. This is exorbitant for newly created women's associations. Moreover, land applicants have to consult the CERP leader and the officer in charge of state-owned land, who are responsible for surveying the plots of land being applied for. Yet the CERP leader lives over fifty kilometres away from certain villages that are members of the Rural Council. The resources allocated to the CERP are insufficient and its officials have difficulties travelling around.

Illiteracy affects 78 per cent of the rural councillors. The Rural Councils may be chaired by an illiterate or have a single literate member who is saddled with all the administrative responsibilities. Despite awareness-raising workshops on the role of the Rural Council, the legal language and the complexity of the texts discourage many rural councillors. Fortunately, CERP officers carry out praise-worthy support work for the Rural Councils.

Illiteracy also affects 95 per cent of women. Women represent 25 per cent of the rural councillors on the Medina Ndiathbe Rural Council. All the female rural councillors are illiterate. So even though their presence in politics is felt, women's participation is limited by illiteracy. The female rural councillors are perceptive of women's needs but are not able to satisfy them.

Comparative Study of the State of Women's Land Ownership

Serer women are the best-off in terms of land ownership, followed by Wolof women and Peul women. The major distinction of Serer women is that they can inherit land directly from their mothers, which is not the case with Wolof and Peul women. Both among the Wolof and the Serer, succession and the allocation of land by rural councillors are referred to as the main modes of land acquisition by women. Among the Peul, on the other hand, the allocation of land by the PIV is women's major mode of land acquisition. Among the Peul, land shortage is unknown, while in the other two research sites land shortage is the main impediment to land acquisition by women. Similarly, land speculation can only be observed among the Wolof.

Socio-cultural inertia is present, particularly among the Peul. It is limited among the Wolof and the Serer. In all three research sites, customary law exists and prevails over religious (Islamic) law and statutory law. The administrative authorities and the locally elected representatives are not always ready to implement the law on the national domain, except in cases of conflict over land.

In theory as well as in practice, Christianity is favourable for women's land ownership. Theoretically, Islam is as well. However, in reality its provisions relative to succession are not well respected, especially among the Peul.

Except among some Peul rural councillors of Medina Ndaithbe, the access of women's associations to land is accepted. The RIG assists women's associations in accessing land, for example, to the extent of making arrangements with land-owners.

Finally, women in all three research sites expressed the need to have land, but were not always ready to face the obstacles confronting them.

Factors Determining Women's Land Ownership

Women's access to and ownership of land is not an accident. Some determining factors were noted, including the socio-cultural environment; women's level of organisation; the attitudes of religious and administrative authorities; the attitudes of locally elected representatives; and the support of development programmes, projects and NGOs.

As seen among the Peul of Medina Ndiathbe, having abundant land does not *ipso facto* mean that women will become landowners. Tradition has to be taken into account. In the research sites with an unfavourable cultural or customary environment, women's land ownership faces many problems. These are compounded when religious and statutory law are subordinated to customary law.

The enviable state of women's land ownership among the Serer of Joal-Fadiouth owes more to customary attitudes and laws that valorise women than it does to religious and statutory law. Were it not for the existence of matriarchy, Serer women's land ownership would probably be the same as that of their Wolof and Peul.

The results of this study illustrate the validity of the saying, 'united we stand, divided we fall'. Individual women's applications for land have little chance of being satisfied compared to applications emanating from women's associations. This was particularly confirmed by the case of the RIG. And administrative authorities clearly expressed their support for collective women's applications.

Unfortunately, female leadership is weak and is not likely to encourage the promotion of rural women. Furthermore, women do not have the means to combine their efforts and engage in common struggle to resolve common problems (including accessing the means of production in general and land in particular). So far, women's associations have operated in a disorganised manner. Their level of organisation is linked to their level of education and training.

The bias of religious authorities is crucial. If the religious authorities insisted on the implementation of Islamic law on inheritance and landed property, women would have a better lot. For the fact that almost all Serer women are landowners may also be explained by the favourable attitude of Christianity towards women and its non-discrimination.

The sub-prefects and CERP heads, as administrative authorities, are supposed to provide technical assistance to rural councillors, particularly with regard to the interpretation of texts and the delimitation of land. In the research sites where they cooperate with women's associations, the results are favourable.

In their responsibility to represent the interests of the population and to allocate and revoke land, locally elected representatives are well placed to understand women's difficulties and provide appropriate solutions. But, as seen with the RIG, conceptions of constituents and the level of education and training among the rural councillors are critical. The Peul Rural Council of Medina Ndiathbe is more inclined to respect customary law than to comply with the law on the national domain. It is less sensitive to women's needs, despite the presence of female rural councillors.

As was the case with the women's association of Cascas, USE contributed to ensuring women's access to land. Without the support of this NGO, what would the fate be of the 446 members of the association? Elsewhere, Africare and the Project on Community Management of National Resources (PGCRN) are also helping women to obtain land to try new development programmes and projects. Africare deals only with women's associations holding title deeds to land issued by the rural community. Once this condition is satisfied, it will provide financial and technical support.

PART III Recommendations Recognising Senegalese Women's Land Rights

In the foreword to the National Action Plan for Senegalese women 1997–2000, the Ministry in Charge of Women, Children and Family Affairs noted that

> the solution is not to live in the past, because it is recognised today that a fossilised society is a society condemned to degenerate. Senegal is experiencing a radical change as witnessed by the multiplicity of ideas disseminated around it, and the riches of its human resources which constitute its greatest asset in the struggle against poverty and for the institution of a lasting development.

The role of women in the Senegalese economy, both in the urban and rural areas, as well as in all sectors of economic activity (particularly agriculture), is important. Women represent 52 per cent of Senegal's population. This should be reflected in similar levels of participation in decision-making and access to the means of production, including land. Marginalising women economically and politically, while using them as an uninformed and untrained electoral and labour resource, is a mistake. Now that Senegal is decentralising and pursuing strategic economic reforms, the centrality of Senegalese women to development must be acknowledged.

Yet this empirical study shows violations of Senegalese women's land rights. Women are confronted with difficulties in appropriating the land they cultivate, and consequently in achieving economic empowerment.

Women, and traditional religious and administrative authorities, as well as locally elected representatives and civil society, should combine efforts to promote and protect Senegalese women's land rights and thus obtain a better future for Senegalese women. In so doing, the general and specific recommendations outlined below should be adopted.

General Recommendations

Concerning women Women's promotion can only be achieved with their active and genuine participation. The following are important for both women and their organisations.

With an overall illiteracy rate of 78 per cent, it is difficult for women to face development challenges. The right to education is enshrined in the Senegalese Constitution. The education and training of women should be privileged, to ensure the ability to fight stereotypes and poverty, and to encourage the development of strong female leadership and the strong representation of women in decision-making.

Guaranteeing women's land rights is impossible unless women know those rights and are intellectually prepared to defend them. Having informed and well-trained women is not enough. Strong female leadership is necessary to challenge socio-cultural inertia.

Women's land rights struggles have little success because of the absence of unifying institutional frameworks for collective action. It is encouraging to observe that women's associations and movements are developing in Senegal. But the qualitative changes necessary for women's promotion cannot be left to the state and development partners. Organisations of well-educated women, such as the Association of Female University Graduates and the Association of Women Lawyers have a role to play, as do federative umbrellas, including the Federation of Senegalese Women's Associations (FAFS) created in 1977 and FNGPF formed in 1987. The latter is composed of some 4,000 women's associations with about 500,000 members.

At present, 75 per cent of poor households are situated in the rural areas. According to the provisions of the law on the national domain, land should be allocated on the basis of the need for productive return. Therefore, if women do not have the financial resources to develop land allocated to them, they run the risk of having the land revoked by the Rural Councils. There is a need to increase women's economic capacity for this reason. In addition, the more that women contribute financially to the upkeep of families, the more they develop their negotiating abilities and the greater the rights they acquire.

At only 9 per cent, women are insufficiently represented in rural and municipal councils. In the present legislature, only 10 per cent of parliamentarians are women. As these are the bodies within which major strategic decisions are taken, women stand to gain by actively participating in decision-making. With the increase of regionalisation, the decentralised participation of women in decision-making should not be excluded.

Concerning civil society These recommendations are aimed at national, regional and international NGOs, particularly those concerned with human rights in general and women's rights in particular.

It is important to provide programmes and projects that mainstream gender. For example, the World Bank's Literacy Project – Priority Women (PAPF) aims to reduce the illiteracy rate of rural women by 5 per cent. And the African Network for Integrated Development (RADI) has developed a programme on rural women's legal rights.

The gender and development approach should be encouraged to examine power relations between the sexes and their different roles. Some NGOs, such as Oxfam, have already recommended this approach and refuse to support programmes, projects or programmes in which women are pushed into the background.

Specific Recommendations

The empirical study discussed in this chapter attests to disproportionate gender relations between men and women. These relations have been socially constructed, with custom and/or tradition playing a fundamental role in that construction. To change these gender relations with respect to women's land ownership, use can be made of custom, religion and the law.

Using the law The Convention on the Elimination of All Forms of Discrimination Against Women (CEDAW) can be used to promote Senegalese women's land ownership.

CEDAW was adopted in 1979 by the UN General Assembly and ratified by Senegal in 1985. It demands that all practices that violate women's equality rights, no matter how rooted in culture and/or tradition, should be eradicated. CEDAW therefore calls on governments to work for the transformation not only of statutory law, but of customary and religious law, to achieve equality between men and women. As a signatory of CEDAW, Senegal should therefore take all appropriate measures to neutralise and develop customary law.

To achieve this, consciousness-raising and functional literacy should be re-inforced, in order to end prejudices and stereotypes maintaining that women do not need economic resources such as land because men support them. The mind-sets of both men and women need to be addressed, particularly among the Peul people. Women's promotion should not be viewed as an attack on men or as a threat, but simply as a reality to be dealt with.

As the Minister for Women, Children and Family Affairs declared:

> it is clear that the hoped-for developments will create imbalances, which need to be taken into account to make progress. Improving the situation of women and young girls has to necessarily go through the implementation of changes beneficial to society as a whole. These changes will result in the loss of certain privileges by some people and can be misunderstood by others – both men and women. We can, therefore, expect resistance from them, but they cannot stop the course of history.

Awareness-raising among traditional and religious authorities is critical, because the rural population of Senegal is both conservative and religious. TOSTAN[4] suggests that regular information sessions aimed at traditional authorities could instil urgency about the need to eradicate discrimination against women. In addition, as Senegal's history demonstrates, no change can occur without the support of traditional and religious authorities. For example, traditional and religious authorities were closely associated with the successful national social mobilisation campaigns against female genital mutilation and HIV/AIDS. A national social mobilisation campaign on women's land ownership could have similar success.

Senegal's laws on the national domain and on the establishment of rural communities need to be harmonised with CEDAW. According to the former law, the two conditions for land allocation are that land should be granted first to inhabitants of the locality, and that it should be allocated to persons able to develop it. This does not seem, a priori, to be unfavourable to the appropriation of land by women. However, as demonstrated by the empirical study, its neutrality does not mainstream gender. In addition, Article 14 of CEDAW, dealing with discrimination against rural women, stipulates that:

> States Parties should take into account the specific problems confronting rural women as well as the important role that these women play in the economic survival of their families, particularly through their work in the non-monetary sectors of the economy, and should take all the appropriate measures to ensure that the provisions of this Convention are applied to women of these areas ... The States undertake to eliminate discrimination against women in the rural areas in order to ensure that they participate, on the basis of equality between men and women, in rural development and in its advantages.

Furthermore, in view of ongoing socio-economic changes and the need for women to access credit, there is need to encourage rural entrepreneurship. The Senegalese Ministry for Women, Children and Family Affairs, in collaboration with other ministries, the private sector and women's associations and movements, should create and support such programmes and projects.

Once these amendments are made, the state should ensure the law is respected by ensuring its implementation. Local authorities, namely the sub-prefect and rural councillors, should ensure that the law is complied with. All applications for land submitted to local authorities should, at risk of being invalidated, necessarily be accompanied by documentary evidence of the application, a technical report and a recommendation from the CERP head. This would preclude the allocation of large areas of land to private farmers. As noted in Abdoul Aziz Diagne's article on the management of land belonging to the national domain, 'the administrative authorities should exercise, much more efficiently, the control which is devolved on them which should apply as much to the legality as to the opportunity of decisions taken by rural councillors in order to put an end to the abuses detected'.

Implementation of the law depends on the rural councillors' level of competence. For example, the violations observed in the application of the law on the national domain are caused both by socio-cultural inertia and the incompetence of a good number of rural councillors. The education and training of rural councillors should thus be ongoing rather than occasional. The use of national languages, as in the pilot project for the promotion of literacy among local representatives and notables, could be beneficial. Gender analysis should be included in such education and training programmes and projects.

Using religion Religion is admittedly often interpreted by men to their advantage and to women's detriment. But religion can also be used by women to defend their land rights.

Christianity (particularly Catholicism) advocates equality rights between men and women and is clear that these rights apply to land ownership. But among the Serer of Joal-Fadiouth, which has a Catholic majority, tradition is more salient and more likely to be implemented. Religious authorities must challenge this tendency among their followers.

The situation is different with Islam. In the seventh century, the emerging Islamic religion found women in a pitiable and tragic situation. In Arab states at the time, women were considered as objects of pleasure and were victims of exploitation, humiliation and injustice. The advent of Islam was a decisive turning point for women. The new religion restored their status and gave them the means to free themselves from servitude to men. For under Islam, women have rights as well as duties.

Today, there are several different interpretations of Islam, some of which reduce women's rights, such as the right to inherit and own land. However, these rights are recognised by Islam without any reservations.

The main method of land acquisition described by Islam is inheritance. Women have the right to inherit from their parents, according to the principle of one share for women and two for men. Similarly, widows may inherit their husbands' property, including land, according to the principle of one-fourth for women if the husbands have no children and one-eighth for women if the husbands have living children. This discrimination is explained by the fact that, in the seventh century, women did not have to work and were supported by men.

Today, however, the situation has changed. Women do over 70 per cent of agricultural work. The contribution of rural and urban women to the economy is undeniable, although it has not been admitted. As a result, the monopolisation of land by men is no longer justified.

Discussions with religious authorities, including the imam of the Wolof's Medina Sabakh mosque, show that Islam is not against its adaptation to the socio-economic or political context. In other words, Islam is not opposed to the development of women's land rights beyond those stipulated by Islamic inheritance law.

Conclusion

This study was an ambitious one, which, beyond the collecting and analysing of empirical data, aims to influence the Senegalese government. It is hoped that it will be a prelude to land law and policy reform to end discrimination against Senegalese women. The value of this study therefore depends upon its follow-up and application.

Notes

1. Land is among the causes of the Casamance conflict. The 1989 Senegalese–Mauritanian conflict stemmed from a land dispute at the border between the two countries.

2. Department of Forecasting and Statistics, Senegalese Ministry of the Economy, Finance and Planning.

3. Droy, Isabelle (1990) *Women and Rural Development*, Paris: Karthala.

4. In 1996–97, this NGO, whose name means 'breakthrough' in the Wolof language, succeeded in eradicating female genital mutilation, a well-established traditional practice in the village of Malikounda, in the Department of Mbour.

SEVEN

Gender, Land and Rights: Contemporary Contestations in Law, Policy and Practice in Uganda

Winnie Bikaako and John Ssenkumba

§ THIS study has included the documentation and interpretation of key aspects of cultural transformation. Foremost of these aspects are the dynamics behind the changing nature of the land rights that women have, through relentless struggle, made society concede.

The study recognises that although the women have won some struggles, much lies ahead and serious obstacles remain. This study seeks to unravel what these obstacles are, how they have been handled hitherto and what needs to be done to ensure desired outcomes. Although activists, scholars and policy-makers have diverse perspectives on effecting cultural transformation, the novelty of this study is the identification of the conjunctions between human rights, law and religion in the context of cultural transformation. These may not be the only variables, or even the most important ones. However, the interplay among them elucidates the explanation of rapid social change and transformation.

Geo-political and Socio-economic Background

Uganda is a landlocked country astride the equator. It lies east of Zaire, south of the Sudan, west of Kenya, north of Tanzania and northeast of Rwanda. It is ethnically linked to all these countries – their international boundaries cut through ethnic groups along the border, dividing extended families. In addition, its location in the Nile basin provides a link to north African countries, like Egypt.

Uganda's total surface area is 236,859 square kilometres, of which 82 per cent is land. Most of this land is flat plateau, between 1,000 and 1,400 metres above sea level, with about 7 per cent being only 1,500 metres above sea level. Its position and diverse topography have given rise to a varied climate, making Uganda rich in flora and fauna and giving its population a range of occupational possibilities. Such an environment gives Uganda much economic potential. With appropriate economic planning and policies, it could develop into a prosperous agricultural and industrial society.

According to the 1991 census, Uganda has a population of 16.7 million people, of whom 51 per cent are female. The country is home to over fifty different ethnic groups, falling into four categories: the Bantu; the Nilotics; the Nilo-Hamites; and the Sudanic ethnic groups. Religion too has shaped Ugandan society and politics. The major religions are Catholicism, Protestantism and Islam. The 1991 census reports that 44.5 per cent of people are Catholics, 39.2 per cent are Protestants, 10.5 per cent are Muslim and 5.9 per cent follow other religions.

The class character of Uganda derives from agriculture, the dominant activity of 90 per cent of the population, who live and work in the countryside or in rural areas on smallholdings. Although about 10 per cent of the population lives and works in the urban areas, most of them have rural homes as well. Uganda has therefore a primarily agrarian economy.

The foundation of the country's economy was laid by the British colonialists, who destroyed whatever enterprise and industry existed in pre-colonial Uganda and introduced cash crops for the benefit of Britain. The economy is still dominated by colonial structures, in spite of their failure to tap Uganda's potential. According to the World Development Report 1997, Uganda has a per capita gross national product (GNP) of USD240 and is ranked the fourteenth poorest state in the world. Low economic performance and civil strife have resulted in an inferior quality of life for most Ugandans.

Evolution of Land Tenure in Uganda: Major Trends

Pre-1900 Customary land tenure prevailed in Uganda before the advent of colonialism. Despite the unifying effect of cultures and customary laws, there was a multitude of customary land tenure systems reflecting the different ethnic groups' legal systems. Available literature suggests an emerging consensus that land ownership under the various customary tenure systems was vested in different entities – the chief or ruler, the tribe, the clan, the family and, in a few cases, the individual. The existence of a dichotomy in customary property laws is also evident. Individual ownership was limited to what an individual had acquired and improved on the land, while the community owned the land or property in its natural state.

Tenure relations under customary land tenure varied, depending on the customs of a given ethnic group. In order to highlight salient features of customary land tenure, attention will be focused on a few ethnic groups broadly representative of all those in Uganda. Customary land tenure systems fell broadly into three categories: communal tenure, clan tenure and 'nomadic' or pastoral tenure.

The communal tenure system was found predominantly in the kingdoms of

Ankole, Buganda, Bunyoro and Toro ethnic groups, which had centralised and feudalistic administration systems. Ownership of land was vested in the ruler, either as an owner or a trustee. The clan tenure system was found, on the other hand, among ethnic groups governed by decentralised administration systems – the Bakiiga ethnic group as well as the Nilotic, Nilo-Hamitic and Sudanic ethnic groups. Traditional rulers did exist in some of these ethnic groups. However, clan elders and leaders had greater influence over the community and over land.

Although homesteads and cultivated fields were owned corporately under both the communal and clan tenure systems, individuals enjoyed specific rights. These included individual rights to homesteads, fields, trees, agricultural products and trapping sites. The tribe and the clan, however, communally owned some resources, namely, uncultivated 'virgin' grasslands, grazing lands and forests within the tribal or clan boundaries, No specific estates, interests or rights were vested in individuals for such resources.

'Nomadic' or pastoralist tenure was prevalent among the Karamoja. The rights to grazing lands were vested in the entire tribe, with no specific rights vested in individuals. However, there were restrictive claims to certain pastures or wells, which could be permanently or seasonally enhanced.

In all the three tenures – communal, clan and pastoralist – there were uncultivated lands which were not subjected to ownership and control. Animals normally used these lands, although among the Nilotic communities such lands constituted hunting lands, ownership of which lay in clans or individuals.

The origin of exclusive claims over land by a tribe or clan was invariably through peaceful settlement, conquest or seizure. The nature of ownership and control exercised by the tribe or the clan did not vary greatly among the different ethnic groups. The head of the tribe or clan naturally became the authority controlling the land in Bunyoro, Busoga and Teso. Through the clan head, the clan exercised rights over the land and their obligations to it. The clan head had the authority to allocate unused land; to allow individuals, both from within and occasionally from outside the clan, to occupy and use unused land; to arrange customary practices such as sowing and harvesting at specific times; and to settle disputes over land. Depending on the specific clan, for instance in Bunyoro, clan heads were paid tributes as marks of prestige for the services provided as leaders.

Men within patrilineal customary tenure systems had absolute inheritance rights to the occupation, possession and use of land. After fulfilling minor pre-emptive customary obligations, men also had absolute rights over the products of the land occupied or cultivated and the right of privacy in their homes. Occupation and use effectively signified indisputable 'ownership'.

These rights did not apply to women. Women did not inherit land. Boys from both monogamous and polygamous marriages usually took over lands allocated to their mothers, by their fathers, for the women's care and use in event of their fathers' deaths. When such boys were still minors, brothers of the deceased fathers normally looked after the women under the deceased men's care as well as their lands until the minors came of age. Surviving wives continued to live on portions of their deceased husbands' lands until they elected to return to their fathers' families or to remarry outside the clan of the deceased husbands. However, in Acholi, Alur, Kigezi and Lango, matrilineal inheritance of land through mothers was practised. Sons were usually allocated lands that were not claimed or occupied as soon as they wanted to grow their own cash crops or marry.

Although Ugandan ethnic groups are patrilineal, there is evidence that some women in a few ethnic groups enjoyed higher status than others in relation to ownership of and control over land. In the kingdoms, women from the royal families owned land. For instance, the Kabaka's (King's) mother and sisters in Buganda had shares in the royal lands. Among the Basoga, daughters of chiefs could inherit from their fathers and become chiefs, implying they became *omukulu wa ulhuya* (family heads) who could own and freely dispose of land.

And in nineteenth-century Toro, women could inherit property, including land and livestock, as well as status as householders from their fathers, if there were no sons. Daughters could be considered before other male relatives. They were free to dispose of their lands so acquired and, if they married, their husbands had no authority over such lands. Disposal of their lands required their permission and these lands were returnable upon divorce. Uxorilocal marriage was practised so that, in effect, they filled several socially important roles that were usually the preserve of men. Where there were sons, daughters could still inherit some of their father's property, even if a smaller share than their brothers'. Essentially, the idea that children, irrespective of sex, should receive part of the father's property was upheld. There is also evidence of several wills where daughters were appointed as heirs to their deceased fathers even when there were living, capable sons. In such cases, daughters as heirs received shares of the property equal to or more than those given to their brothers.

Some women in Toro also enjoyed rights of occupation over customary land, acquired by the granting of requests from the chief. Toro customary law bound the chief to grant, on request, land to adult women, including widows, provided that they proved they had the means to build houses on the land. Married women, however, except in the case of freehold land, would rarely be considered. If they were considered, they would normally get smaller portions than their sons.

1900–74 To achieve their goals and further their aims through indirect rule, the British colonial administration introduced 'new' land tenure systems. In Buganda, the *mailo* tenure system was introduced to extend British colonial administration over hitherto uncolonised areas. Where the British colonial administration did not perceive a specific tenure system as a threat, local populations were allowed to use and own land according to their respective customary tenure systems. Several areas of Uganda thus continued to operate under customary tenure systems. As a result, a multiplicity of land tenure systems emerged. The major tenure systems were the *mailo*, leasehold, freehold and customary tenure systems.

The *mailo* tenure system, introduced through the 1900 Uganda Agreement, was particular to Buganda and parts of Bunyoro. The 1908 Buganda Land Law passed by the *lukiiko* (Buganda Parliament) and approved by the British governor further defined the *mailo* tenure system.

The 1900 Uganda Agreement granted authority for the allocation of land to the *lukiiko*, with chiefs being given the responsibility of determining the beneficiaries to whom land would be allotted. Individual beneficiaries were free to choose the land that they wanted to own before crown land was designated. However, only 4,138 individuals benefited from these allocations. These individuals were issued with provisional certificates for specified amounts of acreage and were then allowed to select land corresponding to those amounts. Under this law, the maximum area that an individual *mailo* owner could own was 30 square miles. A final certificate was issued after land had been surveyed (1904–36), demarcated and entered in the land register.

The 1900 Uganda Agreement, read together with the 1908 Buganda Land Law, made *mailo* lands quasi-freehold, since they were subject to restrictions passed in subsequent legislation by the *lukiiko*. Two major restrictions were imposed over *mailo* owners. First, the 1908 Buganda Land Law prevented *mailo* owners from disposing of their lands to those who did not belong to the Protectorate, the churches or other societies, except with the approval of the governor and the *lukiiko*. The second restriction, through the Land Law, the nature of Succession Law and the 1927 Busuulu and Envujjo Law, specified relations between *mailo* owners and peasants on their lands.

The *mailo* tenure system was a new form of land ownership, resembling the freehold tenure system and introduced in areas where land was previously communally owned. Through the method of land distribution, the beneficiaries of the *mailo* system acquired the most desirable fertile land, while the remaining, less fertile, land became Crown land. Ownership of land necessarily bestowed on *mailo* owners the right to transfer their lands by gift, inheritance or sale to other Africans. In subsequent decades, the provisions for land transactions resulted in mortgages on and sub-divisions and transfers of *mailo* lands. Tenants grew in number on unused *mailo* lands. A large tenant class, commonly known as *bibanja* holders, developed.

Subsequent legislation during the 1900–74 period, including the 1967 Constitution, further entrenched the *mailo* tenure system, albeit with some modifications. The 1967 Constitution, in particular, empowered Parliament to make provision for the regulation of *mailo* lands. The 1967 Constitution also vested ownership of, and control over, all minerals and water on *mailo* lands in the state.

The leasehold tenure system was another colonial innovation. Two forms of leasehold were introduced, statutory and private.

Statutory leaseholds were created under the Crown Lands Ordinance, followed by the 1969 Public Lands Act and later the 1975 Land Reform Decree. The Uganda Land Commission granted statutory leases over public land in rural areas and to urban authorities in urban areas. Holders of customary tenure could be granted, on application to the relevant authority, leasehold tenure in public land they occupied at the time of such application. On conversion, the leases would be subject to modern development conditions.

Private leaseholds were created by private arrangements, made either by individuals or organisations with *mailo* and freehold landowners. The lessor and lessee of private leaseholds privately determined the terms, duration, rental amounts and development conditions. Leases of more than 500 acres granted to non-Africans, whether statutory or private, required the consent of the minister.

Leaseholds grant the right to possession, use or occupation of land for a specified duration. Under the Crown Lands Ordinance, the duration of the leases granted by the Governor to individuals was not to exceed 99 years. All leases are subject to development conditions, mainly for agricultural and building purposes, to be carried out by the lessees. Failure to meet these conditions leads to forfeiture of the leases.

The District and Federal Land Boards, under the 1962 Public Lands Ordinance, were vested with freeholds over all public lands in the districts and federal states. The terms and conditions on which such leases are held have remained the same as under the Crown Lands Ordinance.

In line with the British colonial administration's desire to redefine land in Uganda and encourage individual land ownership by Africans, the freehold tenure system was introduced in parts of the districts known as Ankole, Buganda, Bugisu, Kigezi and Toro.

Freeholds were granted under the 1900 and 1901 Agreements in Toro and Ankole respectively, with titles issued to the allottees later, in accordance with the 1903 Crown Lands Ordinance. Another category of freeholds, 'adjudicated freeholds', was granted in Ankole, Bugisu and Kigezi in accordance with the 1958 Lands Adjudication Rules. Provision for the registration of land titles was to be made on a district basis under the May 1958 Customary Rights of Africans, adjudicated under the Crown Lands (Adjudication) Rules.

The 1962 Public Lands Ordinance, which repealed and replaced the Crown Lands Ordinance, vested all former Crown lands occupied for state purposes in the Uganda Land Commission in freeholds. Management of all former Crown lands in the districts and federal states was vested in the district and federal Land Boards respectively. These Land Boards, under Section 22 of the Public Lands Ordinance, could make grants in freehold or leasehold of public land vested in them, even if such land was occupied under customary land tenure. Customary tenants had to be resettled and could remain on the land until then, or until they were given appropriate compensation, or both. As a result, in Ankole and Kigezi districts these Land Boards granted some public lands as freeholds to tenants. In other districts, however, only leaseholds were granted.

The 1967 Constitution abolished the district and federal Land Boards. The 1967 Constitution vested in the Uganda Land Commission all public land throughout Uganda, *inter alia*, to grant freeholds and leaseholds to individuals. In such grants, the Uganda Land Commission was to act on the advice of District Land Committees. In accordance with the corresponding Act, the Minister for Lands must give his or her consent to the granting of freeholds of public lands of more than 500 acres to an individual, as well as of all public lands in the rural areas. The power of the Uganda Land Commission was thus restricted.

The Act stipulated that, once granted, statutory freeholds must be registered under the Registration of Titles Act, which makes provisions for and stipulates conditions under which such statutory freeholds may be alienated. The Act provides that registered freeholds are equivalent to fee simple absolute possession. For the rights vested in freeholders are the same as the rights of owners of fee simple estates under British land law. Thus, subject to statutory controls, freeholders have the right to everything superjacent and subjacent to their lands. They can lease, mortgage, sell and bequeath their lands. They can alienate them by testamentary disposition or *inter vivos*.

Ugandan freeholds, however, do have statutory and administrative restrictions on the rights of full enjoyment of absolute ownership. As the population increases and pressure on land grows, the state takes on more powers to ensure that land is properly used by those who own it. Absolute ownership does not exist, since what landowners do with their lands has to take the public interest into account. Thus Ugandan freeholders have the following restrictions imposed:

1. All statutory freeholds are subject to development conditions, as contained in the covenants between the grantor and grantee. The grantee is under obligation to develop the land within a stipulated period for the purposes specified on the grant. Any breach of the covenant on the part of the grantee leads to forfeiture of the freehold title (leading to the argument that Ugandan freeholds are equivalent to leaseholds).
2. All mineral and water rights on freeholds are vested in the state. The rights of freeholders are confined to the soil and surface of the land as nothing below the soil belongs to him or her.
3. The Land Transfer Act restricts disposition of land to non-Africans, without the prior consent of the minister.

Freeholds were not widespread. They were limited to a small category of individuals – kings, notables and chiefs, large-scale agricultural developers and some special interest groups such as Catholic and Protestant churches.

Despite the introduction of other tenure systems, customary tenure remains the most widespread tenure system. According to Obol Ochola (1971), customary tenure covers 64 per cent of the total land area. This form of tenure continued to flourish under British colonialism, so long as the protectorate government did not perceive it as a threat. Customary tenants occupied unalienated land, designated as Crown land in the colonial period, that was not converted into *mailo*, leasehold or freehold land.

1975 to the present The 1975 Land Reform Decree abolished *mailo* lands and freeholds. It reduced all *mailo* lands and freeholds to leaseholds by repealing the 1969 Public Lands Act, which had provided for the protection of customary tenants, and granted statutory leases to individuals and organisations for 99 years and 199 years respectively. In practice, however, *mailo* lands and freeholds have continued to feature alongside leaseholds and customary tenants. In effect, the decree remained non-functional except for two aspects. First, it abolished the payment of *busuulu* (ground rent) and *envujjo* (commodity rent). And second, it empowered potential developers who acquired public land to evict customary tenants.

The lax enforcement of the decree may be partly attributed to its conflict with the 1967 Constitution. The 1967 Constitution entrenches the *mailo* tenure system. The decree abolished it, without repealing Article 126 of the 1967 Constitution. The decree was thus rendered unconstitutional. It also effectively nationalised land without compensation, which was contrary to Article 13 of the 1967 Constitution.

Implications of the Colonial Land Tenure Changes for Women's Land Rights

Women's land rights under customary tenure systems were limited to servitude and usufruct. Patrilineality made it impossible for the majority of women to inherit or own land. Women had no control over land. Decision-making was vested in men as heads of families or clans. Even where women were given land by their natal families, they were not allowed to alienate family property. The right of disposition was vested in male family and kinship group heads. These heads were vested with the power to allocate unused land, and controlled any alienation of land to outsiders.

British colonialism greatly impacted customary land tenure systems. Whereas customary tenure systems guaranteed Ugandan women secure user rights, colonial legislation and policy, by exerting pressure on customary tenure systems, altered women's land rights. Family heads, predominantly male, assumed greater autonomy in decisions regarding land access, use and control, thus rendering women's user rights less permanent than before. Family heads assumed more rights, enabling them to alienate land without necessarily consulting the larger family or community. At the same time, British colonialism left intact the patriarchal customs and traditions adhered to by various ethnic groups in Uganda, making it difficult for women to access, inherit and own land. In essence, colonial land laws and policies further strengthened the patriarchal gender relations that existed in Uganda.

Although women did not have rights of control over and disposition of land, they were guaranteed user rights. User rights involved a form of land ownership that deserved to be protected by colonial land law and policy because it was previously well-defined. Post-colonial law and policy should recognise that the value of land can be perceived in terms of use, rather than in terms of abstract legal rights.

Like most post-colonial African states, Uganda is characterised by legal dualism – the existence of an imported 'Western' legal system and customary legal systems specifically pertaining to land and property rights, marriage and succession. There are inevitably conflicts between these two legal systems. Legal dualism makes it possible for a patriarchal society to resist claims for women's rights by vacillating between the two legal systems, successfully neutralising any reforms that might have been instituted. In the words of Mbilinyi (1997):

> it has confined the majority (both male and female) to an arbitrary and contra-dictory world, governed at one moment by universal laws which apply to all citizens, and at another moment by laws, which apply solely to members of a given tribe, clan and ethnic group.

Conceptual and Theoretical Issues

Land rights in development and human rights This study aims to address land rights in economic and social development with particular reference to human rights. It makes use of conceptual and analytical research to examine the broad principles underlying different approaches to land law and land rights in different parts of Uganda and the mechanisms for addressing competing claims to land.

What is new is the establishment of links between land law and land tenure systems on the one hand, and civil, political, economic, social and cultural human rights on the other. Access to land and security of tenure are the basis of livelihoods and subsistence for billions of the world's rural poor. Access and security are thus critical for the realisation of other internationally recognised human rights of the rural poor.

Conflicts proliferate over principles of land law (customary versus statutory), but also over land rights themselves. There is an emerging tension between 'strong' and 'weak' notions of land and property rights. This tension is best manifested in the tension between the civil rights of the landed, and the economic and social rights of the landless, the land poor and precarious tenant farmers.

There is also the tension between extremes of private and public ownership. A middle ground between the two extremes has been struck. Private ownership (side by side with customary ownership) has been recognised, with limitations on the right to private ownership, such as land expropriation in the public interest. With the present trend towards privatisation, public ownership is diminishing. With international pressure and the national adoption of structural adjustment, land law and policies are to be determined by the market. There is renewed pressure to replace customary (communal) land ownership with private (individual) land ownership, in the interest of agricultural productivity. Thus there is renewed concern about preserving the land security associated with customary tenure systems, to avoid further accentuating rural landlessness and poverty and deepening inequalities.

There is documentation of the civil and political rights abuses deriving from land conflicts. However, the wider legal and policy issues relating to land distribution and tenure have not been addressed substantively. There are real difficulties with land law and policy from a human rights perspective. For one thing, land rights do not easily fit the distinctions commonly drawn between civil and political human rights on the one hand, and economic, social and cultural human rights on the other. Land rights, whether to specific lands or to the benefits derived from those lands, depend on ownership and control. Individuals and groups who own specific lands, with titles duly registered, have civil and political land rights. But the individuals dependent on those lands for survival, who have no alternative means of subsistence, must also be considered to have economic, social and cultural land rights. There is a direct connection. Yet the concept of land rights is still ambiguous and fragile. Statutory law provides for the recognition of land as property subject to private land ownership. But it does not take into account the functions of land other than as property, which would imply placing limitations on the private ownership of land.

As a consequence, the human rights approach has not been immediately relevant to arguments for particular types of land tenure systems. Such as approach, however, is of value in determining the moral weight of competing land rights, when claims made by those who need land, but do not own it, are pitted against claims of those who own land, but do not necessarily need it. This is a new dimension to the analysis of land rights, changing the focus from bundles of human rights associated with particular tenure systems to the relationship between tenure systems and the realisation of fundamental human rights.

It must be noted that there has been a shift in the human rights approach since the adoption of the Universal Declaration of Human Rights in 1948. The early emphasis on the protection of property rights changed in the 1950s and 1960s to an emphasis on the need to limit property rights in the public interest. This was consistent with development strategies emphasising redistributive economic and social policies, including land reform policies. The commitment to land reform policies, based on the functions of property, was echoed in a number of Declarations adopted by the United Nations and its specialised agencies throughout the

1970s. The conceptualisation of the right to development underlined the indivisibility of human rights and the interlinkages between civil and political human rights on the one hand, and economic, social and cultural human rights, on the other. Emphasis was also placed on equality of opportunity and equity in development. This was based on efforts to actualise economic, social and cultural human rights. Land rights were seen as key to achieving the right to food, particularly for vulnerable groups. Measures like the protection of usufruct land rights, and the curtailment of absentee landlordism, were examples of what was done in this respect.

The tension between different human rights approaches as they relate to property (including land) rights has shifted in the post-Cold War period. Human rights have now become contentious in North–South relations. While the North emphasises private property rights, the legitimacy of existing private property rights (especially to land) is under scrutiny in the South. The trend is towards security of private land rights in the interest of efficiency and productivity. In some cases, this has been due to internal pressure, for example, peasants demanding security of tenure. But external pressure has also played a part. Funding agencies and international financial institutions (IFIs) have called for the liberalisation of land tenure systems under structural adjustment programmes. The trend towards the liberalisation and privatisation of land has culminated in a dilemma. How is balance to be achieved between security and productivity on the one hand, and customary security and equality on the other? And how to improve women's customary land rights?

Ultimately, that is the question. Human rights should be used to press for more equitable land law and policy. Land law and policy reform must cater to the competing needs of various sections of the population. Access, security and reform are fundamental human rights concerns.

Women and land tenure systems When discussing women's land rights, the first distinction drawn is usually that between matrilineal and patrilineal systems. In matrilineal systems, women, like men, had usufruct land rights based on their position within their matrilineage. They could exercise these usufruct rights when not married, during marriage and upon divorce or widowhood. They could inherit land and pass it on to their children. Women could also acquire and maintain property over which their husbands had no rights.

In patrilineal systems, followed by most ethnic groups in Uganda, women's land rights were dependent on their relationships to males, usually fathers, brothers, husbands or sons. In most cases, women did not inherit land in their own right. When they did, they inherited less land than their brothers. It was mainly through marriage that women acquired user rights to land, with husbands assigning particular lands for cultivation to each of their wives. Besides producing for family needs, women, in some instances, had the discretion to exchange or sell the surplus.

Upon widowhood, women acted as guardians or trustees for minor children until a male heir became of age and could take charge. Women with adult sons were largely assured of continued user rights to land, in contrast to childless women or women who bore only daughters, whose position was precarious. In the ethnic groups where widow inheritance was practised, widow inheritance ensured continuing user rights for women to the lands they had cultivated during marriage. Refusal to marry the successor meant termination of user rights to land.

User rights deteriorated under British colonialism. The biggest change was in the larger lineage's ownership and control of land through inheritance, which was contracted to the immediate and individual family. Statutory law was instrumental in this change and new property laws were introduced and recognised. But at the same time, customary law resisted and some old property laws survived. For example, the pledge (a traditional concept) can be viewed against a mortgage (a modern concept). A pledge is redeemable regardless of time, which is not the case with a mortgage.

Women have not been passive in the face of this change and have seized the available alternatives. This partly explains the refusals to enter into marriage, the high rates of desertion and divorce and the resort to independent income avenues in the informal sector.

Methodology The methodology used was the case study. A careful selection of areas representative of the dynamics related to the four existing land tenure systems in the country led to the central and western regions. From each of the two regions a district was randomly selected: the Bushenyi and the Mubende districts.

Bushenyi, formerly part of the Ankole kingdom, is situated in the western region of Uganda. The 1991 national census indicates that it has a population of 736,361 and a population density of 150 persons per square kilometre. The major land tenure systems found here are the customary and leasehold land tenure systems.

Mubende district is situated in the central region of Uganda, which is historically a largely Buganda region. Mubende district, according to the 1991 national census, has a total population of 500,976 and a population density of 89 persons per square kilometre. The major land tenure systems prevailing in the district are the customary and *mailo* land tenure systems.

From each of the two districts, using multistage random sampling, two parishes were selected: Mazinga and Kakanju parishes in Kakanju sub-county, Bushenyi district; and Nakaseta and Lutete parishes in Sekannyonyi sub-county, Mubende district.

Bearing in mind the nature of our study, a male-to-female sex ratio of 1:2 was used when selecting the 80 households and 70 households in Bushenyi and Mubende districts respectively. A structured questionnaire with open-ended questions was administered to each of these households. In each of the two selected parishes, in-depth interviews were conducted, with the help of an interview guide, with ten opinion leaders, half of whom were women. Additionally, two focus group discussions were conducted in each district. Gender was considered when undertaking the focus group discussions, in view of the fact that most women did not feel comfortable talking openly in the presence of their husbands or of men known to their husbands. The average size of the focus group discussions was 15 persons, and they comprised parish and village leaders of local councils and women councils as well as opinion leaders from the church and local women's groups.

Historical perspectives of women's land status were derived from oral submissions from four knowledgeable elders; historical ethnographies; colonial documents obtained from the National Archives; and legal sources (mainly court records). Contemporary law was drawn from legal documents (court records and the Hansards) and commentaries, current parliamentary debates and accounts of women leaders, both at the national and local levels. District reports and records were also consulted.

Secondary sources included literature available in the libraries at Makerere University's Faculty of Law and the Ministry of Gender and Community Development. Non-governmental organisation (NGO) libraries included those of Action for Development (ACFODE), the Centre for Basic Research (CBR), the Federation of Women Lawyers (FIDA), the Foundation for Human Rights Initiative (FHRI), the Human Rights and Peace Centre (HURIPEC), ISIS-WICCE, Uganda Gender Resource Centre (UGRC) and Uganda Land Alliance.

Continuous data analysis was carried out during the data collection period. In the course of analysis, bearing in mind the tentative themes conceived at the beginning of the project, the outstanding themes that emerged from the study were identified. The data obtained were coded, entered and analysed through cross-tabulations from the Statistical Package for Social Sciences (SPSS).

Having collected data from the two districts and compiled the findings, a simplified version of the findings in Bushenyi district was presented to a local workshop in Bushenyi, at which further recommendations were made by the participants. These recommendations, together with the findings from both Bushenyi and Mubende, were presented to a workshop in Kampala for activists, academics and the media. At this workshop, specific law and policy reform proposals were made. The summary of findings and proposals from the entire research process will be circulated to lobbyists and policy-makers.

Land Rights in Central and Western Uganda

Legal and policy issues Historically, both customary and statutory law have governed women's land status. Customary laws, under customary tenure systems, provided access to land and effective land security for women. Descent was traced and property inherited patrilineally, implying that customary law allowed only men to inherit and own land. Women married to lineage members were guaranteed security of user rights to land. This, however, is not the case today.

Statutory law, on the other hand, guaranteed women the right to purchase, own and dispose of property in their own right. In an attempt to streamline inheritance, the Succession (amendment) Decree No. 22/1972 provided for slightly improved inheritance of property (including land) for women. The law guarantees wives' unequitable rights to 15 per cent of their husbands' estates when they die intestate. In polygamous marriages, all legal wives share the 15 per cent in equal proportions. The widows also enjoy the right to occupy matrilineal homes until they remarry or die. In addition, the Succession Decree gives the right of inheritance to dependant female relatives, the right to apply for letters of administration of deceased husbands' property and the right to challenge unfair wills or obtain grant of probate.

Practice, however, does not reflect the enabling legal provisions. Only 7 per cent of Ugandan land is owned by women. Access of women to land remains difficult, since it depends on the woman's male relations and their socio-economic status. At the national level, most of the 16 per cent of households without access to land are female-headed households.

Women's land rights: voices of rural women The research findings indicate that women's concerns regarding land rights revolve around four major issues: the nature of women's land rights; the position of women in land; the consequences of gender inequality in land rights; and the lack of effective conflict-resolution mechanisms.

Women of both Ankole and Buganda enjoy transient rights to land, as a result of their land rights being appended to those of male relations. Women's land rights tend to be fragile and are defined by several factors. The research findings reflect a causal relationship between women's land rights and factors such as age and marital status, whether they have borne children and the sex of the children, as well as their sexual conduct.

Table 7.1 Factors determining women's land rights

	Bushenyi				Mubende				Total			
	Yes	%	No	%	Yes	%	No	%	Yes	%	No	%
Children	39	79.6	10	20.4	69	98.6	1	1.4	108	90.8	11	9.2
Length of marriage	57	77	17	23	67	95.7	3	4.3	124	86.1	20	13.9
Marital status	36	73.5	13	26.5	69	98.6	1	1.4	105	88.2	14	11.8

Women's land rights are essentially pegged to the institution of marriage, making marriage a determinant of their ability to enjoy land rights. Unmarried daughters tend to have more secure access and greater claims to their parents' estates than married women. A high 88.2 per cent of respondents contend that the rights of married women differ from those of unmarried women. However, the degree of secure access to and control over matrimonial estates depends on the type of marriage (customary, cohabitation, religious) and the success of the marriage (relations of the spouses).

Nearly all the respondents, 90.8 per cent, affirm that women with children, especially male children, are assured of more secure rights to matrimonial estates than childless women. The relationship between length of marriage, number of children and security of women's land rights is confirmed by 88.3 per cent of the respondents (see Table 7.1).

Within the Banyankore and Baganda ethnic groups, women's independent rights to own land are not automatic. Sons take precedence over daughters, when fathers are determining who the beneficiaries should be, how much each beneficiary should get and when beneficiaries should receive shares. Women's rights to inherit land are viewed in terms of their responsibilities to nurture the children of the deceased. Preference is given to children over their mothers in the event of the deaths of male household heads. Succession to land by either brothers (for natal estates) or children (for matrimonial estates) does not guarantee the security of women's land rights. Women's inferior position has meant inferior status on land.

Lack of secure access to, and limited ownership of and control over land has resulted in the socially inferior and economically impoverished status of women in these ethnic groups, as in the rest of Uganda. Women's claims to land remain insignificant and unprotected, in spite of the fact that women in Uganda provide 70–80 per cent of all agricultural labour in agriculture and over 90 per cent of labour in food crop production and processing. Lack of protection of women's access to land and lack of other land rights has direct implications for the development of agriculture and the economy as a whole. Solutions to poverty and underdevelopment depend on addressing the gender dimensions of land rights.

Women's lack of access to, ownership of and control over land has created additional strains. There is an increasing degree of prostitution, sexual harassment, domestic violence, marital instability, separation and divorce arising directly from land rights concerns. In Mubende, 83.3 per cent of respondents attest to conflict emanating from gender inequality in land rights. This is why 93.9 per cent of the respondents in both Bushenyi and Mubende believe that the solution to stability and development of Uganda lies in redressing gender inequalities in land rights.

Existing conflict resolution mechanisms are ineffective in protecting women's interests in land. These include Customary Courts, Local Council Courts and courts of law. These courts are male-dominated and tend to favour males. Their processes are often corrupt, expensive, lengthy and too technical for women, to the extent that the majority of women who have sought recourse through them either withdraw or lose their cases. Women are discouraged from seeking recourse in this way by the lack of economic means and the lack of success so far achieved.

Access to and control over land will be addressed below as the means by which women's land rights can be understood. The present status of women's legal rights to land, and the mechanisms and obstacles that perpetuate gender inequalities in access to and control over land, will be examined.

Women's access to land Today, throughout Uganda, women have the statutory legal right to inherit land. But the degree to which they can exercise that right in practice is constrained by several factors, foremost among which are the necessity for male mediation and the dominance of customary practice.

Women's access to land is dependent on their male relations, who own and/or control land. In Bushenyi, none of the women interviewed holds land independent of male relations. Women in Bushenyi only gain access to land as daughters, sisters, wives, mothers or daughters-in-law. In Buganda, however, a few women do own land independent of their male relations. In Bushenyi, 97.5 per cent of the respondents have access to land, 38.8 per cent through family ownership and the rest through individual ownership.

From Table 7.2, it is observed that 69.9 per cent and 38.5 per cent of the respondents' land holdings in Bushenyi and Mubende respectively fall under customary acquisition – family access, donations and inheritance. The rest gain access through land markets: the landholdings accessed through purchase are 28.2 per cent in Bushenyi and 59.7 per cent in Mubende. Households that access land through borrowing are only 5.8 per cent in Bushenyi and 10.3 per cent in Mubende.

Donation of land The largest number of respondents (43.8 per cent) in Bushenyi gain access to land through donations. Under this mode of acquisition, a father

Table 7.2 Modes of land acquisition

	Bushenyi		Mubende		Total	
	No.	%	No.	%	No.	%
Inheritance	6	5.8	12	15.4	18	9.9
Purchase	23	22.4	40	51.3	63	34.8
Donation	35	34.0	17	21.8	52	28.7
Borrowing	6	5.8	8	10.3	14	7.7
Family access	31	30.1	1	1.3	32	17.7
Landless	2	1.9	0	0	2	1.1
Total	103	100	78	100	181	100

gives part of his (ancestral) land to his son when he marries. This acquired piece of land provides a basis on which a new family is built, ensuring the continuation of a particular family or clan. On the death of the father, the son automatically inherits the land, which he received as a donation/gift. Depending on the role he will play in future (for example, being responsible as the heir for the surviving family), the availability of undistributed land, the family size and the father–son relationship, this son may receive another share of land on the death of his father. The clan elders responsible for distribution of the deceased's estate make the final decision.

Donation is one of the major means by which land is customarily acquired. As a 46-year-old male respondent observes, 'custom specifies particular means through which land is obtained – a grown-up son receives a share of his father's land, on which he can build a house for himself, his wife and children'. The implication is that only sons can and do receive donated land as a means to expand the family or clan.

To confirm ownership rights over donated land, the father, in the presence of other family members and clan elders, indicates the manner in which he intends to distribute his land among his children. A 50-year-old woman observes that 'whenever a father decides to give a share of his land to his son, he invites the clan elders and together they mark the boundaries with *emigorora* [specific short trees which, customarily, are used to mark boundaries]'.

Inheritance of land A deceased father is almost always succeeded by a male, regardless of whether such a male is a collateral relative. This is in contrast to daughters who may be 'linear descendants' and who, under statutory law, are given preference to collateral relatives. Through his will, the deceased distributes his land between the heir (who retains the largest portion) and those sons who previously did not benefit from donations (mainly unmarried sons). Depending on the land available for distribution and the father–son relationships, married sons may also partake of the land, but the priority is the unmarried sons.

Succession is effected through either an oral or a written will. In the former case, an (ageing) father invites clan elders physically to witness the distribution of his land to his children. On his death, the clan elders are expected to implement the wishes of the deceased. In event of the absence of a will, clan elders are empowered to distribute the deceased's land, using customarily recognised criteria. One of the sons, normally the eldest, is the heir. As such, he is given full responsibility over the family and property of the deceased. In cases where the father distributed his property among his children, the heir does not have jurisdiction over the distributed land, except where the deceased charges him with the express responsibility of enforcing restrictions he had made. In the absence of a son, clan elders may choose to give the land to the brother(s) of the deceased. Today, the most common practice is that land is divided among the boys of the family.

Prior to British colonialism, the inheritance of property, including land, was governed by custom. In Buganda, although custom did give inheritance rights to land, it did not provide for equality in gender relations. Patriarchy meant that the Baganda, while recognising women's land rights, made them conditional upon guarantees that this land would remain in the family (and consequently the clan) of either the father or the husband. The Baganda assumed that women did not need independent land rights, since they were assured of usufruct rights as daughters, wives or widows.

Tracing lineage through male descent, the Banyankore and the Baganda do not allow daughters to become heirs to their fathers. Only sons (or, in their absence, other male relatives) can become heirs to their fathers. Daughters have transient land rights, since, upon marriage, it is taken for granted that they will move to reside in their husbands' homes. It is in their husbands' homes that most of their adult contributions of labour are made. Consequently, it is from there that their shares should be taken. This is reinforced by the fact that daughters whose marriages are stable usually take a very long time to pay visits to their parents!

Even when they cannot be heirs to their fathers, daughters in Ankole and Buganda have long been getting shares from their parents' estates. In a few families where there are no sons, the daughters are occasionally given all the property and the male heirs remain titular figureheads. Where there are sons, fathers have been found to give daughters smaller shares than their brothers, because it is deemed that men shoulder bigger responsibilities within families. Responding to the proportion of land bequeathed to daughters compared to sons, a 40-year-old man, like several other respondents in Bushenyi, observed that 'traditionally, if you had two sons and eight daughters, each boy would get his separate share, while the eight girls will get only a single share'.

Reduced influence of customary law Today, however, customary law on inheritance in Ankole and Buganda is no longer universally applied. There are no longer hard and fast rules, but wide variations as to how property is divided within and among families.

Whereas the justification for giving daughters smaller shares than sons of parental estates was that girls were likely to get additional shares from their marriages, some parents had a contrary argument. They contended that it is easier for sons to acquire property and that this could not be said of daughters, who faced many constraints and had fewer opportunities to accumulate property.

To some extent, daughters are gaining recognition as useful members of families. They are given 'rewards' for faithfully caring for their parents, or for being able to complement family needs through labour and money. Their usefulness is compared to that of sons or male heirs who are viewed as irresponsible and opportunistic. This is because sons and male heirs have been noted for selling most, or all, of the lands bequeathed to them. As such, parents have shifted preference for sons alone to their daughters, whom they consider as not being dominated by 'get rich quick' attitudes.

Increasingly, parents are also giving their daughters shares of their estates on grounds of marriages becoming unstable. Such shares are offered as cushions for daughters in cases of failed marriages. On widowhood, the male members of the deceased husbands' families have increasingly taken to ganging up against widows, sending them away from their matrimonial homes. According to FIDA, 40 per cent of the cases brought to them in 1995 were related to harassment of widows and property grabbing by male relatives of deceased husbands. As insurance against the vagaries of marriage, parents are finding it increasingly necessary to reserve shares for each daughter. To strengthen the protection of their daughters' land rights, parents are forced to specify what they have given to their daughters (and sons) while they are still alive, so that there are as many witnesses to such transfers as possible. This is important in light of rampant tampering with wills, often through outright forgery.

As a mode of access to land for women, inheritance presents several problems. There are usually conflicts in respect of perceived partiality in sharing out inherited land. In addition, daughters seldom reside on or near their inherited land, which means that often their brothers – particularly the heirs – act not only as custodians but exercise effective ownership of and control over this land. Further, when parents die when daughters are already married, it is common for daughters not to be considered at all. Those who are unmarried are given shares in their parents' estates. And finally, parents expect their daughters to get shares of their husbands' estates, while husbands expect that their wives will receive shares of their parents' estates. This leaves women stranded in between, with each party shunning responsibility on the pretext that the other will take it up.

In Bushenyi, there is an emerging trend of substituting land donations and bequests with education. This is based on the assumption that education exposes children to greater opportunities. Parents are increasingly reluctant to consider educated children as beneficiaries of their estates, especially through donations. They would rather sell off excess land than allocate it to educated children.

Marital status and land access Battered wives who are unable to remain married, separated women and divorced women who leave of their own accord or are forced out by their husbands, do automatically access their fathers' estates. A 30-year-old separated woman states that

> if you are not married or have left marriage for any reason, your brothers may deny you access to family land. If you have a bad parent, he may choose to side with them, thus denying you access. Even if you have returned home after a misunderstanding with your husband or your husband has divorced or aban-

doned you and you return with your children, they may not be bothered. In spite of the clan elders' intervention on your behalf, the father may either be obstinate or will give you a small inadequate piece of land.

Conversely, the practice of obtaining shares from both the natal and matrimonial estates, found in a few cases, constitutes an advantage for women, notwithstanding the fact that they may not exercise effective control over either of these shares. Widows' inheritance of the estates of their deceased husbands is not automatic. In many cases, it is conditional upon factors (see Table 7.1) such as the length of time that they have spent in marriage (the longer the better), whether one has begotten children in marriage (the more the better) and, in Buganda, whether the children are male or female (the more boys the better). In polygamous homes, this last factor is significant for the division of property, although the usual practice has been that the senior wife (the one married first) is accorded priority. The sharing out of property among wives in a polygamous family is hazardous.

Blatant discrimination was found against women who had not mothered any child in marriage. A range of excuses was offered in justification, the most cited being that the reason for wives being allowed to exercise access rights to land as widows was to look after children, especially those who were still minors. According to this view, children enable women to have stakes in family estates upon deaths of husbands. The question put crudely was: 'Whose interests would a childless widow look after?' This was stressed in cases where the widows were still attractive and young enough to catch the attention of other suitors, from outside the family or clan. A few exceptional cases were found among the Banyankore in Bushenyi, where the family or clan could decide to apportion some of the deceased's estate to a childless widow, on account of her good conduct during marriage.

From the above, it is clear that customary inheritance law has shifted from the hereditary right of sons to inherit land, to a consideration of the right of daughters and wives to inherit land (albeit of unequal shares), to an individual determination of what best suits whom. Customary inheritance law is no longer automatic. As a 40-year-old man observes,

> originally only boys were given a share of their parents' estate … these days, girls are also beneficiaries of land through succession … currently, however, parents are discouraging their children from being heavily dependent on the natal estate … they are left to acquire their own land, as responsible grown-ups.

However, although change is occurring, its extent is still minimal.

When children who are no longer minors need independent sources of income and there is surplus family land, fathers may conditionally allow them to use their lands for specific reasons and for specified periods. Under such arrangements, there is no clear permanent demarcation of land – it is used only temporarily, in accordance with the fathers' specifications. In Bushenyi, 38.8 per cent have access to land under such arrangements. Land, however, is increasingly being individualised, reducing the opportunities for individuals to access land in this way.

The research findings indicate that the concept and practice of access to family land is steadily disappearing. Family (ancestral) land is land that has been handed down several generations through the male lineage. As a result of this customary practice, sons deem their right to family land as automatic. There is growing conflict generated by sons' demands for land even when fathers are not prepared to distribute it. In Bushenyi, in the absence of alternative opportunities for male youth to access independent income, irrespective of their levels of education, several of them demand land even when they are not yet married or in the process of marrying. There are cases where existing conflict resolution mechanisms are resorted to for arbitration. In a focus group discussion conducted exclusively with men in Bushenyi, 72.7 per cent insisted that such claims by their sons were not legitimate in customary terms. The rest (27.3 per cent), who were mainly youth with no secure access to land, were convinced that their rights were customary. One elderly man argued that

> customarily, a male child should not claim ownership rights to land when the father is still living ... even when a son obtains a piece of his father's land on or after marriage, he should not consider it as ownership. This son enjoys only use and occupation rights until he succeeds to it, after the death of his father, by way of an oral will that is executed by specific clan members (commonly paternal uncles).

The increasing population and consequent land scarcity have reduced individuals' access to family and communal land and their opportunities for acquiring adequate land sizes. This has necessitated venturing into acquiring land from more than one source, with or without explicit costs. In Bushenyi, 28.9 per cent of the households, and 16.4 per cent of those in Mubende, have pursued more than one avenue of accessing land. Their need for land exceeds land available

Table 7.3 Land size

	Bushenyi		Mubende	
	No.	%	No.	%
Less than 1	8	10	2	2.9
1–5	35	43.8	39	55.7
6–10	23	28.7	9	12.9
11–20	4	5	4	5.7
Over 20	2	2.5	2	2.9
No response	8	10	14	20
Total	80	100	70	100

through customary acquisition. Thus there is increased dependency on borrowing and purchase as modes of access (see Table 7.2).

This has also resulted in the extinction of communal lands in Bushenyi, as individuals have claimed all such lands. Depending on the location and size of their lands, some individuals now depend on their lands for resources previously acquired from communal lands (such as building materials of clay and poles, firewood, medicinal herbs and water). Where individuals' lands lack such resources, they depend either on the goodwill of neighbours or relatives or on purchase (water for domestic purposes is not sold).

The average size of land accessed by individual households is 3.9 hectares in Bushenyi and 4.3 hectares in Mubende district. Table 7.3 shows the land sizes of households interviewed. The majority of households has access to 1–5 acres in both Bushenyi and Mubende, followed by those in the category of 6–10 acres. In Bushenyi, most households practise mixed farming – growing food and cash crops and rearing cross-bred animals which do not require large grazing lands.

Purchase of land Although access to and ownership of land in Uganda is increasingly being acquired through purchase, women have not taken advantage of land markets as a mode of accessing land for various reasons. In Bushenyi and Mubende respectively, 28.8 per cent and 42.9 per cent of households have acquired their land through land markets. Land markets seem to be growing with the increasing population, increasing land scarcity, advent of a monetary economy and modernisation. The almost half of land purchases have been made in the last decade (see Table 7.4). Land purchases have been made either individually by household heads, the majority of whom are male, or jointly by husbands and wives, from the proceeds of their agricultural produce. The latter is common when the family is seeking additional land.

Although Ugandan statutory law is clear that women are as free as men to own and dispose of property, including land (Registration of Titles Act Cap 205,

Table 7.4 Period when land was acquired

	Bushenyi		Mubende		Total	
	No.	%	No.	%	No.	%
10 years	36	45.0	32	45.7	68	45.3
11–20 years	15	18.8	14	20.0	29	19.3
21–30 years	18	22.5	4	5.7	22	14.7
30 years	7	8.7	11	15.7	18	12.0
No response	4	5.0	9	12.9	13	8.7
Total	80	100	70	100	150	100

1964, of the Laws of Uganda), in practice women have not accessed land markets. The introduction of private ownership has merely shifted control over land from communal ownership to individual male ownership.

Women's lack of access to land markets can be explained by the shortage of funds, due to their income-generating activities being confined to the kitchen and garden. Where they can muster resources with which to purchase land, they have had to do so discreetly, because most husbands perceive their wives' independent acquisition of property, particularly land, as first steps towards preparing for independent existence. This is the same reason why husbands try to ensure that their wives have no independent sources of income.

Given this, women have used several strategies to purchase land. In Buganda, some women arrange to rear domestic animals secretly, especially cows, goats and pigs, at relatives' homes, have them sold and then gradually and secretly purchase land without the knowledge of their husbands. Although this is effective, it has an inherent problem – women become vulnerable to dispossession because they often purchase the land in the names of brothers or sons, who can take advantage of this to declare the land theirs. Potential sellers are often reluctant to sell to women without the approval and consent of their husbands or male relative, sometimes for fear of being wrongly accused of having sexual relationships with the women. Women who are forced to transact land stealthily are also vulnerable to the vendors. The transactions involve assurances that the vendors will not disclose the transactions to their husbands, implying the possibility of betrayal by the vendors.

The study came across 'liberal' husbands who felt that their wives had every right to own property independently, including land, while in marriage. But beneath their outward sense of fairness hidden reasons were detected, such as their perceptions that this property would be for the good of their children and, in some cases, themselves, especially where their incomes were inadequate for the family's needs.

With respect to incomes, the gender division of labour in Bushenyi is such that wives are usually responsible for food crops and husbands for cash crops and livestock. Wives' chances of acquiring money are thus reduced from the beginning. Even where wives have surplus produce that could be marketed to earn income, power relations in the majority of the homes mean that husbands exercise exclusive discretion over use of family income.

Interestingly, most men claimed joint ownership of property, especially land, independently acquired by women during marriage, while at the same time they denied their wives reciprocal ownership of what they themselves acquired after marriage. The men reasoned that they deserve a share of their wives' property, since conditions in the home facilitate women's acquisition of it. Husbands are secretive about their own land transactions, to the extent that their wives are often ignorant of these transactions. They can sell off part of their lands without consulting their wives, just as they can buy other lands without their wives' knowledge. The result of withholding information from one's spouse about land transactions is that it is difficult for the other spouse to follow up when the owner dies.

Thus, as far as land markets are concerned as a means of accessing land, married women are again constrained, although subtly. Single, separated or divorced women are relatively free to transact land.

Borrowing land Another means of accessing land for women is borrowing. Land is lent mainly by those who have land in excess of what they can use. Needless to mention, this is a short-term and tenuous form of access.

Among the challenges faced by women who wish to borrow, is the fact that most people in a position to lend land are men. As such, women cannot effectively negotiate with them. Borrowing also imposes obligations on the borrowers, terms that are more or less equivalent to sharecropping. Those who lend land expect, as a matter of right, that the borrowers are morally (and sometimes obligatorily) bound to give some of the produce to the lenders. Some lenders fix this before-hand, irrespective of the fact that the risks inherent to farming make it impossible to be certain about eventual yields. Lenders lend either marginal land that is not productive, or land with overgrown bush, so that the borrowers will clear and use it for only one or two seasons before it reverts to the lenders. Lenders also lend land they are sure will act as buffer zones between their gardens and vermin. Besides, people are reluctant to lend land because there have been cases where borrowers have claimed ownership in the event of the death of the lenders. All this makes it hopeless for women to rely on borrowing as a secure mode of access to land.

Access to land is increasingly difficult as the population rises and land becomes scarce. With growing individualisation and further fragmentation, the prospect of gaining access to family land becomes dimmer. Customary modes of access to land (donation, inheritance and family access) are being replaced by the individual relationships that landowners (fathers and husbands) enjoy with intended bene-ficiaries (children and wives). The means to access land through land markets (purchase) is dependent on surplus income. And as dependency on land markets grows, fewer people (those who can afford them) can cope. In Mubende, the *mailo* tenure system presents an additional dimension to landlord–tenant relations.

Women in particular are faced with problems hindering their access to land. The major problem is that custom necessitates women's access to land through male mediation. Women are no longer guaranteed secure access. Their access is conditional upon several factors and is limited by the interplay of custom and modernisation. For example, not all married women within polygamous marriages have lands that they can subsist on. As a 56-year-old woman observes, 'a husband cannot provide land for his new wives. This is because he is economically in-capacitated and fewer and fewer co-wives are able to live together in harmony.'

Denial of women's land rights and limited access to land is therefore due to patrilineality and the socio-economic context within which customary and statutory law operate. Culture denies women in Uganda access to personal property, through discriminatory attitudes, customary divorce and inheritance law. The traditional division of rights and responsibilities places women in an inferior position – that of dependence on men. Women are further disadvantaged by their poor economic status. Particularly in the context of land scarcity, land markets tend to favour those with the least need but the greatest resources, at the expense of those with the greatest need and the least resources, and provide no guaranteed alternative livelihoods.

Irrespective of statutory law, women are systematically disadvantaged in practice in all the main modes of access to land. In practice, customary law prevails. Women have not been militant about enforcing their rights of access, because they have accepted the status quo and are consoled by the fact that they are assured of some usufruct land rights.

Women's control over land   There is controversy as to whether or not women need independent land rights. In mainstream development and economic thinking, employment has hitherto been taken as the principal measure and guarantee of women's economic status. This has obscured another measure and guarantee – that of property ownership and control. To argue that women need independent land rights is to challenge the assumption that women's economic needs and interests can be adequately catered for through employment and other forms of income generation. There has also been an assumption that the household is a unit of congruent interests, among whose members the benefits of available resources are shared equitably, irrespective of gender. To argue that women require a specific focus, distinct from that of men, is to challenge that assumption. It is necessary to look beyond the distribution of property among households to its distribution between men and women within households. It is also vital to ascertain not only who owns property, but who controls it. For, from the above discussion of factors affecting access, it is clear that equality in the legal right to own property does not guarantee equality in ownership, and that ownership does not guarantee control. The distinctions between law and practice and between ownership and control are critical for gender analysis. There are barriers to exercising both women's legal rights to land, and women's effective control over what they own.

In examining control, this study delineates the actualisation of rights vested in male and female members of households. This entails unravelling the power relations within families with respect to who determines what use is made of available resources, particularly land, what activities are carried out on the land and what is done with the products from land. The study finds that these three situations are linked to, and are often a direct result of, a still rigid gender division of labour within families.

Customarily, land was a communal asset passed on through the male lineage. The introduction of private ownership changed control over land from communal to individual male ownership. This change did not affect the position of women, who remained subordinate and could only use land, not own it. The exclusion of women from property ownership rested on the need to preserve family property within the male lineage.

The research findings in Bushenyi indicate that married women have the right to use resources available on family land such as firewood, grass, water and any other resource required for their families. Wives have the rights to use land belonging to their husbands to grow food crops consumed by their families. They determine what food produce is enough for their families and what surplus is available for sale. They also grow cash crops and participate in rearing livestock, depending on the availability of their husbands and/or supplementary labour. Husbands, however, are responsible for determining what cash crops are to be grown. Women's right to decision-making over production and over income from the proceeds of production is not absolute (See Table 7.5). Wives do not have the right to the income derived from the sale of surplus food or cash crops, or from animal products such as milk and meat. They cannot decide on the use to which the proceeds can be put, without consent from their husbands.

The power that wives enjoy over production decisions and income relates to surplus food crops. That power is limited, as they have to consult with their husbands on the disposal of such surplus.

Table 7.5 Authority within a family

| | Father (all power) | | | | Mother (some power) | | | |
| | Bushenyi | | Mubende | | Bushenyi | | Mubende | |
	No.	%	No.	%	No.	%	No.	%
Production decisions	26	32.5	52	74.3	37	46.3	10	14.3
Disposal of produce	6	7.7	51	72.9	17	21.8	7	10
Income from produce	57	71.3	45	64.3	10	12.5	18	25.7

| | Other family members (some power) | | | | Both (some power) | | | |
| | Bushenyi | | Mubende | | Bushenyi | | Mubende | |
	No.	%	No.	%	No.	%	No.	%
	8	10	4	5.7	9	11.3	4	5.7
	5	6.4	1	1.4	50	64.1	11	15.7
	4	5	7	10	9	11.3	0	0

As regards the gender division of labour, gender roles are still defined by custom, with some tasks defined as women's and others as men's. Even where role inversion has occurred in practice, the definition of such roles remained stereotyped, with stigma associated to that role inversion.

Two major tendencies were observed. Men are responsible for cash crops and livestock rearing, while women are responsible for food crops. Interestingly, despite the gender division of labour, men still have the final say as to whether women are free to dispose of surplus food crops in markets or not, and over use of the money so earned. The main domestic chores and the welfare of family members is the responsibility of wives, leaving husbands the opportunity to carve out public roles outside homes. The fact that women have to look after homes gives them some control over land use. But men exercise the ultimate veto. There was an incident in Mubende where the cause of a separation was a woman's refusal to tolerate any longer the restrictive injunctions from her husband regarding land use.

There is an upward trend towards joint responsibility and control within homes between spouses, but this is more visible in homes where wives are making contributions to family incomes or play a role in the acquisition of family property. There is also a trend to consult, or at least inform wives, before husbands undertake decisions affecting families. Decisions to dispose of family lands are now increasingly having to be sanctioned by women. Therefore, although the dominant trend both in Bushenyi and Mubende is for men, as heads of households, to exercise superior rights in gender relations, those relations and women's involvement in decision-making actually vary from home to home.

Control of land also depends on the mode of land acquisition and is currently evidenced in three ways – through activities carried out on the land, land transactions and decisions made about income generated from products sold.

According to Table 7.6, 32.5 per cent and 60 per cent of respondents in Bushenyi and Mubende respectively have restrictions on land transactions imposed on them by the previous or current landowners. Restrictions on land use are imposed on 40 per cent of respondents in Bushenyi and 51.4 per cent in Mubende.

Where land has been inherited or purchased, the owner (controlling authority) is the head of the household. Depending on the land tenure system, those who

Table 7.6 Control of land

| | Bushenyi | | Mubende | | Bushenyi | | Mubende | | Total |
	No.	%	No.	%	No.	%	No.	%	No.
Restriction on land transactions	26	32.5	42	60	54	67.5	28	40	150
Restriction on land use	32	40	36	51.4	48	60	34	48.6	150

have acquired land through purchase generally have no conditions attached to it. Ownership belongs to individual heads of households, who are male in most cases. Individual ownership is premised on the perception that the interests of the family shall be catered for, since the family is considered as a fixed and necessary institution founded on principles of caring and sharing. In reality, however, the family is an institution based on unequal power relations and is a possible site of conflict. Depending on the position that an individual occupies within the family, different rights within the household may be enjoyed.

Among the Banyankore, where land has been received as a donation or gift or has been borrowed from fathers, fathers remain the owners (controlling authorities). They determine the nature of rights that individuals hold on the donated/borrowed land. Individuals who acquire their land through donations from their fathers are given land with specified boundaries. This land, more often than not, is given to sons when they marry, so as to nurture their new families. Individuals who acquire donated land are normally free to build houses, grow crops and rear livestock. They are, however, not allowed to lend out, mortgage or sell this land, without conferring with their fathers from whom they acquired it. On the fathers' deaths, the individuals inherit the land and may do with it what they please. However, women inheriting from fathers and husbands are not allowed to mortgage or sell inherited land. They are expected to maintain the land until they choose to leave their marital homes, or until their deaths. In such circumstances, their sons reclaim the land.

Unlike those who acquire donated land, those who are granted temporary use rights by their male relations (fathers, brothers or husbands) on family land are dependent on the owners for continued use. No specific boundaries are drawn under such arrangements. The owners are free to allocate any portion as and when they feel like so doing. The owners restrict the activities that the individuals can carry out on the borrowed land. Such restrictions include those related to the construction of permanent houses or any other structures, growing cash crops or trees, utilising resources such as building materials and firewood, and so on. Disposal of land through lease, mortgage or sale is completely out of the question. Temporary rights are limited to user rights and improvements derived from labour.

On both donated and borrowed land, the owners (controlling authorities) retain the right to terminate the rights enjoyed by the beneficiaries. Fathers are free to dispossess their sons of land if the latter's misconduct is unacceptable to the former. Misconduct is not necessarily related to the (mis)use of land – it can be related to the respect that sons give their parents (especially their fathers), to the relationships of sons with the parents and, sometimes, to the conduct of sons towards entire families or clans. Fathers may decide to punish their sons by dispossessing them of land previously given to them. Sons are therefore denied the means of basic survival and stripped of status, because they have failed to conform to societal norms of society as perceived by fathers.

Types of control Control is exercised at various levels. In Mubende, where the *mailo* tenure system prevails, control is exercised on two levels – the family and community. The *ttaka* (owners of the land) impose restrictions on their tenants on acquiring land, and they also depend on the manner in which the tenants have accessed land. Such conditions include the absence of the tenants' right to lease, mortgage or sell the land, to build permanent structures such as houses, to grow or harvest trees and to grow specific crops, especially perennial crops. Tenants access the *ttaka* through a premium and regular (commonly annual) rent determined by the owners. On complying with the restrictions set by the owners, tenants are considered *kibanja* owners. They are the legal owners of developments on the *kibanja* and those interests are transferable to persons of their choice. Tenants can dispose of those interests through sale, provided that they inform the owners of transactions carried out on their allocated *ttaka*.

At the family level, in spite of differences among the tenure systems, the relations pertaining are defined by custom. It is not surprising to discern similarities in both research sites with regard to the rights of family members within households, particularly with respect to gender.

Land obtained through inheritance confers specific rights on individuals. Under customary tenure systems, successors are free to do anything they like with land. They can lease, mortgage or sell the land. They can use the land in a manner that they choose. These rights are also enjoyed by the beneficiaries of donations and purchases. There are, however, variations according to the individuals involved in exchanging the land. For instance, fathers may, through their wills, instruct their heirs never to mortgage or sell the land bequeathed. This applies largely to women benefiting from both natal and matrimonial estates. The purpose for which such restrictions are imposed is to ensure that family (ancestral) lands are maintained within families or clans. Some women, whose land was obtained through donation or inheritance, may be free to lend but never to sell such land. Similarly, the right to mortgage or use the land to build permanent structures may be restricted.

Among the Banyankore and the Baganda, patrilineality is the main reason for the denial of women's right to inherit and own land. Women possess only user rights to land in their marital homes. All women with access to land enjoy various land rights due to their particular relationships with the owners (male relatives). Since their rights to land are appended to males (fathers, brothers and husbands), women do not possess full control over land, even when the particular land in question was bought with proceeds of the wives' labour.

Where the deceased owner dies intestate, the clan elders appoint an heir, normally the eldest son. The heir takes over all the rights and responsibilities of the deceased. He acquires decision-making power (control). The clan elders also appoint a caretaker to 'inherit' (take care of) the widow. An heir may take over a widow if she is not his mother. In instances where the elder brother of the deceased is the appointed heir, he can also be caretaker of the widow. In such a case, the heir can have sexual relations and produce children with her. If the widow refuses to be inherited, she loses access to all or part of the property and, sometimes, is chased out of the matrimonial home. The heir reserves the right to recover bridewealth when the widow decides to leave the matrimonial home.

Wills, whether oral or written, have offered some protection to the widows and children of deceased husbands. Families therefore depend on the goodwill of deceased husbands to protect their property from in-laws. The research findings indicate that most wills are respected. In some cases, where wills seem to favour widows, in-laws either change the will to suit their interests or hide them so that the contents are not disclosed. Tampering with wills is more common where widows are barren, or are given more property than other dependants, or where poor relations exist between widows and in-laws.

Most women whose husbands have obtained holdings through purchase do not enjoy the same rights as their husbands. They are free to occupy and cultivate matrimonial lands. But they may need to consult the brother(s) of the deceased before building permanent structures on those lands, continuing to cultivate them, or selling them after their husbands' deaths. A 30-year-old woman observes that 'a woman is not free to undertake projects that may be initiated by women's clubs, on her husband's land ... if they are big projects especially, like brick making, my husband will say that I am spoiling his land.'

Acquiring land through the family access mode thus places restrictions on the beneficiaries. Their rights to land are only usufruct, as several respondents indicate. 'I can only dig a garden of food crops and graze my few goats,' says a 33-year-old male. 'My father controls the activities that I can do on his land,' says a single woman with a child. 'I can only dig my garden of potatoes, but cannot sell, lend, mortgage or give it away to anyone as a gift ... I am not even supposed to plant long-term (perennial) crops like bananas, coffee or trees,' says a 24-year-old man, married with one child. 'I can use resources from my father's forest ... occasionally, he can allow me to sell some trees to generate some money that enables me to purchase personal items,' concludes a 22-year-old single man.

Effect on agricultural production From female producers' point of view, the fact that male non-producers are controlling authorities over land, both at the micro family level and the macro national level, points to an obstacle hindering development through agricultural production. Women argue that production is affected by the lack of recognition and utilisation of women's experience obtained from managing land. Decisions are arbitrarily made by men, according to their interests, needs and priorities, which may not conform to those of female producers and their families.

Such decisions include those related to the use of land. Women lack the authority to determine what use land should be put to, in spite of their being the production managers on land. They also lack the authority to determine what use income derived from the produce is put to. Although several women were reluctant to admit, in the presence of their husbands, that they have little or no control over the income earned from farming, during the focus group discussions it was made clear that ultimate authority lies with their fathers or husbands. In Bushenyi, 81.3 per cent of the respondents claim that income derived from family produce is spent on family needs and that decisions on income use are largely determined by male household heads. This is also evidenced by the gender division of labour, where men are not actively engaged in income-generating activities away from the farms, their work being confined to the growing of cash crops and livestock rearing through zero-grazing. Women are left to grow food crops. One respondent, a 30-year-old single mother, attempts to describe the nature of authority within a typical family in Bushenyi as follows:

> My father is the individual with full authority. In circumstances where other members' decisions are rendered important, my father's authority is followed by my brothers – my mother has very limited authority, while I, because I am a girl, have no authority whatsoever.

Among the Baganda, the first practical implication of women's change of residence upon marriage, to join their husbands' homes, is that the husbands will already have acquired the infrastructure for their homes – a house and some land. Many women pointed out that this explains their powerlessness relative to their husbands. In Mubende, for example, the nature of gender relations is significantly altered in cases where the two spouses reported making joint contributions to acquire matrimonial property, particularly land. And where women had acquired the land, they exercise relative discretion in decision-making in their homes. This finding does not apply to Bushenyi, where joint contributions and responsibility depend on the particular power relations between individual couples.

Male respondents argue that they need control over land and its produce because they have specific societal roles to perform. For example, men are tax-payers and need to control the sources of family income to ensure that they meet this obligation. But custom also depicts women as being frail and unable to manage property adequately. They are considered to be vulnerable. One male respondent reasoned that women cannot be empowered with the authority to carry out land transactions since they are easily duped. Like the majority of male respondents, he agrees with the tradition that fathers and husbands should be the sole authorities on land transactions, land use and the use of family income.

There are several implications of women's lack of control. Women are essentially servants on the land of their male relations. Although they cannot independently own land, they are expected to provide unpaid labour for their families. According to the custom governing both the Banyankore and the Baganda, women cannot, and must not, need land for their own sake. Land is accessed to protect the welfare of others – parents, husbands (and their relatives) and children before women's own welfare is considered. Their interests in land are measured in terms of children. If women do not have children to nurture, they are considered as having no justification for making land claims. This is why the rights to continued use and occupation of deceased husbands' land depend on women's conduct as perceived by their husbands and relatives. The sexuality and sexual conduct of women contribute to their land rights. Women who are 'disrespectful' by being unaccepting of their husbands' extramarital sexual relationships, and women suspected of having extramarital sexual relationships or of having mothered children who are not their husbands', are likely to suffer by being denied even minimal land rights of occupancy and/or use.

Women's loss of land rights There are several ways in which individuals lose land rights. In particular, control over individual family members is exercised by heads of households through their control over land.

As fathers gain improved rights as a result of individualisation of land in Uganda, children must ensure that their relations with their fathers are maintained. Trustworthy and well-behaved children are more likely to retain use or ownership land rights than irresponsible and ill-mannered ones.

In Bushenyi, children commonly lose their rights of access, use or control when they perform 'illegal' land transactions. Fathers may give their sons access to land with specified conditions. Sons may lose land rights if they choose to sell part or all of the land without their fathers' (or, in their absence, their clan elders') consent. Ill-mannered children (disrespectful or abusive towards their fathers) and irresponsible children (drunkards or lazy and uncooperative children) may also lose land rights. Fathers may curse, dispossess or disinherit such children. And such children will not receive shares of their fathers' land even when their fathers die. Fathers may pay money to release their sons from prison (by paying bribes to law enforcement officers or court officials), and then decide to forfeit distribution of land to those sons to compensate themselves. Children may also lose land rights upon the deaths of their fathers if surviving relatives choose to deny them land rights. In a few cases, irresponsible fathers may also sell off all or part of their lands, or chase away their children with their mothers in favour of new children and wives.

Children within the family retain user rights to parental land after marriage when their relationships with their fathers are good and when there is adequate land on which to grow crops, or, in a few cases, to rear animals such as goats and cows. Table 7.7 indicates that 71 per cent of both sons and daughters who get married lose their rights to their parents' lands. The reasons for this differ in terms of gender. Although sons, under Kinyankole custom, lose rights over the natal lands after marriage, because they receive independent shares of land upon marriage for them and their families to subsist on, this does not apply to daughters. A 50-year-old female respondent, commenting on a daughter's loss of rights to the parental estate, remarks that your parents and clan believe that your share (of land) is in your husband's estate ... once you are married, they think that whenever you go back to your father's home you are a mere visitor, no longer part of them ... so you have no rights over the (parents') estate as a married woman.

Today, however, there is a change of attitude among parents towards daughters' retaining rights to their lands after they are married. This change is premised on increased marital instability and separation, the perceived reliability of daughters to maintain family property (unlike that of sons, who are believed to be interested in selling it off) and the appreciation of daughters' contributions towards the parents after their marriages. Therefore, daughters retain rights to their parents' land either as cushions against marital failure or as rewards for their contributions towards their parents' welfare. This is why in Ankole and Buganda, single (unmarried, separated/divorced and dispossessed) women are now the major custodians of *ebijja* (family burial grounds).

In event of their fathers' death, daughters' land rights – in spite of their fathers' wishes to have them retain rights – are not guaranteed. Their brothers and uncles may usurp land bequeathed to them. These relatives may also change the nature of rights previously enjoyed over land by imposing fresh conditions on how to use and dispose of the land in question.

Similarly, a woman may lose rights to her husband's lands for several reasons, by means of the control over land that either her husband or his surviving relatives (in case of the husband's death) enjoy. Where women do not conform to customary requirements such as fulfilling reproductive and productive functions, they may be dismissed and replaced with other women. They may then be denied access to their natal lands.

Husbands may have misunderstandings with their wives and choose to abandon them or chase them away. Husbands may also choose to remarry and displace their wives with other women. They may choose to live with several wives on the same piece of land, thus reducing the shares of land available to previous wives, and sometimes certain rights on their shares of land. In some cases, the 'senior' (in terms of length of marriage) wife may be resettled on another piece of land belonging to the husband that is not developed or is marginal, and thus inadequate

Table 7.7 Retention of rights in parents' estates

	Yes		No		Total	
	No.	%	No.	%	No.	%
Male	8	18.2	36	81.8	44	30.3
Female	34	33.7	67	66.3	101	69.7
Total	42	29	103	71.0	145	100

or insufficient. Customarily, a woman who separates from her husband auto-matically loses claim to her husband's lands. Abandoned wives and widows cannot remarry or bear children with other men if they are to retain claims to their husbands' lands. On her husband's death, a widow may lose her rights over her husband's land to surviving successors– her children and their paternal uncles.

Through men's sole and sometimes incorrect decision-making, wives and families may lose land rights. Men can mortgage individual and land and fail to repay the loans. Men may wrong other community members and have to meet community obligations by using land for income. To illustrate the control that other community members have over 'family' land, in a case in Bushenyi a man caught committing adultery was made to sign an agreement, witnessed by Local Council officials, that he had sold off his land to the husband of the woman with whom the 'offence was committed'.

In Bushenyi, the circumstances under which land rights are lost are where women (wives) separate from or divorce their husbands (22.5 per cent), where the controlling authorities (fathers/brothers) dispossess the users of the land (31.3 per cent) for misconduct or illegal land transactions and where the government repos-sesses land for development purposes. Rights over land can also be lost where the controlling authorities (fathers/husbands) sell off land either for selfish reasons or through distress (42.3 per cent).

Changes in customary land law and practice   What the respondents perceive as changes in customary law and practices that were discriminatory on the basis of gender are highlighted below, and the factors causing these changes are pointed out.

Representing the view of the majority of respondents, a 24-year-old Youth Council chair observes that

> (President) Museveni's government has brought about major changes … since his government came to power, and through education, people in society have realised that all children are the same and should be treated equally … people have realised that, in most cases, if a girl gets married and the marriage fails, she has nowhere to go to. This has caused most girls to resort to prostitution, to suffer from AIDS and subsequently, death … so, if they have land, they would not suffer.

A 49-year-old retired grade III teacher and chair of a Local Women's Council laments that

> broken marriages are several these days due to poverty, lack of education, heavy drinking and redundancy of many men … leading to the suffering of women. So parents have opted for giving their daughters a share of their land so that they do not suffer … people have realised that given some opportunities, girls are as equally useful as boys.

To explain the reasons for the positive attitudinal change towards securing women's access rights to parental land, a 30-year-old male respondent remarks that

> in the past, a male adult would get married before getting land and, on getting married, he would receive a share of land from his father as a basis for building and maintaining a family ... today, some children demand for their share from the parents and, when the parents give it to them, most children misuse the land by selling it off and playing 'matatu' (gambling) ... these men consider land as a quick means to obtain income that will solve their immediate needs, in the absence of employment.

The above statements illustrate an emerging trend of parents' consideration of land allocation for their daughters. Fathers' decisions to give daughters shares of land is premised on married daughters' lack of security and control over their husbands' land, and the lack of confidence that fathers have in their sons regarding the preservation of family land. There is a growing realisation that the absence of equal opportunities ensures that women remain subordinate and unprivileged in society. The change of attitude and practice signifies a shift from daughters being viewed as 'property', to being viewed as people who can have access to family property. Daughters' access to natal land, however, does not necessarily imply control. Rather, daughters who have benefited from access have other land rights, especially of disposal, restricted.

A (limited) possibility for childless women to retain rights to their husbands' land exists. Such rights depend on the goodwill of their husbands or their relatives in the event of the husbands' death.

A few women, especially in Buganda, have resorted to risking their marriages by purchasing land independently of their husbands. These women have independent sources of income facilitating access to land markets. All such land purchases, however, are carried out secretly. It is easier for women known to be employed to acquire independent property than it is for housewives who are assumed to have no independent income.

A few widows can, and have, inherited their husbands' land, with relatively greater degrees of autonomy and control. This signifies a shift from getting no share at all, to getting a smaller share (belonging to widows and their youngest sons) with specific restrictions concerning use and disposal, and finally to receiving all land with considerable autonomy and control. One female respondent, a beneficiary, comments that

> I am the head of the family, after the death of my husband ... when I die, my children will take over all the property. Then, when the children are old enough, they will consult the elders who will give each child his share ... all this will be controlled by the heir, the oldest child or any other surviving relative, to whom I will assign the responsibility.

The privatisation of land has reduced the authority that clans have over individual landholdings. Clans, through their elders, retain the right to resolve land disputes and to enforce the will of the deceased through distributing the land belonging to the deceased. Now, with competing needs amid land scarcity and education, attitudes are changing to accommodate the commercialisation of agriculture. Individuals exert more control and influence over the land that they own and, to some extent, the nuclear family has been strengthened.

Struggles to Improve Women's Land Status

Rural women's struggles Apart from about 15 per cent of female respondents in Mubende who openly admitted to the secret purchase of land and other property, married women are still reluctant to disregard customs that restrict them from acquiring independent property. Responding to the question of what they could do as women to improve their land rights, 47.9 per cent of women in Bushenyi and Mubende say that they would join others when the opportunity arose to struggle for their rights, while 12.6 per cent consider any effort, individual or collective, to improve women's land status to be futile. They are pessimistic about the possibility of woman enjoying 'stronger' rights than at present.

Individual efforts include encouraging their husbands to write fair wills, seeking legal assistance from the legal clinics of the FIDA and seeking remedies from the chiefs and Local Council and District Courts. A visit to the District Court showed that fewer land-related cases are being handled there since the Local Council Courts were granted judicial powers to deal with such cases. The District Court in Bushenyi had handled about 16 cases involving gender-related land disputes within a six-year period (1984–90). Of the 13 cases accessed, 15.4 per cent had been technically dismissed, 30.8 per cent had had judgments passed, while 53.8 per cent had been withdrawn before judgment had been passed.

The majority of the cases concerned women who were disgruntled about the inequitable distribution of matrimonial property by their husbands among the wives, or about dispossession of the widows by male relatives. Relatives either forcibly grabbed land from a widow, as in Nakajugo vs. Byasoba, or sold it without the widow's consent, as in Inid Nyamagoye vs. Samu Nyamagoye and Boaz Birungi. In a case exemplifying the former, Yokana Babichengire vs. Edurayi Babichengire, the lawful wife, married for 34 years, complained about a husband who gave her a smaller share in favour of his second wife, in spite of the contribution she had made to the development of the husband's estate. In another case, Harriet Komuruka vs. Rwamuhanda Natukunda and Yorokamu Facian, a chief in the parish took advantage of a widow's vulnerable position and grabbed part of her land, which he then sold to the widow's uncle.

From the above, it can be argued that women's individual struggles to improve their land status take the form of frustrated ineffective conflict-resolution mechanisms that do not necessarily protect the interests of vulnerable women. The majority of the women who have sought recourse through the courts have not received it – they have either withdrawn their cases or ended up losing them. Either the cases have dragged on, involving increased costs, or the demands made by the courts, whether official or not, have discouraged them. Court technicalities have also discouraged individual women – 15.4 per cent could not benefit from fair hearings because their cases were technically dismissed.

Regarding the collective efforts that women are making to strengthen their landholdings, 35.3 per cent admitted that nothing was being done collectively, while 54.6 per cent argued that they were indeed doing something collectively. Collective efforts include organising seminars and workshops through women's associations, together with women's and other national organisations, that sensitise them about women's rights and provide information on how to improve their status. The majority were optimistic about the elected women's representatives in Parliament, whom they saw as having the mandate to address the interests and rights of their constituents.

The majority of female respondents point to customary institutions and practices as denying them the opportunity to organise effectively. The stigma associated with 'forceful' women, the lack of access to information, the lack of commitment to the women's movement and the fear of losing their homes, especially when they have no alternative, are considered as obstacles to the struggles of rural women. Their disadvantaged position is worsened by the lack of adequate finances to carry out those struggles and to fall back on, in the event of being adversely affected during those struggles.

As a result, the majority of women expect solutions 'from without'. Rural women's dependence on the state and on other sympathetic individuals or organisations to struggle for their rights, is apparent in their recommendations for change and their identification of factors responsible for existing change.

The pessimism that most women feel about the possibility for change was based on futile previous attempts. Whereas most women had viewed the Local Councils at their inception as new local institutions sympathetic to their cause, their experience is that the Local Councils are 'faithful' defendants of men's interests. The reluctance (and refusal) of the Local Councils to interfere with 'private' matters, the frequent rulings made against cases presented to the Local Council courts and the bribes required for their intervention were cited as further obstacles to their struggles.

Other key actors The inequality of land rights restricts women's sense of belonging and what they can do with land. But apart from the individual and collective efforts undertaken by the female respondents, there are other efforts, made by other key actors.

According to the respondents, the state has played a role in tilting the balance in their favour. The most significant contribution attributed to the state is its deliberate effort to make women visible by giving them voices in public decision-making. Since coming to power in 1986, the National Resistance Movement (NRM) government has created openings for women in public decision- and policy-making. A woman vice-president was appointed by the president and a few cabinet posts have been filled by women. Women in each district are represented at a national level by a female member of Parliament. At the local level, each of the Local Councils (village, parish, sub-country, division and municipality and district) must ensure that a third of its posts are filled by women. Women's Councils have also been formed from local to national levels. A 45-year-old Local Council women's representative notes that 'as Local Council women leaders, we can talk in Local Council meetings, make decisions and plans at all levels. We can talk and the men listen … signifying a change from previous attitudes and practices where men used to say that the women cannot and must not talk amongst men.'

The respondents, especially the women, appreciate the advisory and leadership functions that women leaders have played in their struggles. These women leaders, with their knowledge and connection to the authorities, have encouraged women with land-related matters to confront the authorities with a view to improving women's status. Increased women's representation on Local Councils is viewed as a blessing for women with cases in previously male-dominated Local Council Courts.

Women's lack of access to and control over land restricts their access to credit and marketing facilities, limits their decision-making over agricultural production and their control over benefits. This has a negative effect on women's production capacity. Women's Councils are considered to be tools for the raising of women's productive capacity. These councils have concentrated on increasing income-generation opportunities for their constituents. They have arranged sensitisation seminars and workshops, training sessions and the input of professional expertise to programme and project development, to improve women's status at both at the micro and macro levels. Women's groups, like the 'Bika Oguze' in Bushenyi, have initiated credit and saving schemes for their members. On the whole, the state's provision of a sympathetic and helpful environment for women's struggles is commended by the vulnerable women in the two districts.

The state's efforts to elevate women's status through deliberate measures such as ensuring women's access to education through affirmative action (giving an additional 1.5 points to female students seeking to enter the university), guaranteeing a third of the positions of all local government structures to women and ensuring women's representation in Parliament through affirmative action have not only increased women's visibility, but have enhanced the impact that they are able to exert within the realm of public decision- and policy-making. The measures have increased understanding of and sympathies for women's concerns at various levels.

However, most men still believe that gender equality is meant to overturn their traditional status. Gender equality has been interpreted by most men, together with some women sympathisers (especially those of the older generation, who are interested in maintaining the status quo), as being disruptive of family harmony. This is why about 60 per cent of respondents are against gender equality and the manner in which it is being promoted. From the perspective of the respondents, gender equality needs more than legislation and enforcement. It can only be sustained by mutual love and respect, and is subject to complex contestations and negotiations within individual families. This is important, since domestic gender and power relations are subject to subtle factors that vary from family to family.

The mediation of women's access to land through men has been addressed, both in the 1995 Constitution and the subsequent 1998 Land Bill. But the gap between law and practice means that a lot remains to be done. For example, women's freedom to buy land can only be exercised if women have as much money as men, which is not the case. Women's associations and organisations, especially in the rural areas, do have an important function economically to empower women to enable them meet the expectations raised by their legal empowerment.

Women's associations and organisations also have the important function of building support among and for women. The provision of specialised services to rural women by women's organisations like ACFODE, which sensitises women to the issues and opportunities; FIDA, which provides legal aid; and the Uganda Women's Finance and Credit Trust (UWFCT), which extends credit to women, is important.

There are also umbrella organisations comprised of rural women's associations. Such umbrellas play a role in women's struggle for land, for instance in asserting women's inheritance claims and struggles by the landless. These umbrellas have created conditions of solidarity for collective action that have shifted women's struggles from covert individual efforts to overt collective efforts. However, even under such umbrellas there are class, ethnic and religious divisions, which sometimes culminate in conflicts. For example, middle-income and rich peasant households are perceived as enjoying class-related advantages over women of low-income peasant households, in terms of rights enjoyed and benefits gained.

A loose coalition of women's non-governmental organisations (NGOs) is lobbying for a gender-responsive land tenure system and justifiably criticised the main provisions of the 1998 Land Bill. Their most significant proposal was that, to ensure equality between man and women in marriage, all matrimonial property, especially land, should be registered jointly in the names of both spouses. Needless to say, this proposal was resisted by most men. If consensus could be reached, it would go a long way to altering or redressing the imbalance in gender relations within families.

Compared to customary law and practices, religion and statutory law have not visibly ensured equality or inequality between men and women regarding land. Religion has not been used in defence of women's rights. However, at a general level, Christianity is perceived as treating women as equal to men. In contrast, Islam is perceived as assigning women inferior positions to men. But there is appreciation of the fact that Islam specifies that women get definite shares of their parental and husbands' estates (including land), unlike Christianity. However, the research findings were that whatever the religious and statutory provisions, the tendency is for customary provisions to override them. As most prejudices against women are embodied in custom, critical efforts need to be concentrated on customary change. This means ideological engagement, a process likely to be harder than struggles at other levels.

Women's interests in land Two further questions will be considered. First, what the respondents perceive as issues requiring attention to effect changes towards improving women's land status. And second, the 1998 Land Bill in relation to those recommendations. The hope is that the emergent recommendations will be responsive to the interests and needs of Uganda.

The research findings indicate that women need interests in land that ensure they can control what the land is used for, the land transactions and the manner in, and purpose for which, the income so derived is used. In order to realise these interests in land, women's secure access to land should be guaranteed and their control over land and its products confirmed. There are various views, however, on how this could be achieved. To appreciate these views, an attitudinal survey of both sexes was conducted, from which the following can be discerned. Although the majority (88.5 per cent) was in favour of women's right to shares of land to

Table 7.8 Attitudes to a woman's right to share part of the estate

		(%)
Women	Some share	37.7
Men	Bigger share	34.4
Both	Equal share	16.4
Women	No share	11.5

Table 7.9 Opinions about the source of land distributed to women

	(%)
Marital estate	54.5
Parental estate	45.5

which they belong by kin, in which they have interests and to which they have contributed, respondents were reluctant to state that gender equality should apply in land distribution.

In light of societal change and the necessity for similar change in customary law and practices, there is little resistance to women acquiring rights to natal and matrimonial land.

A significant number of respondents were against gender equality in principle, since it contravened customary law and practices (Table 7.12). Gender equality is considered from the respondents' perspective. The majority supported widows receiving shares of marital land (Table 7.13). The majority favoured joint owner-ship of marital lands (Table 7.14).

Other safeguards suggested against women's dispossession of natal and marital lands include:

- Sharing decision-making about land. All immediate family members who are of majority age should be involved in decision-making about the property of the family.

Table 7.10 Attitudes towards the number of shares a woman should get

	(%)
Single share (either natal or marital estate)	60
Double share (both natal and marital estates)	40

Table 7.11 Attitudes towards the right of a childless wife to the matrimonial estate

Attitudes	%
Yes (should get a share)	63
No (should not benefit)	32.6
It depends	4.3

Table 7.12 Attitudes towards gender equality

Attitudes	%
Yes	27.6
No	48.3
It depends	10.3
Do not understand	13.8

- Sharing labour. All family members should contribute to labour on family land.
- Sharing decision-making about income. Consultation and shared decision-making should happen with respect to income derived from the land's produce.
- Popularising the manner of land distribution, by landowners before their deaths. All immediate and extended family members should know the manner in which land is to be distributed.
- Guaranteeing all children's land rights. All children must receive shares of marital lands.
- The writing of valid wills recognised by statutory law.

Key actors and land rights struggles All key actors (stakeholders) should contribute towards the struggle for gender equality in land rights, as follows:

- The state should legislate and implement land laws ensuring gender equality in land rights.
- The state, parliamentarians, religious organisations and NGOs should, through mass sensitisation, educate people (especially women) about their land rights, the existing land laws and their implications for gender equality.

Table 7.13 Attitudes towards a widow sharing the marital estate

Attitudes	%
Yes	88.2
No	5.9
It depends	5.9

Table 7.14 Attitudes towards joint ownership of the marital estate

Attitudes	%
Yes	83.3
No	16.7

Table 7.15 Attitudes towards women's involvement in women's groups

Attitudes	%
Yes	55
No	45

- Land use planning and management should begin at the family level, with all family members of majority age participating in decision-making.
- Women should build their confidence by involving themselves in the public sphere rather than confining themselves (or allowing themselves to be confined) to the domestic/private sphere.

Respondents are both for and against women joining associations and organisations geared towards improving their status. Men's opinions on this are premised on their perceptions of the (material) benefits that families derive from such involvement (Table 7.15).

- Both men and women should attend and make use of sensitisation and educational efforts, so that land rights struggles are approached from the basis and strength of knowledge.
- NGOs should strengthen women's bargaining positions by providing sustainable income-generating methods such as credit and infrastructural and technical support.

Land management and conflict resolution

- All family members should be involved in decision-making about family land.
- Clan involvement in land distribution and conflict-resolution should be phased out gradually in favour of community-based organisations representative of (previously) marginalised groups like women, women with disabilities and children.
- Land management and conflict-resolution mechanisms at all levels should include women and be gender-responsive.
- All members of Local Councils should be sensitised about women's land rights, in order to strengthen their knowledge about issues affecting their lives.

The 1998 Land Bill in Perspective

There is currently an inclination to support women's rights in the economic, legal, political and social spheres. The 1995 Constitution entrenches women's rights. Article 26(11) guarantees women the right to own personal property, while Article 33(6) prohibits cultures, customs, laws and traditions against women's dignity, interests and welfare or that undermine their status. In spite of that, however, the 1996 Tenure and Control of Land Bill does not sufficiently address women's plight.

The current draft Land Bill is based on the 1995 Constitution, which vested land in Ugandan citizens according to the four existing land tenure systems and the recommendations of the 1989 Study of Land Tenure and Agricultural Development carried out by the Land Technical Committee. This proposed reform of Ugandan land law is therefore geared towards land privatisation, and aims at greater security of private land rights in the interests of the greater efficiency demanded by the modernisation goal of the NRM government. This also matches external pressures to liberalise land tenure systems under structural adjustment programmes.

The limitation of this approach, which is in accordance with civil code ownership and freehold land tenure, is the failure to recognise the needs of the majority of rural peasants, who need land for survival. To what extent does the emphasis on efficiency enhance women's land rights? Similarly, to what extent does this emphasis respond to existing change, competing demands and needs, which require balancing equity and efficiency? How can fair claims procedures be established when land was originally expropriated and distributed contrary to principles of international human rights law, without fair compensation?

The Land Technical Committee's recommendations are unduly and almost exclusively based on economic criteria and disregard the consequences of their recommendations. These recommendations are best described as inequitable – they favour those with the least need but the greatest resources, at the expense of those with the greatest need and least resources, without guaranteeing alternative livelihoods.

The implication of the 1998 Land Bill is that the majority of smallholding peasants who depend on land for survival will have no option but to sell their land and labour. Ownership of land will be concentrated in the hands of fewer (and absentee) landowners and there are no checks proposed to hinder exploitative rent relations for land use. Traditional structures, such as families, lineages and clans that govern land matters are disregarded, yet they are key to upholding citizen interests.

Struggles over land also manifest the problems inherent in Uganda's dualistic legal system. The 1998 Land Bill attempts, on the one hand, to promote national and international business interests by liberalising and privatising land and securing protection private land rights. On the other, it seeks to provide safeguards to protect community interests, particularly of the majority peasants, based on customary law and practices. The result is a failure to abolish patriarchal customary law and practices that discriminate against women.

The 1998 Land Bill purportedly caters for women's interests in Clauses 4, 6, 11 and 13. Clause 13(1) imposes restrictions on land transfers by family members. It states that no person shall sell, exchange, pledge, mortgage, lease or give away land *inter vivos* or, in the case of a married couple, enter into any other transaction on land without prior written consent of the spouse in occupation of the land. In the case of a non-married person having children, the consent of his or her child of majority age in occupation of the land is sought, while in cases where the children in occupation of the land are below the age of majority, the consent of the committee is obligatory.

However, 'consent' is based on the assumption that all parties have equal power relations in marriage, which is not the case. Rather, given the unequal gender-based power relations, women's consent is presumed to be automatic once their husbands have made decisions. Withholding consent places women at risk of being abused or abandoned. Without equitable land interests, women cannot give consent or restrict transfer of land. The clause is also silent about polygamous marriages, which have been legalised by the Customary Marriages Decree and the Mohammedan Act. And finally, prior written consent presupposes literacy. Thus the illiterate, mostly women, will not be able to give their consent.

The 1998 Land Bill is premised on the assumption that women's access to land will automatically be addressed once land ownership rights are resolved. This ignores women's interests as land users whose protected user rights under customary law and practices have gradually been eroded. Women's interests in land continue to be undervalued and their contribution to agricultural production remains invisible. The perception that women are dependants has continuously informed official policies and plans related to land use and management.

The need to ensure women's secure access to land in light of the fact that they are the major land users, providing 70–80 per cent of labour in agricultural production and over 90 per cent in food crop production and processing, is disregarded. Women in Uganda are reported to own only 7 per cent of land. This disproportionately low share of land ownership has direct implications on women's productivity in agriculture and women's control over the products of their labour.

The solution seems to lie in a compromise position – away from completely abolishing customary law and practices and away from leaving land to the market. Existing customary law and practices should be gradually replaced by notions of 'communities' as they exist today, as multiethnic, pluralistic, urban and rural. Communities should have the power to control and regulate land within their boundaries. Community members, through their representatives, should have control of and be able to regulate land through district and national land mechanisms that are accountable to Parliament. Specific measures are needed to ensure equal and effective participation of women and men, young and old, in decision-making on land at every level.

Conclusion

Contemporary land tenure relations exhibit diversities that reflect cultural, economic, political and social conditions resulting from increased commodity production and the penetration of and integration into global capitalism. The transformation process demonstrates the resistance of males to support women in respect of land tenure relations. However, maintenance of the status quo has implications for development and human rights.

The conclusion of this study therefore is that gender relations and women's economic, political and social positions are the outcomes of processes of bargaining and contestation. These processes may not always be discernible or explicit. They involve both cooperation and conflict and take place in different arenas, from the household to the community, to the market and the state. These arenas are interlinked in such a way that change in one arena impinges on others. For instance, strengthening of women's bargaining power in the community gives them greater bargaining power within the household. But women's ability to improve their power position has been circumscribed by a history of entrenching inequality in the construction of gender, in the distribution of property and in public decision-making. This has relegated women to the role of takers and not makers of norms and laws.

This implies that the necessary change will require simultaneous struggles over gender roles, private and public decision-making and property (including land) rights. The hierarchical character of gender relations, within and outside the household, based on the unequal access of women and men to economic, political and social power, must be challenged. Land rights are thus a critical entry point to challenge unequal gender relations and power.

How these struggles need to be conducted is a complex question with no easy answers. It cannot be entirely resolved outside praxis. To establish women's land rights requires not only removing existing gender inequalities in statutory law, but also ensuring that that law is implemented. Women's ability to claim and retain their land rights, including effective control over land, needs to be strengthened. The complexity of noted obstacles and their contextual variability preclude simple prescriptions and specific strategies. These will evolve through localised campaigns. In such campaigns, the compelling force of human rights could play a pivotal role.

Part II

Key Land Rights Issues and Recommendations

EIGHT

Cameroon: Overcoming Custom, Discrimination and Powerlessness

The Status of Women in Cameroon

Fifty-two per cent of Cameroon's population are women, yet they occupy only 5.6 per cent of the seats in Parliament.[1] Despite the fact that Cameroon ratified the international Convention on the Elimination of All Forms of Discrimination Against Women (the Women's Convention) on 23 August 1994 and has a Constitution that provides for the 'protection' and 'encouragement' of women, the status of Cameroonian women remains poor. Patriarchal and traditional leadership patterns, the colonial legacy of underdevelopment, illiteracy as well as ignorance of their rights, are some of the factors contributing to women's low legal, political and socio-economic status. There are also several pieces of discriminatory legislation that proscribe the property rights of women and undermine their constitutional rights.

Traditionally, in all of Cameroon's indigenous cultures, the public space is considered to be a male domain. Women have little say in public matters and therefore virtually no decision-making powers in respect of resource distribution at the communal level.

At the domestic level, women enjoy some limited decision-making power because of their spiritual and economic roles. Owing to their role as childbearers, some Cameroonian communities, such as the Fali, believe that God has given women the role of 'uniting with the soil' (Bigombe Logo and Bikie 1998: 27). Economically, women are responsible for farming activities, small trading, fishing and sometimes hunting. They also enjoy limited influence in female-controlled spaces such as water wells and women's associations. Women control the process of organising and managing matrimonial ties. All the indigenous communities are polygamous, and men's economic status is judged by the number of wives they have. It is prestigious for a man to have many wives. As a consequence of bride-price and polygamy, women are objectified and commodified. They are considered to be part of the assets and/or property of a man and a key means of wealth acquisition.

Women's economic independence, even at the domestic level, is greatly circumscribed by Cameroon's discriminatory matrimonial and trade legislation. The Civil Code makes the man the head of the household, with immense powers over his wife and children in every aspect. Under the Civil Ordinance, a husband has a right to 'oppose his wife's choice to exercise a commercial activity' (Mungwa 2000: 32). Section 7 of the Trade Act permits a man to 'terminate [his] wife's business activity, by a simple notification of his opposition to the registrar of the competent court' (Mungwa 2000: 32). Men enjoy the right to dispose of, mortgage or sell all property without their wives' consent, under sections 1421 and 1428 of the Civil Code. The laws governing divorce apply double standards under sections 229 and 230 of the Civil Code. While a man may divorce his wife in a single case of adultery, a woman must establish that her husband has '"habitually" had extra-marital intercourse, or that he has committed the act inside the matrimonial home'. Upon the death of her husband, a woman must prove that she contributed to the acquisition of jointly owned property to inherit it (Mungwa 2000: 32). Thus, although women are responsible for several economic activities at the domestic level, they hardly enjoy the benefits of them.

Fortunately, through various civil society initiatives, women are gradually freeing themselves from the burdens of traditional patriarchal cultural restrictions. Cameroonian women are increasingly engaged in activities positively affecting their social positions and therefore leading to their emancipation and autonomy. There is an increase in women's organisations that agitate for women's rights, such as the Association of Women Jurists and the *tontines*, mutual savings groups. Some of the *tontines* have succeeded in launching credit unions, popular banks and saving banks where access to loans for women is facilitated.

However, the advancement of women in Cameroon is greatly hampered by the high incidence of illiteracy. While there is an appreciable improvement in the provision of education services to girls and women, Cameroon is still one of the countries in which over 25 per cent of women are illiterate.[2] More rural than urban women are illiterate.[3] Even in the younger generation, the educational gender gap is clear, with 15 per cent of males aged 15–24 being illiterate as compared to 29 per cent of females in the same age bracket.[4] Illiteracy prevents women from exercising their rights, as their access to information is limited.

Much remains to be done in the area of implementing the woman-friendly elements of Cameroonian law and the international conventions that the country is party to. For example, as of March 1999, Cameroon did not have a post-Beijing plan of action. This is just one area of policy reform that would greatly help to improve the status of Cameroonian women ('Index on the Status of Women in Africa' 2000: 51).

Land in Cameroon

The State shall be the keeper of all lands. In that capacity, it can intervene in order to ensure a rational use or in order to take into account the imperative defence of the economic options of the nation. (Article 1 of Ordinance Number 74-1 of 6 July 1974)

Cameroon suffered from and through the colonial occupation by three European powers (Britain, France and Germany), each with its own consequences in respect of land law and use. Whereas the traditional approach towards land in Cameroon was one in which land was perceived as an inalienable communal resource, the Western perception of land is as private property that can be turned to individual benefit. These conflicting perceptions have been an underlying source of tension in Cameroon's land law, and they persist today. The Germans and French both adopted the position that land that was unoccupied was 'vacant without a master' and could therefore be appropriated and alienated by the colonial state for its use. The British adopted the approach that all lands, whether occupied or not, belonged to the natives but were under the control and disposition of the British governor.

The post-colonial Cameroonian state followed the colonial approach towards land ownership. State policy is opposed to customary systems of land management. The legislative and regulatory framework adopted between 1963 and 1970, as well as the land reform of 1974, consolidated the state's ownership of land, with provisions for purchase by individuals and registration of title. Communities enjoy only user rights over land. Basically, there are now two recognised categories of land in Cameroon, the 'non-exploited but occupied lands' and the 'empty virgin lands'.

To guarantee their rights over land, communities can only acquire land by occupation or exploitation and registration. Title to land can be obtained through purchase by mutual agreement, as a gift (donation *inter vivos*), as a legacy or as a state bequest with an obligation to exploit the land. Everything pertaining to the registration of land is dependent on the administrative judge.

Ignorance, the complexity of the registration process and the conditionalities associated with registration have resulted in a situation where the bulk of farmland and pastoral circuits is controlled by the state. Land registration is predominantly an urban phenomenon. Most rural land is not registered. By 1987, fewer than 30,000 of the 1,145,700 rural farms in Cameroon were registered lands (Bigombe Logo and Bikie 1988: 30). Also, the genesis of the land tenure and registration system in the colonial policy of 'lands of the crown', or 'vacant lands without master', has led to a situation where indigenous communities resent the system. Despite the compulsory registration introduced in 1974, most land in Cameroon remains under customary occupation. This insecurity of title hampers peasants' ability to exploit the land fully, as they are vulnerable to exploitation in times of economic crisis, when the elite purchase land, register it and then later on rent the farms to peasants or evict them. Finally, bundles of rights that exist only through customary law such as 'forest use rights' are not protected by existing legislation which does not recognise traditional rights to land.

Women and Land in Cameroon

When talking about land on a traditional or modern scale in Cameroon, one thinks of the man on the front line. Men rule management of land. The women exceptionally come into play depending no more on custom but rather on individual families that try in one way or another to give a reasonable position to their sister or daughter. (Logo and Bikie, this volume, Chapter 1)

Cameroon is a multicultural, multiethnic and multireligious country. However, regardless of whether the regulatory framework and laws governing women's access to control over land emanate from customary, religious or statutory sources, they have one thing in common. They all discriminate against women. In some cases, the discrimination is subtle and, to some extent, a matter of interpretation. In other cases, it is blatant and justified by the gender-based divisions of labour and responsibilities as well as by the different values placed by society on women and men's work. Factors affecting women's access to and control over land include discriminatory laws and practices, ignorance, illiteracy, lack of codification of customary law and the conflict of laws.

Statutory law On the face of it, Cameroon's statutory land law does not discriminate against women. The legislation and regulations governing access to and control over land appear to be gender neutral. The Constitution guarantees all Cameroonian citizens, 'regardless of sex', the right to property. This right to property includes the right to 'use, enjoy and to have all rights guaranteed to all by law' (Bigombe and Logo 1988: 34). Furthermore, the revised Constitution of Cameroon of 18 January 1996 stipulates that the 'nation protects and encourages the woman'.

Nor do the land laws pertaining to such issues as registration, on the surface, discriminate against women. Article 1 of Ordinance Number 74/1 of 6 July 1974, the governing law on land, states that 'the State guarantees to all persons physically or morally possessing lands in property, the right to enjoy and freely deal with it'.

However, both the constitutional right to property and the land law are undermined by Section 7 of the Trade Act and the sections of the Civil Code that authorise a man to interfere with his wife's right to engage in enterprise, thereby preventing her from freely dealing with her land and thus fully enjoying her property.

Due to poverty, ignorance, illiteracy and certain institutional barriers, statutory land law also discriminates against women. The complexity and bureaucratic nature of the process that has to be undertaken to register land makes it a particularly difficult endeavour for an illiterate person. Since the majority of illiterate people in Cameroon are women, as a constituency they suffer from this problem even more. Not only is the problem of registration of title complex, it is slow and expensive. Again, women constitute the majority of the poor, so are further disadvantaged.

Women are therefore unable to defend their rights either in the local or the legal setting. Women also fear retaliation from their families and communities, as well as fearing corruption and the justice system. These internalised attitudes are passed from generation to generation and are the main cause of women's resigned, and apparently compliant, outlooks and opinions.

Customary Laws and Practices

The bulk of land in rural Cameroon is under customary tenure. Customary land systems are more rigid for women than for men. Men are the decision-makers and consequently determine land management. The gender-based division of labour and crop delegation means that women grow less prestigious crops, used primarily for subsistence and food, while men control cash crops. In some regions, such as among the Beti, after a woman is married she no longer has access to family lands, except if the marital contract is broken. She is then entitled to the access and use of her father's land, but only with his permission.

The traditional means of land acquisition are by donation, inheritance and succession. Donated land is primarily received through parental or filial ties and generally takes place between male members of the family. This is a gift of land for long-term use with no pay. Land is usually only donated to a woman by her father when she has had male children outside wedlock. Such a woman can also inherit land if her father so wishes. In both instances, she is only holding the land in trust for her sons, who will assume control as soon as they are adults. Daughters are rarely candidates for donation as it is assumed that they will marry outside the family. Land is normally inherited by sons and, even among them, the eldest son receives the largest portion as he is also supposed to be responsible for the care of his father's widows and unmarried sisters. Where there are no sons, the land passes into the hands of the closest male relatives.

Traditional acquisition for temporary use occurs in the form of a loan. There are many rules regarding specific allocations. The borrower must specify the intended use of the land and some kind of down payment is usually required. Food crops are often popular for loaned land, as the tenureship is not long term. However, when women borrow land, it generally remains unexploited.

Customary laws and practices are not documented and vary even among clans of the same community. The fluctuating nature of traditional land systems means that women's land rights are currently precarious.

Religious laws and practices The predominant religions in Cameroon are the traditional religions, Christianity and Islam. Islam is the most relevant in respect of women's access to and control over land. Under Islamic laws, women do have some property rights. In regard to inheritance, daughters receive half of what their brothers are entitled to, the justification being that the son is responsible for taking care of his sister, whereas the daughter is entitled to exploit her property for herself alone. There is a need to recognise and affirm how few property rights women have under Islamic law, as some Muslim families, rather than give their daughters what they are entitled to, prefer to follow the customary practices under which women have no right to inherit land. Traditional local religions are very rigid towards women. Women do not have a right to land under these laws.

Recommendations

In order to improve and secure women's access to and control over land in Cameroon, the following actions are recommended:

1. Awareness-raising among women regarding their human rights and, in particular, their land rights. It has been clearly demonstrated that Cameroonian women are not aware of the rights that they possess, particularly under the Constitution, and this lack of awareness is exploited. To improve women's access to and control over land, women therefore need to be made conscious of their rights and the legal mechanisms that they can use to enforce them.
2. Devise methods for providing woman-friendly legal aid services to Cameroonian women, since their property is one of the reasons that they are unable to enforce their rights and therefore improve their access to and control over land.
3. Women's and human rights organisations should promote the review, repeal and/or amendment of laws that discriminate against women and inhibit their access to and control over land. In particular, Section 7 of the Trade Act and the sections of the Civil Code pertaining to divorce and inheritance need examination.
4. Women's organisations, human rights organisations and those engaged in agrarian reform work should advocate gender-sensitive and woman-friendly land reform.
5. Promote the recognition, legislation, documentation and enforcement of women's existing rights under Islamic law.
6. Advocate gender-sensitive enforcement mechanisms in respect of laws pertaining to women's land rights.
7. Conduct gender-sensitive human rights training for law enforcement agencies,

particularly the judiciary, who play a key role in the land registration and administration process.

8. Conduct gender-sensitive human rights training for policy-makers and lobby them to institute woman-friendly land reform.

9. Advocate the development of a post-Beijing national plan and policy.

10. Conduct human rights training for women's rights organisations, to enable them effectively to monitor commitments that Cameroon has made in international law.

Notes

1. As of May 1997, women held only 10 out of 180 seats in Cameroon's Parliament. See 'Index on the Status of Women in Africa' (2000), p. 55.

2. Thirty-two per cent of women in Cameroon between the ages of 20 and 24 compared to 78 per cent of women between the ages of 45 and 49 are illiterate, showing an improvement in the access of women to education. See 'Generational Improvement in Women's Education, African Countries', in *The Generation Gap*, 1994, http://www.unicef. org/pon95/wome0009.html

3. In statistics compiled in 1987, approximately 10 per cent of young urban Cameroonian women were illiterate, compared to approximately 40 per cent of rural women. *The World's Women 1995: Trends and Statistics* (1995), p. 91.

4. These figures are based on a 1990 census conducted by the United Nations in several African countries contained in *The World's Women 2000: Trends and Statistics* (2000), p. 87.

References

The information in this chapter is largely based on Patrice Bigombe Logo's and Elise-Henriette Bikie's work, *Women and Land in Cameroon: Questioning Women's Land Status and Claims for Change*. However the African Women's Development and Communication Network (FEMNET) takes full responsibility for the analysis, interpretation and presentation made therein.

Africa Forum: A Journal of Democracy, Leadership and Development, Vol. 4, No. 1, 2000.

Bigombe Logo, Patrice and Elise-Henriette Bikie (1988), *Women and Land in Cameroon, Questioning Women's Land Status Claims for Change*.

'Index on the Status of Women in Africa' (2000) *Africa Forum: A Journal of Democracy, Leadership and Development*, Vol. 4, No. 1.

Mungwa, Alice (2000) 'The Impact of Women's Status on Meaningful Communication: Considerations from the Cameroonian Situation', *Africa Forum: A Journal of Democracy, Leadership and Development*, Vol. 4, No. 1.

The World's Women 1995, Trends and Statistics (1995), New York: United Nations.

The World's Women 2000, Trends and Statistics (2000), New York: United Nations.

NINE

Ethiopia: Women's Status and Land Reform

The Status of Women

If a woman exhibits intelligence, she is taken for a crafty person; if she dares to express her views, she is labelled 'long tongued'; if she happens to be gutsy and vigorous, she is dubbed 'masculine'. Women are, as a whole, viewed as a personification of weakness and as treacherous beings who do their duties if and when they are whipped or beaten. (National Policy on Ethiopian Women, Government of Ethiopia, 1993)

The status of women of Ethiopia is low. Legal, social and economic institutions have rules and structures that discriminate against women, fail to support them in their reproductive roles and deny them equal benefits to men.

It is estimated that only 5 per cent of women have access to trained midwives. Childbirth-related deaths in Ethiopia are among the highest in the world. Ninety-eight per cent of Ethiopian women have no access to family planning, and the average woman gives birth to seven children. Female genital mutilation and early marriages of children below even ten years of age is common. Thirty per cent of women are in polygamous marriages.

Family law states that the husband is the head of the family. The wife owes him obedience in all lawful things that he orders and is expected to submit to his guidance of her conduct. The husband chooses the common residence, although the wife may appeal to family arbitrators if she is against the decision. Where the husband is not in the position to provide his wife with servants, she is bound to carry out the household duties herself. Also, common property, including the wife's income, is to be administered with the husband, although family arbitrators may entrust property administration to the wife in the interests of the family.

These laws assume that a wife is a dependant of the husband and also his property. The provision for family arbitration subjects women to a system of cultural justice that is skewed in favour of men. Other laws that provide for shared family property assume that women know of their husbands' property ownership and income. This is often not the case.

Although women are 50 per cent of the country's population, they constitute only 23 per cent of those in educational institutions and only 8 per cent in undergraduate colleges. Affirmative action policies are now in place for women at university level.

Women in both the rural and urban areas work long hours in menial jobs, with little or no pay. There is variation between the different communities, but in general, women weed, harvest and store crops. In nomadic communities they are responsible for erecting, dismantling and transporting of mobile homes. In addition, women do all housework, including grinding grain, fetching water, gathering firewood and cow dung for fuel, preparing food and raising children. Rural women sometimes work up to 17 hours a day, but are mostly restricted from ownership and control of land and other property. There is no autonomous civil sector pursuing women's rights in Ethiopia. An independent women's movement has started only recently, with the creation of the Ethiopian Women Lawyers' Association (EWLA).

Land in Ethiopia

Land is a critical resource in Ethiopia. Fifty million of the total 58 million population live in the rural areas. Agriculture constitutes 51 per cent of total GDP, 85 per cent of total employment and 85 per cent of total exports.

Land concerns have been central to the policies of all governments of Ethiopia. Land reforms have aimed at facilitating equal distribution, rather than efficiency as defined by neo-classical economics. All land, rural or urban, is vested in the state and in the peoples of Ethiopia. The law does not provide for the sale or exchange of land allotted in rural areas.

Before 1974, most peasants gained access to land through inheritance. At that time, the most visible and significant land arrangement, mainly in the south, was of landlord and tenant. This was the result of significant land ownership provided as gifts of the imperial regime to political and social elites. These elites were often absent and rented their land to peasants or organised sharecropping arrangements. Sharecropping, where the tenants paid between one-third to three-fourths of the output to landowners, was the dominant arrangement. In the north, a communal land tenure system referred to as *rist* existed. Here, anyone who could claim lineage from the first settler or developer of land had the right to own land.

After 1975, the Derg military regime introduced the 'land to the tiller' reforms. Peasants registered for land distribution through newly formed Peasant Associations. Land was allotted on the basis of family size. No household, however, was allowed to own more than the ten-hectare land ceiling. Land could not be transferred by any other means. Hiring of labour was prohibited unless one was a child, widowed, or a woman or child with no breadwinner. In the *rist* tenure system of the north, claims on land on the basis of lineage were abolished. The Derg reforms did not improve the lives of peasants. Also civil war, recurrent drought and famine undermined land reform. Ethiopia has a high population growth rate of 3 per cent. The ever-growing population made land distribution by family size unsustainable, and by 1980 landlessness was a major crisis.

In 1991, the new government introduced new land reforms based on a federal state. The country was divided into ten regions according to ethnicity. The new land reforms that were stipulated in the 1994 Constitution and were to be administered on a regional basis. Households who lost land in redistribution are compensated. However, the valuation of land and property is ambiguous and any compensation is therefore uneven. To date, only the Amhara region has redistributed land in line with federal provisions. The objective of the land redistribution in Amhara is to secure land grabbed by a few bureaucrats and officials of the agricultural cooperatives, but it is alleged to be punitive towards persons associated with the imperial and military regimes. In the Tigray region, minimum land size ceilings for meaningful agricultural activity have been set.

A Federal Land Proclamation of 1997 is yet to be implemented. The proclamation details the roles of regional states in the administration of rural lands. It provides the states with the responsibility of promulgating laws pertaining to the administration of land under their jurisdiction, as long as these do not contradict federal law.

Women and Land

The land reforms of Ethiopia continue to keep women in marginal positions in regard to access and control of land. Prior to 1974, only ruling-class women could own or purchase land. In most of the north, women had the right of inheritance.

The Derg reforms nationalised land. The nationalisation and subsequent distribution of land was based on membership of the Peasant Associations. The heads of households become members of the Associations. Land was distributed to the head of the household, who, for married couples, is the man. This restricted women's women's right to land, particulatly in the case of married women. Female heads of households received only small landholdings. Divorced women, women in polygamous marriages, and the women who came of age after the initial apportionment of land were the most disadvantaged. In the case of polygamous marriages only one wife was registered. When women married and subsequently relocated to their husbands' homes, they lost land, as did those who divorced and had to leave their matrimonial homes.

Women in the north with inheritance rights had strong control of their land, which was vested on the clan. Nationalisation of land and registration of land under the male head of the household deprived them of land ownership and made women completely dependent on their husbands. Women were categorised among groups unable to cultivate, such as the ill and aged. The reforms therefore did not challenge the taboo against women ploughing and sowing.

The emergence of Peasant Associations, through which land was distributed, and judicial tribunes at the local level, contributed to some enhancement of the land rights of divorced women. Also, in some cases land was apportioned separately for husband and wife.

As noted earlier, the post-1991 land reforms have taken place only in the Amhara region. In these reforms, only single women involved in income-generating activities were allocated land. Widows, divorcees or single dependent women were not provided for.

Existing Women's Land Rights Requiring Implementation

Allocation of land Although the 1997 Rural Land Redistribution Proclamation of the Amhara National State provides for the distribution of land equally to both women and men, only men and single women entrepreneurs were allocated land. The women who have land have smaller and more marginal holdings than those of male-headed households. Land administration should be reformed to implement equality in distribution to all Ethiopians, as stipulated in the land proclamation.

Enforcement of minimum age for marriage Information on the legally accepted minimum age for marriage needs to be disseminated and the law enforced. The prevalence of early marriages, even of seven-year-olds, is disadvantageous to women and to their ability to safeguard their interests in marriage. Children and young girls are ill-prepared for marriage. Early marriage results in frequent divorces and the subsequent dispossession of land for many women.

Women's Land Rights Requiring Recognition

... the full and complete development of a country, the welfare of the world and the cause of peace require the maximum participation of women on equal terms with men in all fields. (Convention on the Elimination of All Forms of Discrimination Against Women, 1979)

Direct and equal access and control of land for all women In some regions of the country, such as Oromia, and the Southern Nations, Nationalities and Peoples Region (SNNPR), women can inherit land in the absence of a male sibling. They can also control land in the absence of a husband or other male relative. However, the general trend nationally is that women heads of households with young children or only female children are more disadvantaged than women with male or adolescent children. Those with young children or only daughters have to depend on male relatives or enter into sharecropping arrangements. Women should be able to inherit and control land in their own right.

The Convention on the Elimination of All Forms of Discrimination Against Women (CEDAW) affirms the right of women to equal treatment in land and agrarian reform.

The outlawing of polygamy and recognition of all wives present Polygamous marriages enhance inequalities between men and women. The resources and wealth of a polygamous home belong to the man. These include labour of the wives and products from agriculture. As a result, a polygamous man has greater social and economic status.

The Protestant Church encourages monogamy, and to be accepted into the church converts have to abandon their wives. The welfare of co-wives should be recognised within the Christian ethic and the church should take responsibility for safeguarding these women against marginalisation and destitution.

Men and women have equal rights and responsibilities during a marriage and at its dissolution, as laid down both in CEDAW and the International Covenant on Civil and Political Rights.

Right to plough and sow In most of the country, it is taboo for women to plough or sow. Although during the civil war women in areas under the control of the Tigray Peoples Liberation Front could plough and sow, the end of the war saw a return to dominant beliefs and practices. The inability to plough and sow serves to justify the perception that women cannot control land without a male

---

Newur'news (Taboos)

Parents can be seen as the most important people who can empower their children. They are the ones who can break and do away with the many *newur'news* (taboos) restricting their daughters and sons in their behaviors and actions ... some *newur'news* are culturally and traditionally defined, prevalent in every household, while many are created or done away with (according to the convenience of the male head of household) in individual families. These *newur'news* are used over generations and become part of one's culture and tradition. It is again women and men who can change them or do away with them. And this is why the family is seen as very important for the empowerment of women. The family is the base to create equality between girls and boys by allowing or restricting them equally in their movements and actions. Why can't a girl play football or slaughter chicken and a boy wash dishes or cook the evening meal? (Birke and Fekade 1999)

presence. Attitudes influencing the persistence of this taboo should be addressed through education and the modelling of alternative approaches.

Access to the consumption and marketing of agricultural produce Women cannot grow cereal, consume or sell it without depending on male relations. The inability to handle growing and marketing of plant and animal produce not only reduces the direct income of women, but reduces their ability to widen their networks to enhance further their economic and social status.

CEDAW affirms the same right of both spouses in a marriage to manage, administer and enjoy family property.

Encouragement of fair domestic division of labour With increased environmental degradation, women have to work longer hours to obtain water and fuel. This work, in combination with other domestic labour and agricultural work, creates an imbalanced and unfair gender division of labour.

The 1976 International Covenant on Economic, Social and Cultural Rights affirms fair work conditions, particularly for women.

Encouragement of agricultural activities that women control Women growing backyard vegetables are finding more autonomy for agricultural activity and income. Growing of vegetables and other farm production where women are in control should be expanded into more viable commercial activities.

Distinguishing between residences and farm holdings In rural Ethiopia residences are part of the farm, as they are built close to the cultivation fields. The agrarian reforms did not differentiate land for residence from that for agricultural activities. Without matrimonial homes being dissociated from land, divorced women and single adult women have to live with their parents or reside with siblings.

Create legal and other institutional fallback positions for divorced women Divorced women often have to leave matrimonial lands and do not have any land rights in their natal lands. Divorced women's right to livelihood on farmland should be recognised and institutions set up to support them emotionally with farm and off-farm activities and legal issues.

Indicators of the Social Empowerment of Women

1. Visibility and social presence
   - Influence on 'agenda setting' of the community and public discourse,
   - Competence in negotiation,
   - Access to institutions, administration and banks, etc.

2. Participation in public life
   - Participation in local decision-making bodies – for community affairs as well as local jurisdiction,
   - Taking leadership roles,
   - Influencing the construction and implementation of cultural practices, religion, etc.
3. Respect by other members of the community/village
   - Freedom from violence,
   - Respect for women irrespective of age,
   - Support for promotion of equality,
   - Recognition of women as representatives of the community and community leaders, etc.
4. Organisation
   - Space to develop collective identity and to organise outside of the family,
   - Collective ability for action and public influence,
   - Alliances with other social groups,
   - Relations with state institutions, etc. (Birke and Fekade 1999)

References

Birke, Aster and Fekade, Konjit (1999) *Reflections: Documentation of the Forum for Gender*, Addis Ababa: Heinrich Boll Stiftung.

Convention on the Elimination of All Forms of Discrimination Against Women (1979), New York: United Nations.

Government of Ethiopia (1993) National Policy on Ethiopian Women, Addis Ababa.

Tadesse, Zenebeworke (2003) this volume, Chapter 2.

Tekie, Alemu (2000) *Insecure Land Tenure Regimes and Soil Conservation*, Addis Ababa University.

TEN

Nigeria: The Road to Independent Ownership

The Status of Women in Nigeria

Although a relatively strong and independent women's movement exists in Nigeria, the status of women is low.

In 1995 the adult female literacy rate was 47 per cent, while that of males was 67 per cent. Only about 30 per cent of students in tertiary educational institutions are women. However, a few state governments have implemented educational policies that may increase female participation in education. These policies have included lowering the entry points into educational institutions for females. There has also been an increase in the number of scholarships awarded to females.

Although Nigeria has well-trained health care personnel, there are often insufficient supplies of necessary health equipment and drugs. Between 1990 and 1996, only 31 per cent of births were attended by trained health personnel. Although there have been widespread family planning programmes, the contraceptive prevalence rate is only 6 per cent. It is also estimated that 60 per cent of women in the country have undergone female genital mutilation (FGM). The government of Nigeria has published policy opposing FGM.

Despite the efforts of various non-governmental organisations to encourage women to participate in politics, women continue to participate in elections largely as voters. For example, in the recently aborted elections, only two women deputy governors were elected as compared to 27 male deputy governors. Women's low self-confidence, their limited economic power and the violence associated with elections have contributed to the poor participation of women in the political process (WiLDAF 1994).

Land Tenure and Administration in Northern Nigeria

Northern Nigeria contains about 55 per cent of Nigeria's population and comprises 19 of Nigeria's 37 states. This part of the country is predominantly Muslim, but there is a significant indigenous Christian religious community. Before the advent of British colonialism, much of northern Nigeria was incorporated into the Sokoto Caliphate after Uthman Dan Fodio's jihad of 1804. The Caliphate's land tenure policy vested all control of mineral land in the state. Selling or inheritance was forbidden, but usufruct rights were granted to individuals who were considered worthy. In *waqf* (conquered land), only one-tenth of the harvest was paid to the authorities, while in non-Muslim land tax was paid as well as royalties from mining. Non-Muslims could not sell, bequeath or lease land.

British rule, which began in 1903, brought an end to the Caliphate but retained Islamic law (Sharia). Under Sharia land is considered indispensable to individual and social life, and no person has control over it except for the areas under their use. Land is administered under three categories: occupied land where the occupier assumes complete ownership, unoccupied land and common land (*wafq*) previously acquired by warfare, cessation or treaty but presently acquired after elder consultations with the Emir. *Wafq* lands are used for grazing, markets and leisure activities.

In non-Muslim communities, customary law determines land tenure and its administration. Land is vested in the head of the family or community, but the individual may acquire absolute rights through gifts, clearing or the partitioning of family property.

Statutory land law also came into existence with British colonialism. Statutory land law created Crown lands as the property of the British government and public lands for indigenous use. Statutory land rights are registered in the Lands Division of State Administration and are mainly restricted to urban and government land. This land can be used for the purposes of mortgages and loans. The Land Use Act of 1978 is the most recent statutory land law reform. The purpose of this legislation was to provide land for all Nigerians, to make easier the acquisition of land by the government and to prohibit land speculation and the escalation of land prices. All owners and users of land are required to have a certificate of occupancy, while undeveloped land could be no more than half a hectare per person, with the rest reverting back to the state.

Women and Land in Northern Nigeria

The law assumed gender equality and therefore enforced stereotypes of men as breadwinners and women as dependants. The law did not recognise the de facto land ownership of women. The registration of customary rights threatened women's secondary rights, because these cannot be converted to ownership rights.

Islamic law recognises women as legal entities. Women can acquire, inherit and bequeath land. However, women's inheritance rights are not applied uniformly. For example, while women's land rights are recognised in Sokoto, they are not recognised in Kano. Historically, therefore, religion has been used both to limit and enhance women's land rights. In pre-independence days, the argument used in Kano to deny women their land rights was that 'women should go to live with male relatives'. This was enacted as Sharia law in Kano in 1923, but annulled in 1954.

In spite of the religious injunction against women's rights to inherit property, the general belief by men in the study sites is that women's land rights are unwarranted because women allegedly have no need for lands, as they are usually married and are catered for by their husbands. When women are divorced, according to the men interviewed in Dawakin Tofa and Yabu, their male guardians will look after them. It is also claimed that women have no time for the arduous task of farming (Abdullah and Hamza 1998).

In Muslim areas, therefore, women do not have independent land rights. The response of women to this reflected the dominant male perspective. 'A woman has rights over her personal effects, her husband has rights over her property ... a woman's property is under the control of her husband ... a woman can have independent thinking only when she is divorced and does not have surviving parents or male kin' (Abdullah and Hamza 1998).

In non-Muslim areas, inheritance is traced through male descent and the people who are entitled to inherit are the children of the deceased, his brothers, and his brothers' male children, parents and grandparents. Wives, sisters, aunts and all other female kin are excluded from inheritance. Women have nothing to be inherited and don't inherit as well (Yakubu 1985). Thus a woman's rights to land can be acquired only through marriage or her family. The rights she derives from either status are usufructory, and therefore she cannot alienate the land. On the death of her husband, she is allowed to continue using the land allocated to her by her deceased husband on condition that she marries another member of the family or stays as part of the family. If she decides to opt out of the family, she loses the land. If, because of old age, the woman stays with her children, she will retain her right to use the land. A woman using her family land does not have the right to alienate such land either (Abdullah and Hamza 1998).

The legal status of women's land rights under Christianity is ambiguous. Recent judgments have applied customary inheritance practices. It is civil marriage rather than Christian marriage that is necessary to protect women's land rights.

Yet in spite of the critical role marriage plays in securing land rights for women in the study sites, marriage is a fluid institution. Fifteen of 50 women were divorced and two-thirds of the women had married more than once.

Existing Women's Land Rights Requiring Enforcement

Enforcement of sharia law on women's land rights According to Sharia law, women are entitled to inherit half of the male share, that is, one share to the man's two shares. For widows, this means an eighth for women with children and a quarter if there are no children. This has often been disregarded, resulting in no independent land rights for women. Enforcing Sharia law in this regard will ensure some land security for women.

Women's Land Rights Requiring Recognition and Appropriate Legislation

Enlightenment on women's right to inheritance Customary law on land inheritance is dominant in both Muslim and non-Muslim areas. Customary law is skewed against women and its basis is discriminatory social attitudes towards women. Awareness programmes should be created that challenge these attitudes and highlight case studies where women have been considered as independent entities in inheritance.

Creation of uniform inheritance laws Laws should be created that provide safeguards for women's use and ownership of land uniformly throughout the country. The layers of law based on custom, religion and statutes have contributed to the ambiguity of land administration, particularly for Nigerian women, whose land rights are limited under all legal systems.

Recognition of women's rights to land occupancy Most women's engagement with land is based on occupancy and use rather than on ownership. Land rights acquired through occupancy should be recognised in statutory law. This would ensure women are not dispossessed of land on divorce or widowhood.

References

This chapter is based on Abdullah and Hamza (1998), but the African Women's Development and Communication Network (FEMNET) takes full responsibility for the analysis, interpretation and presentation made here. The sites used in the research were the Maguzawa and Dawakin Tofa local government areas in Kano, the Yabo local government area in Sokoto and southern Zaria, all in northern Nigeria.

Abdullah, Hussaina J. and Hamza, Ibrahim (1998) *Women Need Independent Ownership Rights: Women and Land in Northern Nigeria,*, Atlanta: Emory University Law School.

Status of Women (CD-ROM) (2000), Addis Ababa: United Nations Economic Commission for Africa (UNECA).

Strengthening Linkages for Women's Rights in Africa (1994), Harare: Women in Law and Development in Africa (WiLDAF).

Women and Housing in Nigeria: Issues, Problems and Prospects (1996), Lagos: Women, Law and Development Centre.

Yakubu, M. G. (1985) *Nigerian Land Law*, London: Macmillan.

ELEVEN
Senegal: Land Rights, Culture and Religion

The Status of Women in Senegal

Senegal is a country covering 250,000 square kilometres, with a population of approximately 52 per cent women. Fifty-eight per cent of the total population is under 20 years of age, and the annual population growth rate is 3 per cent, with a global fertility index of six offspring per woman. Seventy-eight per cent of females and 53 per cent of males are estimated to be illiterate. Of those with post-high school education, only 27 per cent are female.[1] Women therefore have little access to wage-earning jobs and 75 per cent of all women are employed in the informal or agricultural sector. Women's work is consequently both invisible and unappreciated. The country's infrastructure is characterised by poor health and education facilities.

Senegal is culturally diverse and has a multi-faith society. Most of Senegal's peoples subscribe to either the Muslim, Christian or indigenous faiths.[2] There are great variations in the status of Senegalese women according to their specific cultures, ethnicities and religions. While some of Senegal's indigenous cultures, such as that of the Peul, are patriarchal, others, like the Serer, are matrilineal. In this predominantly Muslim country, women have certain rights arising from religious laws that have not been recognised and/or implemented. Therefore, to understand fully the status of women in Senegal, it is necessary to examine all aspects of society, including tradition, religion and law.

Statistics suggest that women make up 75 per cent of the Senegalese rural population. They carry out 81 per cent of all agricultural work and produce 70 per cent of all agricultural produce for both domestic use and export.[3] However, Senegalese women own little land, compared to the value of the labour that they provide. Women are assigned to cultivate land, but in many instances are denied possession of it. Tradition, religion and the law uphold this discrimination. The greatest challenges are to secure rights that exist in customary and religious laws, as well as to address gender-based inequalities. These inequalities arise both from customary and religious laws, which have proven to have more force than statutory law in Senegal and have, at times, rendered women's land rights non-existent.

Senegal ratified the International Convention on the Elimination of All Forms of Discrimination Against Women (CEDAW) in 1985 and the Constitution of Senegal allows women to vote. However, by 1998, women filled only 10 per cent of seats in Parliament. Their access to decision-making is therefore limited. Senegalese women have consistently organised to increase their access to decision-making positions, including those in Parliament, and during the April 2001 elections they made some gains in this arena. Out of 120 members, the new Senegalese Parliament has 38 women, bringing their parliamentary representation to 16.7 per cent.[4] Furthermore, women hold several strategic portfolios in the new cabinet, including one in the Ministry of Justice. Senegal is now ranked 38th globally in respect of its percentage of women parliamentarians and is the seventh highest-ranking African country.[5] It is hoped that these MPs will use these positions to improve the lot of the ordinary Senegalese woman.

Land in Senegal

Land serves both spiritual and utilitarian purposes in Senegal. The rich multicultural and multireligious background of the country influences the manner in which land is perceived and utilised. Senegal is a former French colony and was the capital of French-occupied West Africa. Thus the dominant external influence on Senegalese culture and laws is French. However, the interpretation and implementation of French-based statutory laws is influenced by Senegal's pre-colonial cultures and religion. In many parts of Senegal, indigenous legal systems carry more weight than the modern French-based statutory legal system. This works both to the advantage and disadvantage of Senegalese women, depending on whether the pre-colonial culture was patriarchal or matrilineal, with interpretation of statutory law in matrilineal cultures being more advantageous to women.

In Tine and Sy's study of three Senegalese cultures, the Peul, Serer and Wolof, it was found that in two of them, the Serer and Wolof, rights over land are dependent on whether or not one's ancestor was the first to clear and/or cultivate an area. Known as 'land rights by virtue of fire and the axe', these rights vest both spiritual and proprietary powers in those who possess them.

Among the Wolof, there is a distinction between those who possess rights of fire and those who possess rights of the axe. Rights by virtue of fire are acquired through having been the first person to clear the land with fire. The descendant and heir of such an individual is known as the *lamane*, who possesses the right to dispose of the land as he wishes. Among the Wolof, only a man can hold this right. Rights by virtue of the axe are a form of tenancy in which the *lamane* allows a farmer to clear the land in return for payment. An individual who has rights only by virtue of the axe cannot dispose of the land. He has only a right to till it.

The Serer do not distinguish between the rights of fire and the axe. The person who first cleared the land is perceived as having a spiritual connection with the ancestors and with the spirits that protect the land. Amongst the Serer, the *lamane* is:

> One of the priests of the religion of the land, on the initial agreement which he entered into with the spirits of the forest, consolidated by ancestors whose work and fervour have fertilised the soil and who continue to live. (Tine and Sy, this volume, Chapter 6)

The *lamane* is critical to protecting the fertility of the land. In Serer culture, land is passed on matrilineally. Men inherit land from their maternal uncles. Furthermore, rice paddy-fields can be inherited only by women and are passed on from mother to daughter.

Among the Peul, land is considered sacred and therefore cannot be owned by an individual. Land is communally owned. All Peul people have only user rights in respect of land. The right to administer land is passed on through men. The family patriarch is responsible for the distribution of land, with the oldest males in the family being given priority. Women have user rights only through their fathers, husbands, brothers or sons. Due to this communal ownership, land in Peul-dominated areas is rarely bought or sold, as it has not been commodified.

In examining religious laws, the influence of Sharia (Islamic law) on Senegalese women's access to and control over land is important. Under Sharia, outsiders acquire land if they have openly and publicly cultivated it uninterrupted for a period of ten years. If a family member also exploits family land openly for 40 uninterrupted years, the land becomes his or hers by right (Tine and Sy, Chapter 6). There are also elaborate laws governing the inheritance of property when Muslims die intestate.

In addition, environmental concerns must also be taken into consideration in examining land rights in Senegal. The areas of the groundnut basin face acute land shortages due to salination and tannification (Tine and Sy, Chapter 6).

The National Law 64-46 of 17 June 1964 guides the overall distribution and disposal of land. This law classifies land into four broad categories, according to urban and rural needs, the purpose of national development and the protection of nature. These categories are urban, local, classified and pioneer areas. The administration of rural land (the local areas) falls under the authority of indigenous populations through their elected representatives on Rural Councils. The Rural Councils are organs of the Rural Communities, charged with the responsibility of overseeing land allocation and revocations. Rural Communities were set up under the National Law 72-25 of 19 April 1972 and are defined as: '[Composed] of a certain number of villages belonging to the same locality, bound by solidarity, due particularly to proximity, having common interests and able to find the resources necessary for their development.'

Decisions of the Rural Councils are enforceable only after approval by the sub-prefect. Two basic principles govern the allocation of land. First, priority should be given to inhabitants of the locality. Second, land is allocated to a legal person provided he or she develops it. An allocation can only be revoked on the basis of absence of development or integration into state-owned land.

Women and Land in Senegal

Senegalese women's control over land is limited, whether one examines their situation under the customary, religious or statutory legal systems. Most women only have user rights, except for women living in Serer areas, where, due to the tradition of matriarchy regarding rice paddy-fields, the majority of women own some land.

With regard to ownership, Serer women are by far the most well-off, followed by the Wolof and the Peul. The major distinctive feature among the Serer is that women can inherit land directly from their mothers, which is not the case among the Wolof and the Peul. Empirical research on women's access to and control over land in Senegal found that women's land ownership in the locations under study varied from 32 per cent among the Peul to 42.85 among the Wolof and 88.46 per cent among the Serer (Tine and Sy, Chapter 6).

A combination of different factors has led to this situation. First, customary law tends to prevail over both religious and statutory law in Senegal (however, customary law is not always negative and religious and statutory law are not always equitable). The fact that virtually no women in the Peul areas own land and the majority of women in the Serer do own land can be attributed to the differences in customary law in these areas. Inequitable customary, religious and legal practices, poverty, illiteracy and land shortages are all contributory factors to women's access to and control over land.

Under both Peul and Wolof customary law, women cannot own land. Land is communal property under Peul customary law. Nobody owns it, but men control its administration and distribution. Since land cannot be owned or purchased, women are unable to inherit or acquire it (although in a small number of cases, land has been allocated to women's groups for their use). In the Wolof areas, women are traditionally not allowed to own land. But a small number of women have inherited land from their deceased husbands (under Islamic law) while others have purchased it either individually or through women's groups (under statutory law). However, the Wolof areas of the country face acute land shortages and the *lamanes* tend to engage in illegal land speculation. Under Serer customary law, rice paddy-fields can be inherited only by women. In addition, the Rural Councils tend to favour the allocation of land to women's groups for their use. However, the Serer areas also face the problem of land shortages due to tannification and salination. Thus, land is not 'bought' – rather, the Rural Councils allow individuals and groups to use land. And in so doing, they try to accommodate and prioritise the needs of women's groups.[6]

In the Wolof and Peul areas, the influence of Sharia law must be taken into consideration. Under Sharia, women are allowed to own property and land is not distinguished from other forms of property. The main method of land acquisition under Islam is through inheritance. The principle applied is one share for a woman and two for the man. Where a Muslim man dies intestate, his widow can inherit his property, including land, according to this principle. Thus a widow inherits a quarter of the property if the deceased husband had no children, and an eighth of the property where there are living children of the deceased (Tine and Sy, Chapter 6). The principle of one share for a woman and two for a man is applied in distributing property between the children of a deceased Muslim man who has died intestate. The justification given for this is that the woman utilises her share only for herself, while the man is responsible for the upkeep of the family.[7] Where there is a valid will, a Muslim person can bequeath property as he or she pleases. There are instances of positive use of Sharia. For example, in the Wolof areas, most of the women who have inherited property have done so as a result of adherence to Sharia.

Poverty and illiteracy are obstacles to implementation of positive religious and statutory law. In order to be allocated land under statutory law, it is necessary not only to be able to purchase it, but also to be able to develop it. Seventy-five per cent of Senegal's poor people live in the rural areas (Tine and Sy, Chapter 6). Poverty thus prevents women from acquiring land, even in situations where statutory law is complied with. And when they have land, they are sometimes not able to fulfil the conditions of allocation.

Since statutory law is written in French, it is complicated and difficult to follow. The majority of rural councillors are illiterate and therefore resort to customary law. Even where women sit on the rural councils, they do not wield much power. As a consequence, women lose out in areas where customary law discriminates against them. The dominance of negative customary law over other forms of law has proven to be particularly detrimental in the Peul areas. Aside from woman-friendly customary law, in the Serer areas, the fact that the rural councillors are literate enhances the status of women.

Recommendations

In order to improve Senegalese women's access to and control over land, the following measures are recommended:

1. Improve women's access to education and training. The fact that 78 per cent of Senegalese women are illiterate is a contributory factor to their poverty. Emphasis should be placed on functional literacy in order to ensure that women understand their rights.
2. Facilitate the setting up of strong women's organisations and engage in leader-

ship training to ensure that women's organising and leadership capacities are strengthened. Even in areas where their individual requests were not responded to, women's groups seemed to have success in gaining access to land.

3. Increase women's economic capacity by improving their access to credit and developing their negotiation and management skills. For women to fulfil the legal requirement to develop land, they need the financial resources to do so.

4. Encourage women to enter decision-making through the Rural and Municipal Councils and improve the leadership skills of women already in those councils. Currently women constitute only 9 per cent of the members of Rural and Municipal Councils and they are not particularly active (Tine and Sy, Chapter 6). Yet these councils are responsible for making decisions in respect of land allocation and distribution.

5. Encourage literacy courses for councillors and incorporate gender analysis and gender mainstreaming training into all courses for councillors.

6. Consult and work with the *ulama* (Muslim scholars) on the issue of women's land rights.

7. Target religious and local authorities in awareness-raising campaigns and enlist them as allies in enhancing women's access to and control over land.

8. Incorporate into Senegal's domestic laws and policies those articles of CEDAW that promote women's access to and control over land. For example, Articles 5 and 14 pertain to the eradication of discriminatory socio-cultural practices and the elimination of discrimination against women in rural areas.

Notes

1. Ministry of National Education (1995).

2. Ninety-eight per cent of the country's population subscribe to either the Christian or Muslim faiths; see Chapter 6.

3. The Food and Agriculture Organisation (FAO), quoted in Chapter 6, p. 207. See also the Department of Forecasting and Statistics, Senegalese Ministry of the Economy, Finance and Planning, quoted in Chapter 6, p. 207.

4. See (1 July 2001), 'Women in National Parliaments', at http://www.ipu.org/wmn-e/classifhtm

5. Based on statistics and a comparative analysis conducted by the Inter-Parliamentary Union, see http://www.ipu.org/wmn-e/classifhtm

6. Tine and Sy observed that the Rural Council in Nguenienne is 'favourable to applications emanating from women's associations and deploys a lot of effort to find land for them, even if this means making arrangements with landowners'.

7. Tine and Sy observed that: 'In the seventh century, the emerging Islamic religion found women in a tragic and pitiable situation ... Discrimination [in the distribution of property], which is favourable to men, was explained by the fact that women did not have to work and were supported by men ... We have no choice but to observe that today the situation has changed. Women do over 70 per cent of farming work. Discussions we have had with religious leaders, including the Imam of the Medina Sabakh mosque, show that

Islam is not against the adaptation of Muslim rites to the socio-economic or even political context of the moment.'

References

This chapter is largely based on Ngoné Diop Tine and Mohamadou Sy's work, 'Women and Land in Africa: A Case Study from Senegal', published as Chapter 6 of this book. However, the African Women's Development and Communication Network (FEMNET) takes full responsibility for the analysis, interpretation and presentation made here.

Inter-Parliamentary Union (1 July 2001) 'Women in National Parliaments', http://www.ipu. org/wmn-e/classifhtm

TWELVE
Uganda: The Search for Secure Land Tenure

The Status of Women in Uganda

In Uganda, there exists a formal and institutional recognition of the role and the rights of women in national development comparable to few other countries in Africa. There is affirmative action for women in parliamentary elections, with some seats contested only by women. Eighteen per cent of members of Parliament are women and 13 per cent of senior government ministers.

However, Uganda is an underdeveloped country, where only an estimated 38 per cent of women have access to trained health personnel during childbirth. Only about 15 per cent of Ugandan women use contraceptives, while half a million women have undergone female genital mutilation (FGM).

HIV/AIDS is a major concern. In some cases, infected male spouses have sold off matrimonial property, to the detriment of women and children. Because of AIDS-related deaths, single young women head 49 per cent of households. Infected widows are often rejected and chased from homes. Succession law makes it illegal to evict a widow from the matrimonial home, where she is expected to live with her children until she dies, remarries or leaves voluntarily. However, customary practices such as widow inheritance, where relatives control the property of a deceased male family member, have contributed to women's marginalisation.

Women have the statutory right to own land and other property. However, women customarily have no proprietary rights to land. They get access and user rights to economically significant resources through marriage. Women often lack the collateral necessary to obtain loans to buy land themselves. Some banks also deny women loans unless a male relation has guaranteed them. And women's contribution to marital property acquisition is often not recognised, because marital property is usually registered in the man's name.

In other cases, women have not enforced their rights. One key reason is the limited knowledge about existing laws and land rights among the majority of women. Increasing this knowledge is difficult due to high illiteracy among women – 50 per cent of women in Uganda are illiterate as compared to 26 per cent of men (WiLDAF 1994).

Land in Uganda

Uganda has a range of land tenure categories, including customary land, *mailo* land (landlord–tenant, a tenure no longer officially recognised but dominant), freehold, leasehold and public land.

The *mailo* tenure system was created under colonialism. Although scrapped by the law, it is still dominant in the Buganda area of central Uganda. *Mailo* land was under the authority of the Buganda kingdom's Parliament – the *lukiko*. At that time, a *mailo* landowner could not dispose of his land to a person outside the protectorate. Within the *mailo* system, tenants – the *bibanja* holders – grew. Land was also organised in leasehold and freehold tenure, conditional upon construction or agricultural development. Customary tenure is the oldest and most widespread form of tenure, estimated to cover 64 per cent of Uganda's total land area.

The Land Reform Decree (LRD) of 1975 abolished the *mailo* and freehold land tenure systems. Land was nationalised and rents on *mailo* land abolished. However, the LRD was non-functional in many ways because it conflicted with the Constitution of 1967 which had entrenched the *mailo* system. The LRD also facilitated the eviction of customary tenants by developers who acquired public land. In effect, the nationalisation of public land without compensation was facilitated by the LRD.

A bill drafted in 1998 sets the new legal provisions for land access, ownership and transfer. This bill, based on the revised Constitution of 1995, vests land in Ugandan citizens according to four land tenure systems (exclusive of *mailo*) and the recommendations of a Land Tenure and Agricultural Development study carried out by the Land Technical Committee. The proposed land law reform shows a marked trend towards land privatisation and greater security of private land rights in the interests of increased land use efficiency. These reforms are consistent with the liberal economic reforms of funding agencies and the modernisation goals of the government of the National Resistance Movement (NRM). In effect, it proposes that land reform, premised on the market, should disregard social concerns such as the need of the majority of peasants in the rural areas to have land for survival. The market logic behind land reform thus caters for efficiency, with little regard for equity. The bill favours those with the least need but the greatest resources, at the expense of those with the greatest need but without resources – those with no guarantee of alternative forms of livelihood. The proposed land bill also disregards traditional structures such as clans, lineage and families that have in the past upheld the land interests of all Ugandans.

Women and Land

Like most post-colonial African states, the legal system of Uganda is characterised by dualism – the co-existence of a statutory legal system and an indigenous customary legal system pertaining to marriage, inheritance and property rights, including rights over land.

Pressure has been exerted on customary land tenure systems by this dualism. In the post-colonial era, customary land tenure systems vested authority over land in elders of the clan or leaders of the tribe. Women were protected from landlessness by this authority, in the event of marital conflict, divorce or widowhood. However, with the undermining of customary legal systems by colonial administrations, (male) family heads obtained greater autonomy in decisions regarding access to and control over land. Traditional patriarchy was thus essentially left intact, but with systems for checks and balances destroyed.

Post-colonial land tenure systems that favour private land titles also fail to recognise gender inequities and inequalities within families, ensuring that statutory family law is in favour of men. For example, the proposed 1998 land bill stated that no person shall sell, exchange, pledge, mortgage, lease or give away land without the prior consent of the spouse in occupation of the land. However, the notion of consent is based on the assumption that both spouses have equal power within marriage, which is not the case in Uganda – or indeed, in most of Africa.

The result is insecure land use and control. The contradictions posed by dualism with respect to land tenure work so as to lock women out of the land. Women are locked out of land tenure by statutory law, which is biased in favour of men, and by customary law, which is based on an unaccountable and patriarchal ethos.

Security of land tenure for women, who are the dominant land users, is an economic growth principle perhaps even stronger than that of making land a marketable commodity. Women's land rights need to be protected by replacing the elder's courts for both customary and statutory land law with collective family ownership of land. Collective ownership of land by the family (men, women and perhaps even adult children) should be created. The names of the family members should be entered in the title deeds.

Denial of Women's Access to and Control over Land and Income

Custom depicts women as being unable to manage property adequately. Supposedly frail and weak, women are considered more vulnerable to the environment. There is also the perception that women are more easily duped in transactions involving land. Men also argue that they need to have control over land and its products to fulfil the gender-based roles prescribed to them by society. For instance, as men are traditionally the taxpayers within the family, they say that they need to control the family's income in order to ensure that they meet this obligation.

The result of these prejudices is that women become servants on or mere users of the land of their male relatives. They provide unpaid labour in exchange for their occupation and use of land. Their rights to land are dependent on their marital status and children. If they have no children, they are considered to have no justification for claims to land.

Consequences of Gender Inequality in Land Rights

1. These inequalities keep women poor and of low socio-economic status.
2. Women's claims to land are made insignificant and remain unprotected, despite women's use of land resulting in the provision of 70–80 per cent of labour in agriculture and 90 per cent of labour with respect to food crops and food processing.
3. Increasing prostitution, sexual harassment, domestic violence, marital instability, separation and divorced marriage instability directly arise from land rights issues.

Exceptional land rights under statutory law: secret land purchases by women Women's lack of access to and control over land can be explained by a shortage of funds due to their income-generating activities being confined to the kitchen and the garden. When women can obtain resources to purchase land, they purchase it discreetly. This is because many husbands view their wives' independent acquisition of property, particularly land, as their first steps towards preparing for an independent existence.

In Buganda, some women arrange to rear domestic animals secretly, especially goats, pigs and cows at the home of a relative. They have them sold and then secretly purchase land without the knowledge of their husbands.

This secret purchase approach, which serves to create land ownership for women, has inherent problems. The women often have to purchase land in the names of male relatives, and are therefore vulnerable to dispossession. Also, vendors are sometimes unwilling to sell land to women for fear of being accused of taking other men's wives. In an effort to maintain secrecy on the part of the vendor, women become vulnerable to manipulation.

Secret land purchasing does not, therefore, increase women's vulnerability in regard to access to and control over land. Instead, customary and statutory institutions should be created to secure women's land rights.

Exceptional land rights under customary law: women in Buganda and Ankole Although women have statutory rights to inherit land, in practice these rights are constrained. Succession is supposed to be effected through either an oral or written will. But customary law and practice prevails, under which women are not regarded as legitimate landowners or managers. Even where women may inherit land, male mediation is required. A deceased father is almost always succeeded by a male relative, regardless of whether such a male is a collateral relative or not. One of the sons, normally the eldest, is the heir. In the absence of a son, the elders may choose to give the land to the brother(s) of the deceased. This is at the expense of daughters, who may be linear descendants and who in statutory law are given preference over collateral relatives.

Even though daughters in Buganda and Ankole cannot be heirs to their fathers, they have long been getting shares from their parents' estate. In families where there were no sons, the daughters were given property, with the male heir remaining largely a figurehead. Recently, in both Buganda and Ankole, daughters have also been rewarded with land on the basis of their usefulness to the family. Daughters supporting their families with labour or money are inheriting land. Also, there are increased shares to daughters in recognition of their insecurity with the increased number of unstable marriages.

Existing Land Rights Requiring Enforcement

Customary inheritance for women 'An abandoned wife, a separated wife or a widow cannot choose to remarry or bear children from another man if she is to retain or claim her husband's estate.' Although in areas such as Buganda and Ankole daughters have long received shares of their parents' estate, most women depend on male relations to access land. While statutory law's preference in land transfer is to collateral relatives, under customary law it is always through the male.

Improved safeguards for wills Although it is an offence to meddle with a deceased person's estate, wills are often tampered with in cases where widows are given more property.

Effective conflict resolution mechanisms for women Customary courts, local council courts and courts of law are ineffective for women. The legal process is expensive, technical and lengthy. The process is invariably presided over by men. Women often end up withdrawing or losing their cases.

Women's Land Rights Requiring Recognition and Legislation

Relaxation of gender roles and division of labour Gender roles with respect to the division of labour within and without the home are rigidly determined according to custom. Though domestic gender relations may be configured differently from home to home, men as the heads of households exercise superior rights in gender relations.

Recognition of sexual equality Women's sexual conduct contributes to the recognition of women's rights to land. If a woman is deemed to be disrespectful to her husband or suspected of having extramarital relations, her land rights may be curtailed. Similar behaviour by men does not elicit the same punishment for men.

Access to and control over land for women independent of marriage Women's land rights are tied in both customary and statutory law to marriage. Women's sexual conduct and marital status should not be used as criteria to grant women access to and control over land.

Access to and control over land for women independent of their reproductive roles Land is availed to women due to their reproductive role – the responsibility to nurture children – and not in their own right. In the succession of land by children, sons take precedence over daughters and even this does not generate security of woman's rights to land. There is discrimination against childless, married women on the death of their husbands, especially if the woman is young and able to remarry. For example, in Buganda and Ankole, inheritance of women is conditional upon their remaining in the home, and remarriage is discouraged. The number and sex of women's children should also not be used as criteria to grant women access to and control over land.

Recognition of women's right to income derived from land Women often grow food and cash crops consumed by the family and sold outside of the family. However, despite this, husbands tend to control the income thus derived and make the decisions about its utilisation.

Outlawing widow inheritance In some parts of the country, women are inherited – sexually and materially – in the event of widowhood by a male relative of the deceased. Refusal to be taken over results in the loss of access to land or in dismissal from the home.

References

This chapter is based on the work of Winnie Bikaako and John Ssenkumba, titled 'Gender, Land and Rights: Contemporary Contestations in Law, Policy and Practice in Uganda', published as Chapter 7 in this book. However, the African Women's Development and Communication Network (FEMNET) takes full responsibility for the analysis, interpretation and presentation made here.

Status of Women (2000) (CD-ROM), Addis Ababa: United Nations Economic Commission for Africa (UNECA).

Strengthening Linkages for Women's Rights in Africa (1994), Harare: Women in Law and Development in Africa (WiLDAF).

APPENDIX
Women's Rights under International Law and Policy

Convention on the Elimination of All Forms of Discrimination Against Women (1979)

The full and complete development of a country, the welfare of the world and the cause of peace require the maximum participation of women on equal terms with men in all fields.

Discrimination against women

Article 1. For the purposes of the present Convention, the term 'discrimination against women' shall mean any distinction, exclusion or restriction made on the basis of sex which has the effect or purpose of impairing or nullifying the recognition, enjoyment or exercise by women, irrespective of their marital status, in a basis of equality of men and women, of human rights and fundamental freedoms in the political, economic, social, cultural, civil or any other field.

All measures shall be taken for women to exercise and enjoy their human rights

Article 3. State Parties shall take in all fields, in particular in the political, social, economic and cultural fields, all appropriate measures, including legislation, to ensure the full development and advancement of women, for the purpose of guaranteeing them the exercise and enjoyment of human rights and fundamental freedoms on a basis of equality with men.

Eradication of socio-cultural sex-based discrimination

Article 5. State Parties shall take all appropriate measures:

a. To modify the social and cultural patterns of conduct of men and women, with a view to achieving the elimination of prejudices and customary and all other practices which are based on the idea of inferiority or the superiority of either of the sexes or on stereotyped roles for men and women.

Equality of men and women in rural areas

Article 14.2. State Parties shall take all appropriate measures to eliminate discrimination against women in rural areas in order to ensure, on a basis of equality of men and women, that they participate in and benefit from rural development and, in particular, shall ensure to such women the right:

i. To participate in the elaboration and implementation of development planning at all levels;
j. To have access to adequate health care facilities, including information, counselling and services in family planning;
k. To benefit directly from social security programmes;
l. To obtain all types of training and education, formal and non-formal, including that relating to functional literacy, as well as, *inter alia*, the benefit of all community and extension services, in order to increase their technical proficiency;
m. To organise self-help groups and cooperatives in order to obtain equal access to economic opportunities through employment or self-employment;
n. To participate in all community activities;
o. To have access to agricultural credit and loans, marketing facilities, appropriate technology and equal treatment in land and agrarian reform as well as in land resettlement schemes;
p. To enjoy adequate living conditions, particularly in relation to housing, sanitation, electricity and water supply, transport and communications.

Women's equality with men before the law
Article 15
5. State Parties shall accord to women equality with men before the law.
6. State Parties shall accord to women, in civil matters, a legal capacity identical to that of men and the same opportunities to exercise that capacity. In particular, they shall give women equal rights to conclude contracts and to administer property and shall treat them equally in all stages of procedure in courts and tribunals.
7. State Parties agree that all contracts and all other private instruments of any kind with a legal effect, which is directed at restricting the legal capacity of women, shall be deemed null and void.
8. State Parties shall accord to men and women the same rights with regard to the law relating to the movement of persons and the freedom to choose their residence and domicile.

Elimination of discrimination in marriage
Article 16.1. State Parties shall take all appropriate measures to eliminate discrimination against women in all matters relating to marriage and family relations and in particular shall ensure, on a basis of equality of men and women:

i. The same right to enter into marriage;
j. The same right freely to choose a spouse and to enter into marriage only with their free and full consent;

k. The same rights and responsibilities during marriage and its dissolution;
l. The same rights and responsibilities as parents, irrespective of their marital status, in matters relating to their children; in all cases the interests of the children shall be paramount;
m. The same rights to decide freely and responsibly on the number and spacing of their children and to have access to the information, education and means to enable them to exercise these rights;
n. The same rights and responsibilities with regard to guardianship, wardship, trusteeship and adoption of children, or similar institutions where these concepts exist in national legislation; in all cases the interests of the child shall be paramount;
o. The same personal rights as husband and wife, including the right to choose a family name, a profession and occupation;
p. The same rights for both spouses in respect of the ownership, acquisition, management, administration, enjoyment and disposition of property, whether free of charge or for a valuable consideration.

Vienna Declaration and Programme of Action, World Conference on Human Rights (1993)

Women's rights are human rights

18. The human rights of women and the girl-child are an inalienable, integral and indivisible part of universal human rights. The full and equal participation of women in political, civil, economic, social and cultural life, at the national, regional and international levels, and the eradication of all forms of discrimination on grounds of sex are priority objectives of the international community.

Women's full participation in the development process

36. The World Conference on Human Rights urges the full and equal enjoyment by women of all human rights and that this be a priority for Governments and for the United Nations. The World Conference on Human Rights also underlines the importance of the integration and full participation of women as both agents and beneficiaries in the development process, and reiterates the objectives established on global action for women towards sustainable and equitable development set forth in the Rio Declaration on Environment and Development and chapter 24 of Agenda 21, adopted by the United Nations Conference on Environment and Development (Rio de Janeiro, Brazil, 3–14 June 1992).

Enhanced information dissemination and procedures for enhancing women's equality and safeguarding their human rights

40. Treaty and monitoring bodies should disseminate necessary information to enable women to make more effective use of existing implementation procedures

in their pursuits of full and equal enjoyment of human rights and non-discrimination. New procedures should also be adopted to strengthen implementation of the commitment to women's equality and the human rights of women.

The Commission on the Status of Women and the Committee on the Elimination of Discrimination Against Women should quickly examine the possibility of introducing the right of petition through the preparation of an optional protocol to the Convention on the Elimination of All Forms of Discrimination Against Women. The World Conference on Human Rights welcomes the decision of the Commission on Human Rights to consider the appointment of a Special Rapporteur on Violence Against Women at its fiftieth session.

A woman's right to accessible and adequate health care

41. The World Conference on Human Rights recognises the importance of the enjoyment by women of the highest standard of physical and mental health throughout their life span. In the context of the World Conference on Women and the Convention on the Elimination of All Forms of Discrimination Against Women, as well as the Proclamation of Tehran of 1968, the World Conference on Human Rights reaffirms, on the basis of equality between women and men, a woman's right to accessible and adequate health care and the widest range of family planning services, as well as equal access to education at all levels.

Increased women's access to decision-making processes and posts

43. The World Conference on Human Rights urges Governments and regional and international organisations to facilitate the access of women to decision-making posts and their greater participation in the decision-making process. It encourages further steps within the United Nations Secretariat to appoint and promote women staff members in accordance with the Charter of the United Nations, and encourages other principal and subsidiary organs of the United Nations to guarantee the participation of women under conditions of equality.

International Convention on Civil and Political Rights (1966)

Equal rights and responsibilities in marriage

Article 23

4. State Parties to the present Covenant shall take appropriate steps to ensure equality of rights and responsibilities of spouses as to marriage, during marriage and at its dissolution. In the case of dissolution, provision shall be made for the necessary protection of children.

Equality before the law irrespective of sex

Article 26

All persons are equal before the law and are entitled without any discrimination to the equal protection of the law. In this respect, the law shall prohibit any discrimination and guarantee to all persons equal and effective protection against discrimination on any ground such as race, colour, sex, language, religion, political or other opinion, national or social origin, property, birth or other status.

Part III

The Advocacy Process: The Example of Ethiopia

THIRTEEN
Women's Access to and Control over Land in Ethiopia: The First Workshop

Rachel Kagoiya, Atsango Chesoni and L. Muthoni Wanyeki

Acknowledgements

The African Women's Communication and Development Network (FEMNET) thanks the participants' committed and enthusiastic participation in the workshop, which was inspiring for us all.

FEMNET also thanks Melakou Tegegn of the Panos Institute of Eastern Africa and Yoseph Tesfaye of the Horn of Africa Peace Centre for identifying participants and coordinating logistics in Addis Ababa. Zenebeworke Tadesse's research on women's land rights in Ethiopia created the basis for this investigation into Ethiopian women's access to and control over land. We are grateful to Professor Tilahun Teshome, Dean of Law at the Addis Ababa University, for taking the time to elaborate on Ethiopian law in relation to women's access to and control over land. We thank Tassew Shiferaw, who gave a brief presentation on the Ethiopian policy-making structure.

Without the support of Emory University's Law and Religion Programme and the Ford Foundation, this workshop would not have been possible. We are particularly grateful to Dr Abdullahi An-Na'im for his continued support of FEMNET's advocacy programme's work through this project on culture, religion and human rights.

Atsango Chesoni coordinated and facilitated this workshop, and Rachel Gaceci wrote the workshop report.

Contents

4.0   Defining regulation (law and policy)
5.0   Summary of the study on women's land rights in Ethiopia
6.0   Update on current regulation on women's property rights in Ethiopia
7.0   Defining advocacy and lobbying
8.0   Feedback on the advocacy and lobbying packages
9.0   Strategies to advance women's access to and control over land in Ethiopia
10.0 Evaluation
11.0 Annexes
      Workshop Programme
      Questionnaire for the assessment of the advocacy and lobbying packages
      Participants

1.0 Introduction

The workshop in Addis Ababa, Ethiopia was held under the auspices of a joint project between Emory University, Atlanta, USA and the African Women's Development and Communication Network (FEMNET), Nairobi, Kenya. Support for the project comes from the Ford Foundation. The project aims to improve women's access to and control over land in Africa through research on the impact of customary, religious and statutory laws on women's access to and control over land in five African countries – Cameroon, Ethiopia, Nigeria, Senegal and Uganda. On the basis of the research, advocacy and communications follow-up work is being done, with Ethiopia being chosen as a pilot for this follow-up work.

The 14 participants at the workshop were drawn from Ethiopia. The resource persons were Atsango Chesoni, a consultant with FEMNET, and Professor Tilahun Teshome, Dean of the Faculty of Law at Addis Ababa University. Melakou Tegegn, Regional Director of the Panos Institute of Eastern Africa, and Yoseph Tesfaye of the Horn of Africa Peace Centre, identified and mobilised participants and assisted with logistics. Follow-up workshops to develop a national advocacy plan and to engage with Ethiopian policy-makers on this plan were planned for 2001.

Atsango Chesoni, FEMNET's consultant, opened the workshop and gave a brief introduction to FEMNET's activities. Set up in 1988, FEMNET is a regional membership organisation with its headquarters in Nairobi, Kenya. Its goal is to share experiences, information and strategies among African women's non-governmental organisations (NGOs) through networking, advocacy, training and communications, so as to advance African women's development, equality and other women's human rights.

Since its inception, FEMNET has played a leadership role for African women's NGOs in regional and international policy-making. It was the African regional focal point for the Fourth World Conference on Women held in Beijing, China in 1995 and has continued to play a key role in monitoring the implementation both of the African and global Platforms for Action, which arose from the Beijing process.

This workshop on women's access to and control over land in Ethiopia was organised by FEMNET, with the assistance and support of Melakou Tegegn of the Panos Institute of Eastern Africa. The Panos Institute is one of three African offices of an international organisation based in London, UK. The Institute works on communications to disseminate information and knowledge. For example, Eastern Africa is home to large communities of pastoralists, to whom the Panos Institute provides information through participatory radio. The Institute also focuses on the environment, gender and HIV/AIDS.

1.1 The Project on Women's Land Rights through Communication and Advocacy

This workshop is one of the activities being undertaken by FEMNET's advocacy programme's project on securing women's land rights through communication and advocacy. The Law and Religion Programme at Emory University initiated the project and undertook the first research phase in partnership with African women researchers in five countries – Cameroon, Ethiopia, Nigeria, Senegal and Uganda. The Law and Religion Programme enlisted the assistance of FEMNET to complete the second communications and advocacy phase. The project seeks to enhance African women's access to and control over land by:

1. Commissioning research that examines and analyses women's land rights from cultural, religious and human rights perspectives in five African countries – Cameroon, Ethiopia, Nigeria, Senegal and Uganda. Research has been completed by African women scholars from the five respective countries, with Zenebeworke Tadesse undertaking the research in Ethiopia.
2. Developing communications and advocacy packages intended for use at the national level in lobbying for African women's access to and control over land. Based on the five research studies, advocacy and lobbying packages are being developed for each of the five countries.
3. Ethiopia has been chosen as the pilot country for the testing of the advocacy and lobbying packages, as well as for advocacy work based on these packages. To this end, the project will hold advocacy training and advocacy workshops in Ethiopia with stakeholders and policy-makers respectively to test the draft packages, develop a national advocacy plan and engage policy-makers with that plan.

1.2 Workshop Objectives

The workshop's objectives are to:

• Identify and amend any inaccuracies contained in the Ethiopian advocacy and lobbying package.

- Refine and finalise the format and content of the Ethiopian advocacy and lobbying package.
- Develop a national plan for action on land law and policy from a women's human rights perspective.
- Identify advocacy and lobbying strategies that would enhance women's access to and control over land.

2.0 Defining Human Rights[1]

Participants defined human rights as:

- Rights possessed by virtue of being human beings;
- Rights that cannot be imposed or denied by or to others, for example, the right to life;
- The right to live in a safe environment (the right to security);
- The right to speak (freedom of expression);
- Restrictive against the government because they prevent it (the state) from interfering in our lives in certain ways, for example, the right to make decisions and to choose.

In summary, human rights are rights we all possess by virtue of being human. They are the birthright of all human beings. They include fundamental rights agreed upon and articulated in national constitutions, regional and international instruments. Regional and international instruments that recognise human rights include African Charter on Human and Peoples' Rights and the United Nations Conventions.

Human rights are dynamic – fundamental rights can be interpreted more broadly and new rights can be recognised by communities and states and given legal protection. However, not all human rights are recognised; for example, underdeveloped countries are still fighting for the rights to development and peace to be recognised internationally.

2.1 How are International Human Rights Instruments Reinforced and Their Implementation Monitored?

International and regional human rights instruments are enforced and their implementation monitored through various mechanisms:

- The United Nations Human Rights Commission which monitors the International Convention on Civil and Political Rights and the International Convention on Economic, Social and Cultural Rights.
- The United Nations Committee on the Elimination of All Forms of Discrimination Against Women (CEDAW) which monitors the Convention on the Elimination of All Forms of Discrimination Against Women (the Women's Convention).

- The Organisation of African Unity's African Commission on Human and Peoples' Rights, which monitors the African Charter on Human and Peoples' Rights.
- International and regional mechanisms such as the United Nations Special Rapporteur on Violence Against Women and the Organisation of African Unity's Special Rapporteur on Women's Rights.
- Courts of law.
- Human rights commissions within countries.

Both the United Nations' Convention on Economic, Social and Cultural Rights and the Women's Convention have been ratified in Ethiopia and incorporated into its domestic law. This is unlike Kenya, which has ratified both Conventions but not incorporated them into domestic law. In Kenya, then, they are used only as standards for reference.

2.2 Challenges Encountered in Using the Human Rights Framework

Some of the challenges encountered in using the human rights framework include:

- The institutionalisation of the principle of universality. Human rights violations in Africa are often justified on the basis that human rights are elitist and Western. However, an examination of the evolution of human rights illustrates that our various cultures and peoples have contributed to the elaboration of all rights.
- The institutionalisation of the principle of the indivisibility of rights. Historically, there has been a tendency to privilege the promotion of the first generation of rights (civil and political rights) over others (economic, social and cultural rights). Traditional human rights organisations have tended to focus on civil and political rights, whereas within Africa these are perceived as a privilege of the elite, with development not being perceived as a human right. However, one human right cannot be granted while denying another. Human rights are indivisible.
- There is still need to develop indicators for monitoring the implementation of economic, social and cultural rights so as to make them justiciable (legally usable).
- In respect of the so-called third generation of rights (the rights to development and peace), there is still a struggle to ensure their legal recognition and protection.
- The integration of women's human rights. Although the Universal Declaration of Human Rights states that all peoples should enjoy human rights irrespective of race, sex, etc., the reality is that human rights practice has been gendered. Furthermore, the human rights framework traditionally did not sufficiently

address sexism and questions of gender. Thus various gender-specific human rights instruments and mechanisms such as CEDAW and the Special Rapporteur on Violence Against Women, have been evolved.
- The popularisation of the human rights framework and public education on how to use it.

3.0 Defining Women's Human Rights[2]

Participants were asked what the phrase 'women's human rights' meant to them. They observed that:

- Human rights apply to women's rights.
- Women's rights are human rights, which all women should enjoy by virtue of being human beings.
- Although there are gender imbalances, women should enjoy their own rights, for example, around access to and control of resources.

The Ethiopian Constitution guarantees both women and men the right to equality. However, in practice, human rights instruments are gendered and women have no equal access to their rights even within institutions that promote human rights. The reality of gender-based disparities also prevents women from enjoying their rights.

The need to address women's rights has been met in several ways, for example, by creating woman-specific human rights instruments such as the Women's Convention.

Participants identified some women's human rights instruments and mechanisms as:

- The Convention on the Elimination of All Forms of Discrimination Against Women (the Women's Convention).
- The Special Rapporteur on Violence Against Women, which is an international mechanism. The Special Rapporteur collects data and information on violence against women. One participant expressed concern that this mechanism may be undermined, since it appears to require those seeking redress to exhaust locally available legal avenues. However, the new optional protocol to the Women's Convention enables women to seek redress with the CEDAW committee directly.
- Women-friendly policies that can be enforced by translating them into practice, for example, the Ethiopian Gender Policy.
- Affirmative Action, which was defined as a mechanism by which women, because of their historical marginalisation, are given preference over men so as to achieve gender parity.
- Mainstream human rights commissions.

3.1 Challenges Encountered in Implementing Women's Human Rights

Challenges encountered in implementing women's human rights were identified as follows:

- lack of recognition of women's rights as human rights;
- sexism within the mainstream human rights movement;
- lack of a standardised feminist approach to the documentation of women's human rights violations;
- lack of understanding of human rights methodology and language among women's rights activists;
- the need to strengthen CEDAW through the optional protocol. CEDAW is currently the treaty with the most reservations. So women's human rights activists have successfully campaigned for the creation of an optional protocol to the treaty to strengthen it. The challenge now lies in ensuring that state parties to the convention now ratify the protocol as well. And, as was noted by a participant, there is a danger that new mechanisms can undermine older ones;
- the need to translate the Declaration on the Elimination of All Forms of Violence Against Women into a treaty;
- lobbying for the acceptance of the gender-specific protocol for the African Charter on Human and Peoples' Rights.

One participant questioned why, despite all the international mechanisms we have, gender disparities still exist? Participants responded by noting the following:

- The existence of a disparity between individual and collective discourse. The evolution of human rights did not consider women's human rights. Two sets of discourse thus exist: discourse which focuses on individual rights and does not address women's issues, and discourse which focuses on collective rights and is concerned with women's rights. Over time, the former has dominated, tending to write off collective rights and thus women's rights.
- At the 1993 Human Rights Conference in Vienna, despite their public posturing, some countries would not accept the fundamental principle that women's rights are human rights. The USA, for example, has not ratified the Women's Convention.
- Some countries have not ratified various human rights instruments and gross violations of human rights continue. Again, the majority of countries that sign and ratify human rights instruments do not implement them. This illustrates the hypocrisy of political systems – why do they want to pose as respecting human rights?
- There is lack of political will for implementation. This manifests itself in many

ways. For example, Ethiopia has one of the best constitutions, but its enforcement and implementation mechanism is poor. Again, the laws and policies are not popularised and people end up feeling that they do not own their own laws. Also, some laws are superimposed without the government getting views from the people. There is therefore a need for the evolution of consultative law and policy-making.

Another participant asked if a radical change could be expected overnight. Participants responded by noting that every law and policy within a country should be practical, with the government and other implementing bodies being committed to its implementation. As this is not the case, a radical change cannot be expected.

In summary, although we are expected to enjoy human rights irrespective of our class, race or sex, the practice of human rights has been gendered. Many women's rights organisations are not familiar with the human rights framework, while mainstream human rights organisations have historically tended to focus on first generation rights, and on non-gender-specific violations of such rights.

Women's rights are human rights. During the 1993 Human Rights Conference in Vienna, women's human rights activists successfully promoted the concept that women's rights are indeed human rights. The member states of the United Nations acknowledged that violence against women is a human rights violation and that states are responsible for ensuring redress to victims, whether the violence is perpetrated by public or private actors.

4.0 Defining Regulation (Law and Policy)

Participants were divided into groups of four and five and asked to write on Visualisation in Participatory Process (VIPP) cards their understanding of policy. The following was observed:

- Policy is a mechanism that is used to implement laws.
- Policy is a guideline that is issued to solve a particular social problem.
- Policy is a set of forward-looking guidelines on issues of national concern, which may be translated into binding laws.
- Policy is a defined framework under which actions can be taken by given groups.
- Policy is a mechanism used to address/implement desired concerns/issues.

Participants agreed that policies could be institutional, national and international and relate to our workplaces, our societies and even our homes. Policies contain rules, which, if translated into law, are binding. To hold others accountable to a policy, it is important to have it written down. However, we do have oral policies, for example, customary laws in our communities.

In summary, it was noted that policy is a statement of intent. It can be written, oral or even unstated. Policies govern and regulate the way we work and live at individual and household levels, the workplace, national and international levels. Policies are guidelines or frameworks for how we live and work with each other.

4.1 The Ethiopian National Policy Structure (Tassew Shifraw)

The national gender policy was issued in 1995 to coordinate efforts to address the problems of women that result from their historical marginalisation and thus to lift women's status. The policy is an intervention into women's issues. As a result, a women's affairs sub-sector office was established in the Prime Minister's office. It is held at this high level for fear of marginalising women's issues.

The structure is as follows:

Prime minister's office
↓
Women's affairs sub-sector
↓
12 women's departments
↓
Regional women's officers
↓
Civil service commission
↓
Regional bureaus
↓
Associations, civic organisations,
NGOs and women's groups

The Prime Minister makes policies, and all others within the hierarchy implement. Each Women's Affairs sub-sector department is accountable to a specific ministry. There is a biannual meeting, which helps in assessing the implementation of policies.

5.0 Summary of the Study on Women and Land Rights in Ethiopia[3]

Zenebeworke Tadesse begins by examining both the international and local context with respect to women and land rights. She notes that land reforms have been premised both internationally and in Ethiopia on the myth that the household is a unit within which equal access to land takes place. However, access to resources is not equal, and the framework does not consider that women are not fully on board. Factors that influence the bargaining power of women within the household unit are:

- income earning ability;
- the value placed on the contributions of other members of the household.

Other arenas outside of the home also influence the bargaining power of women within the household unit. For example, Agarwal (1994: 62; see p. 93) is quoted in the study as having identified five factors that determine a rural person's fallback:

- private ownership and control over assets, especially arable land;
- access to employment and other income-earning means;
- access to communal resources such as village commons and forests;
- access to traditional external social support systems;
- access to support from NGOs and the state.

Other factors outside the home also influence this bargaining power. For example, heads of households are equated with male heads, despite the emergence of female-headed households and their relative disadvantages. In addition, the household is seen as the only arena for women's work, yet there are other arenas such as women's work in subsistence agriculture. There is a need for analysis of and change in policies based on the household.

Tadesse goes on to explain the gender-based division of labour and its implications in terms of access to and control over land. Cross-culturally, the division of reproductive labour is homogenised, that is, women are seen as tools for domestic work. On the other hand, the division of productive labour is heterogenised. Entrenched ideologies that support the gender-based division of labour remain. There is a need to change this division and to transform cultural norms defining what is women's work and what is men's work.

Land reform is a generic term that denotes a wide array of policy-led structural changes, such as granting access to land, changing ownership patterns and rights by the state and its subsidiary agents. These reforms are aimed at maintaining the status quo, advancing national bourgeois revolutions, giving land to peasants, or inducing change.

Tadesse gives general observations on land reform in several countries, including some in sub-Saharan Africa, Asia and Latin America. Women work longer hours than men because of their double responsibilities and workload – they do productive work on their own fields, unremunerated family labour and reproductive labour. Land reform that does not address women's domestic or reproductive labour is therefore likely to increase women's workload without a commensurate increase in women's assets. In addition, the allocation of land to male-headed households tends to increases the practice of polygamy, since more land means the need for more women's unremunerated productive labour.

Tadesse categorises the land tenure and reforms in Ethiopia into three periods: pre-1974; 1975–1991; and 1991–present. Prior to the agrarian reform of 1975, the land tenure system and the concomitant production relations were heterogeneous. In most parts of the country, peasants gained access to land through inheritance or through corporate groups consisting of individuals tracing their descent from a certain ancestor. Around this time, the social relationship that existed was that of landlord–tenant. Most women had inheritance rights, and ruling-class women received land as gifts and/or were able to purchase land.

Ethiopia in 1974 experienced what was known as 'land to the tiller' reform. This reform was launched by the military regime in 1975 and was aimed at ending the exploitation of peasants to promote the economy. However, it accelerated poverty, because land was distributed according to family size and registered under male-headed households. By using the household as the unit of allocation, the policy assumed that households were the same and failed to consider intra-house-hold distribution relations. It assumed that the gender-based division of labour in agriculture was immutable, and classified women together with persons whom, due to illness or age, could not personally cultivate their holding. Thus the reform did not challenge the cultural taboo against women ploughing and sowing.

The military government ended in 1991 and Ethiopia became a federal state with ten regional national states based on ethnicity. The federal government has issued a new proclamation known as the Federal Rural Land Administration Proclamation, which makes provision for the enactment of a land administration law by each Regional Council. The proclamation provides for the 'free assignment of holding rights both to peasants and nomads, without differentiation of the sexes'. In addition to giving women legal rights to land, the new government has set forth principles of equality between men and women in the areas of political, cultural, educational and economic rights in the Constitution. However, since its issuance, the Proclamation has not been implemented.

5.1 Gender-equitable Land Reform

Gender-equitable land reform requires:

- The conscientisation of women about new land laws.
- The reform of customary law that discriminates against women.
- Establishment of structures of governance and local institutions to promote women's active participation in decision-making and to challenge traditional power relations.
- Special measures to advance the interests of rural women, such as access to credit, information and technical knowledge and markets.

5.2 Barriers to Women's Access to and Control over Land

- Girls' lack of access to educational facilities.
- Ignorance of women's rights (even when they hold positions of importance, for example in the Regional Councils).
- The persistence of sexist cultural practices such as early marriages and polygamy, which militate against women's access to and control over land.
- Religious laws such as those under Islam that do not entitle women to equal inheritance rights.
- The entrenched gender-based division of agricultural labour.
- Gendered time-use patterns, that is, women's double responsibilities.
- The lack of effective implementation of positive neutral legislation. On paper, Ethiopian women have land rights that are not practised.
- The lack of recognition of the value of women's labour by policy-makers.
- The fact that Ethiopian land reform has followed the international trend of using the household as a unit of allocation, ignoring power relations within that unit that mediate women's access to resources.
- The erosion of usufructary rights by the land reform processes.
- The locational dimension of land rights in respect of women's rights to land in natal areas. Agrarian reform did not differentiate between land for residence and for agricultural activities. Thus women lose their homes if they become divorced, because residences are built close to cultivation fields.
- The focus of NGO and state actors on women's practical needs in the provision of services without attempting to provide technical agricultural information, knowledge, information, financing and markets.

6.0 Update on Current Regulation on Women's Property Rights in Ethiopia (Professor Tilahun Teshome)[4]

In Ethiopia, land ownership during the imperial era was categorised into:

- communal land owned by communities;
- private land owned by individuals/pastoralists;
- state land owned by the government.

The most important legal instrument is the Constitution of the Federal Democratic Republic of Ethiopia (FDRE), and Articles 40 and 41 pertain to property rights:

- Article 40(3): rural and urban lands and all natural resources are public property. However, the definition of 'natural resources' is controversial.
- Articles 40(1) and 41(3): private property is defined as property other than land

and natural resources. This implies that the most important forms of property in Ethiopia are not private property;

- Articles 40(4) and 40(5): peasants and pastoralists have only usufructary rights.

Previous laws, like the Proclamation Number 31/1975 given by the government on Public Ownership and Rural Lands, stated that 'rural Land is the collective property of the Ethiopian People', that is, state property. However, nothing is said in the Constitution on the rights of peasants to transfer their usufructary rights by way of bequest, assignment, sale or any other mode of transfer. Nor does the Constitution define the notion of 'landholding'.

Proclamation Number 89/1997, the Rural Land Administration Proclamation, in Article 2(3) defines holding rights and speaks of the rights of peasants to:

- Use land for agriculture only.
- Lease their holdings.
- 'While the right remains in effect', bequeath it to his family members.

As per Article 6(1), land may be redistributed by decisions of the Regional Councils. This provision, coupled with the phrase 'while the right remains in effect' under Article 2(3), is an indication of the fact that a peasant's landholding does not have any permanent guarantee in law.

The right to bequeath land in use is also restricted by the phrase 'family members', as defined by Article 2(5), which includes only dependants. We also do not find any provision in the Constitution and the proclamation on the right of farmers to borrow money by offering their landholding as collateral.

The federal government gives power to the different regions in Ethiopia to come up with their own Land Distribution Proclamation to include regional peculiarities, but the only regions that have done this are Amhara Region, which has a proclamation to provide for the reallotment of possession of rural land known as the Amhara Proclamation Number 16/1996; and Tigray Region, which has a proclamation to provide for land utilisation known as the Tigray Proclamation Number 23/1997.

The institutions empowered to implement the Amhara land redistribution Proclamation are Peasant Associations, in partnership with the:

- Land Possession Verifying Committee (Article 14);
- Family Size Verifying Committee (Article 15);
- Land Allocating Committee (Article 16);
- Kebele Committee (Articles 30 and 31).

As pertains to women's land rights, the laws focus only on male-headed households. There is a need to revisit the bargaining power of spouses in the management and administration of common property, child care and support, social interactions, etc. On the other hand, the FDRE Constitution, Articles 35(3) and 35(7), says that 'women have equal rights with men with respect to the use, transfer, administration and control of land'. But the issue is how feasible implementation is under existing conditions for:

- Granting access to land.
- Changing ownership patterns.
- Cultural taboos against women ploughing and sowing.
- The notion of the 'male breadwinner', and so on.

There are also some shortcomings of the Rural Land Proclamation of 1975, such as that it:

- Registers women under male heads of households.
- Ignores intra-household distribution relations.
- Fails to address the problems of polygamous unions, divorced and aged women.
- Fails to appreciate the current attitude towards and the minimum role of women in deciding land use priorities and in the control of produce.
- Classifies women with persons who do not cultivate land.
- Insufficiently addresses the problem of landlessness on account of population growth and land supply limitation.

Again the paraphrase in Article 4(5) reads 'no person may use hired labour to cultivate his holding with the exception of a woman with no other adequate means of livelihood or sick, old or minor children'. Sexist provisions of the Rural Land Proclamation have not been repealed.

Teshome concluded by noting that Tadesse's study is detailed and an important tool for policy-makers in Ethiopia. He summarised, in Amharic, a newspaper article that he had written to emphasise issues of land. There is a need to re-examine not only rural land issues but also urban land issues. Various alternatives should be considered to:

- Facilitate the provision of ownership rights to both rural and urban land, currently under state control.
- Allow private urban land ownership.
- Divide the land in agricultural areas in a fair and equitable manner, allowing full ownership for the residents.
- Allow the land in pastoralist areas to be used collectively, allowing full communal ownership by the residents.
- Allow the lands that are not agricultural or pastoralist to be leased or sold to investors.
- Recognising the non-uniformity of land utilisation policies within the different regions, allow the regions to issue their own relevant laws and policies.

Some of these alternatives may require constitutional amendments, and a participatory constitutional amendment process should be instituted with respect to land.

7.0 Defining Advocacy and Lobbying[5]

When asked to define advocacy, participants observed that it is:

- To make something known (awareness-raising).
- To publicise.
- To make change (pressurise).
- To stand by and fight for an objective/for others.

Lobbying, on the other hand, is:

- A technique of advocacy.
- Approaching or availing somebody or something so as to achieve advocacy.
- A system to change others' attitudes or to convince others.
- Influencing others positively.

In summary, advocacy is done whenever and wherever change needs to occur. It is the range of actions taken to highlight problems perceived, to present solutions to address them and ensure the acceptance of those solutions (lobbying is one of those actions).

7.1 Systematising Advocacy

- Advocate on the basis of data.
- Set clear advocacy objectives. They should be specific and measurable and clearly outline what to change, by how much, by whom and by when.
- Develop advocacy coalitions.
- From the data available and the objectives set, develop clear messages; target audiences and strategies to reach them.

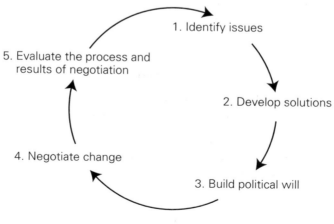

1. Identify issues

5. Evaluate the process and results of negotiation

2. Develop solutions

4. Negotiate change

3. Build political will

Advocacy is a dynamic process

- Make persuasive presentations.
- Evaluate the advocacy effort.

8.0 Feedback on the Advocacy and Lobbying Packages

Participants were given a questionnaire to help them in analysing the draft advocacy and lobbying packages. The following includes their responses to the various questions.

8.1 Language

In respect of the language used in the packages, participants made the following observations:

- The language is simple.
- The language is simple in understanding the main concepts in the study.
- The language is simple, but needs a little explanation, for example, with phrases such as customary practices, statutory laws, etc.
- The language not simple because of the lack of know-how about legal issues.
- The language is not simple for broad audiences such as women's rights organisations.
- Most of the participants found the language gender-sensitive.
- A few participants found the language inclusive. However, the majority pointed out that:
  - It does not address illiterate women.
  - It does not address pastoralists.
  - It does not address the sick, those with disabilities or the aged.
- Most participants agreed that the package should be translated into regional languages, especially Amharigna, Oromigna and Tigrigna, for ease of understanding.

8.2 Content

Most participants agreed that there was enough content and liked the package the way it was. However two participants noted that the package should include:

- The new federal structure of Ethiopia;
- Statistics as to land ownership of families, single women, etc., which are comparative between regions;
- Case studies;
- Interviews;
- If possible, pictures and photographs.

8.3 Accuracy

Generally, participants found the package accurate. However, a few inaccuracies were identified:

- Page 5, line 2, 'prior to 1974, only ruling-class women could own or purchase land ... ' This is untrue, as anyone with money could buy and own land.
- Page 3, the part that deals with family law, which has been revised, should be clarified.
- Page 3, last paragraph, 'they constitute 23 per cent of those in educational institutions. Only 8 per cent are women in undergraduate colleges ... ' This is incorrect, as the numbers are less.
- Where statistics are given, they should be appropriately referenced.

8.4 Potential Usefulness

Most participants agreed that they would use the package, since they work for gender organisations. The media participants saw the package as a good tool for creating awareness and for integrating women's issues nationally. They would use it to advocate women's rights to own and control land.

8.5 Other Comments

- Each Ethiopian culture should be treated independently, not generally.
- The map of Ethiopia on the cover page should be the current one.
- The package should emphasise harmful traditional practices, which undermine women's rights and cause psychological trauma, for example, female genital mutilation (FGM), early marriage, etc.
- The package should also include property rights and the right to shelter.
- The package, being the first of its kind, is useful to brief the public or target a specific audience.
- Continuity of the package should be ensured through follow-up activities quarterly or annually.
- The number of participants should be increased.

The participants did not like the fact that the package tries to cover the whole country, yet only three regions were studied in the research on which it is premised. They liked:

- The format and the basic content of the package;
- The style of writing;
- The quotations from *Reflections on Gender* in Ethiopia;
- The manner in which the package identifies different inaccurate policies;

- The recognition of women's land rights;
- The equality given to both men and women.

9.0 Strategies to Advance Women's Access to and Control over Land in Ethiopia

Participants were divided into two groups to identify:

- Two areas of *law* that need to be changed to enhance women's access to and control over land in Ethiopia;
- Two areas of *national policy* that need to be changed to enhance women's access to and control over land in Ethiopia;
- Two *strategies* that could be used to influence those areas of law and policy;
- *Important actors* necessary to influence change in respect to those laws and policies.

9.1 Laws and Policies Needing Change

As far as the participants knew, no law or policy denies women access to and control over land in Ethiopia. However, the following problems were identified that need to be addressed:

- Cultural practices around the gender-based division of labour and ownership patterns in which women are meant to cook and own utensils and men to plough and own land;
- Gender-biased attitudes underrating women's work. For example, women work about 17–18 hours a day and this is not recognised;
- The lack of awareness about the existence of favourable laws and policies;
- The implementation of favourable laws and policies.

9.2 Strategies

Awareness-raising:

- Create awareness about the land proclamation, particularly with respect to rural land, and the new family law, by using the mass media.

Advocacy

- Create pressure groups for advocacy, for example, with the Ethiopia Women Lawyers Association (EWLA), PMO/WAO, etc.
- Create a network including civic organisations, NGOs, parliamentarians and the government to:
- Reflect on and exchange ideas/information and avoid duplication.

- Assess laws and follow up on/monitor their implementation.
- Campaign against gender-biased attitudes in school curriculum seeking a gender-sensitive curriculum and materials.

Training

- Conduct training for different target audiences such as youth, religious leaders, women policy-makers, etc;
- Conduct legal literacy programmes, seminars, workshops, etc.

9.3 Important Actors

- Influential women such as traditional birth attendants (TBAs);
- Women's organisations;
- Peasant associations;
- Development organisations;
- Civic organisations;
- The youth;
- Community leaders;
- Traditional associations such as Ider leaders;
- Religious and social leaders;
- Other policy-makers such as legislators.

10.0 Evaluation

The facilitator thanked all the participants for attending both sessions and for their patience and active participation. She explained that the workshop was important to test the advocacy and lobbying packages, which will be used in other countries. She was particularly grateful to Melakou Tegegn and Joseph Tesfaye for their assistance and support. She welcomed criticisms of the workshop from the participants as well as suggestions for the follow-up workshops.

The following were their responses:

- Overall, the workshop was good and beneficial. As it was the first of its kind, participants learnt a lot.
- The facilitator was thanked for her clarity, organisation and patience as well as for involving participants through discussions and sharing.
- Tadesse's research and the presence of Professor Teshome was appreciated.
- The small number of participants were facilitated free discussions.
- The workshop was a capacity-building one, which encouraged the confidence of its participants.
- There is need for earlier communication with respect to the follow-up workshops.

- The workshop length could be extended to five days.
- The use of English restricted many from active participation. There is a need for a translator to facilitate broader participation.
- The participants should be increased to include people with knowledge on laws and policies.

The outputs of the workshop should include:

- A reworking of the advocacy and lobbying package to make it more accurate.
- The distribution of the report and the reworked package to the participants.
- Follow-up workshops that will include policy-makers.

11.0 Annexes

11.1 Workshop Programme

11.2 Questionnaire for the Assessment of the Advocacy and Lobbying Packages

Please use capital letters and print out your responses. If the space allocated in this form is too little for a particular question, please feel free to write more on another sheet and return it with your questionnaire.

Name:

Organisation:

Contacts (postal address, telephone number, fax number and email address):

Analyse the package for the following:

1. Language
a. Is the language simple enough for a broad and popular audience that is not necessarily trained in the fields of law, policy-making or media?
b. Is the language gender-sensitive? If not, how is it insensitive?
c. Is the language inclusive? If not, what groups does it exclude (for example, people with disabilities, people from particular ethnicities, etc.) and how?
d. Should the idea of translation of the packages into indigenous languages be considered and if so which ones?

2. Content
a. Does the package contain too much or too little material?
b. If there is too much material, what would you throw out?
c. If there is too little material, what would you include?

3. Accuracy
a. Is the information in the package accurate and correct? If not please list the inaccuracies that you have noted.

4. Potential Usefulness
a. Would you or the organisation you work for be able to use this package? If so why? If not why not?

5. Any Other Comments

11.3 List of Participants

1. Genet Baraki: Ethiopian Women's Lawyers' Association (EWLA), Awassa Branch
2. Akeza Berhanu: Women's Association of Tigray (WAT)
3. Menna Bisrat: Addis Ababa Educational Media
4. Atsango Chesoni: African Women's Development and Communications Network (FEMNET)
5. Tsige Deresse: EWLA
6. Rachel Gaceci: FEMNET
7. Ali Hassen: National Committee on Traditional Practices of Ethiopia (NCTPE)
8. Meselech Mariam: Agricultural Bureau
9. Genet Mitike: Ethiopian Media Women's Association (EMWA)
10. Ellene Mocria: EMWA
11. Tassew Shiferaw: Women's Affairs Sub-sector, Prime Minister's Office
12. Melakou Tegegn: The Panos Institute of Eastern Africa
13. Yoseph Tesfaye: Horn of Africa Peace Centre
14. Professor Tilahun Teshome: Faculty of Law, Addis Ababa University
15. Girma Tessema: House of Peoples Representatives
16. Meseret Wondimagnege: WAT

Notes

This workshop was organised by the African Women's Development and Communications Network (FEMNET), in partnership with Emory University, the Ford Foundation and the Panos Institute of Eastern Africa, at Addis Ababa, Ethiopia, 28–29 December 2000.

1. During this session, Atsango Chesoni's paper 'What are Human Rights? Why Should We Care About Them?' was distributed to participants.

2. Based on Atsango Chesoni's paper 'What are Women's Human Rights?'

3. Unfortunately, Zenebeworke Tadesse was unable to attend the workshop. Atsango Chesoni therefore presented a summary of her study on 'Women's Land Rights in Ethiopia'.

4. Based on the presentation and notes of Professor Tilahun Teshome, Dean of the School of Law, Addis Ababa University.

5. Based on a paper by L. Muthoni Wanyeki, FEMNET's Executive Director, titled 'Lobbying and Advocacy'.

FOURTEEN

Enhancing Ethiopian Women's Access to and Control over Land: The Second Workshop

Atango Chesoni and Grace Githaiga

Acknowledgements

This workshop, on women's access to and control over land, was organised by the African Women's Development and Communications Network (FEMNET), in partnership with the Panos Institute of Eastern Africa, and held in Addis Ababa, Ethiopia from 17–22 July 2001. It is the result of a regional research and advocacy process on culture, religion and human rights, initiated by the Law and Religion Programme of Emory University in Atlanta, GA. The advocacy component of the process was coordinated by FEMNET.

FEMNET is grateful to the consultant for the women and land project, Atsango Chesoni, and to its staff member, Mary Wandia, as well as the resource persons who made the workshops a success. They are Meaza Ashenafi, Konjit Fekade, Genet Mitike and Melakou Tegegn. FEMNET is also grateful to the rapporteur for the workshops, Grace Githaiga.

A big thank you to all the participants for attending and sharing experiences. Particular thanks go to Deberitu and the women from the provinces who gave us their personal experiences and stories.

Finally, special thanks to the Ford Foundation for supporting these workshops through the Law and Religion Programme of Emory University and to Dr Abdullahi An-Na'im for initiating this exciting project.

Contents

What is gender?
What is gender mainstreaming?

Day 2

What is policy?
Who makes policies and laws in Ethiopia?
Current policies and laws pertaining to Ethiopian women's property rights
What is lobbying and advocacy?

Day 3

Analysing the Ethiopian advocacy and media packages
Constraints to Ethiopian women's access to and control over land and strategies
    to overcome them
Women and land reform in Ethiopia

Day 4

Strategies for effective advocacy
Role of monitoring and evaluation
Gender-responsive indicators

Day 5

Plan of action
Evaluation

Appendix
Participants

DAY 1: 17 July 2001

The workshop was opened by Atsango Chesoni, the consultant responsible for the women and land project under the advocacy programme of the African Women's Development and Communication Network (FEMNET), based in Nairobi, Kenya. She introduced FEMNET as an regional organisation formed in 1988 after the Fourth World Conference on Women, held in Beijing, China. FEMNET was the African focal point during the Dakar and Beijing processes and is mandated to coordinate activities of African women's organisations at the regional and international level to follow up on the Dakar and Beijing Platforms for Action. FEMNET aims to network organisations concerned with status of women in Africa so as to advocate policies in all sectors that support women's human rights.

Chesoni explained that this workshop is one of the activities under FEMNET's advocacy programme's women and land project. The project aims to communicate research done in five African countries (Cameroon, Ethiopia, Nigeria, Senegal and Uganda) on culture, religion and human rights as they impact on African women's access to and control over land. Ethiopia was chosen to pilot advocacy activities around the research findings.

Melakou Tegegn, the executive director of the Panos Institute in Addis Ababa, Ethiopia, then gave a brief background to the Panos Institute. This organisation's headquarters are in London, UK. Its objectives are to communicate and disseminate development information, for example, around the environment, health and pastoralist issues in Ethiopia. It also focused on women's human rights and has gone into partnership with the Ethiopian Media Women's Association (EMWA) to host a monthly Gender Forum, bringing together interested individuals and organisations to discuss and reflect on gender issues.

FEMNET and the Panos Institute are collaborating on this project on Ethiopian women's access to and control over land in Ethiopia. In Ethiopia, customary law governs land ownership and women's rights to own land are not upheld. Current statutory law does not recognise the land rights of both women and men. However, the situation is worse for women. There has to be affirmative action with respect to land distribution to rectify this situation.

Dr Konjit Fekade, a gender consultant, then began the session with an exercise to introduce the participants. Each participant was given a piece of paper, asked to pair up and to sketch an image of their partners as well as write down their partners' names, the organisations they work for, their job titles and interests. They then had to introduce their partners to the rest of the room. Participants were drawn from different parts of Ethiopia and included accountants, environmentalists, gender coordinators and officers, heads of women's organisations, journalists and editors.

Participants then proposed and agreed on the following ground rules to ensure the workshop remained focused and achieved its objectives:

- To be punctual.
- To participate and share ideas.
- To make brief points.
- To address issues rather than personalities.
- To contribute to energisers.

What are Human Rights?

Meaza Ashenafi, Executive Director, Ethiopian Women Lawyers' Association (EWLA)

Ashenafi began by noting the importance of the workshop to Ethiopian women. She then asked whether participants understood what human rights were. She asked why it was necessary to know what human rights were, and the participants noted the following:

- Knowing our human rights helps us to demand and exercise our human rights.
- Knowing what rights are available helps us know which rights are neglected.
- Having knowledge helps people differentiate between what is available and what is not and, as a result, we can ask for protection of unavailable rights from the government.
- Accessing knowledge is a human right and, as stated in the United Nations Universal Declaration on Human Rights, every citizen is entitled to protection.
- Individuals who know about their rights can decide on how to protect against their infringement.
- Individuals' rights should not be violated.
- Knowledge about the dignity of human beings, human rights principles and the history of the development of human rights and their implementation is important.

Human rights education is therefore necessary for every human being, but more so for those individuals and groups who are vulnerable to human rights abuses and/or violations. To understand human rights better, we have to relate our lives to them. This is a continuous process of changing our attitudes and thinking about human rights issues. Everyone needs to change their attitudes to be able to exercise their own human rights and to ensure others are given their human rights. Institutions with responsibility for human rights protection include the police, the judiciary and civil society, including community-based organisations (CBOs), NGOs, disabled, minority and women's and labour organisations.

Human rights are the rights available to human beings by virtue of their being human. They are natural rights, which a human being acquires simply through birth. Being human is about the use of language to communicate intelligence. Human traits can be developed or diminished. To develop these traits, education, health, and so on are necessary. Human rights ensure the development of human traits and are based on the underlying notion that all individuals are free and equal.

Human rights principles

- Inalienability: human rights are inalienable and cannot be separated from human beings.
- Universality: human rights are universal and are available to all individuals and peoples without discrimination on the basis of gender, political affiliation, race, religion, and so on.
- Indivisibility: human rights are indivisible and all rights are dependent on other rights. There are no hierarchies of human rights. And human rights cannot be applied selectively (this does not mean that all countries have accepted and implemented all rights contained in the Universal Declaration and the international human rights conventions).

Human rights categories

Civil and political rights, which include the rights to:

- Life, freedom and equality;
- Citizenship and property;
- Movement;
- Expression, organisation and voting;
- Protection from inhuman treatment;
- Equality before the law and a competent judiciary.

Economic, social and cultural rights, which include the rights to:

- Education;
- Employment, leisure, leave, labour organising and social security;
- Good standards of living.

Human rights in Ethiopia Human rights in Ethiopia are derived from international and regional human rights declarations and treaties, and respect human rights principles. The Ethiopian law of 1930 (in the Ethiopian calendar) abolished slavery. The Ethiopian Constitution of 1948 gave recognition to human rights. The Transitional Charter of 1991 incorporated the Universal Declaration of 1948. And the present Constitution of 1995 also incorporates human rights. It notes that:

- Human rights are part of Ethiopia's Constitution.
- The Constitution shall follow international human rights practice.
- All government employees are to protect human rights.

Human rights conventions pertinent to women have been elaborated at the international level since 1950. Ethiopia has ratified most of them, including:

- The Convention on the Elimination of Slavery and the Slave Trade (1954);
- The Declaration on Women's Political Rights;
- The Convention to Eliminate All Forms of Discrimination Against Women (CEDAW);
- The Convention on the Elimination of Trafficking in Women and Employing Others for Prostitution (1999);
- The International Labour Organisation (ILO)'s Convention on Equal Opportunities in Employment.

There are also more international declarations and conventions relating to women, namely:

- The Declaration to Eliminate all forms of Violence Against Women (1993);
- The International Conference on Population Development (ICPD) (1994);

- The Beijing Declaration and Platform for Action (1995);
- The Vienna Declaration and Platform for Action (1999).

Discussion International conventions are legally binding standards. International declarations are moral standards that states agree to abide by. Both are valuable in the struggle for human rights.

Most states have ratified a number of international human rights agreements. But monitoring implementation has been a problem. Most of these agreements remain on paper and have not been implemented. No state implements all human rights. To ensure implementation, political will must exist. Democracy must also exist, allowing for civic organisation and participation, even at the local level.

In addition, the UN High Commission for Human Rights monitors the progress of states that have ratified human rights agreements. Such states are expected to report to the Commission periodically. This monitoring mechanism is not very effective, as the UN lacks enforcement mechanisms. However, the monitoring mechanism is still useful as it affords opportunities to civil society organisations to counter the reports of governments (this is known as shadow reporting).

An important aspect of human rights is implementation. Ethiopia lacks implementation. In most other states, implementation of civil and political rights (requiring non-interference by government in citizens' rights to voice their opinion and to organise) occurs. In a few states, implementation of economic, social and cultural rights (requiring the government's provision of services such as education, health, and so on) also occurs. And in still fewer states, implementation of the rights to development and peace also occurs (underdeveloped countries tend to focus on the right to development, developed countries tend to focus on the right to a healthy environment).

Domestication of international agreements at the national level is important for implementation. For example, Kenya ratified CEDAW. And under Article 2 of the Kenyan Constitution, the right to equality on the basis of sex is provided for. But Kenyan women still lack equal rights. For example, Kenyan women cannot pass on their citizenship to their children. So Kenyan women have been lobbying for substantive equality during the constitutional reform process. So far, one constitutional subsection has been changed and Kenyan women have been included in the Constitutional Review Committee. This kind of change takes a long time. But CEDAW has helped Kenyan women, who have used it in their lobbying and to provide comparative analysis with other African states.

Another example of how international agreements can be used is provided by Ethiopia. Ethiopia was the only African state that was not colonised. It was therefore able to bring cases to the International Court of Justice (ICJ). For example, it tried to bring apartheid South Africa to the ICJ, although it did not succeed.

The view was expressed that the UN condemns human rights violations when it wants to punish states in conflict with a superpower. In addition, the assertion of the universality of human rights has sometimes been used to justify intervention in the internal affairs of states. Human rights are thus sometimes used for political gain. Rather than depend on the UN for enforcement, citizens should struggle with their respective governments for the implementation of human rights. Civil society should take responsibility and avoid facilitating such double standards.

What are Women's Human Rights?

Participants were asked whether they considered women's rights to be human rights. They were then informed that women's rights were noted as human rights in the Vienna Declaration and Programme for Action (1993). For women are human beings, and whatever rights they have are therefore also human rights.

It was necessary to distinguish women's rights from human rights because women have historically been treated differently from men. Equality rights generally note that discrimination on the basis of protected grounds should not hinder the enjoyment of human rights by specific vulnerable groups (children, women, people with disabilities, and so on).

Women's human rights have gradually gained recognition at the international level:

- The Universal Declaration (1945) and the ensuing international human rights conventions explicitly provide that sex should not be a basis for discrimination.
- The Convention on the Political Rights of Women (1954) gives special attention to women's civil and political rights.
- The period 1975–85 was declared the Women's Decade. Progress was made and UN documents from 1979 consistently refer to discrimination against women.
- The Vienna Declaration and Plan of Action (1993) sufficiently addressed the issue of women's human rights.
- The Declaration to Eliminate All Forms of Violence Against Women recognised that violence against women is a human rights issue and, as such, it is the responsibility of states to address it.

CEDAW or the Women's Convention   The CEDAW Committee of the UN monitors implementation of CEDAW or the Women's Convention.

Articles 1–4 provide for:

- A definition of discrimination against women;
- Policies and laws to eliminate discrimination against women;
- The right to undertake actions that guarantee women's human rights (asserting, for example, that affirmative action will not be deemed discriminatory given the historical discrimination against women);
- Affirmative action;

• Addressing cultural and socially based discrimination against women.

Articles 5–9 provide for the responsibilities of states in terms of policy and legal measures and incentives to combat discrimination against women.

Articles 6–15 provide for women's social rights, including trafficking of women, equal access to education, equal access to job opportunities and employment, equal access to health, equality in family law and equality in resourcing and social security schemes. The UN monitors implementation of this.

Women's human rights in Ethiopia The Ethiopian Constitution has recognised women's human rights and the need to impose upon government responsibility for ending discrimination against women. However, statutory law has not yet been substantively amended to bring it in line with the Constitution. There is movement to amend discriminatory laws. But, implementation of even amended laws remains a problem. For example, the introduction of the Family Court has not yet been effective in terms of granting non-discriminatory interpretations.

The participants then brainstormed a list of important women's human rights for Ethiopia, as follows:

• The right to life, the protection of life and protection from violence against women;
• The right to non-discrimination on the basis of sex;
• The right to equality before law;
• The right to economic freedom;
• The right to access to health care;
• The right to access to education;
• The right to freedom of association.

All the above are important. The diversity of the priorities mentioned indicates the interdependency of human rights.

Discussion Human rights violations are usually defended using culture or religion, which creates conflict. The major hindrance to the protection of women's human rights in Ethiopia stems from culture and tradition. For example, in Gambela region, elderly people carry out female genital mutilation (FGM). They are respected. Treating them as criminals is not helpful and so issuing a law against FGM is not a solution. Laws become ineffective when their implementation is not possible. The majority of people still believe in FGM. We should focus on the practitioners. They are few, and changing their attitudes will therefore be easier. If the practitioners know that FGM is a crime, they will refuse to perform it. This would contribute to the decline and eventual elimination of FGM.

In addition, polygamy is accepted and women have no recourse. A woman went to court to complain about her husband taking a second wife and the judge responded: 'So what? I have three wives myself.' We have to sensitise all community members. If the community supports cultural and traditional practices that are harmful to women, there is nobody to complain to about such practices. Before we take cases to court, the people concerned and their families and communities must be aware that they are committing crimes. Asking the communities concerned for advice and ensuring their participation in the amendments to policies and laws is crucial.

Experience Sharing by the Ethiopian Women Lawyers' Association (EWLA)

Case one: abduction A girl was abducted. The culprit was arrested and locked up. After a few days, he was released on a bond. He then abducted her again, taking her to a different area. She stayed with him until the opportunity to escape presented itself. The EWLA representative from Gambela region felt that law enforcement only worked half-heartedly.

Case two: early marriage A 16-year-old girl sought protection from the EWLA. The girl was given shelter, but the police forcibly took her home to be married off. The EWLA sought support from all relevant government officials, who ordered that the marriage be stopped. The parents were jailed. But in the meantime, other family members enforced the marriage.

Case three: exchange of daughters as wives In Oromia region, two fathers exchanged their daughters and took them as wives. In one case, a young girl was given to an 80-year-old man. Her father took the old man's daughter. The first girl ran back to her home. Her father sent her back to the old man. The pattern of running away and being sent back continued. In the end, the girl killed her father.

Case four: making the first wife the wife of the family The practice is that all the male relatives of the bridegroom have sex with the bride on the first day of the wedding. If the bride does not conceive within the wedding period, the practice continues until she becomes pregnant.

Case five: wives being expected to offer sexual services to the family In a part of Ethiopia where Islam is practised, a woman was expected to give sexual services to her brother-in-law when he stayed overnight, as well as to her husband's friends.

Case six: wife inheritance Another example from Gambela region involved the exchange of women among male members of a family. A man inherited the wives of his late brother. When he also died, his step-sons then inherited the wives.

Discussion We must be careful when trying to protect women's human rights not to violate other human rights. For example, the suggestion to forbid the right for bail on a bond would violate a human right. The Ethiopian government has put in place a law forbidding bonds to be granted to citizens accused of taking bribes.

EWLA also has to be careful not to be seen as acting alone. They should cultivate supporters in different communities, so as to work closely with the communities concerned.

What is Gender?

Dr Konjit Fekade, gender consultant

Dr Fekade began the session with an energiser. Participants contributed adjectives to describe both men and women. They then noted that most of those adjectives were actually stereotypes. They felt that the social environment has emphasised stereotyping by encouraging men to be competitive, strong and breadwinners and women to perform housework. Stereotyping is not about women being victims of males. Stereotypes are inherited from our various cultures as norms and values.

These norms and values influence both men and women. For example, the head of the family is the man, who is expected to support the family. Therefore, men are expected to go out and look for work while women are left at home to perform housework. However, there is no reason why women should not go out and look for work while men stay at home to take care of the family. Educating communities to question these norms and values is important.

If women become the family breadwinners, it is feared that women would also become the family decision-makers. This role reversal is therefore not encouraged. But gender analysis stresses that men and women should collaborate at all levels and share decision-making at all levels.

Sex and gender Sex refers to the biological differences between men and women. These differences are generally permanent. Gender refers to the socially constructed roles and responsibilities of women and men. These roles and responsibilities are influenced by expectations and perceptions created by class, culture, custom, economic status, the environment, ethnicity, law, politics, religions and social factors, as well as individual or institutional bias. Gender attitudes and behaviours are learned and can be changed.

Situations in which we see gender differences

- Economic: differences in women's and men's access to credit and loans, employment and control of financial and other productive resources (such as land).
- Educational: differences in educational expectations and opportunities of girls and boys, with family resources directed to boys' rather than to girls' education and girls being streamed into less challenging academic tracks.
- Political: differences in the ways in which women and men assume and share authority and power, with women being more involved at the local level in activities linked to their domestic roles.
- Social: different perceptions of women's and men's social roles, with men being seen as the heads of households and the chief breadwinners and women being seen as caregivers and nurturers.

Discussion Gender is not constructed by men alone, but by society as a whole (including both men and women). However, since gender relations favour men, men tend to support the status quo. Gender is the outcome of socialisation of children by parents and communities. Folklore and proverbs are used to ensure that gender roles attributed to women are viewed as inferior to those attributed to men. Roles that are given to women are assumed to be less important, thus resulting in women's lower social status. Changing socialisation processes will help bring about change. Currently, any deviation from socially accepted gender roles results in degrading name-calling.

Gender roles are also based on power relations. Gender-based divisions of labour differ from culture to culture and even from place to place within the same culture. However, women's roles are consistently subordinate and power relations between men and women remain unequal in favour of men. Even though development has changed some gender-based roles, power relations remain essentially the same, with the only change being in the level and intensity of power inequalities.

Women in some parts of Ethiopia are required to take livestock with them to their marital home. Although this is property given a woman by her parents, once in her marital home, her husband takes control over the property she has brought. Similarly, many working women give their incomes to their husbands. This indicates that economic empowerment alone does not necessarily change power relations between men and women. Attitudinal changes are required for meaningful changes in gender relations.

Group work Participants were divided into three groups and given the task of identifying gender roles and relationships. They were asked to focus on three levels, namely, the home, the community and within organisations. The exercise aimed to examine where decision-making power lies at all three levels. The results are in Table 14.1.

Discussion   There is a need to change the way in which language reflects these gender imbalances, for example, by using 'he' to refer to a person. In one organisation, for example, if the word 'Chairman' is used, a correction is made and conscious efforts are made to change sexist language. EWLA also has done this in its constitution. Sometimes the efforts are cumbersome, so documents have preambles stating that the contents refer to both women and men.

We have to examine the gender relations in our society. There is a disparity in power between men and women, with women generally having less power than men. We need police and law enforcement that ensures parity. Until we create parity between men and women, we cannot talk of gender equality and justice.

Table 14.1 Decision-making power

WOMEN

Levels	Roles
Home	• Childcare • Cleaning • Food preparation • Fetching fuel and water.
Community	• Preparing food during social occasions • Members • Treasurers
Organisation	• Cleaner • Messenger • Secretary • Nurse

MEN

Levels	Roles
Home	• Constructing homes • Constructing fences • Controlling the children's behaviour
Community	• Constructing tents during social occasions • Playing leadership roles • Acting as judges in community affairs • Bosses
Organisation	• Directors • Technicians • Engineers • Pilots

What is Gender Mainstreaming?

Dr Konjit Fekade, gender consultant

Table 14.2 Women in development (WID) and gender and development (GAD)

	Women in development	Gender and development
The approach	• seeks to integrate women into the development process	• seeks to empower women and transform relations between women and men
The focus	• women	• relations between women and men
The problem	• the exclusion of women from the development process	• unequal power relations between women and men, preventing women's full participation in and benefiting from development
The goal	• more efficient and effective development	• women and men sharing decision-making and power • equitable, sustainable development
The strategies	• implement women's components and projects • improve women's ability to manage their households • increase women's productivity and income	• identify and address short-term and income needs determined by women and men to improve their conditions • identify and address women and men's longer-term interests

Definitions of gender mainstreaming Some development organisations interpret gender mainstreaming as meaning that the separate needs and interests of women and men should not be mentioned. Others refer to working at the project level with both women and men as gender mainstreaming. Many development organisations have interpreted gender mainstreaming as meaning that they do not need to maintain separate gender departments or units as individual departments or units have to address gender.

But gender mainstreaming is (and has to be) based on a new vision of gender relations. Mainstreaming requires working to improve the specific situation of women in tandem with that of men. It thus entails a critical review of underlying assumptions about development, its institutions and organisations and the process of allocating opportunities, resources and benefits.

Mainstreaming therefore implies:

* Working with women and men rather than separately with women.
* Including gender in all processes, rather than focusing on women's issues in a separate process.

Table 14.3 Evolution of approaches to women's development

Project goal and time of introduction	Conception of the problem	Conception of the solution	Potential development interventions
Welfare (1950)	• Women's poverty • Women's special needs • Women as a vulnerable group	• Provide support services of nutrition, health, child care	• Feeding programmes • Health and maternity clinics • Immunisation campaigns
Economic self-reliance (1960)	• Women as underemployed, unproductive, dependent, lacking in production skills	• Promote independence and self-reliance • Provide productive skills • Encourage enterprise	• Women's savings, investment and production groups • Income-generating projects for women
Efficiency (1970)	• Women as previously overlooked resources in development • Women as underdeveloped human capital, in need of skills and improved access to resources	• Recognise gender-based divisions of labour • Identify women's actual productive roles • Improve women's access to skills training, technology and resources	• Increase women's access to credit and marketing facilities as well as to technology
Equality (1985)	• Inequality • Discrimination against women in schooling, credit, access to land	• Implement equal opportunities for women in education, access to the factors of production, benefits from production	• Adopt and enforce equal opportunity policies and laws • Affirmative action to promote equal opportunity, equal participation
Empowerment (1985)	• Unequal gender power relations • Male-dominated society • Political and social resistance (both male and female)	• Use strategies of conscientisation, mobilisation for collective action • Expand women's participation in the development process to achieve gender equality in control over productive resources.	• Local level projects that recognise women's roles • Projects concerned with advocacy, democratisation and political action

- Working within existing structures rather than setting up separate structures.

The arguments in support of gender mainstreaming are that:

- Previously, only small resources were allocated to women-specific projects, with the lion's share being expended in gender-blind and male-biased projects.
- Women's subordination does not just affect women as it is structural and impacts on society as a whole.

Table 14.4 Women and empowerment

Levels of empowerment	Description
Control	• Women and men have equal control over factors of production and distribution of benefits, without dominance or subordination
Participation	• Women have equal participation in decision-making about all policies, programmes and projects
Conscientisation	• Women believe that gender roles can be changed and gender equality is possible
Access	• Women gain access to productive skills and resources such as training, credit, land, marketing facilities, public services and benefits on an equal basis with men. Reforms of policies and laws may be prerequisites for such access
Welfare	• Women's material needs, such as food, medical care and income are met

The most important criteria for gender mainstreaming are:

- An organisational commitment at the highest decision-making level to empower women;
- The collection of gender-desegregated data to give a clear picture of the situation of women in relation to men (for example, the number of girls who have dropped out of school, as compared to boys);
- The allocation of resources.

Indicators need to be set so as to gauge whether gender mainstreaming has been successful at both the managerial level and the programme and project levels.

DAY 2: 18 July 2001

What is Policy?

Participants in group discussions defined policy as follows:

- Policy is a directive, a document for the implementation and realisation of laws.
- Policy is a directive, a strategy to solve a given problem, with a detailed plan of execution.
- Policy is a body of principles to guide regulations, rules and actions as well as implementation mechanisms.

There is a difference between policy and law. Policy is both a mechanism used to implement laws and/or a guideline issued to solve a particular social problem. Some policies are translated into law, although there are many policies that do not become law. Policy is not always written down, although written policy is obviously better because it offers guidelines.

Participants then broke into groups to discuss the following:

Group one

1. Explain the policy-making process in an organisation that you work for (choose one organisation). What are the basic steps in making policies for this organisation?

   Policies are initiated, formulated, discussed and approved by the Board of Directors.

2. Are policies written or unwritten?

   Policies are both written and unwritten.

3. Who is involved in the process?

   The policy-making process involves all stakeholders.

4. Of those involved in the process, how many are women?

   There are three women among the five board members and five women among the eleven members of staff.

Group two

1. Give two examples of policies that you have helped to make or know of in your communities.

   In the Amhara region, there is a policy about ceremonies. In the Gambela region, there is a policy on abduction for those who do not have enough bride-price.

2. Are these policies written or unwritten?

   The policy in the Amhara region is written, but the one in the Gambela region is unwritten.

3. What gender implications do these policies have?

   In the Gambela region, under customary law, families must give bride-price.

Group three

1. Give two examples of regional and/or national policies that have implications for gender.
   The national policies on affirmative action, land and family planning and health service provision.
2. Are these policies written or unwritten?
   They are written.
3. Where would you go to find these policies?
   They can be obtained from educational institutions and libraries. With respect to land, what should be looked at is the federal land proclamation number 89/1997: Rural Land Administration Proclamation of the Federal Government. In addition, there are two regional proclamations on land for the Amhara and Tigray regions.

Discussion Group two described the most participatory policy-making process. More women can participate in decision-making on policy because it is a small and fairly democratic organisation. The larger the institution or organisation to be affected by policy, the more complicated, exclusive and undemocratic the policy-making process becomes.

At the community level, generally, rules are clear to everybody. But at the national level, in a society with a large number of illiterate citizens, most of whom are women, involving women in the policy-making process will not happen without planning for it to happen.

In addition, as shown by group three, sometimes both the regional and the national citizenry need to be involved in different although related policy-making processes, for example, with respect to land.

Who Makes Policies and Laws in Ethiopia?

Meaza Ashenafi, Executive Director, EWLA

The Ethiopian government has a federal rather than a unitary structure. Laws are issued by the House of People's Representatives, and the Federation Council interprets the Constitution.

The law-making process of the federal government is as follows. Ministries propose laws to the Law Research Institute of the Ministry of Justice. After consideration, these laws then go to the Council of Ministers for discussion and finally to the House of People's Representatives for adoption.

Policies originated from ministries can either be adopted by the Council of Ministers or by the ministry concerned with the policy, depending on whether or not the policy requires legislation for implementation.

Regional states follow the same process of law- and policy-making.

Discussion In Kenya, the law-making process involves the executive, the legislature and the judiciary. Both the executive and the legislature make laws, while the judiciary interprets implementation of the laws. The President has a lot of power to make law.

For a law to be brought to Parliament, a parliamentarian can move a motion to do so, which can be debated. If the motion passes, the Attorney General's office is given the responsibility of translating the motion into a bill. The bill is taken to Parliament for debate. It goes through a first reading and, if accepted, through a second reading. During these two stages, the public can give its opinions on these bills, either through parliamentarians or through the Attorney-General's office.

If the bill passes the second reading, it becomes a law. However, it must receive presidential assent within 30 days to stand. If he approves it, it becomes a law. If he has a problem with it, he must give his reasons and return it to Parliament for these to be addressed.

A second way of initiating law is through the Law Reform Commission. After a person or group submits their concern to the Law Reform Commission, it is forwarded to the Attorney-General. The Attorney-General is then meant to table the concern in Parliament.

Current Policies and Laws Pertaining to Ethiopian Women's Property Rights

Meaza Ashenafi, Executive Director, EWLA

This session focused on women's property rights with respect to land. If, generally speaking, land rights are not conducive to development, it is difficult to discuss women's land rights and equal access to and control over land.

Land distribution in Ethiopia is on the basis of family heads of households. This affects women's access to and control over land through ownership.

Federal proclamation number 89/1997: Rural Land Administration deals with the administration of land by the regional states. Articles 1, 3, 5 and 10 relate to women.

Distribution of land is still biased in favour of men, because women's access to land is limited to access for female heads of households. There is need for affirmative action to correct the unequal distribution of land on the basis of heads of households. In addition, Article 3 categorises women along with children and people with disabilities. This is degrading.

Discussion In the southern region, customary law prohibits women from inheriting land. Gender-based power relations within households prevent women from exercising control over land. As women do not plough the land, because of customary gender roles, they are forced to rent land. Women are encouraged to become small traders and/or local brewers in order to get land.

It is crucial to implement even existing laws on land. But the major issue is the land tenure system itself. If we do not address the root problem, the rights of women to land cannot be achieved.

What is Lobbying and Advocacy?

Genet Mitike

The goal of advocacy is to influence public policy so as to shape communities better. Advocacy is a dynamic process, in which the aim is to:

- Identify issues;
- Develop solutions;
- Build political will;
- Negotiate change;
- Evaluate the process and results of negotiation.

Forms of advocacy include:

- Lobbying;
- Targeted action campaigns;
- Litigation.

Lobbying involves political beliefs or causes and directly contacting legislators and their staff through phone calls, writing letters, meetings, receptions and/or other events, dinners, and so on.

Targeted action campaigns are major focused efforts in support of an issue over a period of time. This builds and energises members of the campaign, builds relationships with other organisations and gains widespread involvement and/or support. To run a targeted action campaign:

- Decide what you want to accomplish.
- Identify targets for action.
- Create tactics.
- Get messages out.
- Locate and identify resources.

Begin early so that there is time to:

- Learn about the issue.
- Gather additional facts to support your position.
- Build coalitions.
- Educate the media.
- Gain the support of the general public.

When speaking in public on an issue you are advocating for:

- Check the location.

- Arrive early.
- Know the audience and prepare/adjust accordingly.
- Make eye contact.
- Get to and speak on the key points.
- Use facts and quotes.
- Use personal stories to show the issue's importance.
- Keep it short.
- Repeat the main messages in the question and answer session.

When forming advocacy coalitions:

- Discuss your partners' previous experience with coalitions.
- Negotiate shared expectations.
- Share the power and the work.
- Share openly how each group will benefit.
- Celebrate success.
- Plan for constant negotiation.
- Commitment, consistency and continuity are key.

A media plan for advocacy includes:

- Making a press list.
- Meeting with editorial boards.
- Preparing press kits.
- Preparing press releases.
- Writing letters to the editor.
- Writing opinion editorials (op-eds).
- Doing radio and television interviews.
- Preparing and airing public service announcements (PSAs).
- Holding press conferences.
- Making public speeches.

Discussion Advocacy needs to be explained and translated because the words used to describe advocacy often have a negative connotation. Negotiation is a constant part of advocacy.

Group one: organisations involved in advocacy

- The media (there is a need to build capacity within the government media);
- Civil society organisations (which should play a substantive advocacy role, although many are located in the urban areas, many have limited capacity to engage in advocacy and most tend to lack sustainability);
- Women's organisations;
- Educational institutions;
- Professional associations.

Group two: the media's role and weaknesses in advocacy

The government (public) media tend to be active in advocacy only around non-controversial issues, such as children's and women's rights. They are afraid of advocating democratisation and human rights, and need capacity-building in this respect. They also need to coordinate their radio and television coverage with respect to advocating a particular issue.

The private media tend to be sensationalist and to work main for profit. They have limited advocacy capacity.

Alternative media, such as community radio, can (and do) play an advocacy role.

Group three: coordination of advocacy organisations and weaknesses thereof

Existing Ethiopian organisations engaged in advocacy include:

- Publications;
- Radio and television stations;
- Action Professional Associations (APA);
- Dawn of Hope–Ethiopia;
- DTK-Population and Social Marketing;
- EWLA;
- National Committee on Traditional Practices of Ethiopia.

In general, the coordination among these organisations is weak, so there is some duplication of efforts. In addition, they are not very strong, some lack accountability and they also tend to focus on their own areas of work. Coordination of advocacy efforts should be improved.

Tools of Lobbying and Advocacy

Strategically, the following must be identified and/or worked on:

- The credibility of the advocates;
- The issues of the day;
- Friends;
- Policies, laws and the responsible arms of government;
- Alliances with the media;
- The mobilisation of the public (including peasant and urban dwellers' associations, youth associations and professional associations).

Group one: international advocacy

The point of this is to ensure that the international community:

- Is made aware of the oppression of others;

- Gives support to the advocacy struggles within a given state;
- Takes necessary action;
- Engages in advocacy itself;
- Gives legal support to those within the state, if necessary.

Group two: lobbying and advocacy in Ethiopia

There has been lobbying and advocacy in Ethiopia around early marriage, education and HIV/AIDS. The marriage age was increased, and there is a committee taking action to ensure this is implemented. The enrolment of girls has increased, as more schools have been opened. With respect to HIV/AIDS, the government has been supportive in formulating a policy on HIV/AIDS. There has been a campaign on behavioural change, particularly in regard to harmful traditional practices that increase the risk of HIV infection (for example, trying to make circumcision illegal).

Group three: advocacy around women's human rights

Both civil society and the Ethiopian government have advocated women's human rights by:

- Researching issues affecting women;
- Raising the consciousness of women and relevant organisations (through seminars, vigils and workshops);
- Lobbying for improvements in the law and law enforcement (through training of the police).

DAY 3: 19 July 2001

Analysing the Ethiopian Advocacy and Media Packages

Participants studied the advocacy and media packages on women's land rights in Ethiopia, prepared by FEMNET and based on a research paper by Zenebeworke. They critiqued them as follows:

1. What did you like about the package?
- The cover and the layout include the African map.
- The study was been conducted by an Ethiopian national, giving a deeper insight.
- The inclusion of Ethiopia's commitments to international conventions.
- The package discusses women's land rights at the international, regional and national levels.

2. Language
a. Is the language simple enough for a broad and popular audience that is not necessarily trained in the fields of law, policy-making or media?

- English is not our first language, so it is difficult to comment.
- The language used is not clear.
- The language used is not simple and is difficult to understand.
- The language is simple.

b. Is the language gender-sensitive? If not, how is it insensitive?

- It did not answer or deal with gender issues.
- The language is gender-sensitive although some members of the group felt it was not.

c. Is the language inclusive? If not, what groups does it exclude (for example, people with disabilities, particular ethnic nationalities, etc.) and how?

- It did not include all ethnicities or nationalities and people with disabilities.

d. Should the idea of translation of the packages into indigenous languages be considered, and if so, into which ones?

- It should be translated into the major languages.
- It should be translated into Amharinya, Orominya and Tigrinya.

3. Content

a. Did the package contain too much or too little material?

- The content is not adequate.
- It was short and precise.

b. If there is too much material what would you throw out?

- The statistics on the world's population are not necessary.
- The content is too long and it should be short and precise.

c. If too little material what would you include?

- Pictures;
- Comments;
- Case studies;
- Solutions to the problems raised;
- Government efforts on land;
- Ethiopia's family law, using CEDAW as a point of reference.

4. Accuracy: is the information in the package accurate and correct? If not, please list the inaccuracies that you have noted.

- Ethiopia's map not current as it includes Eritrea.
- The statistics are not accurate, specific and updated.
- Outdated laws (family law and the law establishing the federal court) were referred to.
- Social improvement is mentioned more than is the case, so more indicators should be used.

5. Would you or the organisation you work for be able to use this package? If so, why? If not, why not?

- We will use the package for our gender work.

6. Other comments?

- The package should have been given to the participants earlier.
- The picture on the cover does not relate to the issues raise in the package (the woman on the cover is laughing but she should look serious to portray the gravity of the issues).
- The research should be done by professionals and be more extensive.
- The research deals with a specific issue and should have been broader.
- The sample area is limited and does not fully represent Ethiopia.

Constraints to Ethiopian Women's Access to and Control over Land and Strategies to Overcome Them

Challenges and constraints

- Poverty;
- Shortage of land, especially grazing land for pastoralists, due to population pressure and land degradation;
- Land redistribution has not occurred, except in the Amhara and Tigray regions;
- There is no land use policy at either the federal or the regional levels;
- With the exception of the Amhara and Tigray regions, the regions have not formulated policies on land use, management and ownership;
- Lack of detailed directives to ensure implementation of existing policies and laws;
- Harmful traditional practices and customary or traditional laws' prevalence over statutory law;
- Men are considered to be the heads of families;
- Women's lack of control over land, production and its benefits;
- Women's workload;
- The practice of polygamy;
- In some regions, a woman is obligated to marry her deceased husband's brother, so that family land stays under men's control;
- In the Gambela region, daughters do not inherit land;
- Women do not plough, due to gender-based divisions of labour under customary law and backward ploughing technologies.

Strategies

- Developing case studies;
- Lobbying and advocacy for women's land rights;

- Formulating land management and ownership policies in all regions, ensuring fair land distribution to women and that women can inherit land;
- Developing policies on land use in all regions;
- Training on the dangers of harmful traditional practices;
- Training on family planning;
- Consciousness-raising of people who abide by and practise existing policies and laws;
- Empowering women to enjoy their land rights and the benefits from land;
- Introducing appropriate technology to decrease women's workload and so that women can plough (the traditional plough is too difficult and requires too much physical strength).

Women and Land Ownership in Ethiopia

Abaynesh Biru Shibeshi

Women perform equal work in agricultural production. However, their access to land and the benefits of produce are limited. Even though women perform most of the work in livestock, only men get training in animal husbandry. There is a cultural barrier preventing discussion between female farmers and the predominantly male extension workers.

Land ownership desegregated by gender is seen in the following percentages:

Table 14.5 Land ownership desegregated by gender

Region	Men	Women
Afar	92	8
Amhara	83	17
Gambela	78	22
Oromia	83	17
Southern	82	18

In terms of buying land, women have limited access to credit and loans due to lack of information, capital and land to act as collateral. Land inherited by men or bought during a marriage is generally not shared at the time of divorce, as it is viewed as the husband's property. Land inheritance is by sons, on the grounds that daughters move out to their husbands' homes.

An Ethiopian policy on women was formulated in 1994. It is meant to ensure women's equality in all areas so that women benefit from the state's wealth. It suggests a continuous effort to end gender-based inequalities and recommends the development of labour-saving technologies for women.

Further recommendations are that:

- Directives and mechanisms for the implementation of international conventions be created.
- Women's legal rights under the Constitution be implemented.
- Women's equal rights to land and equal benefits from agricultural production be ensured.
- Women's rights with respect to land use, management and ownership be clearly stated.
- Severe punishment for crimes against women be instituted.
- All gender-biased policies be eliminated.
- Women's participation in research be increased.
- Gender-responsible development programmes and projects be formulated.
- Land titles be registered.
- Banking regulations and rules be improved to ensure that women benefit from credit and loan facilities.
- Women be included in agricultural and environmental training.
- Women's equal participation in farmers' associations be assured (and women supported if they want to organise separately).
- Women be trained in economically viable skills.

Women's Access to Land During Land Redistribution in the Amhara Region

Shasha

The population of the Amhara regional state is close to sixteen million, out of which 4.8 million are female. The previous land policy of the Derg did not give women access to land. However, the present land policy of the Ethiopian People's Revolutionary and Democratic Front (EPRDF), expressed in Article 35, no. 6, clearly stipulates the right of women to land ownership. Based on this article, the Amhara state formulated a land redistribution proclamation, Article 16/1989.

During the land redistribution, 403,028 landless farmers were given land. Of these, 135,845 (32.7 per cent) were women. Landless women thus benefited, as the policy targeted women engaged in small trading and single women. The president of the Amhara state said that giving land to single women was aimed at helping them get husbands.

The impacts of this land distribution were that:

- Women's right to land ownership was granted.
- Women have the security of land ownership.
- Those who were previous engaged as daily labourers now get sustained incomes from their land.

- Single women who had difficulties getting married due to being landless now have improved chances.
- Such women, as landowners in their own right, once married, cannot be sent out of their homes by their husbands.

However, apart from these general observations, there is a need to assess the impact of this land distribution in detail. The following constraints affecting women landowners have also been observed:

- Women are not included in training activities or in the provision of improved seeds and fertilisers (only 4.2 per cent received extension support).
- Women landowners still do not plough, due to the lack of oxen and ploughing tools, the fact that traditional ploughing techniques require physical strength and that this practice is not culturally accepted.
- Women therefore depend on men to do their ploughing and have to give up to three-quarter of their land or produce in payment, thereby decreasing their gains and perpetuating their dependence on men.
- In addition, they may suffer from decreased production, because men plough women's land after ploughing their own, sometimes leading to delays in planting.
- Because of the meagre incomes therefore received, some women are inclined to rent their land, thus losing the sense of land ownership and the prestige that goes with it.
- Due to their lack of formal education and information, they cannot read written rental agreements entered into and people invariably deny oral agreements.

Detailed research into the impact of land distribution to women in the Amhara region therefore needs to be carried out.

Women and Land Ownership in the Oromia Region

Arriss

Most of the population in the Oromia region is Muslim and follows Sharia. Yet:

- Women do not inherit land.
- Women are required to give sexual services to their brothers-in-law, friends and male guests.
- During divorce, women do not get their share. They are not allowed to continue to live in the area and usually go back to their parents. However, some women have been able to get their share by going to the Civil Court.
- When a man dies, his brother inherits his wife on the premise that he will love and protect his brother's sons and the property will stay within the family.
- When a woman dies, her sister marries her husband on the same premise that applies with the death of a husband.

Case study: women's land ownership in the Southern region, Deberitu
Deberitu used to work in an elementary school in Aria District in the Oromia region. However, because of ethnic conflict, she had to go back to her parents in the Southern region. Her mother was old at the time her father died. Deberitu therefore had to take responsibility for the family's property. However, her brother, who was married and had his own land, claimed his mother's property by using customary law, which grants inheritance rights only to male children.

The case was brought to the local authorities. Because of their own biases, they did not follow the Constitution, which provides for wives to inherit their husbands' property. They paid lip service to this woman's situation, enabling her brother to continue harassing her. Finally, the local authorities sent the case to the district level, where it sits now.

Case study: women's land ownership in the Oromia region A young woman, 18 years old, had a husband. When he died, his family forced her to marry his younger brother. The young woman was locked in the house for a long time. She finally managed to get out and report the case to the police. The police put the person in prison and EWLA offered her legal services. However, as the family and the community believe in wife inheritance, all kinds of force and pressure are being applied to force her to remain with her brother-in-law.

DAY 4: 20 July 2001

Strategies for Effective Advocacy

Case one: the family law campaign, Ethiopia
Meaza Ashenafi, Executive Director, EWLA
The EWLA's public education on women programme offers free services. It has worked towards changing laws biased against women. This is advocacy work, which has a multiplying effect. Once the EWLA highlights an issue, others join in the cause. The use of media and film have therefore been one key advocacy strategy.

The successes of the ELWA are with respect both to civil law (family law, maternity leave law and pension law for women) and criminal law (regarding punishments for crimes against women). Lessons learnt are to:

- Advocate on the basis of our own expertise (for example, the case of Aberash, who killed the man who had abducted her, was used to highlight not only her case but the plight of Ethiopian women in general, through a British Broadcasting Corporation documentary).
- Assign tasks according to people's attitudes and strong points.
- Provide clear information.
- Make strong alliances.

Case two: How the 'secularist' and the 'Archbishop' found common cause, Kenya

Atsango Chesoni, consultant, FEMNET

This advocacy case study relates to the reformulation of the Kenyan Constitution.

In 1992, Kenyans realised they needed constitutional reform to make the government more democratic. The debates were controversial. The advocacy effort was unusual, in that organisations that do not normally work together joined hands (including human rights organisations and religious organisations from different faiths and sects).

In 1997, the government expressed its interest, but wanted to engage only with the religious organisations. This was naturally dangerous for women's organisations. They began coordinating different women's organisations and recommendations reflecting the women's position were drafted. The organisations' own media, as well as the mainstream media, were used to show that the religious organisations did not necessarily represent all sections of the citizenry. In addition, a religious women's order, the Sisters of Kenya, was approached to join the women's constitutional effort. By working with the Sisters of Kenya, the position of the women's organisations was difficult for the government to dismiss.

The strategy was successful. Discussions were held among the different religious and secular organisations, and resulted in an amendment to Article 82 of the Kenyan Constitution, to include sex as a protected ground on which discrimination cannot occur. Lessons learnt were that it is key to:

- Be creative about using issues and/or situations to our advantage.
- Make contacts with the appropriate people.
- Develop trust to facilitate honest discussion and negotiation.
- Find common ground.

Discussion It is important to note that all advocacy efforts take time to achieve results. It is also important to acknowledge the contributions of all individuals and organisations to a successful advocacy effort.

Building alliances is critical and coordination of those alliances is important. It helps to bring 'experts' on board. It also helps to work with relevant and sympathetic government bodies, particularly those removed from government politics.

Planning for Advocacy

Planning helps us to identify issues, as well as our aims and objectives. It helps us develop our strategy (what issue to raise, when, to whom and by whom, what alliances to make and with whom, what resources we need and from whom, etc.). It helps us keep our direction as well as to monitor and evaluate our progress.

Planning therefore helps us make the maximum use of our resources (budget, labour, time, etc.). It helps us to identify why advocacy is sometimes not sustained, as has happened to some advocacy in Ethiopia.

Role of Monitoring and Evaluation

Monitoring is important. It should be a continuous process as it can be done at four stages, in assessment, planning, implementation and evaluation.

In the assessment stage, problems are identified and discussed with a wide range of stakeholders to ensure that a holistic view of the problems has been achieved. Planning is then done based on identified problems, and seeking out additional information on the issues. During implementation, the monitoring analyses weaknesses and strengths of the activities planned and helps the implementers to improve. Evaluation is done at the conclusion of the activities planned and adjusted.

Gender-responsive Indicators

Dr Konjit Fekade, gender consultant

An indicator is a pointer, which is used to measure changes in a specific condition over a specified period of time. It can provide a look at the results of actions and initiatives. It is an instrument to monitor and evaluate development work.

Input indicators measure the delivery of resources devoted to a project's activities. They are measures to monitor achievement during implementation, and serve primarily to track progress towards the intended results.

Output indicators measure intermediate results, for example, at a point when a funder's involvement in a project is close to completion.

Outcome indicators relate to the longer-term results of the project, after a funder's involvement is completion.

Input, output and outcome indicators can be either quantitative or qualitative. Quantitative indicators are numerical measurements of change, such as the number of women visiting a pre-natal counselling centre. Qualitative indicators relate to people's perceptions, such as opinions regarding alterations in authority, social relations or status. They can be quantified.

To develop a work plan with indicators:

- Identify objectives.
- Identify external factors as enabling or potential risks.
- Decide which types of indicators are appropriate to measure achievement of the objectives and over what time frame.
- Develop qualitative analysis.

Objectives must be clearly developed if indicators are to be used, and indicators should follow objectives closely. There are two types of objectives:

- Objectives of which the results are relatively easily quantifiable (for example, to increase gross enrolment rates by 50 per cent at the primary school level in the project area).
- Objectives of which the results are less easily quantifiable and which will require greater emphasis on qualitative analysis to measure them (for example, to ensure gender equality in the project area).

Quantitative indicators will tell you, for example, how many people participated in a project, but will give little information about the degree, nature and effects of their participation. Qualitative analysis is therefore used to understand social processes, why and how a particular situation came into being and how this situation can be changed in the future. While quantitative indicators will tell you how far your project has succeeded or failed, qualitative analysis will tell you why this result took place, and whether the result was a good one or not.

In developing indicators for objectives, the following guidelines can be used:

- Each stage of the project cycle needs indicators.
- Indicators must fit with objectives.
- Indicators of enabling/risk factors should be included.
- Both quantitative and qualitative indicators are needed.
- Indicators should be developed in a participatory fashion, involving all stakeholders wherever possible.
- All indicators should be gender-desegregated.

Why Gender-responsive Indicators?

- Since mainstream indicators (for example, gross national product) have been used to obscure or undervalue women's contribution to society, quantitative and qualitative gender-sensitive indicators illustrate women's and men's participation in different aspects of social life.
- Gender-responsive indicators measure gender-related changes in society.
- They point out how far, and in what ways, development programmes and projects have met their gender objectives and achieved results related to gender equality.

Examples of gender-responsive indicators include:

1. Social

- Women's control over fertility decisions;
- The number of women in local organisations (for example, women's associations);
- The extent of training among women, as compared to men;
- Women's mobility within and outside their residential locality, as compared with men's mobility.

2. Legal

- The enforcement of legislation related to the protection of women's human rights;
- The number of cases related to women's human rights heard in local courts and the results of such cases;
- The decrease or increase in cases of violence against women.

3. Political

- The percentage of women in the civil service;
- The percentage of seats held by women in decision-making bodies;
- The percentage of women in decision-making positions in government.

DAY 5: 21 July 2001

Plan of Action

1. Mission statement

- To see that Ethiopian women's access to, use of and control over land is equal to that of men.

2. General objectives

- To engage in advocacy to ensure the formulation and implementation of policies that give equal access to, use of and control over land to women.
- To work towards the elimination of harmful traditional attitudes and practices that hinder the implementation of policies on the right of land to women.

3. Specific objectives

- To ensure that existing policies and laws are improved and new policies and laws are formulated to give women access to, use of and control over land within five years.
- To establish coordination between the government and civil society organisations engaged in issues relevant to women's land rights.
- To sensitise 25 per cent of relevant people on policies related to land issues in general and women's land rights in particular within two years.
- To build capacity to enable at least 50 per cent of landless Ethiopian women to acquire land within ten years.
- To minimise harmful traditional attitudes and practices that hinder women's land rights within ten years.

Evaluation

1. Content of the workshop

- Too much 44%
- Too little 12%
- Enough 44%

2. Which section of the programme needs strengthening?

- All sections.
- The human rights section.
- The policy section.
- The advocacy section.
- Women and land ownership issues.

3. Material
- Enough 76%
- Too little 24%

4. Venue of the workshop

- All said that it was comfortable.

5. Other comments about the workshop

a. What did you like about the workshop?
- It dealt with practical issues such as human rights and land.
- It addressed the crucial issue of women's land rights.
- The training methodology.
- It was participatory.

b. What you did not like about the workshop?
- There should have been tables.
- There was not enough time.
- There should have been more experts to discuss the issues.

Appendix

Participants

1. Hebret Abahoy, Ministry of Justice, Addis Ababa
2. Yelfigne Abegaz, Canadian Physicians for Aid and Relief (CPAR), Addis Ababa
3. Zenebech Alamneh, Assosa Branch, Ethiopian Women Lawyers' Association (EWLA)
4. Ellen Alem, EWLA, Addis Ababa
5. Abiye Alemu Environment et Développement en Afrique (ENDA), Addis Ababa, Ethiopia
6. Ismael Arebo, Culture and Information Bureau, Addis Ababa
7. Sammet Arele, Cultural and Information Bureau, Addis Ababa
8. Meaza Ashenafi, EWLA, Addis Ababa

9. Tekabech Assefa, Ethiopian Media Women's Association (EMWA), Addis Ababa
10. Tsehay Belayneh, Dolina Plc, Addis Ababa
11. Letekidan Berhane, the *Ethiopian Herald*, Addis Ababa
12. Menna Bisray, Educational Media Agency, Addis Ababa
13. Atsango Chesoni, African Women's Development and Communication Network (FEMNET), Nairobi, Kenya
14. Rahel Asfaw Demissie, Faculty of Law, Addis Ababa University
15. Shashi Demessie, EWLA, Addis Ababa
16. Tsige Deresse, Adama Branch, Nazarat, Ethiopia
17. Lommi Elalla, Oromia Branch, EWLA, Assela, Ethiopia
18. Tegest Enyew, Awassa Branch, EWLA, Awassa, Ethiopia
19. Konjit Eshenj, Nazarat Branch, EWLA, Nazarat, Ethiopia
20. Dr Konjit Fekade, Addis Ababa University
21. Mulusembet Feleke, Radio Fana, Addis Ababa
22. Deretu Gacheno, Kembata Self-Help Organisation, KMG, Addis Ababa
23. Frehiwot Gebeyehu, Agri-Services Ethiopia, Addis Ababa
24. Mebratu Gebeyehu, Action Professionals' Association for the People (APAP), Addis Ababa
25. Minale Gebeyehu, Radio Fana, Addis Ababa
26. Samson Getahun, Consultant, Addis Ababa
27. Tewolde Geyesus, Lem-Ethiopia, Addis Ababa
28. Original Wocde Giorgis, EWLA, Addis Ababa
29. Grace Githaiga, Kenya Community Media Network (KCOMNET), Nairobi, Kenya
30. Kirubil Hailu, ISD, Addis Ababa
31. Ali Hassen, National Committee on Traditional Practices, Addis Ababa
32. Fetellewerek Kebede, Dire Dawa Branch, EWLA, Dire Dawa
33. Bethelehem Kifle, *Zemen* Newspaper, Addis Ababa
34. Getachew Kitaw, Ethiopian Bar Association, Addis Ababa
35. Etalem Mengeshu, Consultant, Addis Ababa
36. Tibebe Mergia, *The Sun*, Addis Ababa
37. Genet Metike, National Committee on Traditional Practices, Addis Ababa
38. Kebrework Negussie, Bahr Dar Branch, EWLA, Bahr Dar, Ethiopia
39. Helen Seifu, EWLA, Addis Ababa
40. Abaynesh Biru Shibeshi, Agency for Cooperation and Research in Development (ACORD), Addis Ababa
41. Getahun Shibeshi, ENDA-Ethiopia, Addis Ababa
42. Tassew Shiferaw, Women's Affairs Office, Prime Minister's Office, Addis Ababa
43. Makal Simon, Gamballa Branch, EWLA, Gamballa, Ethiopia
44. Melakou Tegegn, Panos Institute of Eastern Africa, Addis Ababa

45. Tilahun Teshome, Addis Ababa University
46. Girma Tessema, House of Peoples' Representatives, Addis Ababa
47. Alemnesh Urga, Jima Branch, EWLA, Jima, Ethiopia
48. Mary Wandia, FEMNET, Nairobi, Kenya

Index